# The U.S. Presidential Election Process

Edited by Paul F. Kisak

# Contents

# Chapter 1

# United States presidential election

The **election of the President and Vice President of the United States** is an indirect vote in which citizens cast ballots for a slate of members of the U.S. Electoral College. These electors cast direct votes for the President and Vice President. If both votes result in an absolute majority, the election is over. If a majority of electors do not vote for President, the House of Representatives chooses the President; if a majority of electors do not vote for Vice President, the Senate votes. Presidential elections occur quadrennially on Election Day, which since 1845 has been the Tuesday after the first Monday in November,[1][2][3] coinciding with the general elections of various other federal, state, and local races. The 2016 U.S. presidential election is scheduled for November 8.

The process is regulated by a combination of both federal and state laws. Each state is allocated a number of Electoral College electors equal to the number of its Senators and Representatives in the U.S. Congress.[4] Additionally, Washington, D.C. is given a number of electors equal to the number held by the least populous state.[5] U.S. territories are not represented in the Electoral College.

Under the U.S. Constitution, each state legislature is allowed to designate a way of choosing electors.[4] Thus, the popular vote on Election Day is conducted by the various states and not directly by the federal government. In other words, it is really an amalgamation of separate elections held in each state and Washington, D.C. instead of a single national election. Once chosen, the electors can vote for anyone, but – with rare exceptions like an unpledged elector or faithless elector – they vote for their designated candidates and their votes are certified by Congress, who is the final judge of electors, in early January. The presidential term then officially begins on Inauguration Day, January 20 (although the formal inaugural ceremony traditionally takes place on the 21st if the 20th is a Sunday).

The nomination process, consisting of the primary elections and caucuses and the nominating conventions, was never specified in the Constitution, and was instead developed over time by the states and the political parties. The primary elections are staggered generally between January and June before the general election in November, while the nominating conventions are held in the Summer. This too is also an indirect election process, where voters cast ballots for a slate of delegates to a political party's nominating convention, who then in turn elect their party's presidential nominee. Each party's presidential nominee then chooses a vice presidential running mate to join with him or her on the same ticket, and this choice is rubber-stamped by the convention. Because of changes to national campaign finance laws since the 1970s regarding the disclosure of contributions for federal campaigns, presidential candidates from the major political parties usually declare their intentions to run as early as the Spring of the previous calendar year before the election.[6] Thus, the entire modern presidential campaign and election process usually takes almost two years.

## 1.1 History

Article Two of the United States Constitution originally established the method of presidential elections, including the Electoral College. This was a result of a compromise between those constitutional framers who wanted the Congress to choose the president, and those who preferred a national popular vote.[7]

Each state is allocated a number of electors that is equal to the size of its delegation in both houses of Congress combined. With the ratification of the 23rd Amendment to the Constitution in 1969, the District of Columbia is also granted a number of electors, equal to the number of those held by the least populous state. However, U.S. territories are not represented in the Electoral College.

Constitutionally, the manner for choosing electors is determined within each state by its legislature. During the first presidential election in 1789, only 6 of the 13 original states chose electors by any form of popular vote.[8] Gradually throughout the years, the states began conducting popular

1

elections to help choose their slate of electors, resulting in the overall, nationwide indirect election system that it is today.

Under the original system established by Article Two, electors could cast two votes to two different candidates for president. The candidate with the highest number of votes (provided it was a majority of the electoral votes) became the president, and the second-place candidate became the vice president. This presented a problem during the presidential election of 1800 when Aaron Burr received the same number of electoral votes as Thomas Jefferson and challenged Jefferson's election to the office. In the end, Jefferson was chosen as the president because of Alexander Hamilton's influence in the House of Representatives. This added to the deep rivalry between Burr and Hamilton which resulted in their famous 1804 duel.

In response to the 1800 election, the 12th Amendment was passed, requiring electors to cast two distinct votes: one for President and another for Vice President. While this solved the problem at hand, it ultimately had the effect of lowering the prestige of the Vice Presidency, as the office was no longer for the leading challenger for the Presidency. The separate ballots for President and Vice President became something of a moot issue later in the 19th century when it became the norm for popular elections to determine a state's Electoral College delegation. Electors chosen this way are pledged to vote for a particular presidential and vice presidential candidate (offered by the same political party). So, while the Constitution says that the President and Vice President are chosen separately, in practice they are chosen together.

The 12th Amendment also established rules when no candidate wins a majority vote in the Electoral College. In the presidential election of 1824, Andrew Jackson received a plurality, but not a majority, of electoral votes cast. The election was thrown to the House of Representatives, and John Quincy Adams was elected to the presidency. A deep rivalry was fermented between Andrew Jackson and House Speaker Henry Clay, who had also been a candidate in the election.

Since 1824, aside from the occasional "faithless elector," the popular vote determines the winner of a presidential election by determining the electoral vote, as each state or district's popular vote determines its electoral college vote. Although the nationwide popular vote does not directly determine the winner of a presidential election, it does strongly correlate with who is the victor. In 52 of the 56 total elections held so far (about 93 percent), the winner of the national popular vote has also carried the Electoral College vote. The winners of the nationwide popular vote and the Electoral College vote differ only in close elections. In highly competitive elections, candidates focus on turning out their vote in the contested swing states critical to winning an electoral college majority, so they do not try to maximize their popular vote by real or fraudulent vote increases in one-party areas.[9]

However, candidates can fail to get the most votes in the nationwide popular vote in a Presidential election and still win that election. In the 1824 election, Jackson won the popular vote, but no one received the majority of electoral votes. According to the 12th Amendment in the Constitution, the House of Representatives must choose the president out of the top 3 people in the election. Clay had come fourth, so he threw his support to Adams, who then won. Because Adams later named Clay his Secretary of State, Jackson's supporters claimed that Adams gained the presidency by making a deal with Clay. Charges of a "corrupt bargain" followed Adams through his term. Then in 1876, 1888 and 2000, the winner of electoral vote lost the popular vote outright. Numerous constitutional amendments have been submitted seeking to replace the Electoral College with a direct popular vote, but none has ever successfully passed both Houses of Congress. Another alternate proposal is the National Popular Vote Interstate Compact, an interstate compact whereby individual participating states agree to allocate their electors based on the winner of the national popular vote instead of just their respective statewide results.

The presidential election day was established on a Tuesday in the month of November because of the factors involved (weather, harvests and worship). When voters used to travel to the polls by horse, Tuesday was an ideal day because it allowed people to worship on Sunday, ride to their county seat on Monday, and vote on Tuesday–all before market day, Wednesday. The month of November also fit nicely between harvest time and harsh winter weather, which could be especially bad to people traveling by horse and buggy.[10]

Until 1937, presidents were not sworn in until March 4 because it took so long to count and report ballots, and because of the winner's logistical issues of moving to the capital. With better technology and the 20th Amendment being passed, presidential inaugurations were moved to noon on January 20–allowing presidents to start their duties sooner.[10]

The Federal Election Campaign Act of 1971 was enacted to increase disclosure of contributions for federal campaigns. Subsequent amendments to law require that candidates to a federal office must file a Statement of Candidacy with the Federal Election Commission before they can receive contributions aggregating in excess of $5,000 or make expenditures aggregating in excess of $5,000. Thus, this began a trend of presidential candidates declaring their intentions to run as early as the Spring of the previous calendar year so they can start raising and spending the money needed for their nationwide campaign.[6]

The first president, George Washington, was elected as an independent. Since the election of his successor, John Adams, in 1796, all winners of U.S. presidential elections have represented one of two major parties. Third parties have taken second place only twice, in 1860 and 1912. The last time a third (independent) candidate achieved significant success (although still finishing in third place) was in 1992.

## 1.2 Procedure

### 1.2.1 Eligibility requirements

Article Two of the United States Constitution stipulates that for a person to serve as President, the individual must be a natural-born citizen of the United States, at least 35 years old, and a resident of the United States for a period of no less than 14 years. A candidate may start running his or her campaign early before turning 35 years old or completing 14 years of residency, but must meet the age and residency requirements by Inauguration Day. The Twenty-second Amendment to the Constitution also sets a term limit: a President cannot be elected to more than two terms.

In addition, the Twelfth Amendment establishes that the Vice-President must meet all of the qualifications of being a President.

Although not a mandatory requirement, Federal campaign finance laws including the Federal Election Campaign Act state that a candidate who intends to receive contributions aggregating in excess of $5,000 or make expenditures aggregating in excess of $5,000, among others, must first file a Statement of Candidacy with the Federal Election Commission.[11] This has led presidential candidates, especially members from the two major political parties, to officially announce their intentions to run as early as the spring of the previous calendar year so they can start raising or spending the money needed for their nationwide campaign.[6] Potential candidates usually form exploratory committees even earlier to determining the feasibility of them actually running.

### 1.2.2 Nominating process

Main articles: United States presidential primary and United States presidential nominating convention
The modern nominating process of U.S. presidential elections currently consists of two major parts: a series of presidential primary elections and caucuses held in each state, and the presidential nominating conventions held by each political party. This process was never included in the

*A 2008 Democratic caucus meeting in Iowa City, Iowa. The Iowa caucuses are traditionally the first major electoral event of presidential primaries and caucuses.*

*The floor of the 2008 Republican National Convention at the Xcel Energy Center in Saint Paul, Minnesota.*

United States Constitution, and thus evolved over time by the political parties to clear the field of candidates.

The primary elections are run by state and local governments, while the caucuses are organized directly by the political parties. Some states hold only primary elections, some hold only caucuses, and others use a combination of both. These primaries and caucuses are staggered generally between January and June before the federal election, with Iowa and New Hampshire traditionally holding the first presidential state caucus and primary, respectively.

Like the general election, presidential caucuses or primaries are indirect elections. The major political parties officially vote for their presidential candidate at their respective nominating conventions, usually all held in the summer before the federal election. Depending on each state's law and state's political party rules, when voters cast ballots for a candidate in a presidential caucus or primary, they may be voting to award delegates "bound" to vote for a candidate at the presidential nominating conventions, or they may simply be expressing an opinion that the state party is not bound to follow in selecting delegates to their respective national convention.

Unlike the general election, voters in the U.S. territories can also elect delegates to the national conventions. Furthermore, each political party can determine how many delegates to allocate to each state and territory. In 2012 for example, the Democratic and Republican party conventions each used two different formulas to allocate delegates. The Democrats based theirs on two main factors: (1) the proportion of votes each state gave to the Democratic candidate in the previous three presidential elections, and (2) the number of electoral votes each state had in the Electoral College.[12] In contrast, the Republicans assigned to each state 10 delegates, plus 3 delegates per congressional district.[13] Both parties then gave fixed amounts of delegates to each territory, and finally bonus delegates to states and territories that passed certain criteria.[12][13]

Along with delegates chosen during primaries and caucuses, state and U.S. territory delegations to both the Democratic and Republican party conventions also include "unpledged" delegates who can vote for whomever they want. For Republicans, they consist of the three top party officials from each state and territory. Democrats have a more expansive group of unpledged delegates called "superdelegates", who are party leaders and elected officials.

Each party's presidential candidate also chooses a vice presidential nominee to run with him or her on the same ticket, and this choice is rubber-stamped by the convention.

### 1.2.3   The popular vote on Election Day

*A Texas voter about to mark a selection for president on a ballot, 2008 Election Day*

Under the United States Constitution, the manner of choosing electors for the Electoral College is determined by each state's legislature. Although each state currently designates electors by popular vote, other methods are allowed. For instance, a number of states formerly chose presidential electors by a vote of the state legislature itself.

However, federal law does specify that all electors must be selected on the same day, which is "the first Tuesday after the first Monday in November," i.e. a Tuesday no earlier than November 2 and no later than November 8.[14] Today, the states and the District of Columbia each conduct their own popular elections on Election Day to help determine their respective slate of electors. Thus, the presidential election is really an amalgamation of separate and simultaneous state elections instead of a single national election run by the federal government.

Like any other election in the United States, the eligibility of an individual for voting is set out in the Constitution and regulated at state level. The Constitution states that suffrage cannot be denied on grounds of race or color, sex or age for citizens eighteen years or older. Beyond these basic qualifications, it is the responsibility of state legislatures to regulate voter eligibility.

Generally, voters are required to vote on a ballot where they select the candidate of their choice. The presidential ballot is a vote "for the electors of a candidate" meaning that the voter is not voting for the candidate, but endorsing a slate of electors pledged to vote for a specific presidential and vice presidential candidate.

Many voting ballots allow a voter to "blanket vote" for all candidates in a particular political party or to select individual candidates on a line by line voting system. Which candidates appear on the voting ticket is determined through a legal process known as ballot access. Usually, the size of the candidate's political party and the results of the major nomination conventions determine who is pre-listed on the presidential ballot. Thus, the presidential election ticket will not list every candidate running for President, but only those who have secured a major party nomination or whose size of their political party warrants having been formally listed. Laws are in effect to have other candidates pre-listed on a ticket, provided that enough voters have endorsed the candidate, usually through a signature list.

The final way to be elected for president is to have one's name written in at the time of election as a write-in candidate. This is used for candidates who did not fulfill the legal requirements to be pre-listed on the voting ticket. It is also used by voters to express a distaste for the listed candidates, by writing in an alternative candidate for president such as Mickey Mouse or comedian Stephen Colbert (whose application was voted down by the South Carolina Democratic Party). In any event, a write-in candidate has never won an election for President of the United States.

Because U.S. territories are not represented in the Electoral College, U.S. citizens in those areas do not vote in the general election for President. Guam has held straw polls for president since the 1980 election to draw attention to this fact.[15]

### 1.2.4   Electoral college

Main article: Electoral College (United States)
Most state laws establish a winner-take-all system, wherein

*Electoral College map showing the results of the 2012 U.S. presidential election. Incumbent Democrat president Barack Obama won the popular vote in 26 states and Washington, D.C. (denoted in blue) to capture 332 electoral votes. Republican challenger Mitt Romney won the popular vote in 24 states (denoted in red) to capture 206 electoral votes.*

the ticket that wins a plurality of votes wins all of that state's allocated electoral votes, and thus has their slate of electors chosen to vote in the Electoral College. Maine and Nebraska do not use this method, opting instead to give two electoral votes to the statewide winner and one electoral vote to the winner of each Congressional district.

Each state's winning slate of electors then meets at their respective state's capital on the first Monday after the second Wednesday in December to cast their electoral votes on separate ballots for President and Vice President. Although Electoral College members can technically vote for anyone under the U.S. Constitution, 24 states have laws to punish faithless electors,[16] those who do not cast their electoral votes for the person whom they have pledged to elect.

In early January, the total Electoral College vote count is opened by the sitting Vice President, acting in his capacity as President of the Senate, and read aloud to a joint session of the incoming Congress, which was elected at the same time as the President.

If no candidate receives a majority of the electoral vote (currently at least 270), the President is determined by the rules outlined by the 12th Amendment. Specifically, the selection of President would then be decided by a ballot of

the House of Representatives. For the purposes of electing the President, each state has only one vote. A ballot of the Senate is held to choose the Vice President. In this ballot, each senator has one vote. The House of Representatives has chosen the victor of the presidential race only twice, in 1800 and 1824; the Senate has chosen the victor of the vice-presidential race only once, in 1836.

If the President is not chosen by Inauguration Day, the Vice President-elect acts as President. If neither are chosen by then, Congress by law determines who shall act as President, pursuant to the 20th Amendment.

Unless there are faithless electors, disputes, or other controversies, the events in December and January mentioned above are largely a formality since the winner can be determined based on the state-by-state popular vote results. Between the general election and Inauguration Day, this apparent winner is referred to as the "President-elect" (unless it is a sitting President that has won re-election).

### 1.2.5   Election calendar

The typical periods of the presidential election process are as follows, with the dates corresponding to the 2016 general election:

- Spring 2015 – Candidates announce their intentions to run, and (if necessary) file their Statement of Candidacy with the Federal Election Commission

- August 2015 to March 2016 – Primary and caucus debates

- February 1 to June 14, 2016 – Primaries and caucuses

- April to August, 2016 – Nominating conventions (including those of the minor third parties)

- September and October, 2016 – Presidential election debates

- November 8, 2016 – Election Day

- December, 2016 – Electors cast their electoral votes

- Early January, 2017 – Congress counts and certifies the electoral votes

- January 20, 2017 – Inauguration Day

## 1.3   Trends

### 1.3.1   Political experience

See also: List of Presidents of the United States by previous experience and List of Presidents of the United States by other offices held

A number of trends in the political experience of presidents have been observed over the years. In recent decades, the presidential nominees of both major parties have been either incumbent presidents, sitting or former vice presidents, sitting or former U.S. Senators, or sitting or former state Governors. The last major nominee from either party who had not previously served in such an office was General Dwight D. Eisenhower, who won the Republican nomination and ultimately the presidency in the 1952 election. Chester A. Arthur had held no federal or statewide office, before becoming Vice President and then President following the assassination of President James A. Garfield in 1881.

The U.S. Secretary of State used to be a stepping-stone to the White House, with five of the six Presidents who served between 1801 and 1841 previously holding that office. However, since 1841, only one Secretary of State has gone on to be President (James Buchanan).

Fourteen Presidents have previously served as Vice President. However, only John Adams (1796), Thomas Jefferson (1800), Martin Van Buren (1836), Richard Nixon (1968) and George H. W. Bush (1988) began their first term after winning an election. Among the remaining nine who began their first term as President according to the presidential line of succession after their respective predecessor died or resigned from office, Theodore Roosevelt, Calvin Coolidge, Harry S. Truman, and Lyndon B. Johnson were reelected. John Tyler, Millard Fillmore, Andrew Johnson, Chester A. Arthur, and Gerald Ford served as President but never won any presidential election. Ford had been appointed to the Vice Presidency through the processes of the Twenty-fifth Amendment and lost the 1976 presidential election, making him the only President to have never been elected to national office.

In the 2008 election, the nominees of both major parties, Barack Obama and John McCain, were sitting U.S. Senators. Before 2008, fifteen presidents previously served in the Senate, including four of the five Presidents who served between 1945 and 1974. However, only two out of those fifteen were sitting U.S. Senators at the time they were elected president (Warren G. Harding in 1920 and John F. Kennedy in 1960). Major-party candidate Senators Andrew Jackson (1824), Lewis Cass (1848), Stephen Douglas (1860), Barry Goldwater (1964), George McGovern (1972), and John Kerry (2004) all lost their elections. Only one sitting member of the House of Representatives has been elected president (James A. Garfield in 1880), although eighteen presidents have been former members of the House.

Despite Obama's tenure, contemporary electoral success has clearly favored state governors. Of the last six presidents, four (Jimmy Carter, Ronald Reagan, Bill Clinton and George W. Bush) have been governors of a state. Geographically, these presidents were from either very large states (California, Texas) or from a state south of the Mason–Dixon line and east of Texas (Georgia, Arkansas). In all, sixteen presidents have been former governors, including seven who were in office as governor at the time of their election to the presidency. Other major-party candidates who were also state governors include Michael Dukakis (1988), and Mitt Romney (2012).

After leaving office, one President, William Howard Taft, served as Chief Justice of the United States. Only two Presidents, John Quincy Adams (serving in the House) and Andrew Johnson (serving in the Senate), have served in Congress after being President. John Quincy Adams however is the only former President to be elected to federal office; when Andrew Johnson served as a Senator, state legislatures appointed the Senators.

### 1.3.2   Technology and media

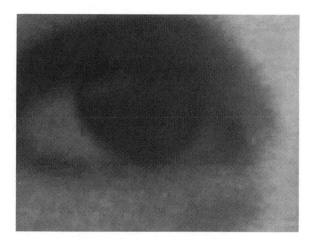

*Lyndon B. Johnson's 1964 "Daisy" advertisement*

Advances in technology and media have also affected presidential campaigns. The invention of both radio and television have given way to the reliance of national political advertisements across those methods of communication. National advertisements such as Lyndon B. Johnson's 1964 commercial "Daisy", Ronald Reagan's 1984 commercial "Morning in America", and George H. W. Bush's 1988 commercial "Revolving Door" became major factors in those respective elections. In 1992, George H. W. Bush's promise of "Read my lips: no new taxes" was extensively used in the commercials of Bill Clinton and Bush's other opponents with significant effect during the campaign.

Since the development of the Internet in the mid-90s, Internet activism has also become an invaluable component of presidential campaigns, especially since 2000. The internet was first used in the 1996 presidential elections, but primarily as a brochure for the candidate online.[17] It was only used by a few candidates and there is no evidence of any major effect on the outcomes of that election cycle.[17]

In 2000, both candidates (George W. Bush and Al Gore) created, maintained and updated their campaign website. But it was not until the 2004 presidential election cycle was the potential value of the internet seen. By the summer of 2003, ten people competing in the 2004 presidential election had developed campaign websites.[18] Howard Dean's campaign website from that year was considered a model for all future campaign websites. His website played a significant role in his overall campaign strategy.[19] It allowed his supporters to read about his campaign platform and provide feedback, donate, get involved with the campaign, and connect with other supporters.[20] A Gallup poll from January 2004 revealed that 49 percent of Americans have used the internet to get information about candidates, and 28 percent said that they use the internet to get this information frequently.[21]

In 2008, the internet became a grassroots and a voice of the people tool-a way for the users to connect with each other and with the campaign, like Dean's website had done in 2004. All of the major candidates had a website and utilized social networking like Facebook and MySpace. The popularity of a candidate could be measured by the number of 'friends' on these sites as well as on websites like Hitwise, which listed the number of hits all of the presidential candidate's websites had each week.

Internet channels such as YouTube were used by candidates to share speeches and ads for free. This also served as a forum for users to attack other candidates by uploading videos of gaffes.[21]

A study done by the Pew Internet & American Life Project in conjunction with Princeton Survey Research Associates in November 2010 shows that 54 percent of adults in the United States used the internet to get information about the 2010 midterm elections and about specific candidates. This represents 73 percent of adult internet users. The study also showed that 22 percent of adult internet users used social network sites or Twitter to get information about and discuss the elections and 26 percent of all adults used cell phones to learn about or participate in campaigns.[22]

E-campaigning as it has come to be called, is subject to very little regulation. On March 26, 2006, the Federal Election Commission voted unanimously to "not regulate political communication on the Internet, including emails, blogs and the creating of Web sites"[23] This decision made only paid political ads placed on websites subject to campaign finance limitations.[24] A comment was made about this decision by Roger Alan Stone of Advocacy Inc. that explain this loophole in the context of a political campaign, "A wealthy individual could purchase all of the e-mail addresses for registered voters in a congressional district . . . produce an Internet video ad, and e-mail it along with a link to the campaign contribution page..Not only would this activity not count against any contribution limits or independent expenditure requirements; it would never even need to be reported"[23]

## 1.4 Criticisms

Main articles: Criticisms of the Electoral College, Criticisms of U.S. presidential primaries and History of U.S. presidential nominating conventions

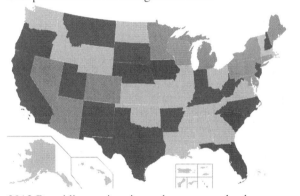

2012 Republican primaries and caucuses calendar.

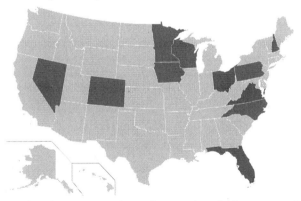

2012 swing states, where the margin of victory was 8 percentage points or less.
States won by Republican Mitt Romney by 0–4 percentage points
States won by Democrat Barack Obama by 0–4 percentage points
States won by Democrat Barack Obama by 4–8 percentage points

Today, the presidential election process remains controversial, with critics arguing that it is inherently undemocratic, and discourages voter participation and turnout in many areas of the country. Because of the staggered nature of the primary season, voters in Iowa, New Hampshire and other small states which traditionally hold their primaries and caucuses first in January usually have a major impact on the races. Campaign activity, media attention, and voter participation are usually higher in these states, as the candidates attempt to build momentum and generate a bandwagon effect in these early primaries. Conversely, voters in California and other large states which traditionally hold their primaries last in June usually end up having no say in who the presidential candidates will be. The races are usually over by then, and thus the campaigns, the media, and voters have little incentive to participate in these late primaries. As a result, more states vie for earlier primaries to claim a greater influence in the process. However, compressing the primary calendar in this way limits the ability of lesser-known candidates to effectively corral resources and raise their visibility among voters, especially when competing with better-known candidates who have more financial resources and the institutional backing of their party's establishment. Primary and caucus reform proposals include a National Primary held on a single day; or the Interregional Primary Plan, where states would be grouped into six regions, and each of the regions would rotate every election on who would hold their primaries first.

With the primary races usually over before June, the political conventions have mostly become scripted, ceremonial affairs. As the drama has left the conventions, and complaints grown that they were scripted and dull pep rallies, public interest and viewership has fallen off. After formerly offering gavel-to-gavel coverage of the major party conventions in the mid-20th Century, the Big Three television networks now only devote approximately three hours of coverage (one hour per night).

Critics also argue that the Electoral College is archaic and inherently undemocratic. With all but two states (the exceptions being Maine and Nebraska) using a winner-take-all system, both the Democratic and the Republican candidates are all but certain to win all the electoral votes from those states whose residents predominantly vote for the Democratic Party or the Republican Party, respectively. This encourages presidential candidates to focus exponentially more time, money, and energy campaigning in a few so-called "swing states", states in which no single candidate or party has overwhelming support. Such swing states like Ohio are inundated with campaign visits, saturation television advertising, get-out-the-vote efforts by party organizers, and debates. Meanwhile, candidates and political parties have no incentive to mount nationwide campaign efforts, or work to increase voter turnout, in predominately Democratic Party "safe states" like California or predominately Republican Party "safe states" like Texas. In practice, the winner-take-all system also both reinforces the country's two-party system and decreases the importance of third and minor political parties.[25] Furthermore, a candidate can win the electoral vote without securing the greatest amount of the national popular vote, such as during the 1824, 1876, 1888, and 2000 elections. In theory, it is possible to secure the necessary 270 electoral votes from just the top 11 populous states and then ignore the rest of the country.

Constitutional amendments, such as the Every Vote Counts Amendment, have been proposed seeking to replace the Electoral College with a direct popular vote, which proponents argue would increase turnout and participation. Other proposed reforms include the National Popular Vote Interstate Compact, an interstate compact without Congressional authorization, whereby individual participating states agree to allocate their electors based on the winner of the national popular vote, instead of voting their respective statewide results. Another proposal is for every state to simply adopt the District system used by Maine and Nebraska: give two electoral votes to the statewide winner and one electoral vote to the winner of each Congressional district. The Automatic Plan would replace the Electors with an automatic tallying of votes to eliminate the faithless elector affecting the outcome of the election. The Proportional Plan, often compared to the District Plan, would distribute electoral votes in each state in proportion to the popular vote, introducing third party effects in election outcomes. The House Plan would require a constitutional amendment to allocate electors based on the House apportionment alone to lessen small state advantage. Direct election plans and bonus plans have in common a higher valuation on the popular vote for president.[26]

## 1.5 Electoral college results

See also: List of United States presidential elections by Electoral College margin and List of United States presidential elections by popular vote margin

The following is a table of electoral college results:

*Political party of each candidate is indicated in parentheses*

*\* Winner received less than an absolute majority of the popular vote.*

*† Losing candidate received a plurality of the popular vote.*

*‡ Losing candidate received an absolute majority of the popular vote.*

*\*\* As the second place winner, was elected Vice President as per the law in effect prior to the ratification of the Twelfth Amendment.*

## 1.6 Voter turnout

See also: Voter turnout in the United States presidential elections

Voter turnout in the 2004 and 2008 elections showed a noticeable increase over the turnout in 1996 and 2000. Prior to 2004, voter turnout in presidential elections had been decreasing while voter registration, measured in terms of voting age population (VAP) by the U.S. Census, has been increasing. The VAP figure, however, includes persons ineligible to vote — mainly non-citizens and ineligible felons — and excludes overseas eligible voters. Opinion is mixed on whether this decline was due to voter apathy [34][35][36] or an increase in ineligible voters on the rolls.[37] The difference between these two measures are illustrated by analysis of turnout in the 2004 and 2008 elections. Voter turnout from the 2004 and 2008 election was "not statistically different," based on the voting age population used by a November 2008 U.S. Census survey of 50,000 households . If expressed in terms of vote eligible population (VEP), the 2008 national turnout rate was 61.7% from 131.3 million ballots cast for president, an increase of over 1.6 percentage points over the 60.1% turnout rate of 2004, and the highest since 1968.[38]

## 1.7 Financial disclosures

Prior to 1967, many presidential candidates disclosed assets, stock holdings, and other information which might affect the public trust.[39] In that year, Republican candidate George W. Romney went a step further and released his tax returns for the previous twelve years.[39] Since then, many presidential candidates – including all major-party nominees since 1980 – have released some of their returns,[40] although few of the major party nominees have equaled or exceeded George Romney's twelve.[41][42]

## 1.8 Presidential coattails

Main article: Coattail effect

Presidential elections are held on the same date as those for all the seats in the United States House of Representatives, the full terms for 33 or 34 of the 100 seats in the United States Senate, the governorships in several U.S. states, as well as many state and local elections. Presidential candidates tend to bring out supporters who then vote for their party's candidates for those other offices. Members of the U.S. Senate or House of Representatives are also more likely to be voted for on a year of the presidential election than a midterm.[43] In effect, these other candidates are said to ride on his coattails.

### 1.8.1 Comparison with other U.S. general elections

[1] This table does not include special elections, which may be held to fill political offices that have become vacant between the regularly scheduled elections.

[2] As well as all six non-voting delegates of the U.S. House.

[3] As well as five non-voting delegates of the U.S. House. The Resident Commissioner of Puerto Rico instead serves a four-year term that coincides with the presidential term.

[4] Both the Governors of New Hampshire and Vermont are each elected to two-year terms. The other 48 state governors serve four-year terms.

- view
- talk
- edit

## 1.9 See also

- American election campaigns in the 19th century
- Elections in the United States
- Most royal candidate theory

**Statistical forecasts**

- PollyVote
- FiveThirtyEight.com
- Electoral-vote.com

## 1.10 Notes

[1] 3 U.S.C. § 1

[2] Caldwell, Leigh Ann (November 4, 2015). "A Viewer's Guide to the Next Year in Presidential Politics". NBC News. Retrieved November 8, 2015.

[3] Cohen, Andrew (October 29, 2012). "Could a Hurricane Like Sandy Postpone the Presidential Election?". The Atlantic. Retrieved November 8, 2015.

[4] Article II, Section 1, Clause 2 of the U.S. Constitution

[5] Twenty-third Amendment to the U.S. Constitution

[6] Jose A. DelReal (April 3, 2015). "Why Hillary Clinton might have just two more weeks or so to announce she's running for president". *Washington Post*. Retrieved April 12, 2015.

[7] Gary Bugh (2010). *Electoral College Reform: Challenges and Possibilities*. Ashgate Publishing, Ltd. p. 40. ISBN 978-0-7546-7751-2.

[8] Out of the 13 original states during the 1789 election, 6 states chose electors by some form of popular vote, 4 states chose electors by a different method, North Carolina and Rhode Island were ineligible to participate since they had not yet ratified the U.S. Constitution, and New York failed to appoint their allotment of electors in time because of a deadlock in their state legislature.

[9] Rose, Douglas Dana. "The Ten Most Competitive American Presidential Elections". *ResearchGate*.

[10] Yan, Holly (6 November 2012). "Why Tuesday, why November, why elephants? Election riddles solved". CNN. Retrieved 9 November 2012.

[11] "2016 Presidential Form 2 Filers" (Press release). Federal Election Commission. Retrieved April 12, 2015.

[12] "Democratic Detailed Delegate Allocation – 2012". *The Green Papers*. Retrieved September 8, 2015.

[13] "Republican Detailed Delegate Allocation – 2012". *The Green Papers*. Retrieved September 8, 2015.

[14] "Sandy unlikely to postpone election". USA Today. Retrieved 31 October 2012.

[15] "Guam Legislature Moves General Election Presidential Vote to the September Primary". Ballot-Access.org. 2008-07-10. Retrieved 2008-09-17.

[16] "Faithless Electors". *FairVote*.

[17] Pollard, Chesebro & Studinski (2009). "The Role of the Internet in Presidential Campaigns". *Communications Studies* **60** (5).

[18] Endres, Warnick (2004). "Text-based Interactivity in Candidate Campaign Web Sites: A case Study from the 2002 Elections". *Western Journal of Communication* **68** (3).

[19] Endres, Warmick (2009). "Text-based Interactivity in Candidate Campaign Web Sites: A case Study from the 2002 Elections". *Western Journal of Communication* **68** (3): 322–342. doi:10.1080/10570310409374804.

[20] Pollard, Chesebro & Studinski, Timothy D.; Chesebro, James W.; Studinski, David Paul (2009). "The Role of the Internet in Presidential Camapigns". *Communications Studies* **60** (5): 574–588. doi:10.1080/10510970903260418.

[21] Pollard, Chesebro & Studinski, Timothy D.; Chesebro, James W.; Studinski, David Paul (2009). "The Role of the Internet in Presidential Campaigns". *Communications Studies* **60** (5): 574–588. doi:10.1080/10510970903260418.

[22] Smith, Aaron. "Pew Internet & American Life Project". *The Internet and Campaign 2010*. Pew Research Center.

[23] Bimbaum, Jeffrey (June 11, 2006). "Loophole a Spigot for E-Mail; Critics Fear Voters Will Be Deluged as Fall Elections Near". *The Washington Post*.

[24] Trent & Friedenberg (2008). *Political Campaign Communication Principles & Practices*. Lanham, MD: Rowman & Littlefield Publishers, Inc.

[25] Jerry Fresia (February 28, 2006). "Third Parties?". Zmag.org. Retrieved August 26, 2010.

[26] Melcher, James P., "Electing to Reform: Maine and the District Plan for Selection of Presidential Electors", 2004, New England Political Science Association. viewed October 23, 2014.

[27] Here a "major candidate" is defined as a candidate receiving at least 1.0% of the total popular vote or more than one electoral vote for elections including and after 1824, or greater than 5 electoral votes for elections including and before 1820.

[28] Both Burr and Jefferson received the same number of electoral votes. The tie was broken by the House of Representatives, sparking a series of events that led to the passing of the Twelfth Amendment

[29] There was a dispute as to whether Missouri's electoral votes in 1820 were valid, because of the timing of its assumption of statehood. The first figure excludes Missouri's votes and the second figure includes them.

[30] None of the four presidential candidates in 1824 received a majority of the electoral vote, so the presidential election was decided by the House of Representatives

[31] Because of the American Civil War, all of the states in rebellion did not participate

[32] Greeley came in second in the popular vote but died before electoral votes were cast. Most of his electors cast votes for Hendricks, Brown, and Jenkins; while another three electoral votes to Greeley were disqualified.

[33] Byrd was not directly on the 1960 ballot. Instead, his electoral votes came from several unpledged electors and a faithless elector. The claim that Kennedy received a plurality of the votes can only be sustained if those votes cast for unpledged Democratic electors are tabulated as Kennedy's, even if they did not vote for him. If these votes are excluded from Kennedy's total, Nixon had the national popular-vote plurality.

[34] "National Voter Turnout in Federal Elections: 1960-1996". Federal Election Commission. 2003-07-29. Retrieved 2007-12-09.

[35] "Election Information: Election Statistics". Office of the Clerk. Retrieved 2007-12-09.

[36] "Voting and Registration Date". U.S. Census Bureau. Retrieved 2007-12-09.

[37] "Voter Turnout Frequently Asked Questions". Elections.gmu.edu. March 12, 2009. Retrieved January 24, 2009.

[38] "2008 Preliminary Voter Turnout". Elections.gmu.edu. March 12, 2009. Retrieved January 24, 2009.

[39] "Income Tax Returns Released for Last 12 Years by Romney", *St. Joseph Gazette*, United Press International, November 27, 1967.

[40] Shaxson, Nicholas (August 2012). "Where the Money Lives". *Vanity Fair*.

[41] Sherman, Amy (August 19, 2012), "Debbie Wasserman Schultz' claim about release of tax returns of major candidates is false, says PolitiFact Florida", *Miami Herald*.

[42] "Romney and the Tax Return Precedent", FactCheck.org, July 19, 2012.

[43] "Government By the People; national, state, and local version" Prentice Hall publishers, by Cronin Magleby O'Brien Light

## 1.11 External links

- The American Presidency Project (UC Santa Barbara: 52,000+ Presidential Documents)

- Electoral College Box Scores

- Teaching about Presidential Elections

- All the maps since 1840 by counties (French language site)

- Dave Leip's Atlas of U.S. Presidential Elections

- History of U.S. Presidential Elections: 1789-2004

- Graphic election results from 1952 to 2008 broken down by state (Java Applet)

- A history of the presidency from the point of view of Vermont Discusses history of American presidential elections with two states as opposite "poles", Vermont, and Alabama

- The Living Room Candidate: A Compilation of Presidential Television Ads

- A New Nation Votes: American Election Returns 1787-1825

- How close were Presidential Elections? - Michael Sheppard, Michigan State University

- Better World Links on the U.S. Presidential Election

- Presidential Elections: Resource Guides from the Library of Congress

- U.S. Election Statistics: A Resource Guide from the Library of Congress

- "Electoral Votes". *New International Encyclopedia*. 1905. This is a tabulation of the electoral votes by election year, and also includes the results for Vice President.

### Statistical forecasts

- Election Projection

- 17 poll composite

- Princeton Election Consortium

- Gallup

# Chapter 2

# Indirect election

**Indirect election** is a process in which voters in an election do not choose between candidates for an office but rather elect persons who will then make the choice. It is one of the oldest form of elections and is still used today for many upper houses and presidents.

Some examples of indirectly elected bodies and individuals include:

- the election of the United States President is an indirect election. Voters elect the electoral college, which then elects the President. The President of Germany is similarly elected by a Federal Convention convened for that purpose. India and several other countries have a President or other largely ceremonial head of state elected by their parliament.

- the Parliamentary Assemblies of the Council of Europe, OSCE, the WEU and NATO - in all of these cases, voters elect national parliamentarians, who in turn elect some of their own members to the assembly

- the German Bundesrat, where voters elect the Landtag members, who then elect the state government, which then appoints its members to the Bundesrat

- most bodies formed of representatives of national governments, e.g. the United Nations General Assembly, can be considered indirectly elected (assuming the national governments are democratically elected in the first place)

- the Indian Rajya Sabha (upper house of parliament) is indirectly elected, largely by state legislatures; Manmohan Singh was a member of the Rajya Sabha but chosen by the majority party in the Lok Sabha (lower house of parliament) as the Prime Minister (2004-2014); as such, Singh as Prime Minister had never won a direct or popular election; introduced as a "technocrat"

- the United States Senate was indirectly elected by state legislatures until, after a number of attempts over the

previous century, the 17th amendment to the constitution was ratified in 1913.

- the election of the government in most parliamentary systems - the voters elect the parliamentarians, who then elect the government including most prominently the prime minister from among themselves

Many republics with parliamentary systems elect their president indirectly (Germany, Italy, Estonia, Latvia, Hungary, India, Israel).

In a Westminster system, the leader of the majority party in the parliament almost always becomes the prime minister. Therefore, it could be said that the prime minister is elected indirectly.

- in the United Kingdom, the Prime Minister usually is a member of the House of Commons, the lower, elected house of Parliament

In Spain, the Congress of Deputies votes on a motion of confidence of the king's nominee (customarily the party leader whose party controls the Congress) and the nominee's political manifesto, an example of an indirect election of the Prime Minister of Spain.

Indirect political elections have been used for lesser national offices, as well. In the United States, most members of the Senate were elected by the legislatures of the states until 1913, when the Seventeenth Amendment instituted direct elections for those office-holders. In France, election to the upper house of Parliament, the Sénat, is indirect, with the electors (called "grands électeurs") being local elected representatives.

The Electoral College of the United States, whose task is to elect a president, is a form of indirect election. However, electors rarely change their actual vote from their pledged vote, and this factor has never made the difference in an election.

## 2.1 See also

- List of democracy and elections-related topics
- Proxy voting
- Delegative democracy
- Double direct election
- Elbridge Gerry

# Chapter 3

# Electoral College (United States)

This article is about the United States Electoral College. For electoral colleges in general, see Electoral college. For other uses and regions, see Electoral college (disambiguation).

*Electoral College map showing the results of the 2012 U.S. presidential election. President Barack Obama (D-IL) won the popular vote in 26 states and the District of Columbia (denoted in blue) to capture 332 electoral votes. Former Governor Mitt Romney (R-MA) won the popular vote in 24 states (denoted in red) to capture 206 electoral votes.*

The **United States Electoral College** is the institution that elects the President and Vice President of the United States every four years. Citizens of the United States do not directly elect the president or the vice president; instead, these voters directly elect designated intermediaries called "electors," who almost always have pledged to vote for particular presidential and vice presidential candidates (though unpledged electors are possible) and who are themselves selected according to the particular laws of each state. Electors are apportioned to each of the 50 states as well as to the District of Columbia (also known as Washington, D.C.). The number of electors in each state is equal to the number of members of Congress to which the state is entitled,[1] while the Twenty-third Amendment grants the District of Columbia the same number of electors as the least populous state, currently three. Therefore, in total, there are currently 538 electors, corresponding to the 435 members

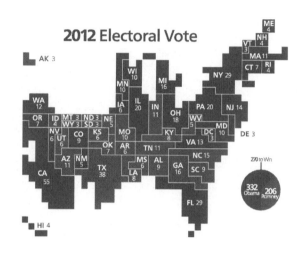

*Cartogram representation of the Electoral College vote for the 2012 election, with each square representing one electoral vote.*

of the House of Representatives and 100 senators, plus the three additional electors from the District of Columbia.

Except for the electors in Maine and Nebraska, electors are elected on a "winner-take-all" basis.[2] That is, all electors pledged to the presidential candidate who wins the most votes in a state become electors for that state. Maine and Nebraska use the "congressional district method", selecting one elector within each congressional district by popular vote and selecting the remaining two electors by a statewide popular vote.[3] Although no elector is required by federal law to honor a pledge, there have only been very few occasions when an elector voted contrary to a pledge.[4][5] The Twelfth Amendment, in specifying how a president and vice president are elected, requires each elector to cast one vote for president and another vote for vice president.

The candidate who receives an absolute majority of electoral votes (currently 270) for the office of president or of vice president is elected to that office. The Twelfth Amendment provides for what happens if the Electoral College fails to elect a president or vice president. If no candidate receives a majority for president, then the House of Representatives will select the president, with each state delegation (instead of each representative) having only one vote. If no candidate receives a majority for vice president, then the Senate will select the vice president, with each senator having one vote. On four occasions, most recently in 2000, the Electoral College system has resulted in the election of a candidate who did not receive the most popular votes in the election.[6][7]

## 3.1 Background

The Constitutional Convention in 1787 used the Virginia Plan as the basis for discussions, as the Virginia delegation had proposed it first. The Virginia Plan called for the Congress to elect the president.[8] Delegates from a majority of states agreed to this mode of election.[9] However, the Committee of Eleven, formed to work out various details including the mode of election of the president, recommended instead that the election be by a group of people apportioned among the states in the same numbers as their representatives in Congress (the formula for which had been resolved in lengthy debates resulting in the Connecticut Compromise and Three-fifths compromise), but chosen by each state "in such manner as its Legislature may direct." Committee member Gouverneur Morris explained the reasons for the change; among others, there were fears of "intrigue" if the president were chosen by a small group of men who met together regularly, as well as concerns for the independence of the president if he was elected by the Congress.[10] Some delegates, including James Wilson and James Madison, preferred popular election of the executive. Madison acknowledged that while a popular vote would be ideal, it would be difficult to get consensus on the proposal given the prevalence of slavery in the South:

> There was one difficulty however of a serious nature attending an immediate choice by the people. The right of suffrage was much more diffusive in the Northern than the Southern States; and the latter could have no influence in the election on the score of Negroes. The substitution of electors obviated this difficulty and seemed on the whole to be liable to the fewest objections.[11]

The Convention approved the Committee's Electoral College proposal, with minor modifications, on September 6, 1787.[12] Delegates from the small states generally favored the Electoral College out of concern that the large states would otherwise control presidential elections.[13]

In *The Federalist Papers*, James Madison explained his views on the selection of the president and the Constitution.

In Federalist No. 39, Madison argued that the Constitution was designed to be a mixture of state-based and population-based government. Congress would have two houses: the state-based Senate and the population-based House of Representatives. Meanwhile, the president would be elected by a mixture of the two modes.[14] Additionally, in the Federalist No. 10, James Madison argued against "an interested and overbearing majority" and the "mischiefs of faction" in an electoral system. He defined a faction as "a number of citizens whether amounting to a majority or minority of the whole, who are united and actuated by some common impulse of passion, or of interest, adverse to the rights of other citizens, or to the permanent and aggregate interests of the community." Republican government (i.e., federalism, as opposed to direct democracy), with its varied distribution of voter rights and powers, would countervail against factions. Madison further postulated in the Federalist No. 10 that the greater the population and expanse of the Republic, the more difficulty factions would face in organizing due to such issues as sectionalism.[15]

Although the United States Constitution refers to "Electors" and "electors", neither the phrase "Electoral College" nor any other name is used to describe the electors collectively. It was not until the early 19th century that the name "Electoral College" came into general usage as the collective designation for the electors selected to cast votes for president and vice president. It was first written into federal law in 1845 and today the term appears in 3 U.S.C. § 4, in the section heading and in the text as "college of electors."[16]

## 3.2 History

### 3.2.1 Original plan

Article II, Section 1, Clause 2 of the Constitution states:

> Each State shall appoint, in such Manner as the Legislature thereof may direct, a Number of Electors, equal to the whole Number of Senators and Representatives to which the State may be entitled in the Congress: but no Senator or Representative, or Person holding an Office of Trust or Profit under the United States, shall be appointed an Elector.

Article II, Section 1, Clause 4 of the Constitution states:

> The Congress may determine the Time of choosing the Electors, and the Day on which they shall give their Votes; which Day shall be the same throughout the United States.

Article II, Section 1, Clause 3 of the Constitution provided for the original fashion by which the president and vice president were to be chosen by the electors. In the original system, the candidate who received a majority of votes from the electors would become president; the candidate receiving the second most votes would become vice president.

The design of the Electoral College was based upon several assumptions and anticipations of the Framers of the Constitution:[17]

1. Each state legislature would determine a system of allocating electors. First systems included legislatures, district plans and direct popular voting.

2. Each presidential elector would exercise independent judgment when voting.

3. Candidates would not pair together on the same ticket with assumed placements toward each office of president and vice president.

4. The system as designed would rarely produce a winner, thus sending the election to Congress.

On these facts, some scholars have described the Electoral College as being intended to nominate candidates from which the Congress would then select a president and vice president.[18]

Each state government is free to have its own plan for selecting its electors, and the Constitution does not require states to popularly elect their electors. Several different methods for selecting electors are described at length below.

### 3.2.2 Breakdown and revision

The emergence of political parties and nationally coordinated election campaigns soon complicated matters in the elections of 1796 and 1800. In 1796, Federalist Party candidate John Adams won the presidential election; by finishing in second place, Democratic-Republican Party candidate Thomas Jefferson, the Federalists' opponent, became the vice president. This resulted in the President and Vice President not being of the same political party.

In 1800, the Democratic-Republican Party again nominated Jefferson for president, and also nominated Aaron Burr for vice president. After the election, Jefferson and Burr both obtained a majority of electoral votes, but tied one another with 73 votes each. Since ballots did not distinguish between votes for president and votes for vice president, every ballot cast for Burr technically counted as a vote for him to become president, despite Jefferson clearly being his party's first choice. Lacking a clear winner by constitutional standards, the election had to be decided by the House of

Representatives pursuant to the Constitution's contingency election provision.

Having already lost the presidential contest, Federalist Party representatives in the lame duck House session seized upon the opportunity to embarrass their opposition and attempted to elect Burr over Jefferson. The House deadlocked for 35 ballots as neither candidate received the necessary majority vote of the state delegations in the House (the votes of nine states were needed for an election). Jefferson achieved electoral victory on the 36th ballot, but only after Federalist Party leader Alexander Hamilton—who disfavored Burr's personal character more than Jefferson's policies—had made known his preference for Jefferson.

Responding to the problems from those elections, the Congress proposed the Twelfth Amendment in 1803—prescribing electors cast separate ballots for president and vice president—to replace the system outlined in Article II, Section 1, Clause 3. By June 1804, the states had ratified the amendment in time for the 1804 election.

### 3.2.3 Fourteenth Amendment

Section 2 of the Fourteenth Amendment allows for a state's representation in the House of Representatives to be reduced to the extent that state unconstitutionally denies people the right to vote.

On May 8, 1866, during a debate on the Fourteenth Amendment, Thaddeus Stevens, the leader of the Republicans in the House of Representatives, delivered a speech on the amendment's intent. Regarding Section 2, he said:[19]

> The second section I consider the most important in the article. It fixes the basis of representation in Congress. If any State shall exclude any of her adult male citizens from the elective franchise, or abridge that right, she shall forfeit her right to representation in the same proportion. The effect of this provision will be either to compel the States to grant universal suffrage or so shear them of their power as to keep them forever in a hopeless minority in the national Government, both legislative and executive.[20]

Federal law (2 U.S.C. § 6) implements Section 2's mandate.

## 3.3 Modern mechanics

### 3.3.1 Summary

Even though the aggregate national popular vote is calculated by state officials, media organizations, and the Federal Election Commission, the people only indirectly elect the president, as the national popular vote is not the basis for electing the president or vice president. The President and Vice President of the United States are elected by the Electoral College, which consists of 538 presidential electors from the fifty states and Washington, D.C.. Presidential electors are selected on a state-by-state basis, as determined by the laws of each state. Since the election of 1824,[21] most states have appointed their electors on a winner-take-all basis, based on the statewide popular vote on Election Day. Maine and Nebraska are the only two current exceptions, as both states use the congressional district method. Although ballots list the names of the presidential and vice presidential candidates (who run on a ticket), voters actually choose electors when they vote for president and vice president. These presidential electors in turn cast electoral votes for those two offices. Electors usually pledge to vote for their party's nominee, but some "faithless electors" have voted for other candidates.

A candidate must receive an absolute majority of electoral votes (currently 270) to win the presidency or the vice presidency. If no candidate receives a majority in the election for president or vice president, that election is determined via a contingency procedure established by the Twelfth Amendment. In such a situation, the House chooses one of the top three presidential electoral vote-winners as the president, while the Senate chooses one of the top two vice presidential electoral vote-winners as vice president.

### 3.3.2 Electors

**Apportionment**

Further information: United States congressional apportionment

A state's number of electors equals the number of representatives and senators the state has in the United States Congress.[22][23] In the case of representatives, this is based on the respective populations. Each state's number of representatives is determined every 10 years by the United States Census. In the case of senators, each state is entitled to two.

Under the Twenty-third Amendment, Washington, D.C. is allocated as many electors as it would have if it were a state, but no more electors than the least populous state. The least populous state (which is Wyoming according to the 2010 Census) has three electors; thus, D.C. cannot have more than three electors. Even if D.C. were a state, its population would entitle it to only three electors; based on its pop-

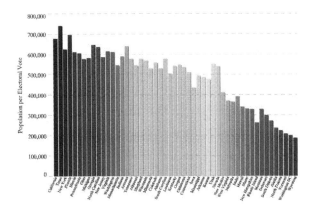

*State population per electoral vote for the 50 states and Washington D.C.*

ulation per electoral vote, D.C. has the second highest per-capita Electoral College representation, after Wyoming.[24]

Currently, there is a total of 538 electors, there being 435 representatives and 100 senators, plus the three electors allocated to Washington, D.C.. The six states with the most electors are California (55), Texas (38), New York (29), Florida (29), Illinois (20) and Pennsylvania (20). The seven smallest states by population—Alaska, Delaware, Montana, North Dakota, South Dakota, Vermont, and Wyoming—have three electors each. This is because each of these states is entitled to one representative and two senators.

**Selection**

Article II, Section 1, Clause 2 of the Constitution requires each state legislature to determine how electors for the state are to be chosen, but it disqualifies any person holding a federal office, either elected or appointed, from being an elector.[25] Under Section 3 of the Fourteenth Amendment, any person who has sworn an oath to support the United States Constitution in order to hold either a state or federal office, and later rebelled against the United States, is disqualified from being an elector. However, the Congress may remove this disqualification by a two-thirds vote in each House.

Candidates for elector are nominated by their state political parties in the months prior to Election Day. In some states, the electors are nominated in primaries, the same way that other candidates are nominated. In some states, such as Oklahoma, Virginia and North Carolina, electors are nominated in party conventions. In Pennsylvania, the campaign committee of each candidate names their candidates for elector (an attempt to discourage faithless electors).[26]

Since the Civil War, all states have chosen presidential electors by popular vote. This process has been normalized to the point that the names of the electors appear on the ballot only in a handful of states.[4][27]

The Tuesday following the first Monday in November has been fixed as the day for holding federal elections, called the Election Day.[28] Forty eight states and Washington, D.C., employ the "winner-takes-all method", each awarding its electors as a single bloc. Maine and Nebraska use the "congressional district method", selecting one elector within each congressional district by popular vote and selecting the remaining two electors by a statewide popular vote. This method has been used in Maine since 1972 and in Nebraska since 1996.[3]

The current system of choosing electors is called the "short ballot." In most states, voters choose a slate of electors, and only a few states list on the ballot the names of proposed electors. In some states, if a voter wants to write in a candidate for president, the voter is also required to write in the names of proposed electors.[26]

After the election each state prepares seven Certificates of Ascertainment, each listing the candidates for president and vice president, their pledged electors, and the total votes each candidacy received.[29] One certificate is sent, as soon after Election Day as practicable, to the National Archivist in Washington D.C. The Certificates of Ascertainment are mandated to carry the State Seal, and the signature of the Governor (in the case of the District of Columbia, the Certificate is signed by the Mayor of the District of Columbia[30]).

## Meetings

The Electoral College never actually meets as one body. Electors chosen on Election Day meet in their respective state capitals (electors for the District of Columbia meet within the District) on the Monday after the second Wednesday in December, at which time they cast their electoral votes on separate ballots for president and vice president.[31][32][33]

Although procedures in each state vary slightly, the electors generally follow a similar series of steps, and the Congress has constitutional authority to regulate the procedures the states follow. The meeting is opened by the election certification official—often that state's secretary of state or equivalent—who reads the Certificate of Ascertainment. This document sets forth who was chosen to cast the electoral votes. The attendance of the electors is taken and any vacancies are noted in writing. The next step is the selection of a president or chairman of the meeting, sometimes also with a vice chairman. The electors sometimes choose a secretary, often not himself an elector, to take the minutes of the meeting. In many states, political officials give short speeches at this point in the proceedings.

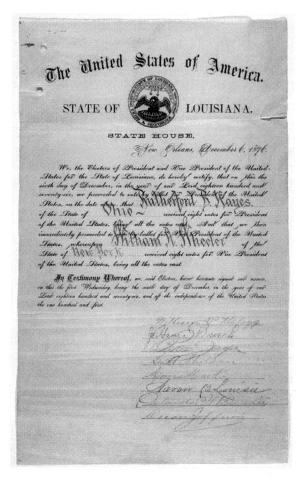

Certificate for the electoral vote for Rutherford B. Hayes and William A. Wheeler for the State of Louisiana

When the time for balloting arrives, the electors choose one or two people to act as tellers. Some states provide for the placing in nomination of a candidate to receive the electoral votes (the candidate for president of the political party of the electors). Each elector submits a written ballot with the name of a candidate for president. In New Jersey, the electors cast ballots by checking the name of the candidate on a pre-printed card; in North Carolina, the electors write the name of the candidate on a blank card. The tellers count the ballots and announce the result. The next step is the casting of the vote for vice president, which follows a similar pattern.

Each state's electors must complete six Certificates of Vote. Each Certificate of Vote must be signed by all of the electors and a Certificate of Ascertainment must be attached to each of the Certificates of Vote. Each Certificate of Vote must include the names of those who received an electoral vote for either the office of president or of vice president. The electors certify the Certificates of Vote and copies of the Certificates are then sent in the following fashion:[34]

- One is sent by registered mail to the President of the Senate (who usually is the vice president);

- Two are sent by registered mail to the Archivist of the United States;

- Two are sent to the state's Secretary of State; and

- One is sent to the chief judge of the United States district court where those electors met.

A staff member of the President of the Senate collects the Certificates of Vote as they arrive and prepares them for the joint session of the Congress. The Certificates are arranged—unopened—in alphabetical order and placed in two special mahogany boxes. Alabama through Missouri (including the District of Columbia) are placed in one box and Montana through Wyoming are placed in the other box.[35]

### Faithlessness

Main article: Faithless elector

A faithless elector is one who casts an electoral vote for someone other than the person pledged or does not vote for any person. Twenty-four states have laws to punish faithless electors. In 1952, the constitutionality of state pledge laws was brought before the Supreme Court in *Ray v. Blair*, 343 U.S. 214 (1952). The Court ruled in favor of state laws requiring electors to pledge to vote for the winning candidate, as well as removing electors who refuse to pledge. As stated in the ruling, electors are acting as a functionary of the state, not the federal government. Therefore, states have the right to govern electors. The constitutionality of state laws punishing electors for actually casting a faithless vote, rather than refusing to pledge, has never been decided by the Supreme Court. While many only punish a faithless elector after-the-fact, states like Michigan also specify that the faithless elector's vote be voided.[36]

As electoral slates are typically chosen by the political party or the party's presidential nominee, electors usually have high loyalty to the party and its candidate: a faithless elector runs a greater risk of party censure than criminal charges.

Faithless electors have not changed the outcome of any presidential election to date. For example, in 2000 elector Barbara Lett-Simmons of Washington, D.C. chose not to vote, rather than voting for Al Gore as she had pledged to do. This was done as an act of protest against Washington, D.C.'s lack of congressional voting representation.[37] That elector's abstention did not change who won that year's presidential election, as George W. Bush received a majority (271) of the electoral votes.

### 3.3.3 Joint session of Congress and the contingent election

The Twelfth Amendment mandates that the Congress assemble in joint session to count the electoral votes and declare the winners of the election.[38] The session is ordinarily required to take place on January 6 in the calendar year immediately following the meetings of the presidential electors.[39] Since the Twentieth Amendment, the newly elected House declares the winner of the election; all elections before 1936 were determined by the outgoing House instead.

The meeting is held at 1:00 pm in the Chamber of the U.S. House of Representatives.[39] The sitting vice president is expected to preside, but in several cases the President *pro tempore* of the Senate has chaired the proceedings instead. The vice president and the Speaker of the House sit at the podium, with the vice president in the seat of the Speaker of the House. Senate pages bring in the two mahogany boxes containing each state's certified vote and place them on tables in front of the senators and representatives. Each house appoints two tellers to count the vote (normally one member of each political party). Relevant portions of the Certificate of Vote are read for each state, in alphabetical order.

Members of Congress can object to any state's vote count, provided that the objection is presented in writing and is signed by at least one member of each house of Congress. An objection supported by at least one senator and one representative will be followed by the suspension of the joint session and by separate debates and votes in each House of Congress; after both Houses deliberate on the objection, the joint session is resumed. A State's certificate of vote can be rejected only if both Houses of Congress vote to accept the objection. In that case, the votes from the State in question are simply ignored. The votes of Arkansas and Louisiana were rejected in the presidential election of 1872.[40]

Objections to the electoral vote count are rarely raised, although it did occur during the vote count in 2001 after the close 2000 presidential election between Governor George W. Bush of Texas and the Vice President of the United States, Al Gore. Vice President Gore, who as vice president was required to preside over his own Electoral College defeat (by five electoral votes), denied the objections, all of which were raised only by several House members and would have favored his candidacy, after no senators would agree to jointly object. Objections were again raised in the vote count of the 2004 elections, and on that occasion the document was presented by one representative and one senator. Although the joint session was suspended, the objections were quickly disposed of and rejected by both Houses of Congress. If there are no objections or all objections are overruled, the presiding officer simply includes a State's votes, as declared in the certificate of vote, in the official tally.

After the certificates from all States are read and the respective votes are counted, the presiding officer simply announces the final result of the vote and, provided that the required absolute majority of votes was achieved, declares the names of the persons elected president and vice president. This announcement concludes the joint session and formalizes the recognition of the president-elect and of the vice president-elect. The senators then depart from the House Chamber. The final tally is printed in the Senate and House journals.

### 3.3.4 Contingent presidential election by House

Pursuant to the Twelfth Amendment, the House of Representatives is required to go into session immediately to vote for president if no candidate for president receives a majority of the electoral votes (since 1964, 270 of the 538 electoral votes).

In this event, the House of Representatives is limited to choosing from among the three candidates who received the most electoral votes. Each state delegation votes *en bloc* – each delegation having a single vote; the District of Columbia does not receive a vote. A candidate must receive an absolute majority of state delegation votes (i.e., at present, a minimum of 26 votes) in order for that candidate to become the *President-elect*. Additionally, delegations from at least two-thirds of all the states must be present for voting to take place. The House continues balloting until it elects a president.

The House of Representatives has chosen the president only twice: in 1801 under Article II, Section 1, Clause 3 and in 1825 under the Twelfth Amendment.

### 3.3.5 Contingent vice presidential election by Senate

If no candidate for vice president receives an absolute majority of electoral votes, then the Senate must go into session to elect a vice president. The Senate is limited to choosing from only the top two candidates to have received electoral votes (one fewer than the number to which the House is limited). The Senate votes in the normal manner in this case (i.e., ballots are individually cast by each senator, not by state delegations). However, two-thirds of the senators must be present for voting to take place.

Additionally, the Twelfth Amendment states that a "major-

ity of the whole number" of senators (currently 51 of 100) is necessary for election.[41] Further, the language requiring an absolute majority of Senate votes precludes the sitting vice president from breaking any tie which might occur,[42] although this is disputed by some legal scholars.[43]

The only time the Senate chose the vice president was in 1837. In that instance, the Senate adopted an alphabetical roll call and voting aloud. The rules further stated, "[I]f a majority of the number of senators shall vote for either the said Richard M. Johnson or Francis Granger, he shall be declared by the presiding officer of the Senate constitutionally elected Vice President of the United States;" the Senate chose Johnson.[44]

### 3.3.6 Deadlocked chambers

If the House of Representatives has not chosen a *president-elect* in time for the inauguration (noon on January 20), then Section 3 of the Twentieth Amendment specifies that the *vice president-elect* becomes acting president until the House selects a president. If there is also no vice president-elect in time for the inauguration, then under the Presidential Succession Act of 1947, the sitting Speaker of the House would become acting president until either the House selects a president or the Senate selects a vice president. Neither of these situations has ever occurred.

### 3.3.7 Current electoral vote distribution

See also: Electoral vote changes between United States presidential elections

The following table shows the number of electoral votes (EV) to which each state and the District of Columbia will be entitled during the 2012, 2016 and 2020 presidential elections:[45] The numbers in parentheses represent the number of electoral votes that a state gained (+) or lost (-) because of reapportionment following the 2010 Census.[46]

*The District of Columbia, though not a state, is granted the same number of electoral votes as the least populous state (which has always been 3) by the Twenty-third Amendment.*

** *Maine and Nebraska electors distributed by way of the Congressional District Method.*

(+) *or* (-) *represents number of electors gained or lost in comparison to 2004 & 2008 electoral college allocation*

## 3.4 Chronological table

Source: http://psephos.adam-carr.net/countries/u/usa/
pres.shtml Note: In 1788, 1792, 1796, and 1800, each
elector cast votes for two Candidates

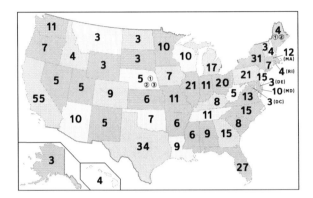

*Number of electors from each state for the 2004 and 2008 pres-
idential elections. 12 electoral votes changed between 18 states,
based on the 2010 census. Eight states lost one electoral vote and
two (New York & Ohio) each lost two electoral votes. Eight states
gained electoral votes, six gained one electoral vote, Florida gained
two & Texas gained four.*

## 3.5 Alternative methods of choosing electors

Before the advent of the short ballot in the early 20th century, as described above, the most common means of electing the presidential electors was through the *general ticket*.
The general ticket is quite similar to the current system
and is often confused with it. In the general ticket, voters
cast ballots for individuals running for presidential elector
(while in the short ballot, voters cast ballots for an entire
slate of electors). In the general ticket, the state canvass
would report the number of votes cast for each candidate for
elector, a complicated process in states like New York with
multiple positions to fill. Both the general ticket and the
short ballot are often considered at-large or winner-takes-all
voting. The short ballot was adopted by the various states
at different times; it was adopted for use by North Carolina
and Ohio in 1932. Alabama was still using the general ticket
as late as 1960 and was one of the last states to switch to the
short ballot.

The question of the extent to which state constitutions may
constrain the legislature's choice of a method of choosing
electors has been touched on in two U.S. Supreme Court
cases. In *McPherson v. Blacker*, 146 U.S. 1 (1892), the
Court cited Article II, Section 1, Clause 2 which states
that a state's electors are selected "in such manner as the

legislature thereof may direct" and wrote that these words
"operat[e] as a limitation upon the state in respect of any
attempt to circumscribe the legislative power." In *Bush v.
Palm Beach County Canvassing Board*, 531 U.S. 70 (2000),
a Florida Supreme Court decision was vacated (not reversed) based on *McPherson*. On the other hand, three dissenting justices in *Bush v. Gore*, 531 U.S. 98 (2000), wrote:
"nothing in Article II of the Federal Constitution frees the
state legislature from the constraints in the State Constitution that created it."[48]

### 3.5.1 Appointment by state legislature

In the earliest presidential elections, state legislative choice
was the most common method of choosing electors. A majority of the states selected presidential electors by legislation in both 1792 (9 of 15) and 1800 (10 of 16), and
half of the states did so in 1812.[49] Even in the 1824 election, a quarter of states (6 of 24) chose electors by legislation. In that election, Andrew Jackson lost in spite of having pluralities of both the popular and electoral votes,[50]
with the outcome being decided by the six state legislatures
choosing the electors. Some state legislatures simply chose
electors, while other states used a hybrid method in which
state legislatures chose from a group of electors elected
by popular vote.[51] By 1828, with the rise of Jacksonian
democracy, only Delaware and South Carolina used legislative choice.[50] Delaware ended its practice the following election (1832), while South Carolina continued using
the method until it seceded from the Union in December
1860.[50] South Carolina used the popular vote for the first
time in the 1868 election.[52]

Excluding South Carolina, legislative appointment was used
in only four situations after 1832:

- In 1848, Massachusetts statute awarded the state's
  electoral votes to the winner of the at-large popular
  vote, but only if that candidate won an absolute majority. When the vote produced no winner between
  the Democratic, Free Soil, and Whig parties, the state
  legislature selected the electors, giving all 12 electoral
  votes to the Whigs.[53]

- In 1864, Nevada, having joined the Union only a
  few days prior to Election Day, had no choice but to
  appoint.[53]

- In 1868, the newly reconstructed state of Florida appointed its electors, having been readmitted too late to
  hold elections.[53]

- Finally, in 1876, the legislature of the newly admitted
  state of Colorado used legislative choice due to a lack
  of time and money to hold an election.[53]

Legislative appointment was brandished as a possibility in the 2000 election. Had the recount continued, the Florida legislature was prepared to appoint the Republican slate of electors to avoid missing the federal safe-harbor deadline for choosing electors.[54]

The Constitution gives each state legislature the power to decide how its state's electors are chosen[50] and it can be easier and cheaper for a state legislature to simply appoint a slate of electors than to create a legislative framework for holding elections to determine the electors. As noted above, the two situations in which legislative choice has been used since the Civil War have both been because there was not enough time or money to prepare for an election. However, appointment by state legislature can have negative consequences: bicameral legislatures can deadlock more easily than the electorate. This is precisely what happened to New York in 1789 when the legislature failed to appoint any electors.[55]

### 3.5.2  Electoral districts

Another method used early in U.S. history was to divide the state into electoral districts. By this method, voters in each district would cast their ballots for the candidate they supported and the winner in each district would receive that electoral vote. This was similar to how states are currently separated by congressional districts. However, the difference stems from the fact that every state always had two more electoral districts than congressional districts. As with congressional districts, moreover, this method is vulnerable to gerrymandering.

### 3.5.3  Proportional vote

Under such a system, electors would be selected in proportion to the votes cast for their candidate or party, rather than being selected by the statewide plurality vote.[56]

### 3.5.4  Congressional District Method

There are two versions of the Congressional District Method: one has been implemented in Maine and Nebraska; another that has been proposed in Virginia. Under the implemented Congressional District Method, the electoral votes are distributed based on the popular vote winner within each of the state's congressional districts; the statewide popular vote winner receives two additional electoral votes.[57]

In 2013, a different version of the Congressional District Method was proposed in Virginia. This version would distribute Virginia's electoral votes based on the popular

vote winner within each of Virginia's congressional districts; the two statewide electoral votes would be awarded based on which candidate won the most congressional districts, rather than on who won Virginia's statewide popular vote.[58]

The Congressional District Method can more easily be implemented than other alternatives to the winner-takes-all method. State legislation is sufficient to use this method.[59] Advocates of the Congressional District Method believe the system would encourage higher voter turnout and incentivize presidential candidates to broaden their campaigns in non-competitive states.[60] Winner-take-all systems ignore thousands of popular votes; in Democratic California there are Republican districts, in Republican Texas there are Democratic districts. Because candidates have an incentive to campaign in competitive districts, with a district plan, candidates have an incentive to actively campaign in over thirty states versus seven "swing" states.[61][62] Opponents of the system, however, argue that candidates might only spend time in certain battleground districts instead of the entire state and cases of gerrymandering could become exacerbated as political parties attempt to draw as many safe districts as they can.[63]

Unlike simple congressional district comparisons, the District Plan popular vote bonus in the 2008 election would have given Obama 56% of the Electoral College versus the 68% he did win, it "would have more closely approximated the percentage of the popular vote won [53%]."[64]

#### Implementation

Of the 43 states whose electoral votes could be affected by the Congressional District Method, only Maine and Nebraska apply it. Maine has four electoral votes, based on its two representatives and two senators. Nebraska has two senators and three representatives, giving it five electoral votes.[65] Maine began using the Congressional District Method in the election of 1972. Nebraska has used the Congressional District Method since the election of 1992.[66][67] Since the 1830s, the only other state to use the system is Michigan, which only used the system for the 1892 presidential election.[57][68][69]

The Congressional District Method allows a state the chance to split its electoral votes between multiple candidates. Before 2008, neither Maine nor Nebraska had ever split their electoral votes.[57] Nebraska split its electoral votes for the first time in 2008, giving John McCain its statewide electors and those of two congressional districts, while Barack Obama won the electoral vote of Nebraska's 2nd congressional district.[70] Following the 2008 split, some Nebraska Republicans made efforts to discard the Congressional District Method and return to the winner-takes-all system.[71] In January 2010, a bill was introduced in the Nebraska legislature to revert to a winner-take-all system;[72] the bill died in committee in March 2011.[73] Republicans had also passed bills in 1995 and 1997 to eliminate the Congressional District Method in Nebraska, but those bills were vetoed by Democratic Governor Ben Nelson.[71]

In 2010, Republicans in Pennsylvania, who controlled both houses of the legislature as well as the governorship, put forward a plan to change the state's winner-takes-all system to a Congressional district method system. Pennsylvania had voted for the Democratic candidate in the five previous presidential elections, so many saw this as an attempt to take away Democratic electoral votes. Although Democrat Barack Obama won Pennsylvania in 2008, he only won a minority of the state's congressional districts.[74][75] The plan later lost support.[76] Other Republicans, including Michigan state representative Pete Lund,[77] RNC Chairman Reince Priebus, and Wisconsin Governor Scott Walker, have floated similar ideas.[78][79]

## 3.6 Contemporary issues

Arguments between proponents and opponents of the current electoral system include four separate but related topics: indirect election, disproportionate voting power by some states, the winner-takes-all distribution method (as chosen by 48 of the 50 states), and federalism. Arguments against the Electoral College in common discussion mostly focus on the allocation of the voting power among the states. Gary Bugh' s research of congressional debates over proposed Electoral College amendments reveals that reform opponents have often appealed to a traditional version of representation, whereas reform advocates have tended to reference a more democratic view.[80]

### 3.6.1 Criticism

**Irrelevancy of national popular vote**

The elections of 1876, 1888, and 2000 produced an Electoral College winner who did not receive at least a plurality of the nationwide popular vote.[81] In 1824, there were six states in which electors were legislatively appointed, rather than popularly elected, so the true national popular vote is uncertain. When no candidate received a majority of electoral votes in 1824, the election was decided by the House of Representatives and so could be considered distinct from the latter three elections in which all of the states had popular selection of electors.[82] The true national popular vote was also uncertain in the 1960 election, and the plurality for

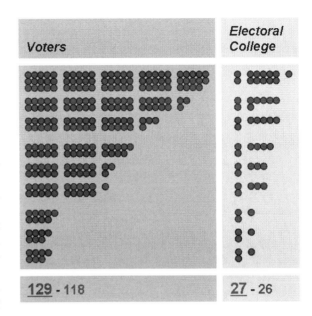

*This graphic demonstrates how the winner of the popular vote can still lose in a hypothetical electoral college system.*

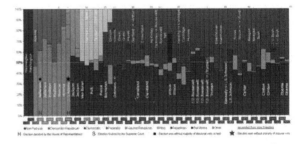

*A bar graph of popular votes in presidential elections, with blue stars marking the four elections in which the winner did not have the plurality of the popular vote. Black squares mark the cases where the electoral vote resulted in a tie, or the winner did not have the majority of electoral votes. An 'H' marks the two cases where the election was decided by the House, and an 'S' marks the one case where the election was finalized by the Supreme Court.*

the winner depends on how votes for Alabama electors are allocated.[83]

Opponents of the Electoral College claim that such outcomes do not logically follow the normative concept of how a democratic system should function. One view is that the Electoral College violates the principle of political equality, since presidential elections are not decided by the one-person one-vote principle.[81] Outcomes of this sort are attributable to the federal nature of the system. Supporters of the Electoral College argue that candidates must build a popular base that is geographically broader and more diverse in voter interests. This feature is not a logical consequence of having intermediate elections of Presidents, but rather the winner-takes-all method of allocating each state's slate of electors. Allocation of electors in proportion to the state's popular vote could reduce this effect.

Scenarios exhibiting this outcome typically result when the winning candidate has won the requisite configuration of states (and thus their votes) by small margins, but the losing candidate captured large voter margins in the remaining states. In this case, the very large margins secured by the losing candidate in the other states would aggregate to well over 50 percent of the ballots cast nationally. In a two-candidate race, with equal voter turnout in every district and no faithless electors, a candidate could win the electoral college while winning only about 22% of the nationwide popular vote. This would require the candidate in question to win each one of the following states by just one vote: Alabama, Alaska, Arizona, Arkansas, Colorado, Connecticut, Delaware, District of Columbia, Hawaii, Idaho, Indiana, Iowa, Kansas, Kentucky, Louisiana, Maine, Maryland, Massachusetts, Minnesota, Mississippi, Missouri, Montana, Nebraska, Nevada, New Hampshire, New Jersey, New Mexico, North Dakota, Oklahoma, Oregon, Rhode Island, South Carolina, South Dakota, Tennessee, Utah, Vermont, Virginia, West Virginia, Wisconsin, and Wyoming.[84]

A result of the present functionality of the Electoral College is that the national popular vote bears no legal or factual significance on determining the outcome of the election. Since the national popular vote is irrelevant, both voters and candidates are assumed to base their campaign strategies around the existence of the Electoral College; any close race has candidates campaigning to maximize electoral votes by capturing coveted swing states, not to maximize national popular vote totals.

> The United States is the only country that elects a politically powerful president via an electoral college and the only one in which a candidate can become president without having obtained the highest number of votes in the sole or final round of popular voting.
> — George C. Edwards, 2011[81]

**Exclusive focus on large swing states**

Main article: Swing state

According to this criticism, the electoral college encourages political campaigners to focus on a few so-called "swing states" while ignoring the rest of the country. Populous states in which pre-election poll results show no clear favorite are inundated with campaign visits, saturation television advertising, get-out-the-vote efforts by party organizers and debates, while "four out of five" voters in the national election are "absolutely ignored," according to one

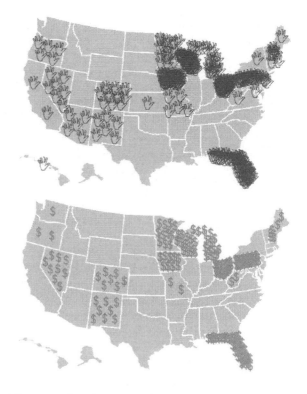

*These maps show the amount of attention given to each state by the Bush and Kerry campaigns during the final five weeks of the 2004 election. At the top, each waving hand represents a visit from a presidential or vice presidential candidate during the final five weeks. At the bottom, each dollar sign represents one million dollars spent on TV advertising by the campaigns during the same time period.*

assessment.[85] Since most states use a winner-takes-all arrangement in which the candidate with the most votes in that state receives all of the state's electoral votes, there is a clear incentive to focus almost exclusively on only a few key undecided states; in recent elections, these states have included Pennsylvania, Ohio, and Florida in 2004 and 2008, and also Colorado in 2012. In contrast, states with large populations such as California, Texas, and New York, have in recent elections been considered "safe" for a particular party—Democratic for California and New York and Republican for Texas—and therefore campaigns spend less time and money there. Many small states are also considered to be "safe" for one of the two political parties and are also generally ignored by campaigners: of the 13 smallest states, six are reliably Democratic, six are reliably Republican, and only New Hampshire is considered as a swing state, according to critic George C. Edwards III.[81] In the 2008 election, campaigns did not mount nationwide efforts but rather focused on select states.[81]

It is possible to win the election by winning eleven states and disregarding the rest of the country. If one ticket were to take California (55 votes), Texas (38), New York (29), Florida (29), Illinois (20), Pennsylvania (20), Ohio (18),

Michigan (16), Georgia (16), North Carolina (15), and New Jersey (14) that ticket would have 270 votes, which would be enough to win. In the close elections of 2000 and 2004, these eleven states gave 111 votes to Republican candidate George W. Bush and 160 votes to Democratic candidates Al Gore and John Kerry. In 2008, the Democratic candidate Barack Obama won nine of these eleven states (for 222 electoral votes), with Republican John McCain taking a combined 49 electoral votes from Texas and Georgia.

Proponents of the Electoral College claim that adoption of the popular vote would shift the disproportionate focus to large cities at the expense of rural areas.[86] Candidates might also be inclined to campaign hardest in their base areas to maximize turnout among core supporters, and ignore more closely divided parts of the country. Proponents of a national popular vote for president dismiss such arguments, pointing out that candidates in popular vote elections for governor and U.S. Senate and for statewide allocation of electoral votes do not ignore voters in less populated areas.[87]

**Discourages turnout and participation**

Except in closely fought swing states, voter turnout is largely insignificant due to entrenched political party domination in most states. The Electoral College decreases the advantage a political party or campaign might gain for encouraging voters to turn out, except in those swing states.[88] If the presidential election were decided by a national popular vote, in contrast, campaigns and parties would have a strong incentive to work to increase turnout everywhere.[89] Individuals would similarly have a stronger incentive to persuade their friends and neighbors to turn out to vote. The differences in turnout between swing states and non-swing states under the current electoral college system suggest that replacing the Electoral College with direct election by popular vote would likely increase turnout and participation significantly.[88]

**Obscures disenfranchisement within states**

According to this criticism, the electoral college reduces elections to a mere count of electors for a particular state, and, as a result, it obscures any voting problems *within* a particular state. For example, if a particular state blocks some groups from voting, perhaps by voter suppression methods such as imposing reading tests, poll taxes, registration requirements, or legally disfranchising specific minority groups, then voting inside that state would be reduced. But the state's electoral count would be the same. So disenfranchisement has no effect on the overall electoral tally. Critics contend that such disenfranchisement is partially ob-

scured by the Electoral College. A related argument is that the Electoral College may have a dampening effect on voter turnout: there is no incentive for states to reach out to more of its citizens to include them in elections because the state's electoral count remains fixed in any event. According to this view, if elections were by popular vote, then states would be motivated to include more citizens in elections since the state would then have more political clout nationally. Critics contend that the electoral college system insulates states from negative publicity as well as possible federal penalties for disenfranching subgroups of citizens.

Legal scholars Akhil Amar and Vikram Amar have argued that the original Electoral College compromise was enacted partially because it enabled the southern states to disenfranchise its slave populations.[90] It permitted southern states to disfranchise large numbers of slaves while allowing these states to maintain political clout within the federation by using the three-fifths compromise. They noted that constitutional Framer James Madison believed that the question of counting slaves had presented a serious challenge but that "the substitution of electors obviated this difficulty and seemed on the whole to be liable to the fewest objections."[91] Akhil and Vikram Amar added that:

> The founders' system also encouraged the continued disfranchisement of women. In a direct national election system, any state that gave women the vote would automatically have doubled its national clout. Under the Electoral College, however, a state had no such incentive to increase the franchise; as with slaves, what mattered was how many women lived in a state, not how many were empowered ... a state with low voter turnout gets precisely the same number of electoral votes as if it had a high turnout. By contrast, a well-designed direct election system could spur states to get out the vote.
>
> — Akhil and Vikram Amar[90]

**Lack of enfranchisement of U.S. territories**

See also: Voting rights in the United States § Overseas and nonresident citizens

Territories of the United States, such as Puerto Rico and Guam, are not entitled to electors in presidential elections. Constitutionally, only U.S. states (per Article II, Section 1, Clause 2) and Washington, D.C. (per the Twenty-third Amendment) are entitled to electors. Guam has held nonbinding straw polls for president since the 1980s to draw attention to this fact.[92][93] This has also led to various scholars concluding that the U.S. national-electoral process is not fully democratic.[94][95]

### Favors less populous states

As a consequence of giving more *per capita* voting power to the less populated states, the Electoral College gives extra power to voters in those states. For example, an electoral vote represents over two times as many people in New York than in South Dakota.[96] In one countervailing analysis about smaller states gaining an Electoral College advantage, the Banzhaf power index (BPI) model based on probability theory was used to test the hypothesis that citizens of small states accrue more election power. It was found that in 1990, individual voters in California, the largest state, had 3.3 times more individual power to choose a President than voters of Montana, the largest of the minimum 3 elector states.[97] Banzhaf's method has been criticized for treating votes like coin-flips, and more empirically based models of voting yield results which seem to favor larger states less.[98]

### Disadvantage for third parties

See also: Duverger's law and Causes of a two-party system

In practice, the winner-take-all manner of allocating a state's electors generally decreases the importance of minor parties.[99] However, it has been argued that the electoral college is not a cause of the two-party system, and that it had a tendency to improve the chances of third-party candidates in some situations.[81]

### Not straightforward

One view is that the electoral college is overly and unnecessarily complex:

> The electoral college does not provide a straightforward process for selecting the president. Instead, it can be extraordinarily complex and has the potential to undo the people's will at many points in the long journey from the selection of electors to counting their votes in Congress.
> — George Edwards, 2011[81]

## 3.6.2 Support

### Prevents an urban-centric victory

Proponents of the Electoral College claim the Electoral College prevents a candidate from winning the presidency by simply winning in heavily populated urban areas. This means that candidates must make a wider geographic appeal than they would if they simply had to win the national popular vote.[100]

### Maintains the federal character of the nation

The United States of America is a federal coalition which consists of component states. Proponents of the current system argue that the collective opinion of even a small state merits attention at the federal level greater than that given to a small, though numerically equivalent, portion of a very populous state. The system also allows each state the freedom, within constitutional bounds, to design its own laws on voting and enfranchisement without an undue incentive to maximize the number of votes cast.

For many years early in the nation's history, up until the Jacksonian Era, many states appointed their electors by a vote of the state legislature, and proponents argue that, in the end, the election of the President must still come down to the decisions of each state, or the federal nature of the United States will give way to a single massive, centralized government.[101]

In his book *A More Perfect Constitution*, Professor Larry Sabato elaborated on this advantage of the Electoral College, arguing to "mend it, don't end it," in part because of its usefulness in forcing candidates to pay attention to lightly populated states and reinforcing the role of the state in federalism.[102]

### Enhances status of minority groups

Instead of decreasing the power of minority groups by depressing voter turnout, proponents argue that by making the votes of a given state an all-or-nothing affair, minority groups can provide the critical edge that allows a candidate to win. This encourages candidates to court a wide variety of such minorities and advocacy groups.[101]

### Encourages stability through the two-party system

Many proponents of the Electoral College see its negative effect on third parties as beneficial. They argue that the two party system has provided stability because it encourages a delayed adjustment during times of rapid political and cultural change. They believe it protects the most powerful office in the country from control by what these proponents view as regional minorities until they can moderate their views to win broad, long-term support across the nation. Advocates of a national popular vote for president suggest that this effect would also be true in popular vote elections. Of 918 elections for governor between 1948 and 2009, for example, more than 90% were won by candidates securing more than 50% of the vote, and none have been won with less than 35% of the vote.[103]

### Flexibility if a presidential candidate dies

According to this argument, the fact that the electoral college is made up of real people instead of mere numbers allows for human judgment and flexibility to make a decision, if it happens that a candidate dies or becomes legally disabled around the time of the election. Advocates of the current system argue that human electors would be in a better position to choose a suitable replacement than the general voting public. According to this view, electors could act decisively during the critical time interval between when ballot choices become fixed in state ballots[104] until mid-December when the electors formally cast their ballots.[105] In the election of 1872, losing Democratic candidate Horace Greeley died during this time interval which resulted in Democratic disarray, but the Greeley electors were able to split their votes for different alternate candidates.[106][107][108] A situation in which the winning candidate died has never happened. In the election of 1912, Vice President Sherman died shortly before the election when it was too late for states to remove his name from their ballots; accordingly, Sherman was listed posthumously, but the eight electoral votes that Sherman would have received were cast instead for Nicholas Murray Butler.[109]

### Isolation of election problems

Some supporters of the Electoral College note that it isolates the impact of any election fraud, or other such problems, to the state where it occurs. It prevents instances where a party dominant in one state may dishonestly inflate the votes for a candidate and thereby affect the election outcome. For instance, recounts occur only on a state-by-state basis, not nationwide.[110] Critics of the current system suggest that the results in a single state – such as Florida in 2000 – can decide the national election and thus not keep any problems in such a state isolated from the rest of the nation.[111]

## 3.7 Proposals for reform or abolition

### 3.7.1 Bayh–Celler Constitutional amendment

The closest the country has ever come to abolishing the Electoral College occurred during the 91st Congress (1969-1971).[112] The presidential election of 1968 resulted in Richard Nixon receiving 301 electoral votes (56% of electors), Hubert Humphrey 191 (35.5%) and George Wallace 46 (8.5%) with 13.5% of the popular vote. However, Nixon had only received 511,944 more popular votes than Humphrey, 43.5% to 42.9%, less than 1% of the national total.[113]

Representative Emanuel Celler (D – New York), Chairman of the House Judiciary Committee, responded to public concerns over the disparity between the popular vote and electoral vote by introducing House Joint Resolution 681, a proposed Constitutional amendment which would have replaced the Electoral College with simpler plurality system based on the national popular vote. With this system, the pair of candidates who had received the highest number of votes would win the presidency and vice presidency providing they won at least 40% of the national popular vote. If no pair received 40% of the popular vote, a runoff election would be held in which the choice of President and vice president would be made from the two pairs of persons who had received the highest number of votes in the first election. The word "pair" was defined as "two persons who shall have consented to the joining of their names as candidates for the offices of President and Vice President."[114]

On April 29, 1969, the House Judiciary Committee voted 28 to 6 to approve the proposal.[115] Debate on the proposal before the full House of Representatives ended on September 11, 1969[116] and was eventually passed with bipartisan support on September 18, 1969, by a vote of 339 to 70.[117]

On September 30, 1969, President Richard Nixon gave his endorsement for adoption of the proposal, encouraging the Senate to pass its version of the proposal which had been sponsored as Senate Joint Resolution 1 by Senator Birch Bayh (D – Indiana).[118]

On October 8, 1969, the *New York Times* reported that 30 state legislatures were "either certain or likely to approve a constitutional amendment embodying the direct election plan if it passes its final Congressional test in the Senate." Ratification of 38 state legislatures would have been needed for adoption. The paper also reported that 6 other states had yet to state a preference, 6 were leaning toward opposition and 8 were solidly opposed.[119]

On August 14, 1970, the Senate Judiciary Committee sent its report advocating passage of the proposal to the full Senate. The Judiciary Committee had approved the proposal by a vote of 11 to 6. The six members who opposed the plan, Democratic Senators James Eastland of Mississippi,

John Little McClellan of Arkansas and Sam Ervin of North Carolina along with Republican Senators Roman Hruska of Nebraska, Hiram Fong of Hawaii and Strom Thurmond of South Carolina, all argued that although the present system had potential loopholes, it had worked well throughout the years. Senator Bayh indicated that supporters of the measure were about a dozen votes shy from the 67 needed for the proposal to pass the full Senate. He called upon President Nixon to attempt to persuade undecided Republican senators to support the proposal.[120] However, Nixon, while not reneging on his previous endorsement, chose not to make any further personal appeals to back the proposal.[121]

On September 8, 1970, the Senate commenced openly debating the proposal[122] and the proposal was quickly filibustered. The lead objectors to the proposal were mostly Southern senators and conservatives from small states, both Democrats and Republicans, who argued abolishing the Electoral College would reduce their states' political influence.[121] On September 17, 1970, a motion for cloture, which would have ended the filibuster, received 54 votes to 36 for cloture,[121] failing to receive the then required two-thirds majority of senators voting.[123] A second motion for cloture on September 29, 1970 also failed, by 53 to 34. Thereafter, the Senate Majority Leader, Mike Mansfield of Montana, moved to lay the proposal aside so that the Senate could attend to other business.[124] However, the proposal was never considered again and died when the 91st Congress ended on January 3, 1971.

### 3.7.2 Every Vote Counts Amendment

Main article: Every Vote Counts Amendment

A joint resolution to amend the United States Constitution, providing for the popular election of the president and vice president under a new electoral system was introduced by Representative Gene Green (D) of Texas on January 4, 2005. Representative Green then again introduced the legislation on January 7, 2009 as H.J.Res. 9.

### 3.7.3 National Popular Vote Interstate Compact

Main article: National Popular Vote Interstate Compact

Several states plus the District of Columbia have joined the National Popular Vote Interstate Compact. Those jurisdictions joining the compact agree to pledge their electors to the winner of the national popular vote. The Compact will not come into effect until a sufficient number of states agree

to the Compact such that a majority (at least 270) of all electors are pledged to the winner of the national popular vote. As of 2016, 10 states and the District of Columbia have joined the compact; collectively, these jurisdictions control 165 electoral votes, which is 61% of the 270 required for the Compact to take effect.[125]

The Compact is based on the current rule in Article II, Section 1, Clause 2 of the Constitution that gives each state legislature the plenary power to determine how it chooses its electors, though some have suggested that Article I, Section 10, Clause 3 of the Constitution requires congressional consent before the Compact could be enforcible.[126]

The first state to join the Compact was Maryland, when Governor Martin O'Malley signed the bill into law on April 10, 2007.[127] New Jersey joined on January 13, 2008, despite objections from Republicans who criticized the bill as undermining federal elections.[128] Illinois passed the law on April 7, 2008.[129] Hawaii joined on May 1, when the legislature overrode a veto from Governor Linda Lingle.[130] On April 28, 2009, the State of Washington joined, when Governor Christine Gregoire signed HB 1598.[131] Massachusetts joined the compact on August 4, 2010, when Governor Deval Patrick signed that state's bill into law.[132] Additionally, the District of Columbia, which has three electoral votes, joined the compact on December 7, 2010.[133] Vermont joined the compact on April 22, 2011, when Governor Peter Shumlin signed that state's bill into law.[134] On August 8, 2011, California joined when Governor Jerry Brown signed a bill adding California to the compact.[135]

## 3.8   See also

- County Unit System

- Electoral vote changes between United States presidential elections

- List of U.S. states and territories by population

- List of United States presidential electors, 2000

- List of United States presidential electors, 2004

- List of United States presidential electors, 2008

- List of United States presidential electors, 2012

- United States presidential election

- United States presidential election maps

# 3.9 Notes

[1] Article II, Section 1, Clause 2 of the Constitution

[2] Morris, Irwin L. (2010). *The American Presidency: An Analytical Approach*. Cambridge University Press. p. 67. ISBN 9781139491624. OCLC 607985767.

[3] The Electoral College – Maine and Nebraska

[4] The Green Papers

[5] Many states have laws designed to ensure that electors vote for pledged candidates, though the constitutionality of these laws has never been positively established. See The Green Papers

[6] Library of Congress - Election Process

[7] US House of Representatives: History, Art & Archives - Electoral College Fast Facts

[8] "Debates in the Federal Convention of 1787: May 29". Avalon Project. Retrieved April 13, 2011.

[9] "Debates in the Federal Convention of 1787: June 2". Avalon Project. Retrieved April 13, 2011.

[10] "Debates in the Federal Convention of 1787: September 4". Avalon Project. Retrieved April 13, 2011.

[11] Records of the Federal Convention, p. 57 Farrand's Records, Volume 2, A Century of Lawmaking for a New Nation: U.S. Congressional Documents and Debates, 1774–1875, Library of Congress

[12] "Debates in the Federal Convention of 1787: September 6". Avalon Project. Retrieved April 13, 2011.

[13] Concerns With The Electoral College

[14] "The Federalist 39". Avalon Project. Retrieved April 13, 2011.

[15] *The Federalist Papers: Alexander Hamilton, James Madison, John Jay* The New American Library, 1961

[16] archives.gov

[17] Chang, Stanley (2007). "Updating the Electoral College: The National Popular Vote Legislation". *Harvard Journal on Legislation* (Cambridge, MA: President and Fellows of Harvard College) **44** (205, at 208).

[18] Berg-Andersson, Richard E. (September 17, 2000). "What Are They All Doing, Anyway?: An Historical Analysis of the Electoral College". *The Green Papers*.

[19] THE FOURTEENTH AMENDMENT from America Book 9 (archived from the original on 2011-10-27)

[20] The selected papers of Thaddeus Stevens, v.2, Stevens, Thaddeus, 1792–1868, Palmer, Beverly Wilson, 1936, Ochoa, Holly Byers, 1951, Pittsburgh: University of Pittsburgh, Digital Research Library, 2011, pp. 135–136

[21] McCarthy, Devin. "How the Electoral College Became Winner-Take-All". *Fairvote*. Retrieved 22 November 2014.

[22] The present allotment of electors by state is shown in the *Electoral vote distribution* section.

[23] The number of electors allocated to each state is based on Article II, Section 1, Clause 2 of the Constitution, subject to being reduced pursuant to Section 2 of the Fourteenth Amendment.

[24] Table 1. Annual Estimates of the Population for the United States, Regions, States, and Puerto Rico: April 1, 2010 to July 1, 2011 in State Totals: Vintage 2011, United States Census Bureau.

[25] Sabrina Eaton (October 29, 2004). "Brown learns he can't serve as Kerry elector, steps down" (PDF). Cleveland Plain Dealer (reprint at Edison Research). Archived from the original (PDF) on July 10, 2011. Retrieved January 3, 2008.

[26] ElectoralVote.com – Current Assigning of Electors Archived January 11, 2015 at the Wayback Machine

[27] Darrell J. Kozlowski (2010). *Federalism*. Infobase Publishing. pp. 33–34. ISBN 978-1-60413-218-2.

[28] 3 U.S.C. § 1 A uniform national date for presidential elections was not set until 1845, although the Congress always had constitutional authority to do so. — Kimberling, William C. (1992) *The Electoral College*, p. 7

[29] "Electoral College Instructions to State Officials" (PDF). National Archives and Records Administration. Retrieved 22 January 2014.

[30] District of Columbia Certificate of Ascertainment

[31] "Twelfth Amendment". FindLaw. Retrieved August 26, 2010.

[32] "Twenty-third Amendment". FindLaw. Retrieved August 26, 2010.

[33] "U.S.C. § 7 : US Code - Section 7: Meeting and vote of electors". FindLaw. Retrieved August 26, 2010.

[34] "U.S. Electoral College – For State Officials". National Archives and Records Administration. Retrieved November 7, 2012.

[35] Associated Press (January 9, 2009). "Congress meets to count electoral votes". MSNBC. Retrieved April 5, 2012.

[36] "Michigan Election Law Section 168.47". Legislature.mi.gov. Retrieved August 26, 2010.

[37] "The Green Papers". The Green Papers. Retrieved August 26, 2010.

[38] "The President of the Senate shall, in the presence of the Senate and House of Representatives, open all the certificates and the votes shall then be counted." *Constitution of the United States: Amendments 11–27*, National Archives and Records Administration

[39] 3 U.S.C. § 15, *Counting electoral votes in Congress*

[40] David A. McKnight (1878). *The Electoral System of the United States: A Critical and Historical Exposition of Its Fundamental Principles in the Constitution and the Acts and Proceedings of Congress Enforcing It*. Wm. S. Hein Publishing. p. 313. ISBN 978-0-8377-2446-1.

[41] "RL30804: The Electoral College: An Overview and Analysis of Reform Proposals, L. Paige Whitaker and Thomas H. Neale, January 16, 2001". Ncseonline.org. Archived from the original on June 28, 2011. Retrieved August 26, 2010.

[42] Longley, Lawrence D.; Pierce, Neal R. (1999). "The Electoral College Primer 2000". New Haven, CT: Yale University Press: 13.

[43] "Election evolves into 'perfect' electoral storm". *USA Today*. December 12, 2000. Retrieved September 20, 2008.

[44] "Senate Journal from 1837". Memory.loc.gov. Retrieved August 26, 2010.

[45] "Apportionment of the U.S. House of Representatives Based on the 2010 Census" (PDF). Washington, D.C.: U.S. Census Bureau. December 21, 2010. Archived from the original (PDF) on 2011-01-24. Retrieved December 21, 2010. Each state's number of electoral votes is equal to its total congressional representation (its number of Representatives plus its two Senators).

[46] "2010 Census: State Population and the Distribution of Electoral Votes and Representatives". thegreenpapers.com. External link in |publisher= (help)

[47] Moore, John L., ed. (1985). *Congressional Quarterly's Guide to U.S. Elections* (2nd ed.). Washington, D.C.: Congressional Quarterly, Inc. pp. 254–256.

[48] *Bush v. Gore*, (Justice Stevens dissenting) (quote in second paragraph)

[49] Moore, John L., ed. (1985). *Congressional Quarterly's Guide to U.S. Elections* (2nd ed.). Washington, D.C.: Congressional Quarterly, Inc. p. 255.

[50] Kolodny, Robin (1996). "The Several Elections of 1824". *Congress & the Presidency* (Washington, D.C.: American University) **23** (2).

[51] "Election 101" (PDF). *Princeton Press*. Princeton University Press. Retrieved 22 November 2014.

[52] Black, Eric (14 October 2012). "Our Electoral College system is weird — and not in a good way". MinnPost. Retrieved 22 November 2014.

[53] Moore, John L., ed. (1985). *Congressional Quarterly's Guide to U.S. Elections* (2nd ed.). Washington, D.C.: Congressional Quarterly, Inc. p. 266.

[54] "Legislative Action?, The NewsHour with Jim Lehrer, November 30, 2000". Pbs.org. Archived from the original on 2001-01-24. Retrieved August 26, 2010.

[55] Moore, John L., ed. (1985). *Congressional Quarterly's Guide to U.S. Elections* (2nd ed.). Washington, D.C.: Congressional Quarterly, Inc. p. 254.

[56] "FairVote". FairVote. Retrieved August 14, 2014.

[57] "Fiddling with the Rules – Franklin & Marshall". Fandm.edu. March 9, 2005. Archived from the original on 2006-05-01. Retrieved August 26, 2010.

[58] Henderson, Nia-Malika; Haines, Errin (January 25, 2013). "Republicans in Virginia, other states seeking electoral college changes". washingtonpost.com. Retrieved January 24, 2013.

[59] "Election Reform" (PDF). Dos.state.pa.us. Archived from the original (PDF) on 2008-05-01. Retrieved August 26, 2010.

[60] McNulty, Timothy (December 23, 2012). "Pennsylvania looks to alter state's electoral vote system". Pittsburgh Post Gazette.

[61] Sabato, Larry. "A more perfect Constitution" viewed November 22, 2014. (archiveed from the original on 2016-01-02)

[62] Levy, Robert A., Should we reform the Electoral College? Cato Institute, viewed November 22, 2014.

[63] "The Electoral College – Reform Options". Fairvote.org. Retrieved August 14, 2014.

[64] Congressional Research Services Electoral College, p.15, viewed November 22, 2014.

[65] "Articles – Upgrading The College". President Elect. September 5, 2004. Retrieved August 26, 2010.

[66] "Methods of Choosing Presidential Electors". Uselectionatlas.org. Retrieved August 26, 2010.

[67] "Nebraska's Vote Change." (April 7, 1991) *The Washington Post*

[68] Skelley, Geoffrey (20 November 2014). "What Goes Around Comes Around?". Sabato's Crystal Ball. Retrieved 22 November 2014.

[69] Egan, Paul (21 November 2014). "Michigan split its electoral votes in 1892 election". Lansing State Journal. Retrieved 22 November 2014.

[70] Tysver, Robynn (November 7, 2008). "Obama wins electoral vote in Nebraska". Omaha World Herald. Retrieved November 7, 2008.

[71] Molai, Nabil (October 28, 2008). "Republicans Push to Change Electoral Vote System". KPTM Fox 42. Archived from the original on 2011-07-13. Retrieved November 4, 2008.

[72] Ortiz, Jean (January 7, 2010). "Bill targets Neb. ability to split electoral votes". Associated Press. Retrieved September 8, 2011.

[73] Kleeb, Jane (March 10, 2011). "Fail: Sen. McCoy's Partisan Electoral College Bill". Bold Nebraska. Archived from the original on May 31, 2012. Retrieved August 9, 2011.

[74] https://www.nytimes.com/2011/09/19/us/politics/pennsylvania-republicans-weigh-electoral-vote-changes.html

[75] Pennsylvania Ponders Bold Democrat-Screwing Electoral Plan

[76] GOP Pennsylvania electoral vote plan might be out of steam – The York Daily Record (archived from the original on 2012-01-31

[77] Gray, Kathleen (14 November 2014). "Bill to change Michigan's electoral vote gets hearing". Detroit Free Press. Retrieved 22 November 2014.

[78] Jacobson, Louis (31 January 2013). "The Ramifications of Changing the Electoral College". Governing Magazine. Retrieved 22 November 2014.

[79] Wilson, Reid (17 December 2012). "The GOP's Electoral College Scheme". National Journal. Archived from the original on 2013-01-08. Retrieved 22 November 2014.

[80] Bugh, Gary E. 2010. "Representation in Congressional Efforts to Amend the Presidential Election System". In *Electoral College Reform: Challenges and Possibilities*, ed. Gary E. Bugh. Burlington, VT: Ashgate Publishers, 5–18.

[81] Edwards III, George C. (2011). *Why the Electoral College is Bad for America* (Second ed.). New Haven and London: Yale University Press. pp. 1, 37, 61, 176–7, 193–4. ISBN 978-0-300-16649-1.

[82] "Electoral College Mischief, The Wall Street Journal, September 8, 2004". Opinionjournal.com. Retrieved August 26, 2010.

[83] "Did JFK Lose the Popular Vote?". RealClearPolitics. October 22, 2012. Retrieved October 23, 2012.

[84] "The trouble with the Electoral College". C.G.P. Grey. Archived from the original on 2012-01-21. Retrieved October 29, 2012.

[85] "It's Time to End the Electoral College : Here's how.". *The Nation*. November 7, 2012.

[86] *Hands Off the Electoral College* by Rep. Ron Paul, MD, December 28, 2004

[87] *Myths about Big Cities and Big States* by National Popular Vote (archived from the original on 2009-08-05)

[88] Nivola, Pietro (January 2005). "Thinking About Political Polarization" (139). Brookings Institution Policy Brief.

[89] Koza, John; et al. (2006). "Every Vote Equal: A State-Based Plan for Electing the President by National Popular Vote" (PDF). p. xvii. Archived from the original (PDF) on 2006-11-13.

[90] Amar, Akhil; Amar, Vikram (September 9, 2004). "The Electoral College Votes Against Equality". *Los Angeles Times*. Archived from the original on 2010-04-15.

[91] Katrina vanden Heuvel (November 7, 2012). "It's Time to End the Electoral College". *The Nation*. Retrieved November 8, 2012. Electoral college defenders offer a range of arguments, from the openly anti-democratic (direct election equals mob rule), to the nostalgic (we've always done it this way), to the opportunistic (your little state will get ignored! More vote-counting means more controversies! The Electoral College protects hurricane victims!). But none of those arguments overcome this one: One person, one vote.

[92] "Guam Legislature Moves General Election Presidential Vote to the September Primary". Ballot-Access.org. 2008-07-10. Retrieved 2014-07-24.

[93] "In Guam, 'Non-Binding Straw Poll' Gives Obama A Commanding Win". NPR. 2012-11-12. Retrieved 2014-07-24.

[94] Torruella, Juan R. (1985), *The Supreme Court and Puerto Rico: The Doctrine of Separate and Unequal*, University of Puerto Rico Press, ISBN 0-8477-3031-X

[95] José D. Román. "Puerto Rico and a Constitutional Right to vote". University of Dayton. Retrieved 2007-10-02. (excerpted from: José D. Román, "Trying to Fit an Oval Shaped Island into a Square Constitution: Arguments for Puerto Rican Statehood", 29 *Fordham Urban Law Journal* 1681-1713, 1697-1713 (April 2002) (316 Footnotes Omitted))

[96] Miroff, Bruce; Seidelman, Raymond; Swanstrom, Todd (November 2001). *The Democratic Debate: An Introduction to American Politics* (Third ed.). Houghton Mifflin Company. ISBN 0618054529.

[97] Mark Livingston, Department of Computer Science. "Banzhaf Power Index". University of North Carolina.

[98] Gelman, Andrew; Katz, Jonathan; Tuerlinckx, Francis (2002). "The Mathematics and Statistics of Voting Power" (PDF). *Statistical Science* **17** (4): 420–435. doi:10.1214/ss/1049993201.

[99] Jerry Fresia (February 28, 2006). "Third Parties?". Zmag.org. Retrieved August 26, 2010.

[100] "Why the Electoral College, P. Andrew Sandlin, December 13, 2000". Lewrockwell.com. December 13, 2000. Retrieved August 26, 2010.

[101] Kimberling, William C. (May 1992). "The Electoral College" (PDF). Federal Election Commission. Retrieved January 3, 2008.

[102] Sabato, Larry (2007). *A More Perfect Constitution* (First U.S. ed.). Walker Publishing Company. ISBN 0-8027-1621-0. Retrieved July 30, 2009.

[103] Majority and Plurality in U.S. Gubernatorial Elections. FairVote.org (2010-04-09). Retrieved on 2013-07-12.

[104] Note: this may be a few days or even weeks before an election; many states cannot change ballots at a late stage.

[105] Note: the day when the electors cast their votes is the first Monday after the second Wednesday in December.

[106] Note: three electoral votes were still cast for Greeley despite being dead.

[107] Ethan Trex (November 4, 2008). "Electoral College for dummies". CNN. Archived from the original on 2013-01-20. Retrieved November 8, 2012. ... In 1872, though, Democrat Horace Greeley died just over three weeks after Ulysses S. Grant thumped him in the election. ... electors who would have voted for Greeley simply spread their 66 votes among other Democratic candidates. ... Thomas Andrews Hendricks actually came in second in the election with 42 electoral votes despite not campaigning for the presidency...

[108] SHELLY FREIERMAN (November 2, 2000). "NEWS WATCH; Looking for Comic Relief? Then Consider the Duke". *The New York Times.* Retrieved November 8, 2012. ... (In 1872, Horace Greeley, opposing Ulysses S. Grant, got zero electoral votes to Grant's 286, but five other candidates received from one to 42 votes each)....

[109] JAMES BARRON (August 27, 2012). "When the Vice Presidency Was a Job for New Yorkers". *The New York Times.* Retrieved November 8, 2012. ... But Sherman died in office, less than a month before the election of 1912.... The Republican Party designated Nicholas Murray Butler ... as the candidate to receive Sherman's votes in the Electoral College...

[110] "The Electoral College: Bulwark Against Fraud". Psych.cornell.edu. Archived from the original on 2000-07-15. Retrieved August 26, 2010.

[111] "Myths about Recounts". National Popular Vote.

[112] For a more detailed account of this proposal read *The Politics of Electoral College Reform* by Lawrence D. Longley and Alan G. Braun (1972)

[113] *1968 Electoral College Results*, National Archives and Records Administration

[114] "Text of Proposed Amendment on Voting". *The New York Times.* April 30, 1969. p. 21.

[115] "House Unit Votes To Drop Electors". *The New York Times.* April 30, 1969. p. 1.

[116] "Direct Election of President Is Gaining in the House". *The New York Times.* September 12, 1969. p. 12.

[117] "House Approves Direct Election of The President". *The New York Times.* September 19, 1969. p. 1.

[118] "Nixon Comes Out For Direct Vote On Presidency". *The New York Times.* October 1, 1969. p. 1.

[119] "A Survey Finds 30 Legislatures Favor Direct Vote For President". *The New York Times.* October 8, 1969. p. 1.

[120] "Bayh Calls for Nixon's Support As Senate Gets Electoral Plan". *The New York Times.* August 15, 1970. p. 11.

[121] "Senate Refuses To Halt Debate On Direct Voting". *The New York Times.* September 18, 1970. p. 1.

[122] "Senate Debating Direct Election". *The New York Times.* September 9, 1970. p. 10.

[123] The Senate in 1975 reduced the required vote for cloture from two-thirds of those voting (66 votes) to three-fifths (60 votes). *See* United States Senate website.

[124] "Senate Puts Off Direct Vote Plan". *The New York Times.* September 30, 1970. p. 1.

[125] National Popular Vote -- 61% of the Way to Activating the National Popular Vote Bill

[126] Neale, Thomas H. Electoral College Reform Congressional Research Service p.21-22, viewed November 23, 2014.

[127] *Dropping out of the electoral college*, CNN, April 10, 2007

[128] "Trenton: State Backs Electoral College Change", *The New York Times,* January 14, 2008, Page B5

[129] "About Governor Blagojevich's signing of HB 1685". Nationalpopularvote.com. Retrieved August 26, 2010.

[130] "About veto override in Hawaii". Nationalpopularvote.com. Retrieved August 26, 2010.

[131] "History of Bill". Apps.leg.wa.gov. Retrieved August 26, 2010.

[132] Leblanc, Steve (August 4, 2010). "Mass. gov. signs national popular vote bill". *The Seattle Times.* Retrieved August 26, 2010.

[133] "Council of the District (Search for B18-0769)". Council of the District of Columbia. 2009. Retrieved December 21, 2010.

[134] "Vermont Is Eighth State to Enact National Popular Vote Bill". BusinessWire. April 22, 2011. Retrieved April 22, 2011.

[135] sacbee.com

## 3.10 External links

- U.S. Electoral College FAQ (www.archives.gov)

- Interactive U.S. Electoral Map

- Historical Documents on the Electoral College

- Electoral Vote

- 270 to win

- Winning The Electoral College

- "Math Against Tyranny"

- The Green Papers: More detailed description of reform proposals

- The Electoral College: How It Works in Contemporary Presidential Elections Congressional Research Service

- Office of the Federal Register

- Joint Session of the 111th Congress for the purpose of certifying the Electoral College ballot count, January 9, 2009 (C-Span video)

- Introductory chapter of *Electoral College Reform: Challenges and Possibilities*

# Chapter 4

# President of the United States

"POTUS" redirects here. For the political talk radio channel, see P.O.T.U.S. (Sirius XM).
For other uses, see President of the United States (disambiguation). For a list, see List of Presidents of the United States.

The **President of the United States of America** (**POTUS**)[7] is the elected head of state and head of government of the United States. The president leads the executive branch of the federal government and is the commander-in-chief of the United States Armed Forces.

The President of the United States is considered one of the world's most powerful people, leading the world's only contemporary superpower.[8][9][10][11] The role includes being the commander-in-chief of the world's most expensive military with the largest nuclear arsenal and leading the largest economy by real and nominal GDP. The office of the president holds significant hard and soft power both in the United States and abroad.

Article II of the U.S. Constitution vests the executive power of the United States in the president. The power includes execution of federal law, alongside the responsibility of appointing federal executive, diplomatic, regulatory and judicial officers, and concluding treaties with foreign powers with the advice and consent of the Senate. The president is further empowered to grant federal pardons and reprieves, and to convene and adjourn either or both houses of Congress under extraordinary circumstances.[12] The president is largely responsible for dictating the legislative agenda of the party to which the president is enrolled. The president also directs the foreign and domestic policy of the United States.[13] Since the founding of the United States, the power of the president and the federal government has grown substantially.[14]

The president is indirectly elected by the people through the Electoral College to a four-year term, and is one of only two nationally elected federal officers, the other being the Vice President of the United States.[15] The Twenty-second Amendment, adopted in 1951, prohibits anyone from ever being elected to the presidency for a third full term. It also prohibits a person from being elected to the presidency more than once if that person previously had served as president, or acting president, for more than two years of another person's term as president. In all, 43 individuals have served 44 presidencies (counting Cleveland's two non-consecutive terms separately) spanning 56 full four-year terms.[16] On January 20, 2009, Barack Obama became the 44th and current president. On November 6, 2012, he was re-elected and is currently serving the 57th term. The next presidential election is scheduled to take place on November 8, 2016. On January 20, 2017, a new president will take office.

## 4.1 Origin

In 1776, the Thirteen Colonies, acting through the Second Continental Congress, declared political independence from Great Britain during the American Revolution. The new states, though independent of each other as nation states,[17] recognized the necessity of closely coordinating their efforts against the British.[18] Desiring to avoid anything that remotely resembled a monarchy, Congress negotiated the Articles of Confederation to establish a weak alliance between the states.[17] As a central authority, Congress under the Articles was without any legislative power; it could make its own resolutions, determinations, and regulations, but not any laws, nor any taxes or local commercial regulations enforceable upon citizens.[18] This institutional design reflected the conception of how Americans believed the deposed British system of Crown and Parliament ought to have functioned with respect to the royal dominion: a superintending body for matters that concerned the entire empire.[18] Out from under any monarchy, the states assigned some formerly royal prerogatives (*e.g.*, making war, receiving ambassadors, etc.) to Congress, while severally lodging the rest within their own respective state governments. Only after all the states agreed to a resolution settling competing western land claims did the Articles take effect on March 1, 1781, when Maryland became the final state to ratify them.

In 1783, the Treaty of Paris secured independence for each of the former colonies. With peace at hand, the states each turned toward their own internal affairs.[17] By 1786, Americans found their continental borders besieged and weak, their respective economies in crises as neighboring states agitated trade rivalries with one another, witnessed their hard currency pouring into foreign markets to pay for imports, their Mediterranean commerce preyed upon by North African pirates, and their foreign-financed Revolutionary War debts unpaid and accruing interest.[17] Civil and political unrest loomed.

Following the successful resolution of commercial and fishing disputes between Virginia and Maryland at the Mount Vernon Conference in 1785, Virginia called for a trade conference between all the states, set for September 1786 in Annapolis, Maryland, with an aim toward resolving further-reaching interstate commercial antagonisms. When the convention failed for lack of attendance due to suspicions among most of the other states, the Annapolis delegates called for a convention to offer revisions to the Articles, to be held the next spring in Philadelphia. Prospects for the next convention appeared bleak until James Madison and Edmund Randolph succeeded in securing George Washington's attendance to Philadelphia as a delegate for Virginia.[17][19]

When the Constitutional Convention convened in May 1787, the 12 state delegations in attendance (Rhode Island did not send delegates) brought with them an accumulated experience over a diverse set of institutional arrangements between legislative and executive branches from within their respective state governments. Most states maintained a weak executive without veto or appointment powers, elected annually by the legislature to a single term only, sharing power with an executive council, and countered by a strong legislature.[17] New York offered the greatest exception, having a strong, unitary governor with veto and appointment power elected to a three-year term, and eligible for reelection to an indefinite number of terms thereafter.[17] It was through the closed-door negotiations at Philadelphia that the presidency framed in the U.S. Constitution emerged.

## 4.2 Powers and duties

### 4.2.1 Article I legislative role

The first power the Constitution confers upon the president is the veto. The Presentment Clause requires any bill passed by Congress to be presented to the president before it can become law. Once the legislation has been presented, the

*President Barack Obama signing legislation at the* Resolute *desk*

president has three options:

1. Sign the legislation; the bill then becomes law.

2. Veto the legislation and return it to Congress, expressing any objections; the bill does not become law, unless each house of Congress votes to override the veto by a two-thirds vote.

3. Take no action. In this instance, the president neither signs nor vetoes the legislation. After 10 days, not counting Sundays, two possible outcomes emerge:

   - If Congress is still convened, the bill becomes law.
   - If Congress has adjourned, thus preventing the return of the legislation, the bill does not become law. This latter outcome is known as the pocket veto.

In 1996, Congress attempted to enhance the president's veto power with the Line Item Veto Act. The legislation empowered the president to sign any spending bill into law while simultaneously striking certain spending items within the bill, particularly any new spending, any amount of discretionary spending, or any new limited tax benefit. Congress could then repass that particular item. If the president then vetoed the new legislation, Congress could override the veto by its ordinary means, a two-thirds vote in both houses. In *Clinton v. City of New York*, 524 U.S. 417 (1998), the U.S. Supreme Court ruled such a legislative alteration of the veto power to be unconstitutional.

### 4.2.2 Article II executive powers

**War and foreign affairs powers**

Perhaps the most important of all presidential powers is the command of the United States Armed Forces as its

*Abraham Lincoln, the 16th President of the United States, successfully preserved the Union during the American Civil War*

commander-in-chief. While the power to declare war is constitutionally vested in Congress, the president has ultimate responsibility for direction and disposition of the military. The present-day operational command of the Armed Forces (belonging to the Department of Defense) is normally exercised through the Secretary of Defense, with assistance of the Chairman of the Joint Chiefs of Staff, to the Combatant Commands, as outlined in the presidentially approved Unified Command Plan (UCP).[20][21][22] The framers of the Constitution took care to limit the president's powers regarding the military; Alexander Hamilton explains this in Federalist No. 69:

> The President is to be commander-in-chief of the army and navy of the United States. ... It would amount to nothing more than the supreme command and direction of the military and naval forces ... while that [the power] of the British king extends to the DECLARING of war and to the RAISING and REGULATING of fleets and armies, all [of] which ... would appertain to the legislature.[23] [Emphasis in the original.]

Congress, pursuant to the War Powers Resolution, must authorize any troop deployments longer than 60 days, although that process relies on triggering mechanisms that have never been employed, rendering it ineffectual.[24] Additionally, Congress provides a check to presidential military power through its control over military spending and regulation. While historically presidents initiated the process for going to war,[25][26] critics have charged that there have been several conflicts in which presidents did not get official declarations, including Theodore Roosevelt's military move into Panama in 1903,[25] the Korean War,[25] the Vietnam War,[25] and the invasions of Grenada in 1983[27] and Panama in 1990.[28]

Along with the armed forces, the president also directs U.S. foreign policy. Through the Department of State and the Department of Defense, the president is responsible for the protection of Americans abroad and of foreign nationals in the United States. The president decides whether to recognize new nations and new governments, and negotiates treaties with other nations, which become binding on the United States when approved by two-thirds vote of the Senate.

Although not constitutionally provided, presidents also sometimes employ "executive agreements" in foreign relations. These agreements frequently regard administrative policy choices germane to executive power; for example, the extent to which either country presents an armed presence in a given area, how each country will enforce copyright treaties, or how each country will process foreign mail. However, the 20th century witnessed a vast expansion of the use of executive agreements, and critics have challenged the extent of that use as supplanting the treaty process and removing constitutionally prescribed checks and balances over the executive in foreign relations. Supporters counter that the agreements offer a pragmatic solution when the need for swift, secret, and/or concerted action arises.

## Administrative powers

Suffice it to say that the President is made the sole repository of the executive powers of the United States, and the powers entrusted to him as well as the duties imposed upon him are awesome indeed.

William Rehnquist, *Nixon v. General Services Administration*, **433 U.S. 425 (1977)** (dissenting opinion)

The president is the head of the executive branch of the federal government and is constitutionally obligated to "take care that the laws be faithfully executed."[29] The executive branch has over four million employees, including members of the military.[30]

Presidents make numerous executive branch appointments: an incoming president may make up to 6,000 before taking office and 8,000 more while serving. Ambassadors, members of the Cabinet, and other federal officers, are all appointed by a president with the "advice and consent" of a majority of the Senate. When the Senate is in recess for at least ten days, the president may make recess appointments.[31] Recess appointments are temporary and expire at the end of the next session of the Senate.

The power of a president to fire executive officials has long been a contentious political issue. Generally, a president may remove purely executive officials at will.[32] However, Congress can curtail and constrain a president's authority to fire commissioners of independent regulatory agencies and certain inferior executive officers by statute.[33]

The president additionally possesses the ability to direct much of the executive branch through executive orders that are grounded in federal law or constitutionally granted executive power. Executive orders are reviewable by federal courts and can be superseded by federal legislation.

To manage the growing federal bureaucracy, Presidents have gradually surrounded themselves with many layers of staff, who were eventually organized into the Executive Office of the President of the United States. Within the Executive Office, the President's innermost layer of aides (and their assistants) are located in the White House Office.

### Juridical powers

The president also has the power to nominate federal judges, including members of the United States courts of appeals and the Supreme Court of the United States. However, these nominations do require Senate confirmation. Securing Senate approval can provide a major obstacle for presidents who wish to orient the federal judiciary toward a particular ideological stance. When nominating judges to U.S. district courts, presidents often respect the long-standing tradition of Senatorial courtesy. Presidents may also grant pardons and reprieves, as is often done just before the end of a presidential term, not without controversy.[34][35][36]

Historically, two doctrines concerning executive power have developed that enable the president to exercise executive power with a degree of autonomy. The first is executive privilege, which allows the president to withhold from disclosure any communications made directly to the president in the performance of executive duties. George Washington first claimed privilege when Congress requested to see Chief Justice John Jay's notes from an unpopular treaty negotiation with Great Britain. While not enshrined in the Constitution, or any other law, Washington's action created the precedent for the privilege. When Richard Nixon tried to use executive privilege as a reason for not turning over subpoenaed evidence to Congress during the Watergate scandal, the Supreme Court ruled in *United States v. Nixon*,

418 U.S. 683 (1974), that executive privilege did not apply in cases where a president was attempting to avoid criminal prosecution. When President Bill Clinton attempted to use executive privilege regarding the Lewinsky scandal, the Supreme Court ruled in *Clinton v. Jones*, 520 U.S. 681 (1997), that the privilege also could not be used in civil suits. These cases established the legal precedent that executive privilege is valid, although the exact extent of the privilege has yet to be clearly defined. Additionally, federal courts have allowed this privilege to radiate outward and protect other executive branch employees, but have weakened that protection for those executive branch communications that do not involve the president.[37]

*President George W. Bush delivering the 2007 State of the Union Address, with Vice President Dick Cheney and Speaker of the House Nancy Pelosi behind him*

The state secrets privilege allows the president and the executive branch to withhold information or documents from discovery in legal proceedings if such release would harm national security. Precedent for the privilege arose early in the 19th century when Thomas Jefferson refused to release military documents in the treason trial of Aaron Burr and again in *Totten v. United States* 92 U.S. 105 (1876), when the Supreme Court dismissed a case brought by a former Union spy.[38] However, the privilege was not formally recognized by the U.S. Supreme Court until *United States v. Reynolds* 345 U.S. 1 (1953), where it was held to be a common law evidentiary privilege.[39] Before the September 11 attacks, use of the privilege had been rare, but increasing in frequency.[40] Since 2001, the government has asserted the privilege in more cases and at earlier stages of the litigation, thus in some instances causing dismissal of the suits before reaching the merits of the claims, as in the Ninth Circuit's ruling in *Mohamed v. Jeppesen Dataplan, Inc.*[39][41][42] Critics of the privilege claim its use has become a tool for the government to cover up illegal or embarrassing government actions.[43][44]

**Legislative facilitator**

The Constitution's Ineligibility Clause prevents the President (and all other executive officers) from simultaneously being a member of Congress. Therefore, the president cannot directly introduce legislative proposals for consideration in Congress. However, the president can take an indirect role in shaping legislation, especially if the president's political party has a majority in one or both houses of Congress. For example, the president or other officials of the executive branch may draft legislation and then ask senators or representatives to introduce these drafts into Congress. The president can further influence the legislative branch through constitutionally mandated, periodic reports to Congress. These reports may be either written or oral, but today are given as the State of the Union address, which often outlines the president's legislative proposals for the coming year. Additionally, the president may attempt to have Congress alter proposed legislation by threatening to veto that legislation unless requested changes are made.

In the 20th century critics began charging that too many legislative and budgetary powers have slid into the hands of presidents that should belong to Congress. As the head of the executive branch, presidents control a vast array of agencies that can issue regulations with little oversight from Congress. One critic charged that presidents could appoint a "virtual army of 'czars' – each wholly unaccountable to Congress yet tasked with spearheading major policy efforts for the White House."[45] Presidents have been criticized for making signing statements when signing congressional legislation about how they understand a bill or plan to execute it.[46] This practice has been criticized by the American Bar Association as unconstitutional.[47] Conservative commentator George Will wrote of an "increasingly swollen executive branch" and "the eclipse of Congress."[48]

According to Article II, Section 3, Clause 2 of the Constitution, the president may convene either or both houses of Congress. If both houses cannot agree on a date of adjournment, the president may appoint a date for Congress to adjourn.

## 4.2.3   Ceremonial roles

As head of state, the president can fulfill traditions established by previous presidents. William Howard Taft started the tradition of throwing out the ceremonial first pitch in 1910 at Griffith Stadium, Washington, D.C., on the Washington Senators' Opening Day. Every president since Taft, except for Jimmy Carter, threw out at least one ceremonial first ball or pitch for Opening Day, the All-Star Game, or the World Series, usually with much fanfare.[49]

The President of the United States has served as the hon-

*President Woodrow Wilson throwing out the ceremonial first ball on Opening Day, 1916*

orary president of the Boy Scouts of America since the founding of the organization.[50]

Other presidential traditions are associated with American holidays. Rutherford B. Hayes began in 1878 the first White House egg rolling for local children.[51] Beginning in 1947 during the Harry S. Truman administration, every Thanksgiving the president is presented with a live domestic turkey during the annual national thanksgiving turkey presentation held at the White House. Since 1989, when the custom of "pardoning" the turkey was formalized by George H. W. Bush, the turkey has been taken to a farm where it will live out the rest of its natural life.[52]

Presidential traditions also involve the president's role as head of government. Many outgoing presidents since James Buchanan traditionally give advice to their successor during the presidential transition.[53] Ronald Reagan and his successors have also left a private message on the desk of the Oval Office on Inauguration Day for the incoming president.[54]

During a state visit by a foreign head of state, the president typically hosts a State Arrival Ceremony held on the South Lawn, a custom begun by John F. Kennedy in 1961.[55] This is followed by a state dinner given by the president which is held in the State Dining Room later in the evening.[56]

The modern presidency holds the president as one of the nation's premier celebrities. Some argue that images of the presidency have a tendency to be manipulated by administration public relations officials as well as by presidents themselves. One critic described the presidency as "propagandized leadership" which has a "mesmerizing power surrounding the office."[57] Administration public relations managers staged carefully crafted photo-ops of smiling presidents with smiling crowds for television cameras.[58] One critic wrote the image of John F. Kennedy was described as carefully framed "in rich detail" which "drew on the power of myth" regarding the incident of PT 109[59] and wrote that Kennedy understood how to use images to further his presidential ambitions.[60] As a result, some political commentators have opined that American voters have unrealistic expectations of presidents: voters expect a president to "drive the economy, vanquish enemies, lead the free world, comfort tornado victims, heal the national soul and protect borrowers from hidden credit-card fees."[61]

### 4.2.4 Critics of presidency's evolution

Main article: Imperial Presidency

Most of the nation's Founding Fathers expected the Congress, which was the first branch of government described in the Constitution, to be the dominant branch of government; they did not expect a strong executive.[62] However, presidential power has shifted over time, which has resulted in claims that the modern presidency has become too powerful,[63][64] unchecked, unbalanced,[65] and "monarchist" in nature.[66] Critic Dana D. Nelson believes presidents over the past thirty years have worked towards "undivided presidential control of the executive branch and its agencies."[67] She criticizes proponents of the unitary executive for expanding "the many existing uncheckable executive powers – such as executive orders, decrees, memorandums, proclamations, national security directives and legislative signing statements – that already allow presidents to enact a good deal of foreign and domestic policy without aid, interference or consent from Congress."[67] Activist Bill Wilson opined that the expanded presidency was "the greatest threat ever to individual freedom and democratic rule."[68]

## 4.3 Selection process

### 4.3.1 Eligibility

See also: Age of candidacy and Natural-born-citizen clause

Article II, Section 1, Clause 5 of the Constitution sets the requirements to hold office. A president must:

- be a natural-born citizen of the United States;[note 1]

- be at least thirty-five years old;

- have been a permanent resident in the United States for at least fourteen years.

A person who meets the above qualifications is still disqualified from holding the office of president under any of the

*George Washington, the first President of the United States*

following conditions:

- Under the Twenty-second Amendment, no person can be elected president more than twice. The amendment also specifies that if any eligible person serves as president or acting president for more than two years of a term for which some other eligible person was elected president, the former can only be elected president once. Scholars disagree whether anyone no longer eligible to be elected president could be elected vice president, pursuant to the qualifications set out under the Twelfth Amendment.[69]

- Under Article I, Section 3, Clause 7, upon conviction in impeachment cases, the Senate has the option of disqualifying convicted individuals from holding federal office, including that of president.[70]

- Under Section 3 of the Fourteenth Amendment, no person who swore an oath to support the Constitution, and later rebelled against the United States, can become president. However, this disqualification can be lifted by a two-thirds vote of each house of Congress.

### 4.3.2 Campaigns and nomination

Main articles: United States presidential primary, United States presidential nominating convention, United States presidential election debates and United States presidential election

The modern presidential campaign begins before the primary elections, which the two major political parties use to clear the field of candidates before their national nominating conventions, where the most successful candidate is made the party's nominee for president. Typically, the party's presidential candidate chooses a vice presidential nominee, and this choice is rubber-stamped by the convention. The most common previous profession by U.S. presidents is lawyer.[71]

Nominees participate in nationally televised debates, and while the debates are usually restricted to the Democratic and Republican nominees, third party candidates may be invited, such as Ross Perot in the 1992 debates. Nominees campaign across the country to explain their views, convince voters and solicit contributions. Much of the modern electoral process is concerned with winning swing states through frequent visits and mass media advertising drives.

### 4.3.3  Election and oath

Main articles: Electoral College (United States) and Oath of office of the President of the United States

The president is elected indirectly. A number of electors,

*A map of the United States showing the number of electoral votes allocated to each state following reapportionment based on the 2010 census; 270 electoral votes are required for a majority out of 538 overall*

collectively known as the Electoral College, officially select the president. On Election Day, voters in each of the states and the District of Columbia cast ballots for these electors. Each state is allocated a number of electors, equal to the size of its delegation in both Houses of Congress combined. Generally, the ticket that wins the most votes in a state wins all of that state's electoral votes and thus has its slate of electors chosen to vote in the Electoral College.

The winning slate of electors meet at its state's capital on

the first Monday after the second Wednesday in December, about six weeks after the election, to vote. They then send a record of that vote to Congress. The vote of the electors is opened by the sitting vice president—acting in that role's capacity as President of the Senate—and read aloud to a joint session of the incoming Congress, which was elected at the same time as the president.

Pursuant to the Twentieth Amendment, the president's term of office begins at noon on January 20 of the year following the election. This date, known as Inauguration Day, marks the beginning of the four-year terms of both the president and the vice president. Before executing the powers of the office, a president is constitutionally required to take the presidential oath:

> I do solemnly swear (or affirm) that I will faithfully execute the Office of President of the United States, and will to the best of my Ability, preserve, protect and defend the Constitution of the United States.[72]

Although not required, presidents have traditionally palmed a Bible while swearing the oath and have added, "So help me God!" to the end of the oath.[73] Further, although the oath may be administered by any person authorized by law to administer oaths, presidents are traditionally sworn in by the Chief Justice of the United States.

### 4.3.4  Tenure and term limits

The term of office for president and vice president is four years. George Washington, the first president, set an unofficial precedent of serving only two terms, which subsequent presidents followed until 1940. Before Franklin D. Roosevelt, attempts at a third term were encouraged by supporters of Ulysses S. Grant and Theodore Roosevelt; neither of these attempts succeeded. In 1940, Franklin D. Roosevelt declined to seek a third term, but allowed his political party to "draft" him as its presidential candidate and was subsequently elected to a third term. In 1941, the United States entered World War II, leading voters to elect Roosevelt to a fourth term in 1944.

After the war, and in response to Roosevelt being elected to third and fourth terms, the Twenty-second Amendment was adopted. The amendment bars anyone from being elected president more than twice, or once if that person served more than half of another president's term. Harry S. Truman, president when this amendment was adopted, was exempted from its limitations and briefly sought a third (a second full) term before withdrawing from the 1952 election.

Since the amendment's adoption, four presidents have served two full terms: Dwight D. Eisenhower, Ronald Rea-

*Franklin D. Roosevelt was elected to four terms before the adoption of the Twenty-second Amendment*

gan, Bill Clinton, and George W. Bush. Barack Obama has been elected to a second term. Jimmy Carter and George H. W. Bush sought a second term, but were defeated. Richard Nixon was elected to a second term, but resigned before completing it. Lyndon B. Johnson was the only president under the amendment to be eligible to serve more than two terms in total, having served for only fourteen months following John F. Kennedy's assassination. However, Johnson withdrew from the 1968 Democratic Primary, surprising many Americans. Gerald Ford sought a full term, after serving out the last two years and five months of Nixon's second term, but was not elected.

### 4.3.5 Vacancy or disability

See also: Twenty-fifth Amendment to the United States Constitution, United States presidential line of succession, Presidential Succession Act and Impeachment in the United States

Vacancies in the office of President may arise under several possible circumstances: death, resignation and removal from office.

Article II, Section 4 of the Constitution allows the House of Representatives to impeach high federal officials, including the president, for "treason, bribery, or other high crimes and misdemeanors." Article I, Section 3, Clause 6 gives the Senate the power to remove impeached officials from office, given a two-thirds vote to convict. The House has thus far impeached two presidents: Andrew Johnson in 1868 and Bill Clinton in 1998. Neither was subsequently convicted by the Senate; however, Johnson was acquitted by just one vote.

Under Section 3 of the Twenty-fifth Amendment, the president may transfer the presidential powers and duties to the vice president, who then becomes acting president, by transmitting a statement to the Speaker of the House and the President *pro tempore* of the Senate stating the reasons for the transfer. The president resumes the discharge of the presidential powers and duties upon transmitting, to those two officials, a written declaration stating that resumption. This transfer of power may occur for any reason the president considers appropriate; in 2002 and again in 2007, President George W. Bush briefly transferred presidential authority to Vice President Dick Cheney. In both cases, this was done to accommodate a medical procedure which required Bush to be sedated; both times, Bush returned to duty later the same day.[74]

Under Section 4 of the Twenty-fifth Amendment, the vice president, in conjunction with a majority of the Cabinet, may transfer the presidential powers and duties from the president to the vice president by transmitting a written declaration to the Speaker of the House and the president *pro tempore* of the Senate that the president is unable to discharge the presidential powers and duties. If this occurs, then the vice president will assume the presidential powers and duties as acting president; however, the president can declare that no such inability exists and resume the discharge of the presidential powers and duties. If the vice president and Cabinet contest this claim, it is up to Congress, which must meet within two days if not already in session, to decide the merit of the claim.

The United States Constitution mentions the resignation of the president, but does not regulate its form or the conditions for its validity. Pursuant to federal law, the only valid evidence of the president's resignation is a written instrument to that effect, signed by the president and delivered to the office of the Secretary of State.[75] This has only occurred once, when Richard Nixon delivered a letter to Henry Kissinger to that effect.

Section 1 of the Twenty-fifth Amendment states that the vice president becomes president upon the removal from office, death or resignation of the preceding president. The Presidential Succession Act of 1947 provides that if the offices of President and Vice President are each either vacant or are held by a disabled person, the next officer in the presidential line of succession, the Speaker of the House, becomes acting president. The line then extends to the President pro tempore of the Senate, followed by every member of the Cabinet. These persons must fulfill all eligibility requirements of the office of President to be eligible to become acting president; ineligible individuals are skipped. There has never been a special election for the office of President.

## 4.4 Compensation

Since 2001, the president has earned a $400,000 annual salary, along with a $50,000 annual expense account, a $100,000 nontaxable travel account, and $19,000 for entertainment.[79][80] The most recent raise in salary was approved by Congress and President Bill Clinton in 1999 and went into effect in 2001.

The White House in Washington, D.C., serves as the official place of residence for the president. As well as access to the White House staff, facilities available to the president include medical care, recreation, housekeeping, and security services. The government pays for state dinners and other official functions, but the president pays for personal, family and guest dry cleaning and food; the high food bill often amazes new residents.[81] Naval Support Facility Thurmont, popularly known as Camp David, is a mountain-based military camp in Frederick County, Maryland, used as a country retreat and for high alert protection of the president and guests. Blair House, located next to the Eisenhower Executive Office Building at the White House Complex and Lafayette Park, is a complex of four connected townhouses exceeding 70,000 square feet (6,500 m$^2$) of floor space which serves as the president's official guest house and as a secondary residence for the president if needed.[82]

For ground travel, the president uses the presidential state car, which is an armored limousine built on a heavily modified Cadillac-based chassis.[83] One of two identical Boeing VC-25 aircraft, which are extensively modified versions of Boeing 747−200B airliners, serve as long distance travel for the president and are referred to as *Air Force One* while the president is on board (although any U.S. Air Force aircraft the President is aboard is designated as "Air Force One" for the duration of the flight). In-country trips are typically handled with just one of the two planes while overseas trips are handled with both, one primary and one backup. Any civilian aircraft the President is aboard is designated Executive One for the flight.[84][85] The president also has access to a fleet of thirty-five U.S. Marine Corps helicopters of varying models, designated *Marine One* when the president is aboard any particular one in the fleet. Flights are typically handled with as many as five helicopters all flying together and frequently swapping positions as to disguise which helicopter the President is actually aboard to any would-be threats.

The U.S. Secret Service is charged with protecting the sitting president and the first family. As part of their protection, presidents, first ladies, their children and other immediate family members, and other prominent persons and locations are assigned Secret Service codenames.[86] The use of such names was originally for security purposes and dates to a time when sensitive electronic communications were not routinely encrypted; today, the names simply serve for purposes of brevity, clarity, and tradition.[87]

- Presidential amenities
- **The White House**
- **Camp David**
- **Blair House**
- **State car**
- **Air Force One**
- **Marine One**

## 4.5 Post-presidency

*Presidents Richard Nixon, Ronald Reagan, Gerald Ford, and Jimmy Carter share a drink in the Blue Room in October 1981. (Reagan was the incumbent President at the time)*

Beginning in 1959, all living former presidents were granted a pension, an office, and a staff. The pension has increased numerous times with Congressional approval. Retired presidents now receive a pension based on the salary of the current administration's cabinet secretaries, which was $199,700 each year in 2012.[88] Former presidents who served in Congress may also collect congressional pensions.[89] The Former Presidents Act, as amended, also provides former presidents with travel funds and franking privileges. Prior to 1997, all former presidents, their spouses, and their children until age 16 were protected

*Presidents Jimmy Carter, Bill Clinton, Barack Obama and George W. Bush, at the dedication of the George W. Bush Presidential Library in 2013.*

by the Secret Service until the president's death.[90][91] In 1997, Congress passed legislation limiting secret service protection to no more than 10 years from the date a president leaves office.[92] On January 10, 2013, President Obama signed legislation reinstating lifetime secret service protection for him, George W. Bush, and all subsequent presidents.[93] A spouse who remarries is no longer eligible for secret service protection.[92]

Some presidents have had significant careers after leaving office. Prominent examples include William Howard Taft's tenure as Chief Justice of the United States and Herbert Hoover's work on government reorganization after World War II. Grover Cleveland, whose bid for reelection failed in 1888, was elected president again four years later in 1892. Two former presidents served in Congress after leaving the White House: John Quincy Adams was elected to the House of Representatives, serving there for seventeen years, and Andrew Johnson returned to the Senate in 1875. John Tyler served in the provisional Congress of the Confederate States during the Civil War and was elected to the Confederate House of Representatives, but died before that body first met.

Presidents may use their predecessors as emissaries to deliver private messages to other nations or as official representatives of the United States to state funerals and other important foreign events.[94][95] Richard Nixon made multiple foreign trips to countries including China and Russia and was lauded as an elder statesman.[96] Jimmy Carter has become a global human rights campaigner, international arbiter, and election monitor, as well as a recipient of the Nobel Peace Prize. Bill Clinton has also worked as an informal ambassador, most recently in the negotiations that led to the release of two American journalists, Laura Ling and Euna Lee, from North Korea. Clinton has also been active politically since his presidential term ended, working with

his wife Hillary on her 2008 and 2016 presidential bids and President Obama on his reelection campaign.

- Living former presidents, in order of service

  - **Jimmy Carter**
    39th (1977–81)
    October 1, 1924

  - **George H. W. Bush**
    41st (1989–93)
    June 12, 1924

  - **Bill Clinton**
    42nd (1993–2001)
    August 19, 1946

  - **George W. Bush**
    43rd (2001–09)
    July 6, 1946

### 4.5.1 Presidential libraries

Main article: Presidential library
Since Herbert Hoover, each president has created a

repository known as a presidential library for preserving and making available his papers, records and other documents and materials. Completed libraries are deeded to and maintained by the National Archives and Records Administration (NARA); the initial funding for building and equipping each library must come from private, non-federal sources.[97] There are currently thirteen presidential libraries in the NARA system. There are also presidential libraries maintained by state governments and private foundations, such as the Abraham Lincoln Presidential Library and Museum, which is run by the State of Illinois.

As many presidents live for many years after leaving office, several of them have personally overseen the building and opening of their own presidential libraries, some even making arrangements for their own burial at the site. Several presidential libraries therefore contain the graves of the president they document, such as the Richard Nixon Presidential Library and Museum in Yorba Linda, California and the Ronald Reagan Presidential Library in Simi Valley, California. The graves are viewable by the general public visiting these libraries.

## 4.6   Timeline of Presidents

This is a graphical timeline listing of the Presidents of the United States.

## 4.7   See also

### 4.7.1   Lists relating to the United States presidency

List of Presidents of the United States

Lists of candidates for President of the United States
Lists of fictional Presidents of the United States
Lists of honors and awards received by Presidents of the United States
Lists of United States judicial appointments by president
Vice presidency of the United States-related lists
List of Presidents of the United States
List of Presidents of the United States by age
American Presidents: Life Portraits
List of United States presidential assassination attempts and plots
Assassination threats against Barack Obama
List of autobiographies by Presidents of the United States
List of burial places of Presidents of the United States
List of nicknames used by George W. Bush
List of United States presidential candidates
List of children of the Presidents of the United States
List of Presidents of the United States by education
List of U.S. counties named after U.S. Presidents
List of Presidents of the United States by date of birth
List of Presidents of the United States by date of death
List of Presidents of the United States who died in office
Living First Ladies of the United States
List of United States Presidential firsts
List of Presidents of the United States who were Freema-

sons
Handedness of Presidents of the United States
Heights of presidents and presidential candidates of the United States
Historical polling for U.S. Presidential elections
Historical rankings of Presidents of the United States
U.S. Presidential IQ hoax
Bibliography of Thomas Jefferson
List of Presidents of the United States by judicial appointments
Bibliography of Abraham Lincoln
List of observances in the United States by presidential proclamation
List of official vehicles of the President of the United States
List of photographs of Abraham Lincoln
List of U.S. military vessels named after Presidents
List of United States presidential elections by popular vote margin
List of White House security breaches
Living Presidents of the United States
Lyndon B. Johnson bibliography
Bibliography of William McKinley
List of meetings between the Pope and the President of the United States
List of United States Presidents by military rank
List of Presidents of the United States by military service
List of multilingual presidents of the United States
List of Presidents of the United States by name
List of United States Presidents by net worth
List of nicknames of United States Presidents
Richard Nixon bibliography
North American Leaders' Summit
List of books and films about Barack Obama
United States presidential pets
List of places named for Dwight D. Eisenhower
List of places named for Andrew Jackson
List of places named for Thomas Jefferson
List of places named for James Monroe
List of places named for James K. Polk
List of places named for George Washington
List of United States Presidents on currency
List of Presidents of the United States by previous experience
List of Presidents of the United States by home state
List of Presidents of the United States by political affiliation
List of Presidents of the United States by other offices held
List of Presidents of the United States by occupation
List of Presidents of the United States by time in office
Ronald Reagan bibliography
Religious affiliations of Presidents of the United States
List of residences of Presidents of the United States
List of Presidents of the United States who owned slaves

### 4.7.2 Presidential administrations

- Presidency of George Washington

- Presidency of Thomas Jefferson

- Presidency of Andrew Jackson

- Presidency of Abraham Lincoln

- Presidency of Ulysses S. Grant

- Presidency of Theodore Roosevelt

- Presidency of Dwight D. Eisenhower

- Timeline of the presidency of John F. Kennedy

- Presidency of Richard Nixon

- Presidency of Ronald Reagan

- Presidency of Bill Clinton

- George W. Bush's first term as President of the United States

- George W. Bush's second term as President of the United States

- Presidency of Barack Obama

### 4.7.3 Categories

- Category:United States presidential history

### 4.7.4 Articles

- Curse of Tippecanoe

- Executive Office of the President of the United States

- Imperial Presidency

- *The Imperial Presidency*

- Imperiled presidency

- President of the Continental Congress

- Presidential $1 Coin Program

- Second-term curse

- United States presidential line of succession in fiction

- Vice President of the United States

- White House Office

## 4.8 Notes

[1] Foreign-born American citizens who met the age and residency requirements at the time the Constitution was adopted were also eligible for the presidency. However, this allowance has since become obsolete.

## 4.9 References

[1] "How To Address The President; He Is Not Your Excellency Or Your Honor, But Mr. President". *The New York Times.* August 2, 1891.

[2] "USGS Correspondence Handbook - Chapter 4". Usgs.gov. July 18, 2007. Retrieved November 15, 2012.

[3] "Models of Address and Salutation". Ita.doc.gov. Retrieved September 4, 2010.

[4] HEADS OF STATE, HEADS OF GOVERNMENT, MINISTERS FOR FOREIGN AFFAIRS, Protocol and Liaison Service, United Nations. Retrieved on November 1, 2012.

[5] The White House Office of the Press Secretary (September 1, 2010). "Remarks by President Obama, President Mubarak, His Majesty King Abdullah, Prime Minister Netanyahu and President Abbas Before Working Dinner". *WhiteHouse.gov.* Retrieved July 19, 2011.

[6] "Exchange of Letters". Permanent Observer Mission of Palestine to the United Nations. September 1978. Retrieved July 19, 2011.

[7] Safire, William (October 12, 1997). "On language: POTUS and FLOTUS". *New York Times*. New York: The New York Times Company. Retrieved May 11, 2014.

[8] "The Most Powerful Man in the World is a Black Man – The Los Angeles Sentinel". Lasentinel.net. Retrieved September 4, 2010.

[9] "Who should be the world's most powerful person?". *The Guardian* (London). January 3, 2008.

[10] Jon Meacham (December 20, 2008). "Meacham: The History of Power". *Newsweek*. Retrieved September 4, 2010.

[11] Fareed Zakaria (December 20, 2008). "The NEWSWEEK 50: Barack Obama". *Newsweek*. Retrieved September 4, 2010.

[12] "Transcript of the Constitution of the United States – Official". Archives.gov. Retrieved September 4, 2010.

[13] Pfiffner, J. P. (1988). "The President's Legislative Agenda". *Annals of the American Academy of Political and Social Science* **499**: 22–35. doi:10.1177/0002716288499001002.

[14] The Influence of State Politics in Expanding Federal Power,' Henry Jones Ford, Proceedings of the American Political Science Association, Vol. 5, Fifth Annual Meeting (1908) Retrieved March 17, 2010.

[15] Our Government • The Executive Branch, The White House.

[16] "The Executive Branch". Whitehouse.gov. Retrieved January 27, 2009.. Grover Cleveland served two non-consecutive terms, so he is counted twice; as the 22nd and 24th presidents.

[17] Milkis, Sidney M.; Nelson, Michael (2008). *The American Presidency: Origins and Development* (5th ed.). Washington, D.C.: CQ Press. pp. 1–25. ISBN 0-87289-336-7.

[18] Kelly, Alfred H.; Harbison, Winfred A.; Belz, Herman (1991). *The American Constitution: Its Origins and Development* **I** (7th ed.). New York: W.W. Norton & Co. pp. 76–81. ISBN 0-393-96056-0.

[19] Beeman, Richard (2009). *Plain, Honest Men: The Making of the American Constitution*. New York: Random House. ISBN 0-8129-7684-3.

[20] "DOD Releases Unified Command Plan 2011". *United States Department of Defense*. April 8, 2011. Retrieved February 25, 2013.

[21] 10 U.S.C. § 164

[22] Joint Chiefs of Staff. About the Joint Chiefs of Staff. Retrieved February 25, 2013.

[23] Hamilton, Alexander. *The Federalist* #69 (reposting). Retrieved June 15, 2007.

[24] Christopher, James A.; Baker, III (July 8, 2008). "The National War Powers Commission Report" (PDF). The Miller Center of Public Affairs at the University of Virginia. Retrieved December 15, 2010. No clear mechanism or requirement exists today for the president and Congress to consult. The War Powers Resolution of 1973 contains only vague consultation requirements. Instead, it relies on reporting requirements that, if triggered, begin the clock running for Congress to approve the particular armed conflict. By the terms of the 1973 Resolution, however, Congress need not act to disapprove the conflict; the cessation of all hostilities is required in 60 to 90 days merely if Congress fails to act. Many have criticized this aspect of the Resolution as unwise and unconstitutional, and no president in the past 35 years has filed a report "pursuant" to these triggering provisions.

[25] "The Law: The President's War Powers". *Time*. June 1, 1970. Retrieved September 28, 2009.

[26] Alison Mitchell (May 2, 1999). "The World; Only Congress Can Declare War. Really. It's True". *The New York Times*. Retrieved November 8, 2009. Presidents have sent forces abroad more than 100 times; Congress has declared war only five times: the War of 1812, the Mexican War, the Spanish-American War, World War I and World War II.

[27] Alison Mitchell (May 2, 1999). "The World; Only Congress Can Declare War. Really. It's True". *The New York Times*. Retrieved November 8, 2009. President Reagan told Congress of the invasion of Grenada two hours after he had ordered the landing. He told Congressional leaders of the bombing of Libya while the aircraft were on their way.

[28] Michael R. Gordon (December 20, 1990). "U.S. troops move in panama in effort to seize noriega; gunfire is heard in capital". *The New York Times*. Retrieved November 8, 2009. It was not clear whether the White House consulted with Congressional leaders about the military action, or notified them in advance. Thomas S. Foley, the Speaker of the House, said on Tuesday night that he had not been alerted by the Administration.

[29] "Article II, Section 3, U.S. Constitution". *law.cornell.edu*. Legal Information Institute. 2012. Retrieved August 7, 2012.

[30] "The Executive Branch". *The White House website*. Retrieved October 17, 2010.

[31] *National Labor Relations Board v. Noel Canning*, 572 U.S. __ (2014).

[32] *Shurtleff v. United States*, 189 U.S. 311 (1903); *Myers v. United States*, 272 U.S. 52 (1926).

[33] *Humphrey's Executor v. United States*, 295 U.S. 602 (1935) and *Morrison v. Olson*, 487 U.S. 654 (1988), respectively.

[34] David Johnston (December 24, 1992). "Bush Pardons 6 in Iran Affair, Aborting a Weinberger Trial; Prosecutor Assails 'Cover-Up'". *The New York Times*. Retrieved November 8, 2009. But not since President Gerald R. Ford granted clemency to former President Richard M. Nixon for possible crimes in Watergate has a Presidential pardon so pointedly raised the issue of whether the President was trying to shield officials for political purposes.

[35] David Johnston (December 24, 1992). "Bush Pardons 6 in Iran Affair, Aborting a Weinberger Trial; Prosecutor Assails 'Cover-Up'". *The New York Times*. Retrieved November 8, 2009. The prosecutor charged that Mr. Weinberger's efforts to hide his notes may have 'forestalled impeachment proceedings against President Reagan' and formed part of a pattern of 'deception and obstruction.'... In light of President Bush's own misconduct, we are gravely concerned about his decision to pardon others who lied to Congress and obstructed official investigations.

[36] Peter Eisler (March 7, 2008). "Clinton-papers release blocked". USA TODAY. Retrieved November 8, 2009. Former president Clinton issued 140 pardons on his last day in office, including several to controversial figures, such as commodities trader Rich, then a fugitive on tax evasion charges. Rich's ex-wife, Denise, contributed $2,000 in 1999 to Hillary Clinton's Senate campaign; $5,000 to a related political action committee; and $450,000 to a fund set up to build the Clinton library.

[37] Millhiser, Ian (June 1, 2010). "Executive Privilege 101". Center for American Progress. Retrieved October 8, 2010.

[38] "Part III of the opinion in *Mohamed v. Jeppesen Dataplan*". Caselaw.findlaw.com. Retrieved November 29, 2010.

[39] Frost, Amanda; Florence, Justin (2009). "Reforming the State Secrets Privilege" (PDF). American Constitution Society. Retrieved October 8, 2010.

[40] Weaver, William G.; Pallitto, Robert M. (2005). "State Secrets and Executive Power". *Political Science Quarterly* (The Academy of Political Science) **120** (1): 85–112. doi:10.1002/j.1538-165x.2005.tb00539.x. Use of the state secrets privilege in courts has grown significantly over the last twenty-five years. In the twenty-three years between the decision in Reynolds [1953] and the election of Jimmy Carter, in 1976, there were four reported cases in which the government invoked the privilege. Between 1977 and 2001, there were a total of fifty-one reported cases in which courts ruled on invocation of the privilege. Because reported cases only represent a fraction of the total cases in which the privilege is invoked or implicated, it is unclear precisely how dramatically the use of the privilege has grown. But the increase in reported cases is indicative of greater willingness to assert the privilege than in the past.

[41] Savage, Charlie (September 8, 2010). "Court Dismisses a Case Asserting Torture by C.I.A". *The New York Times*. Retrieved October 8, 2010.

[42] Finn, Peter (September 9, 2010). "Suit dismissed against firm in CIA rendition case". *The Washington Post*. Retrieved October 8, 2010.

[43] Greenwald, Glenn (February 10, 2009). "The 180-degree reversal of Obama's State Secrets position". *Salon*. Retrieved October 8, 2010.

[44] American Civil Liberties Union (January 31, 2007). "Background on the State Secrets Privilege". ACLU. Retrieved October 8, 2010.

[45] Eric Cantor (July 30, 2009). "Obama's 32 Czars". *The Washington Post*. Retrieved September 28, 2009.

[46] Dana D. Nelson (October 11, 2008). "The 'unitary executive' question". *Los Angeles Times*. Retrieved October 4, 2009.

[47] Transcript – Ray Suarez; et al. (July 24, 2006). "President's Use of 'Signing Statements' Raises Constitutional Concerns". PBS Online NewsHour. Retrieved November 11, 2009. The American Bar Association said President Bush's use of "signing statements," which allow him to sign a bill into law but not enforce certain provisions, disregards the rule of law and the separation of powers. Legal experts discuss the implications.

[48] George F. Will – op-ed columnist (December 21, 2008). "Making Congress Moot". *The Washington Post*. Retrieved September 28, 2009.

[49] Duggan, Paul (April 2, 2007). "Balking at the First Pitch". *The Washington Post*. p. A01.

[50] "2007 Report to the Nation". Boy Scouts of Amercica. 2007. Retrieved September 23, 2009.

[51] Grier, Peter (April 25, 2011). "The (not so) secret history of the White House Easter Egg Roll". *The Christian Science Monitor*. Retrieved May 6, 2011.

[52] Hesse, Monica (November 21, 2007). "Turkey Pardons, The Stuffing of Historic Legend". *The Washington Post*. Retrieved May 14, 2011.

[53] Gibbs, Nancy (November 13, 2008). "How Presidents Pass The Torch". *Time*. Retrieved May 6, 2011.

[54] Dorning, Mike (January 22, 2009). "A note from Bush starts morning in the Oval Office". *Chicago Tribune*. Retrieved May 6, 2011.

[55] James A. Abbott and Elaine M. Rice (1998). *Designing Camelot: The Kennedy White House Restoration*. Van Nostrand Reinhold. pp. 9–10. ISBN 0-442-02532-7.

[56] "The White House State Dinner" (PDF). *The White House Historical Association*. Retrieved May 14, 2011.

[57] Rachel Dykoski (November 1, 2008). "Book note: Presidential idolatry is "Bad for Democracy"". Twin Cities Daily Planet. Retrieved November 11, 2009. Dana D. Nelson's book makes the case that we've had 200+ years of propagandized leadership...

[58] John Neffinger (April 2, 2007). "Democrats vs. *Science*: Why We're So Damn Good at Losing Elections". *Huffington Post*. Retrieved November 11, 2009. ...back in the 1980s Lesley Stahl of 60 Minutes ran a piece skewering Reagan's policies on the elderly ... But while her voiceover delivered a scathing critique, the video footage was all drawn from carefully-staged photo-ops of Reagan smiling with seniors and addressing large crowds ... Deaver thanked ... Stahl...for broadcasting all those images of Reagan looking his best.

[59] Dana D. Nelson (2008). "Bad for democracy: how the Presidency undermines the power of the people". U of Minnesota Press. ISBN 978-0-8166-5677-6. Retrieved November 11, 2009. in rich detail how Kennedy drew on the power of myth as he framed his experience during World War II, when his PT boat was sliced in half by a Japanese...

[60] Dana D. Nelson (2008). "Bad for democracy: how the Presidency undermines the power of the people". U of Minnesota Press. ISBN 978-0-8166-5677-6. Retrieved November 11, 2009. Even before Kennedy ran for Congress, he had become fascinated, through his Hollywood acquaintances and visits, with the idea of image... (p.54)

[61] Lexington (July 21, 2009). "The Cult of the Presidency". *The Economist*. Retrieved November 9, 2009. Gene Healy argues that because voters expect the president to do everything ... When they inevitably fail to keep their promises, voters swiftly become disillusioned. Yet they never lose their romantic idea that the president should drive the economy, vanquish enemies, lead the free world, comfort tornado victims, heal the national soul and protect borrowers from hidden credit-card fees.

[62] Michiko Kakutani (book reviewer) (July 6, 2007). "Unchecked and Unbalanced". *The New York Times*. Retrieved November 9, 2009. the founding fathers had 'scant affection for strong executives' like England's king, and ... Bush White House's claims are rooted in ideas "about the 'divine' right of kings" ... and that certainly did not find their 'way into our founding documents, the 1776 Declaration of Independence and the Constitution of 1787.'

[63] "The Conquest of Presidentialism". *Huffington Post*. August 22, 2008. Retrieved September 20, 2009.

[64] interview by David Schimke (September–October 2008). "Presidential Power to the People – Author Dana D. Nelson on why democracy demands that the next president be taken down a notch". *Utne Reader*. Retrieved September 20, 2009.

[65] Ross Linker (September 27, 2007). "Critical of Presidency, Prof. Ginsberg and Crenson unite". The Johns-Hopkins Newsletter. Retrieved November 9, 2009. presidents slowly but surely gain more and more power with both the public at large and other political institutions doing nothing to prevent it.

[66] Michiko Kakutani (book reviewer) (July 6, 2007). "Unchecked and Unbalanced". *The New York Times*. Retrieved November 9, 2009. UNCHECKED AND UNBALANCED: Presidential Power in a Time of Terror By Frederick A. O. Schwarz Jr. and Aziz Z. Huq (authors)

[67] Dana D. Nelson (October 11, 2008). "Opinion–The 'unitary executive' question – What do McCain and Obama think of the concept?". *Los Angeles Times*. Retrieved September 21, 2009.

[68] Scott Shane (September 25, 2009). "A Critic Finds Obama Policies a Perfect Target". *The New York Times*. Retrieved November 8, 2009. There is the small, minority-owned firm with deep ties to President Obama's Chicago backers, made eligible by the Federal Reserve to handle potentially lucrative credit deals. 'I want to know how these firms are picked and who picked them,' Mr. Wilson, the group's president, tells his eager researchers.

[69] See: Peabody, Bruce G.; Gant, Scott E. (1999). "The Twice and Future President: Constitutional Interstices and the Twenty-Second Amendment". *Minnesota Law Review* (Minneapolis, MN: Minnesota Law Review) **83** (565).; alternatively, see: Albert, Richard (2005). "The Evolving Vice Presidency". *Temple Law Review* (Philadelphia, PA: Temple University of the Commonwealth System of Higher Education) **78** (811, at 856–9).

[70] See GPO Annotated U.S. Constitution, 2002 Ed., at 611 & nn. 772–773.

[71] International Law, US Power: The United States' Quest for Legal Security, p 10, Shirley V. Scott - 2012

[72] U.S. Const. art. II, § 1, cl. 8.

[73] "Judge doesn't ban "God" in inaugural oath". Associated Press. January 15, 2009. Retrieved August 18, 2012.

[74] Guardian, "Bush colonoscopy leaves Cheney in charge", July 20, 2007.

[75] 3 U.S.C. § 20

[76] "Presidential and Vice Presidential Salaries, 1789+". University of Michigan. Archived from the original on June 6, 2011. Retrieved October 7, 2009.

[77] Relative Value in US Dollars. *Measuring Worth*. Retrieved May 30, 2006.

[78] Dept. of Labor Inflation Calculator. *Inflation Calculator*. Retrieved August 10, 2009.

[79] "How much does the U.S. president get paid?". *Howstuffworks*. Retrieved July 24, 2007.

[80] Salaries of Federal Officials: A Fact Sheet. *United States Senate* website. Retrieved August 6, 2009.

[81] Bumiller, Elizabeth (January 2009). "Inside the Presidency". *National Geographic*. Retrieved June 24, 2012.

[82] "President's Guest House (includes Lee House and Blair House), Washington, DC". Retrieved September 30, 2009.

[83] New Presidential Limousine enters Secret Service Fleet U.S. Secret Service Press Release (January 14, 2009) Retrieved on January 20, 2009.

[84] Air Force One. White House Military Office. Retrieved June 17, 2007.

[85] Any U.S. Air Force aircraft carrying the president will use the call sign "Air Force One." Similarly, "Navy One", "Army One", and "Coast Guard One" are the call signs used if the president is aboard a craft belonging to these services. "Executive One" becomes the call sign of any civilian aircraft when the president boards.

[86] "Junior Secret Service Program: Assignment 7. Code Names". National Park Service. Retrieved August 18, 2007.

[87] "Candidate Code Names Secret Service Monikers Used On The Campaign Trail". CBS. September 16, 2008. Retrieved November 12, 2008.

[88] Schwemle, Barbara L. (October 17, 2012). "President of the United States: Compensation" (PDF). Congressional Research Service. Retrieved January 10, 2013.

[89] "Former presidents cost U.S. taxpayers big bucks". *Toledo Blade*. January 7, 2007. Retrieved May 22, 2007.

[90] 18 U.S.C. § 3056

[91] "Obama signs bill granting lifetime Secret Service protection to former presidents and spouses". The Associated Press. January 10, 2013. Retrieved January 10, 2013.

[92] "United States Secret Service: Protection". United States Secret Service. Retrieved October 8, 2014.

[93] "Obama signs protection bill for former presidents". *The Washington Times*. January 10, 2013. Retrieved August 14, 2013.

[94] "Shock and Anger Flash Throughout the United States". Associated Press. March 31, 1981. Retrieved March 11, 2011.

[95] "FOUR PRESIDENTS". Reagan Presidential Library, National Archives and Records Administration. Retrieved April 3, 2011.

[96] Biography of Richard M. Nixon, The White House.

[97] 44 U.S.C. § 2112

## 4.10 Further reading

- Balogh, Brian and Bruce J. Schulman, eds. *Recapturing the Oval Office: New Historical Approaches to the American Presidency* (Cornell University Press, 2015), 311 pp.

- Bumiller, Elisabeth (January 2009). "Inside the Presidency". *National Geographic* **215** (1): 130–149.

- Couch, Ernie. *Presidential Trivia.* Rutledge Hill Press. March 1, 1996. ISBN 1-55853-412-1

- Lang, J. Stephen. *The Complete Book of Presidential Trivia.* Pelican Publishing. 2001. ISBN 1-56554-877-9

- Greenberg, David. *Republic of Spin: An Inside History of the American Presidency* (W. W. Norton & Company, 2015). xx, 540 pp.

- Leo, Leonard – Taranto, James – Bennett, William J. *Presidential Leadership: Rating the Best and the Worst in the White House.* Simon and Schuster. 2004. ISBN 0-7432-5433-3

- *Presidential Studies Quarterly*, published by Blackwell Synergy, is a quarterly academic journal on the presidency.

- Świątczak, Wasilewska, Iwona. *"The Toughest Season in the White House": The Rhetorical Presidency and the State of the Union Address, 1953–1992.* Ph.D. thesis. University of Helsinki, 2014. ISBN 978-951-51-0248-5. 978-951-51-0249-2 Online version.

### 4.10.1 Primary sources

- Waldman, Michael – Stephanopoulos, George. *My Fellow Americans: The Most Important Speeches of America's Presidents, from George Washington to George W. Bush.* Sourcebooks Trade. 2003. ISBN 1-4022-0027-7

- Jacobs, Ron. Interview with Joseph G. Peschek and William Grover, authors of *The Unsustainable Presidency*, a book offering an analysis of the role the US President plays in economics and politics

## 4.11 External links

**Official**

- "Executive Office of the President". Retrieved January 21, 2009.

- "White House". Retrieved October 7, 2005.

**Presidential histories**

- A New Nation Votes: American Election Returns, 1787–1825 Presidential election returns including town and county breakdowns

- "American Presidents: Life Portraits". *C-SPAN*. Retrieved February 13, 2016. Companion website for the C-SPAN television series: *American Presidents: Life Portraits*

- "Presidential Documents from the National Archives". Retrieved March 21, 2007. Collection of letters, portraits, photos, and other documents from the National Archives

- "The American Presidency Project". *UC Santa Barbara*. Retrieved October 7, 2005. Collection of over 67,000 presidential documents

- The History Channel: US Presidents

**Miscellaneous**

- "All the President's Roles". *Ask Gleaves*. Retrieved October 20, 2006. Article analyzing a president's many hats

- Hauenstein Center for Presidential Studies Educational site on the American presidency

- "Presidents' Occupations". Retrieved August 20, 2007. Listing of every President's occupations before and after becoming the Commander in Chief

- "The Masonic Presidents Tour". *The Masonic Library and Museum of Pennsylvania*. Retrieved October 7, 2005. Brief histories of the Masonic careers of Presidents who were members of the Freemasons

- "The Presidents". *American Experience*. Retrieved March 4, 2007. PBS site on the American presidency

- Presidents of the United States: Resource Guides from the Library of Congress

- Shapell Manuscript Foundation Images of documents written by U.S. presidents

# Chapter 5

# Vice President of the United States

The **Vice President of the United States** (**VPOTUS**) is the second-highest position in the executive branch of the United States, after the president.[1] The executive power of both the vice president and the president is granted under Article Two, Section One of the Constitution. The vice president is indirectly elected, together with the president, to a four-year term of office by the people of the United States through the Electoral College.[2] The vice president is the first person in the presidential line of succession, and would normally ascend to presidency upon the death, resignation, or removal of the president.[3]

The vice president is also president of the United States Senate,[4] and in that capacity, only votes when it is necessary to break a tie. While Senate customs have created supermajority rules that have diminished this constitutional tie-breaking authority, the vice president still retains the ability to influence legislation; for example, the Deficit Reduction Act of 2005 was passed in the Senate by a tie-breaking vice presidential vote.[4][5][6] Additionally, pursuant to the Twelfth Amendment, the vice president presides over the joint session of Congress when it convenes to count the vote of the Electoral College.[2]

While the vice president's only constitutionally prescribed functions aside from presidential succession relate to their role as President of the Senate, the office is commonly viewed as a component of the executive branch of the federal government. The United States Constitution does not expressly assign the office to any one branch, causing a dispute among scholars whether it belongs to the executive branch, the legislative branch, or both.[7][8][9][10] The modern view of the vice president as a member of the executive branch is due in part to the assignment of executive duties to the vice president by either the president or Congress, though such activities are only recent historical developments.[7]

## 5.1 Origin

The creation of the office of vice president was a direct consequence of the Electoral College. Delegates to the Philadelphia Convention gave each state a number of presidential electors equal to that state's combined share of House and Senate seats. Yet the delegates were worried that each elector would only favor his own state's favorite son candidate, resulting in deadlocked elections that would produce no winners. To counter this potential difficulty, the delegates gave each presidential elector two votes, requiring that at least one of their votes be for a candidate from outside the elector's state; they also mandated that the winner of an election must obtain an absolute majority of the total number of electors. The delegates expected that each elector's second vote would go to a statesman of national character.[11]

Fearing that electors might throw away their second vote to bolster their favorite son's chance of winning, however, the Philadelphia delegates specified that the runner-up would become vice president. Creating this new office imposed a political cost on discarded votes and forced electors to cast their second ballot.[11]

## 5.2 Roles of the vice president

The Constitution limits the formal powers and role of vice president to becoming president, should the president become unable to serve, prompting the well-known expression "only a heartbeat away from the presidency", and to acting as the presiding officer of the U.S. Senate. Other statutorily granted roles include membership of both the National Security Council and the Board of Regents of the Smithsonian Institution.[12][13]

### 5.2.1   President of the United States Senate

As President of the Senate, the vice president has two primary duties: to cast a vote in the event of a Senate deadlock and to preside over and certify the official vote count of the U.S. Electoral College. For example, in the first half of 2001, the Senators were divided 50-50 between Republicans and Democrats and Dick Cheney's tie-breaking vote gave the Republicans the Senate majority.

**Regular duties**

As President of the Senate (Article I, Section 3, Clause 4), the vice president oversees procedural matters and may cast a tie-breaking vote. There is a strong convention within the U.S. Senate that the vice president should not use their position as President of the Senate to influence the passage of legislation or act in a partisan manner, except in the case of breaking tie votes. As President of the Senate, John Adams cast twenty-nine tie-breaking votes, a record no successor except John C. Calhoun ever threatened. Adams's votes protected the president's sole authority over the removal of appointees, influenced the location of the national capital, and prevented war with Great Britain. On at least one occasion Adams persuaded senators to vote against legislation he opposed, and he frequently addressed the Senate on procedural and policy matters. Adams's political views and his active role in the Senate made him a natural target for critics of George Washington's administration. Toward the end of his first term, a threatened resolution that would have silenced him except for procedural and policy matters caused him to exercise more restraint in hopes of seeing his election as President of the United States.

In modern times, the vice president rarely presides over day-to-day matters in the Senate; in their place, the Senate chooses a President pro tempore (or "president for a time") to preside in the vice president's absence; the Senate normally selects the longest-serving senator in the majority party. The President pro tempore has the power to appoint any other senator to preside and in practice, junior senators from the majority party are assigned the task of presiding over the Senate at most times.

Except for this tie-breaking role, the *Standing Rules of the Senate* vest *no* significant responsibilities in the vice president. Rule XIX, which governs debate, does not authorize the vice president to participate in debate, and grants only to members of the Senate (and, upon appropriate notice, former presidents of the United States) the privilege of addressing the Senate, without granting a similar privilege to the sitting vice president. Thus, as *Time* magazine wrote during the controversial tenure of Vice President Charles G. Dawes, "once in four years the Vice President can make a little speech, and then he is done. For four years he then

has to sit in the seat of the silent, attending to speeches ponderous or otherwise, of deliberation or humor."[14]

**Recurring, infrequent duties**

The President of the Senate also presides over counting and presentation of the votes of the Electoral College. This process occurs in the presence of both houses of Congress, generally on January 6 of the year following a U.S. presidential election.[15] In this capacity, only four vice presidents have been able to announce their own election to the presidency: John Adams, Thomas Jefferson, Martin Van Buren, and George H. W. Bush. At the beginning of 1961, it fell to Richard Nixon to preside over this process, which officially announced the election of his 1960 opponent, John F. Kennedy. In 2001, Al Gore announced the election of his opponent, George W. Bush. In 1969, Vice President Hubert Humphrey would have announced the election of his opponent, Richard Nixon; however, on the date of the Congressional joint session (January 6), Humphrey was in Norway attending the funeral of Trygve Lie, the first elected Secretary-General of the United Nations.[16]

In 1933, incumbent Vice President Charles Curtis announced the election of House Speaker John Nance Garner as his successor, while Garner was seated next to him on the House dais.

The President of the Senate may also preside over most of the impeachment trials of federal officers. However, whenever the President of the United States is impeached, the US Constitution requires the Chief Justice of the United States to preside over the Senate for the trial. The Constitution is silent as to the presiding officer in the instance where the vice president is the officer impeached.

### 5.2.2   Succession and the Twenty-Fifth Amendment

The U.S. Constitution provides that should the president die, become disabled while in office or removed from office, the "powers and duties" of the office are transferred to the vice president. Initially, it was unclear whether the vice president actually became the new president or merely an acting president. This was first tested in 1841 with the death of President William Henry Harrison. Harrison's vice president, John Tyler, asserted that he had succeeded to the full presidential office, powers, and title, and declined to acknowledge documents referring to him as "Acting President." Despite some strong calls against it, Tyler took the oath of office as the tenth President. Tyler's claim was not challenged legally, and so the Tyler precedent of full succession was established. This was made explicit by Section

*John Tyler was the first vice president to assume the presidency following the death of his predecessor. In doing so, he insisted that he was the president, not merely an acting president.*

1 of the Twenty-fifth Amendment to the U.S. Constitution, ratified in 1967.

Section 2 of the Twenty-fifth Amendment provides for vice presidential succession:

> *Whenever there is a vacancy in the office of the Vice President, the President shall nominate a Vice President who shall take office upon confirmation by a majority vote of both Houses of Congress.*

Gerald Ford was the first vice president selected by this method, after the resignation of Vice President Spiro Agnew in 1973; after succeeding to the presidency, Ford nominated Nelson Rockefeller as vice president.

Another issue was who had the power to declare that an incapacitated president is unable to discharge his duties. This question had arisen most recently with the illnesses of President Dwight D. Eisenhower. Section 3 and Section 4 of the amendment provide means for the vice president to become acting president upon the temporary disability of the president. Section 3 deals with self-declared incapacity of the president. Section 4 deals with incapacity declared by the joint action of the vice president and of a majority of the Cabinet.

*President Lyndon Johnson is sworn in, following the assassination of President John Kennedy.*

While Section 4 has never been invoked, Section 3 has been invoked three times: on July 13, 1985 when Ronald Reagan underwent surgery to remove cancerous polyps from his colon, and twice more on June 29, 2002 and July 21, 2007 when George W. Bush underwent colonoscopy procedures requiring sedation. Prior to this amendment, Vice President Richard Nixon informally assumed some of President Dwight Eisenhower's duties for several weeks on each of three occasions when Eisenhower was ill.

### 5.2.3 Informal roles

The extent of any informal roles and functions of the vice president depend on the specific relationship between the president and the vice president, but often include tasks such as drafter and spokesperson for the administration's policies, adviser to the president, and being a symbol of American concern or support. The influence of the vice president in this role depends almost entirely on the characteristics of the particular administration. Dick Cheney, for instance, was widely regarded as one of President George W. Bush's closest confidants. Al Gore was an important adviser to President Bill Clinton on matters of foreign policy and the environment. Often, vice presidents are chosen to act as a "balance" to the president, taking either more moderate or radical positions on issues. Under the American system the president is both head of state *and* head of government, and the ceremonial duties of the former position are often delegated to the vice president. The vice president is often assigned the ceremonial duties of representing the president and the government at state funerals or other functions in the United States. This often is the most visible role of the vice president, and has occasionally been the subject of ridicule, such as during the vice presidency of George H. W. Bush. The vice president may meet with other heads of state or attend state funerals in other countries, at times when the administration wishes to demonstrate concern or support but cannot send the president themselves. Many vice presidents have lamented the lack of meaningful work in their role, from the very first vice president, John Adams, who said "My country has in its wisdom contrived for me the most insignificant office that ever the invention of man contrived or his imagination conceived."[17] John Nance Garner, who served as vice president from 1933 to 1941 under President Franklin D. Roosevelt, claimed that the vice presidency "isn't worth a pitcher of warm piss."[18] Harry Truman, who also served as vice president under Roosevelt, said that the office was as "useful as a cow's fifth teat."[19]

**Office as stepping stone to the presidency**

In recent decades, the vice presidency has frequently been used to launch bids for the presidency. The transition of the office to its modern stature occurred primarily as a result of Franklin Roosevelt's 1940 nomination, when he captured the ability to nominate his running mate instead of leaving the nomination to the convention. Prior to that, party bosses often used the vice presidential nomination as a consolation prize for the party's minority faction. A further factor potentially contributing to the rise in prestige of the office was the adoption of presidential preference primaries in the early 20th century. By adopting primary voting, the field of candidates for vice president was expanded by both the increased quantity and quality of presidential candidates successful in some primaries, yet who ultimately failed to capture the presidential nomination at the convention.

Of the thirteen presidential elections from 1956 to 2004, nine featured the incumbent president; the other four (1960, 1968, 1988, 2000) all featured the incumbent vice president. Former vice presidents also ran, in 1984 (Walter Mondale), and in 1968 (Richard Nixon, against the incumbent vice president, Hubert Humphrey). The first presidential election to include neither the incumbent president nor the incumbent vice president on a major party ticket since 1952 came in 2008 when President George W. Bush had already served two terms and Vice President Cheney chose not to run. Richard Nixon is also the only non-sitting vice president to be elected president, as well as the only person to be elected president and vice president twice each.

## 5.3   Selection process

*John Adams, the first Vice President of the United States*

### 5.3.1   Eligibility

The Twelfth Amendment states that "no person constitutionally ineligible to the office of President shall be eligible to that of Vice President of the United States."[20] Thus, to serve as vice president, an individual must:

- Be a natural-born U.S. citizen;

- Be at least 35 years old

- Have resided in the U.S. at least 14 years.[21]

### 5.3.2   Disqualifications

Additionally, Section 3 of the Fourteenth Amendment denies eligibility for any federal office to anyone who, having sworn an oath to support the United States Constitution, later has rebelled against the United States. This disqualification, originally aimed at former supporters of the Confederacy, may be removed by a two-thirds vote of each house of the Congress.

Under the Twenty-second Amendment, the President of the United States may not be *elected* to more than two terms. However, there is no similar such limitation as to how many times one can be elected vice president. Scholars disagree whether a former president barred from election to the presidency is also ineligible to be elected or appointed vice president, as suggested by the Twelfth Amendment.[22][23] The issue has never been tested in practice.

Also, Article I, Section 3, Clause 7 allows the Senate, upon voting to remove an impeached federal official from office, to disqualify that official from holding any federal office.

### 5.3.3 Residency limitation

While it is commonly held that the president and vice president must be residents of different states, this is not actually the case. Nothing in the Constitution prohibits *both* candidates being from a single state. Instead, the limitation imposed is on the members of the Electoral College, who must cast a ballot for at least one candidate who is not from *their own* state.

In theory, the candidates elected could both be from one state, but the electors of that state would, in a close electoral contest, run the risk of denying their vice presidential candidate the absolute majority required to secure the election, even if the presidential candidate is elected. This would then place the vice presidential election in the hands of the Senate.

In practice, however, residency is rarely an issue. Parties have avoided nominating tickets containing two candidates from the same state. Further, the candidates may themselves take action to alleviate any residency conflict. For example, at the start of the 2000 election cycle Dick Cheney was a resident of Texas; Cheney quickly changed his residency back to Wyoming, where he had previously served as a U.S. Representative, when Texas governor and Republican presidential nominee George W. Bush asked Cheney to be his vice presidential candidate.

### 5.3.4 Nominating process

Though the vice president need not have any political experience, most major-party vice presidential nominees are current or former United States Senators or Representatives, with the occasional nominee being a current or former Governor, a high-ranking military officer, or a holder of a major post within the Executive Department. The vice presidential candidates of the major national political parties are formally selected by each party's quadrennial nominating convention, following the selection of the party's presidential candidates. The official process is identical to the one by which the presidential candidates are chosen, with delegates placing the names of candidates into nomination, followed by a ballot in which candidates must receive a majority to secure the party's nomination.

In practice, the presidential nominee has considerable influence on the decision, and in the 20th century it became cus-

tomary for that person to select a preferred running mate, who is then nominated and accepted by the convention. In recent years, with the presidential nomination usually being a foregone conclusion as the result of the primary process, the selection of a vice presidential candidate is often announced prior to the actual balloting for the presidential candidate, and sometimes before the beginning of the convention itself. The first presidential aspirant to announce his selection for vice president before the beginning of the convention was Ronald Reagan who, prior to the 1976 Republican National Convention announced that Richard Schweiker would be his running mate. Reagan's supporters then sought to amend the convention rules so that Gerald R. Ford would be required to name his vice presidential running mate in advance as well. The proposal was defeated, and Reagan did not receive the nomination in 1976. Often, the presidential nominee will name a vice presidential candidate who will bring geographic or ideological balance to the ticket or appeal to a particular constituency.

The vice presidential candidate might also be chosen on the basis of traits the presidential candidate is perceived to lack, or on the basis of name recognition. To foster party unity, popular runners-up in the presidential nomination process are commonly considered. While this selection process may enhance the chances of success for a national ticket, in the past it often insured that the vice presidential nominee represented regions, constituencies, or ideologies at odds with those of the presidential candidate. As a result, vice presidents were often excluded from the policy-making process of the new administration. Many times their relationships with the president and his staff were aloof, non-existent, or even adversarial.

The ultimate goal of vice presidential candidate selection is to help and not hurt the party's chances of getting elected. A selection whose positive traits make the presidential candidate look less favorable in comparison can backfire, such as in 1988 when Democratic candidate Michael Dukakis chose experienced Texas Senator Lloyd Bentsen, and in 2008 when Republican candidate John McCain picked dynamic Alaska Governor Sarah Palin. However, Palin also hurt McCain when her interviews with Katie Couric led to concerns about her fitness for the presidency.[24] In 1984, Walter Mondale picked Geraldine Ferraro whose nomination became a drag on the ticket due to repeated questions about her husband's finances. Questions about Dan Quayle's experience and temperament were raised in the 1988 presidential campaign of George H.W. Bush, but he still won. James Stockdale, the choice of third-party candidate Ross Perot in 1992, was seen as unqualified by many, but the Perot-Stockdale ticket still won about 19% of the vote.

Historically, vice presidential candidates were chosen to

provide geographic and ideological balance to a presidential ticket, widening a presidential candidate's appeal to voters from outside his regional base or wing of the party. Candidates from electoral-vote rich states were usually preferred. However, in 1992, moderate Democrat Bill Clinton (of Arkansas) chose moderate Democrat Al Gore (of Tennessee) as his running mate. Despite the two candidates' near-identical ideological and regional backgrounds, Gore's extensive experience in national affairs enhanced the appeal of a ticket headed by Clinton, whose political career had been spent entirely at the local and state levels of government. In 2000, George W. Bush chose Dick Cheney of Wyoming, a reliably Republican state with only three electoral votes, and in 2008, Barack Obama mirrored Bush's strategy when he chose Joe Biden of Delaware, a reliably Democratic state, likewise one with only three electoral votes. Both Cheney and Biden were chosen for their experience in national politics (experience lacked by both Bush and Obama) rather than the ideological balance or electoral vote advantage they would provide.

The first presidential candidate to choose his vice presidential candidate was Franklin Delano Roosevelt in 1940.[25] The last not to name a vice presidential choice, leaving the matter up to the convention, was Democrat Adlai Stevenson in 1956. The convention chose Tennessee Senator Estes Kefauver over Massachusetts Senator (and later president) John F. Kennedy. At the tumultuous 1972 Democratic convention, presidential nominee George McGovern selected Senator Thomas Eagleton as his running mate, but numerous other candidates were either nominated from the floor or received votes during the balloting. Eagleton nevertheless received a majority of the votes and the nomination, though he later resigned from the ticket, resulting in Robert Sargent Shriver becoming McGovern's final running mate; both lost to the Nixon-Agnew ticket by a wide margin, carrying only Massachusetts and the District of Columbia.

In cases where the presidential nomination is still in doubt as the convention approaches, the campaigns for the two positions may become intertwined. In 1976, Ronald Reagan, who was trailing President Gerald R. Ford in the presidential delegate count, announced prior to the Republican National Convention that, if nominated, he would select Senator Richard Schweiker as his running mate. This move backfired to a degree, as Schweiker's relatively liberal voting record alienated many of the more conservative delegates who were considering a challenge to party delegate selection rules to improve Reagan's chances. In the end, Ford narrowly won the presidential nomination and Reagan's selection of Schweiker became moot.

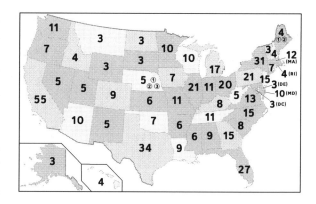

*A map of the United States showing the number of electoral votes allocated to each state as of the 2000 United States Census. This map applied for the 2004 and 2008 elections; it notes that Maine and Nebraska distribute electoral by way of the Congressional District Method. 270 electoral votes are required for a majority out of 538 overall.*

### 5.3.5   Election, oath, and tenure

Main article: Electoral College (United States)

Vice presidents are elected indirectly in the United States. A number of electors, collectively known as the Electoral College, officially select the president. On Election Day, voters in each of the states and the District of Columbia cast ballots for these electors. Each state is allocated a number of electors, equal to the size of its delegation in both Houses of Congress combined. Generally, the ticket that wins the most votes in a state wins all of that state's electoral votes and thus has its slate of electors chosen to vote in the Electoral College.

The winning slate of electors meet at its state's capital on the first Monday after the second Wednesday in December, about six weeks after the election, to vote. They then send a record of that vote to Congress. The vote of the electors is opened by the sitting vice president, acting in his capacity as President of the Senate and read aloud to a joint session of the incoming Congress, which was elected at the same time as the president.

Pursuant to the Twentieth Amendment, the vice president's term of office begins at noon on January 20 of the year following the election. This date, known as Inauguration Day, marks the beginning of the four-year terms of both the president and vice president.

Although Article VI requires that the vice president take an oath or affirmation of allegiance to the US Constitution, unlike the president, the United States Constitution does not specify the precise wording of the oath of office for the vice president. Several variants of the oath have been used since 1789; the current form, which is also recited by Senators,

Representatives and other government officers, has been used since 1884:

> I, A— B—, do solemnly swear (or affirm) that I will support and defend the Constitution of the United States against all enemies, foreign and domestic; that I will bear true faith and allegiance to the same; that I take this obligation freely, without any mental reservation or purpose of evasion; and that I will well and faithfully discharge the duties of the office on which I am about to enter. So help me God.[26]

The term of office for vice president is four years. While the Twenty-Second Amendment generally restricts the president to two terms, there is no similar limitation on the office of vice president, meaning an eligible person could hold the office as long as voters continued to vote for electors who in turn would renew the vice president's tenure. A vice president could even serve under different administrations, as George Clinton and John C. Calhoun have done.

### 5.3.6 Original election process and reform

***Four vice presidents:*** *L-R, outgoing President Lyndon B. Johnson (the 37th Vice President), incoming President Richard Nixon (36th), (Everett Dirksen administering oath), Spiro Agnew incoming vice president (39th), and outgoing Vice President Hubert Humphrey (38th), January 20, 1969*

Under the original terms of the Constitution, the electors of the Electoral College voted only for office of president rather than for both president and vice president. Each elector was allowed to vote for two people for the top office. The person receiving the greatest number of votes (provided that such a number was a majority of electors) would be president, while the individual who received the next largest number of votes became vice president. If no one received a majority of votes, then the House of Representatives would choose among the five candidates with the largest numbers of votes, with each state's representatives together casting a single vote. In such a case, the person who received the highest number of votes but was not chosen president would become vice president. In the case of a tie for second, then the Senate would choose the vice president.[27]

The original plan, however, did not foresee the development of political parties and their adversarial role in the government. For example, in the election of 1796, Federalist John Adams came in first, but because the Federalist electors had divided their second vote amongst several vice presidential candidates, Democratic-Republican Thomas Jefferson came second. Thus, the president and vice president were from opposing parties. Predictably, Adams and Jefferson clashed over issues such as states' rights and foreign policy.[28]

A greater problem occurred in the election of 1800, in which the two participating parties each had a secondary candidate they *intended* to elect as vice president, but the more popular Democratic-Republican party failed to execute that plan with their electoral votes. Under the system in place at the time (Article II, Section 1, Clause 3), the electors could not differentiate between their two candidates, so the plan had been for one elector to vote for Thomas Jefferson but *not* for Aaron Burr, thus putting Burr in second place. This plan broke down for reasons that are disputed, and both candidates received the same number of votes. After 35 deadlocked ballots in the House of Representatives, Jefferson finally won on the 36th ballot and Burr became vice president.[29]

This tumultuous affair led to the adoption of the Twelfth Amendment in 1804, which directed the electors to use separate ballots to vote for the president and vice president.[20] While this solved the problem at hand, it ultimately had the effect of lowering the prestige of the vice presidency, as the office was no longer for the leading challenger for the presidency.

The separate ballots for president and vice president became something of a moot issue later in the 19th century when it became the norm for popular elections to determine a state's Electoral College delegation. Electors chosen this way are pledged to vote for a particular presidential and vice presidential candidate (offered by the same political party). So, while the Constitution says that the president and vice president are chosen separately, in practice they are chosen together.

If no vice presidential candidate receives an Electoral College majority, then the Senate selects the vice president, in accordance with the United States Constitution. The

Twelfth Amendment states that a "majority of the whole number" of Senators (currently 51 of 100) is necessary for election.[30] Further, the language requiring an absolute majority of Senate votes precludes the sitting vice president from breaking any tie which might occur.[31] The election of 1836 is the only election so far where the office of the vice president has been decided by the Senate. During the campaign, Martin Van Buren's running mate Richard Mentor Johnson was accused of having lived with a black woman. Virginia's 23 electors, who were pledged to Van Buren and Johnson, refused to vote for Johnson (but still voted for Van Buren). The election went to the Senate, where Johnson was elected 33-17.

### 5.3.7 Salary

The vice president's salary is $230,700.[32] The salary was set by the 1989 Government Salary Reform Act, which also provides an automatic cost of living adjustment for federal employees.

The vice president does not automatically receive a pension based on that office, but instead receives the same pension as other members of Congress based on his position as President of the Senate.[33] The vice president must serve a minimum of five years to qualify for a pension.[34]

Since 1974, the official residence of the vice president and their family has been Number One Observatory Circle, on the grounds of the United States Naval Observatory in Washington, D.C.

### 5.3.8 Vacancy

See also: Impeachment in the United States, Twenty-fifth Amendment to the United States Constitution and List of Vice Presidents of the United States

Article I, Section 2, Clause 5 and Article II, Section 4 of the Constitution both authorize the House of Representatives to serve as a "grand jury" with the power to impeach high federal officials, including the president, for "treason, bribery, or other high crimes and misdemeanors." Similarly, Article I, Section 3, Clause 6 and Article II, Section 4 both authorize the Senate to serve as a court with the power to remove impeached officials from office, given a two-thirds vote to convict. No vice president has ever been impeached.

Prior to ratification of the Twenty-fifth Amendment in 1967, no provision existed for filling a vacancy in the office of vice president. As a result, the vice presidency was left vacant 16 times—sometimes for nearly four years—until the next ensuing election and inauguration: eight times due to the death of the sitting president, resulting in the vice

*John C. Calhoun was the first vice president to resign from office.*

presidents becoming president; seven times due to the death of the sitting vice president; and once due to the resignation of Vice President John C. Calhoun to become a senator.

Calhoun resigned because he had been dropped from the ticket by President Andrew Jackson in favor of Martin Van Buren, due primarily to conflicting with the President over the issue of nullification. Already a lame duck vice president, he was elected to the Senate by the South Carolina state legislature and resigned the vice presidency early to begin his Senate term because he believed he would have more power as a senator.

Since the adoption of the Twenty-Fifth Amendment, the office has been vacant twice while awaiting confirmation of the new vice president by both houses of Congress. The first such instance occurred in 1973 following the resignation of Spiro Agnew as Richard Nixon's vice president. Gerald Ford was subsequently nominated by President Nixon and confirmed by Congress. The second occurred 10 months later when Nixon resigned following the Watergate scandal and Ford assumed the presidency. The resulting vice presidential vacancy was filled by Nelson Rockefeller. Ford and Rockefeller are the only two people to have served as vice president without having been elected to the office, and Ford remains the only person to have served as both vice president and president without being elected to either office.

> Once the election is over, the Vice President's usefulness is over. He's like the second stage of a rocket. He's damn important going into orbit, but he's always thrown off to burn up in the atmosphere.
>
> — An aide to Vice President Hubert Humphrey.[35]

The Twenty-Fifth Amendment also made provisions for a replacement in the event that the vice president died in office, resigned, was removed from office via impeachment conviction or succeeded to the presidency. The original Constitution had no provision for selecting such a replacement, so the office of vice president would remain vacant until the beginning of the next presidential and vice presidential terms. This issue had arisen most recently when the John F. Kennedy assassination caused a vacancy from November 22, 1963, until January 20, 1965, and was rectified by Section 2 of the Twenty-Fifth Amendment.

## 5.4 Growth of the office

*Though prominent as a Missouri Senator, Harry Truman had been vice president only three months when he became president; he was never informed of Franklin Roosevelt's war or postwar policies while vice president.*

*Vice President Dick Cheney met with Vice President-elect Joe Biden at Number One Observatory Circle on November 13, 2008, representing a transition between vice presidencies.*

For much of its existence, the office of vice president was seen as little more than a minor position. Adams, the first vice president, was the first of many who found the job frustrating and stupefying.[36] Thomas R. Marshall, the 28th vice president, lamented: "Once there were two brothers. One ran away to sea; the other was elected Vice President of the United States. And nothing was heard of either of them again."[37] His successor, Calvin Coolidge, was so obscure that Major League Baseball sent him free passes that misspelled his name, and a fire marshal failed to recognize him when Coolidge's Washington residence was evacuated.[38] When the Whig Party asked Daniel Webster to run for the vice presidency on Zachary Taylor's ticket, he replied "I do not propose to be buried until I am really dead and in my coffin."[39] This was the second time Webster declined the office, which William Henry Harrison had first offered to him. Ironically, both of the presidents making the offer to Webster died in office, meaning the three-time presidential candidate could have become president if he had accepted either. Since presidents rarely died in office, however, the better preparation for the presidency was considered to be the office of Secretary of State, in which Webster served under Harrison, Tyler, and later, Taylor's successor, Fillmore.

For many years, the vice president was given few responsibilities. Garret Hobart, the first vice president under William McKinley, was one of the very few vice presidents at this time who played an important role in the administration. A close confidant and adviser of the president, Hobart was called "Assistant President."[40] However, until 1919, vice presidents were not included in meetings of the President's Cabinet. This precedent was broken by President Woodrow Wilson when he asked Thomas R. Marshall to preside over Cabinet meetings while Wilson was in France negotiating the Treaty of Versailles.[41] President

Warren G. Harding also invited his vice president, Calvin Coolidge, to meetings. The next vice president, Charles G. Dawes, did not seek to attend Cabinet meetings under President Coolidge, declaring that "the precedent might prove injurious to the country."[42] Vice President Charles Curtis was also precluded from attending by President Herbert Hoover.

In 1933, Franklin D. Roosevelt raised the stature of the office by renewing the practice of inviting the vice president to cabinet meetings, which every president since has maintained. Roosevelt's first vice president, John Nance Garner, broke with him at the start of the second term on the Court-packing issue and became Roosevelt's leading political enemy. In 1937, Garner became the first vice president to be sworn in on the Capitol steps in the same ceremony with the president, a tradition that continues. Prior to that time, vice presidents were traditionally inaugurated at a separate ceremony in the Senate chamber. Gerald R. Ford and Nelson A. Rockefeller, who were both appointed to the office under the terms of the 25th amendment, were inaugurated in the House and Senate chambers, respectively.

Garner's successor, Henry Wallace, was given major responsibilities during the war, but he moved further to the left than the Democratic Party and the rest of the Roosevelt administration and was relieved of actual power. Roosevelt kept his last vice president, Harry Truman, uninformed on all war and postwar issues, such as the atomic bomb, leading Truman to remark, wryly, that the job of the vice president was to "go to weddings and funerals." Following Roosevelt's death and Truman's ascension to the presidency, the need to keep vice presidents informed on national security issues became clear, and Congress made the vice president one of four statutory members of the National Security Council in 1949.

Richard Nixon reinvented the office of vice president. He had the attention of the media and the Republican party, when Dwight Eisenhower ordered him to preside at Cabinet meetings in his absence. Nixon was also the first vice president to formally assume temporary control of the executive branch, which he did after Eisenhower suffered a heart attack on September 24, 1955, ileitis in June 1956, and a stroke in November 1957.

Until 1961, vice presidents had their offices on Capitol Hill, a formal office in the Capitol itself and a working office in the Russell Senate Office Building. Lyndon B. Johnson was the first vice president to be given an office in the White House complex, in the Old Executive Office Building. The former Navy Secretary's office in the OEOB has since been designated the "Ceremonial Office of the Vice President" and is today used for formal events and press interviews. President Jimmy Carter was the first president to give his vice president, Walter Mondale, an office in the West Wing of the White House, which all vice presidents have since retained. Because of their function as Presidents of the Senate, vice presidents still maintain offices and staff members on Capitol Hill.

Though Walter Mondale's tenure was the beginning of the modern day power of the vice presidency, the tenure of Dick Cheney saw a rapid growth in the office of the vice president. Vice President Cheney held a tremendous amount of power and frequently made policy decisions on his own, without the knowledge of the President.[43] After his tenure, and during the 2008 presidential campaign, both vice presidential candidates, Sarah Palin and Joe Biden, stated that the office had expanded too much under Cheney's tenure and both had planned to reduce the role to simply being an adviser to the president.[44]

## 5.5  Post–vice presidency

The five former vice presidents now living are:

- **Walter Mondale**
  42nd (1977–1981)
  January 5, 1928

- **George H. W. Bush**
  43rd (1981–1989)
  June 12, 1924

  - **Dan Quayle**
  44th (1989–1993)
  February 4, 1947

  - **Al Gore**
  45th (1993–2001)
  March 31, 1948

  - **Dick Cheney**
  46th (2001–2009)
  January 30, 1941

Four vice presidents have been elected to the presidency immediately after serving as vice president: John Adams, Thomas Jefferson, Martin Van Buren and George H. W. Bush. Richard Nixon, John C. Breckinridge, Hubert Humphrey and Al Gore were all nominated by their respective parties, but failed to succeed the presidents with whom they were elected, though Nixon was elected president eight years later. Some former vice presidents have sought other offices after stepping down as vice president. John C. Calhoun resigned as vice president to accept election as US Senator from South Carolina. Hannibal Hamlin, Andrew Johnson, Alben Barkley and Hubert Humphrey were all elected to the Senate after leaving office. Levi P. Morton, vice president under Benjamin Harrison, was elected Governor of New York after leaving office.

Two vice presidents served under different presidents. George Clinton served under both Thomas Jefferson and James Madison, while John C. Calhoun served under John Quincy Adams and Andrew Jackson. In the modern era, Adlai Stevenson I became the first former vice president to seek election with a different running mate, running in 1900 with William Jennings Bryan after serving under Bryan's rival, Grover Cleveland. He was also narrowly defeated for Governor of Illinois in 1908. Charles W. Fairbanks, vice president under Theodore Roosevelt, sought unsuccessfully to return to office as Charles Evans Hughes' running mate in 1916.

Richard Nixon unsuccessfully sought the governorship of California in 1962, nearly two years after leaving office as vice president and just over six years before becoming president. Walter Mondale ran unsuccessfully for president in 1984, served as U.S. Ambassador to Japan from 1993 to 1996, and then sought unsuccessfully to return to the Senate in 2002. George H. W. Bush won the presidency, and his vice president, Dan Quayle, sought the Republican nomination in 2000. Al Gore also ran unsuccessfully for the presidency in 2000, turning to environmental advocacy afterward. Cheney had previously explored the possibility of running for president before serving as vice president, but chose not to run for president after his two terms as vice president.

Since 1977, former presidents and vice presidents who are elected or re-elected to the Senate are entitled to the largely honorific position of Deputy President pro tempore. So far, the only former vice president to have held this title is Hubert Humphrey following his return to the Senate. Walter Mondale would have been entitled to the position had his 2002 Senate bid been successful.

Under the terms of an 1886 Senate resolution, all former vice presidents are entitled to a portrait bust in the Senate wing of the United States Capitol, commemorating their service as presidents of the Senate. Dick Cheney is the most recent former vice president to be so honored.

Former vice presidents are eligible for pensions, and have been entitled to Secret Service personal protection since 2008.[45] Former vice presidents traditionally receive Secret Service protection for up to six months after leaving office, by order of the Secretary of Homeland Security.[46] In 2008, a bill titled the "Former Vice President Protection Act" was passed by Congress and signed into law by President Bush.[47] It provides six-month Secret Service protection by law to a former vice president and family. According to the Department of Homeland Security, protection for former vice president Cheney has been extended numerous times because threats against him have not decreased since his leaving office.[48]

## 5.6 Timeline of vice presidents

This is a graphical timeline listing of the Vice Presidents of the United States.

## 5.7 See also

- List of Vice Presidents of the United States
- List of Vice Presidents of the United States by age
- Office of the Vice President of the United States

## 5.8 Notes and references

[1] "U.S. Senate - No HTTPS".

[2] U.S. Const. amend. XII, § 1.

[3] U.S. Const. amend. XXV, § 1.

[4] U.S. Const. art. I, § 3, cl. 4.

[5] "U.S. Senate: Legislation & Records Home > Votes > Roll Call Vote". Senate.gov. Retrieved October 30, 2011.

[6] Oleszek, Walter J. CRS7-5700 Super-Majority Votes in the Senate Congressional Research Service, April 12, 2010

[7] Goldstein, Joel K. (1995). "The New Constitutional Vice Presidency". *Wake Forest Law Review* (Winston Salem, NC: Wake Forest Law Review Association, Inc.) **30**: 505.

[8] Reynolds, Glenn Harlan (2007). "Is Dick Cheney Unconstitutional?". *Northwestern University Law Review Colloquy* (Chicago: Northwestern University School of Law) **102**: 110.

[9] Garvey, Todd (2008). "A Constitutional Anomaly: Safeguarding Confidential National Security Information Within the Enigma That Is the American Vice Presidency". *William & Mary Bill of Rights Journal* (Williamsburg: Publications Council of the College of William and Mary) **17**: 565.

[10] Subhawong, Aryn (2008). "A Realistic Look at the Vice Presidency: Why Dick Cheney Is An "Entity Within the Executive Branch"". *Saint Louis University Law Journal* (Saint Louis: Saint Louis University School of Law) **53**: 281.

[11] Albert, Richard (2005). "The Evolving Vice Presidency". *Temple Law Review* (Philadelphia, PA: Temple University of the Commonwealth System of Higher Education) **78**: 811, at 816–19.

[12] 50 U.S.C. § 402

[13] 20 U.S.C. § 42

[14] "President Dawes," Time Magazine, December 14, 1924.

[15] 3 U.S.C. § 15

[16] "St. Petersburg Times, January 7, 1969, p.6-A". News.google.com. January 7, 1969. Retrieved October 30, 2011.

[17] Adams, John (19 December 1793). "Letter from John Adams to Abigail Adams, 19 December 1793". *Massachusetts Historical Society*. Retrieved 3 October 2014.

[18] "John Nance Garner quotes". Retrieved August 25, 2008.

[19] "Nation: Some Day You'll Be Sitting in That Chair". *Time.com*. 29 November 1963. Retrieved 3 October 2014.

[20] Wikisource:Additional amendments to the United States Constitution#Amendment XII

[21] See: U.S. Const. art. II, §1, cl. 5; see also, U.S. Const. amend. XII, §4.

[22] See: Peabody, Bruce G.; Gant, Scott E. (1999). "The Twice and Future President: Constitutional Interstices and the Twenty-Second Amendment". *Minnesota Law Review* (Minneapolis, MN: Minnesota Law Review) **83**: 565.

[23] See: Albert, Richard (2005). "The Evolving Vice Presidency". *Temple Law Review* (Philadelphia, PA: Temple University of the Commonwealth System of Higher Education) **78**: 811, at 856–59.

[24] Nagourney, Adam (September 30, 2008). "Concerns About Palin's Readiness as Big Test Nears". New York Times. p. A16. Retrieved April 9, 2011.

[25] The "Veepstakes": Strategic Choice in Presidential Running Mate Selection, by Lee Sigelman and Paul J. Wahlbeck, American Political Science Review, December 1997

[26] See: 5 U.S.C. § 3331; see also: Standing Rules of the Senate: Rule III

[27] Wikisource:Constitution of the United States of America#Section 1 2

[28] "Electoral College Box Scores 1789–1996". National Archives and Records Administration. Retrieved July 30, 2005.

[29] "Electoral College Box Scores 1789–1996". National Archives and Records Administration. Retrieved July 30, 2005.

[30] "RL30804: The Electoral College: An Overview and Analysis of Reform Proposals, L. Paige Whitaker and Thomas H. Neale, January 16, 2001". Ncseonline.org. Archived from the original on June 28, 2011. Retrieved August 26, 2010.

[31] Longley, Lawrence D.; Pierce, Neal R. (1999). "The Electoral College Primer 2000". New Haven, CT: Yale University Press: 13.

[32] "Current salary information". Usgovinfo.about.com. Retrieved March 13, 2011.

[33] http://www.senate.gov/reference/resources/pdf/RL30631.pdf

[34] Emily Yoffe (January 3, 2001). "Pension information". Slate.com. Retrieved August 9, 2009.

[35] Quoted by Light 1984 cited in Sigelman and Wahlbeck 1997. JSTOR

[36] "John Adams". Retrieved August 9, 2011.

[37] "A heartbeat away from the presidency: vice presidential trivia". Case Western Reserve University. October 4, 2004. Retrieved September 12, 2008.

[38] Greenberg, David (2007). *Calvin Coolidge*. Macmillan. pp. 40–41. ISBN 0-8050-6957-7.

[39] Binkley, Wilfred Ellsworth; Moos, Malcolm Charles (1949). *A Grammar of American Politics: The National Government*. New York: Alfred A. Knopf. p. 265.

[40] "Garret Hobart". Retrieved August 25, 2008.

[41] Harold C. Relyea (February 13, 2001). "The Vice Presidency: Evolution of the Modern Office, 1933–2001" (PDF). Congressional Research Service.

[42] "U.S. Senate Web page on Charles G. Dawes, 30th Vice President (1925–1929)". Senate.gov. Retrieved August 9, 2009.

[43] Kenneth T. Walsh (October 3, 2003). "Dick Cheney is the most powerful vice president in history. Is that good?". U.S. News and World Report. Retrieved September 13, 2015.

[44] "Full Vice Presidential Debate with Gov. Palin and Sen. Biden". YouTube. Retrieved October 30, 2011.

[45] "Internet Public Library: FARQs". Retrieved August 25, 2008.

[46] "LARRY KING LIVE: Interview with Al, Tipper Gore". *CNN*. Retrieved August 25, 2008.

[47] "Former Vice President Protection Act of 2008". Opencongress.org. Retrieved August 9, 2009.

[48] "President Barack Obama authorizes extended Secret Service guard for former VP Dick Cheney". *Daily News* (New York). July 21, 2009.

## 5.9 Further reading

- Goldstein, Joel K. (1982). *The Modern American Vice Presidency*. Princeton University Press. ISBN 0-691-02208-9.

- Tally, Steve (1992). *Bland Ambition: From Adams to Quayle—The Cranks, Criminals, Tax Cheats, and Golfers Who Made It to Vice President*. Harcourt. ISBN 0-15-613140-4.

## 5.10 External links

- White House website for the Vice President

- Vice-President Elect Chester Arthur on Expectations of VP Shapell Manuscript Foundation

- A New Nation Votes: American Election Returns 1787–1825

# Chapter 6

# United States presidential primary

For the ongoing presidential primaries, see Democratic Party presidential primaries, 2016 and Republican Party presidential primaries, 2016.

The series of **presidential primary elections and cau-**

*Voters checking in at a 2008 Washington state Democratic caucus held at Eckstein Middle School in Seattle*

**cuses** held in each U.S. state and territory is part of the nominating process of United States presidential elections. This process was never included in the United States Constitution; it was created over time by the political parties. Some states hold only primary elections, some hold only caucuses, and others use a combination of both. These primaries and caucuses are staggered generally between either late-January or early-February, and mid-June before the general election in November. The primary elections are run by state and local governments, while caucuses are private events that are directly run by the political parties themselves. A state's primary election or caucus is usually an indirect election: instead of voters directly selecting a particular person running for President, they determine how many delegates each party's national convention will receive from their respective state. These delegates then in turn select their party's presidential nominee.

Each party determines how many delegates are allocated to each state. Along with those delegates chosen during the primaries and caucuses, state delegations to both the Democratic and Republican conventions also include "unpledged" delegates, usually current and former elected officeholders and party leaders, who can vote for whomever they want.

This system of presidential primaries and caucuses is somewhat controversial because of its staggered nature. The major advantage is that candidates can concentrate their resources in each area of the country one at a time instead of campaigning in every state simultaneously. However, the overall results may not be representative of the U.S. electorate as a whole: voters in Iowa, New Hampshire and other small states which traditionally hold their primaries and caucuses first usually have a major impact on the races, while voters in California and other large states which traditionally hold their primaries last in June generally end up having no say because the races are usually over by then. As a result, more states vie for earlier primaries to claim a greater influence in the process.

## 6.1   Process

Both major political parties of the U.S.—the Democratic Party and the Republican Party—officially nominate their candidate for President at their respective national conventions. Each of these conventions is attended by a number of delegates selected in accordance with the given party's bylaws. The results of the presidential primaries and caucuses bind many of these delegates, known as pledged delegates, to vote for a particular candidate.[1] Both parties also have a group of unpledged delegates, also known as superdelegates, generally being current and former elected officeholders and party leaders.

64

*A 2008 Washington state Democratic caucus held in the school lunchroom of Eckstein Middle School in Seattle. In some states like Washington, voters attend local meetings run by the parties instead of polling places to cast their selections.*

### 6.1.1 Types of primaries and caucuses

Franchise in a primary or caucus is governed by rules established by the state party, although the states may impose other regulations.

While most states hold primary elections, a handful of states hold caucuses. Instead of going to a polling place, voters attend local private events run by the political parties, and cast their selections there. The advantage of caucuses is that the state party runs the process directly instead of having the state and local governments run them. The disadvantage is that most election laws do not normally apply to caucuses.[2]

Nearly all states have a *binding* primary or caucus, in which the results of the election legally *bind* some or all of the delegates to vote for a particular candidate at the national convention, for a certain number of ballots or until the candidate releases the delegates. Some binding primaries are *winner-take-all* contests, in which all of a state's delegates are required to vote for the same candidate. In a *proportional vote*, a state's delegation is allocated in proportion to the candidates' percent of the popular vote. In many of those states that have proportional vote primaries, a candidate must meet a certain threshold in the popular vote to be given delegates.[1]

A handful of states practice *non-binding* primaries or caucuses, which may select candidates to a state convention, which then in turn selects delegates to the national convention. A couple of states like Iowa have an additional step in their *non-binding* primaries or caucuses where voters instead elect delegates to *county* conventions. The county conventions then in turn elect delegates to the state conventions, and so on.

In many states, only voters registered with a party may vote in that party's primary, known as a closed primary. In some states, a semi-closed primary is practiced, in which voters unaffiliated with a party (independents) may choose a party primary in which to vote. In an open primary, any voter may vote in any party's primary. In all of these systems, a voter may participate in only one primary; that is, a voter who casts a vote for a candidate standing for the Republican nomination for president cannot cast a vote for a candidate standing for the Democratic nomination, or vice versa. A few states once staged a blanket primary, in which voters could vote for one candidate in multiple primaries, but the practice was struck down by the U.S. Supreme Court in the 2000 case of *California Democratic Party v. Jones* as violating the freedom of assembly guaranteed by the First Amendment.[3]

### 6.1.2 Delegate selection rules

Both the Democratic Party and the Republican Party usually modify their delegate selection rules between presidential elections, including how delegates are allocated to each state and territory.

Under the current Democratic Party selection rules, adopted in 2006, pledged delegates are selected under proportional representation, which requires a candidate have a minimum of 15% of a state's popular vote to receive delegates. In addition, the Democratic Party may reject any candidate under their bylaws. Each state publishes a Delegate Selection Plan that notes the mechanics of calculating the number of delegates per congressional district, and how votes are transferred from local conventions to the state and national convention.[4] Since the 2012 Democratic primaries, the number of pledged delegates allocated to each of the 50 U.S. states and Washington, D.C. is based on two main factors: (1) the proportion of votes each state gave to the Democratic candidate in the last three presidential elections, and (2) the number of electoral votes each state has in the United States Electoral College. States who schedule their primary or caucus later in the primary season may also get additional bonus delegates.[5]

The Republican Party's rules since 2008 leave more discretion to the states in choosing a method of allocating pledged delegates. As a result, states variously applied the statewide winner-take-all method (e.g., New York), district- and state-level winner-take-all (e.g., California), or proportional allocation (e.g., Massachusetts).[6] Changes in the rules before 2012 brought proportional representation to more states. Also, three delegates are allocated for each congressional district. For at-large ones elected statewide, each state gets at least 10, plus additional bonus delegates based on whether it has a Republican governor, it has GOP majorities in one or all chambers of its state legislature, and whether it has GOP majorities in its delegation to the U.S. Congress, among other factors.[7]

Each party's bylaws also specify which current and former elected officeholders and party leaders qualify as unpledged delegates. Because of possible deaths, resignations, or the results of intervening or special elections, the final number of these superdelegates may not be known until the week of the convention.

## 6.2   Calendar

Campaigning for President often begins almost a year before the New Hampshire primary, almost two years before the presidential election. This is largely because federal campaign finance laws including the Federal Election Campaign Act state that a candidate who intends to receive contributions aggregating in excess of $5,000 or make expenditures aggregating in excess of $5,000, among others, must first file a Statement of Candidacy with the Federal Election Commission.[8] Thus, presidential candidates officially announce their intentions to run that early so they can start raising or spending the money needed to mount their nationwide campaigns.[9]

During the first six months of the year, primaries and caucuses are separately held in each state, Puerto Rico, insular areas, and the District of Columbia, Each party sets its own calendar and rules, and in some cases actually administers the election. However, to reduce expenses and encourage turnout, the major parties' primaries are usually held the same day and may be consolidated with other state elections. The primary election itself is administered by local governments according to state law. In some cases, state law determines how delegates will be awarded and who may participate in the primary; where it does not, party rules prevail.[10]

Since the 1970s, states have held increasingly early primaries to maximize their leverage[11] (see *Front-loading and compression* below). In reaction to these moves, both the Democratic and Republican National Committees imposed a timing tier system of scheduling rules, stripping states of delegates if they move their primaries early, such as the case in both the Florida Democratic primary and the Florida Republican primary in 2008.

The election dates for 2016, up to and including Super Tuesday are as follows:

- February 1: Iowa caucus (both parties)

- February 9: New Hampshire primary (both parties)

- February 20: Nevada Democratic caucuses and South Carolina Republican primary

- February 23: Nevada Republican caucuses

- February 27: South Carolina Democratic primary

- March 1: Super Tuesday: Primaries/caucuses for both parties in several states

### 6.2.1   Iowa and New Hampshire

Main articles: Iowa caucuses and New Hampshire primary
The first binding event, in which a candidate can secure

*A 2008 Democratic caucus meeting in Iowa City, Iowa. The Iowa caucuses are traditionally the first major electoral event of presidential primaries and caucuses.*

convention delegates, is traditionally the Iowa caucus, usually held in late January or early February of the presidential election year. It is generally followed by the New Hampshire primary, the first primary by tradition since 1920 and by New Hampshire state law. New Hampshire law states the primary shall be held "on the Tuesday at least seven days immediately preceding the date on which any other state shall hold a similar election." The Iowa caucuses are not considered to be "a similar election" under New Hampshire's law because the former uses caucuses instead of primary elections. Should any other state move its primary too close to New Hampshire's, or before, the New Hampshire Secretary of State is required to reschedule the primary accordingly.[12]

In recent elections, the Iowa caucuses and New Hampshire primary have garnered over half the media attention paid to the entire selection process.[13] After Iowa and New Hampshire, the front runners then attempt to solidify their status, while the others fight to become #2.[14]

Because these states are small, campaigning takes place on a much more personal scale. As a result, even a little-known, underfunded candidate can use "retail politics" to meet intimately with interested voters and perform better than expected. The Iowa caucuses and New Hampshire primary have produced a number of headline-making upsets in history:[15]

- Harry S. Truman ended his re-election bid in 1952 after losing the New Hampshire primary.[16]

- Lyndon Baines Johnson dropped his 1968 reelection bid after performing far below expectations in the New Hampshire primary.

- In the 1972 Democratic primaries, George McGovern was initially considered a dark horse but he had better-than-expected second-place finishes in Iowa and New Hampshire and eventually won the nomination; frontrunner Edmund Muskie who won both contests instead lost momentum.

- George H. W. Bush won the Iowa caucus in 1980, leading him to claim that he had "Big Mo" (momentum) over frontrunner Ronald Reagan. However, Reagan won the New Hampshire primary and several others to take the nomination. In the 1988 Republican presidential nomination, Bush, serving as Reagan's vice president, unexpectedly finished third in Iowa which Bob Dole won. Dole was also leading in New Hampshire polls but ended up losing that primary as he failed to counterattack ads from Bush. Bush had no serious trouble clinching the nomination afterward.

- Gary Hart was initially not considered a serious contender in 1984, which featured former Vice President Walter Mondale as the frontrunner. However, Hart had a respectable showing in Iowa and then stunned Mondale in New Hampshire, the latter where Hart had started campaigning months earlier. This resulted in a long primary battle, with Mondale eventually emerging as the nominee after Super Tuesday III.

- Pat Buchanan's 2nd place showing in the 1992 and win in the 1996 New Hampshire primaries coincided with the weakness of the future nominees, incumbent George H. W. Bush, and Senator Bob Dole respectively, Bush and Dole subsequently lost the general election.

- In 1992, then Governor Bill Clinton's better-than-expected second-place finish in New Hampshire salvaged his campaign and he went on to win the nomination, following on to be elected President with a 43% plurality.

- Senator John McCain upset George W. Bush in the New Hampshire primary in 2000, Bush's frontrunner campaign had initially not expected serious opposition after other potential candidates like Elizabeth Dole

and Dan Quayle decided not to run. McCain's new-found momentum ended after his defeat in the South Carolina primary (see below), and though he pulled out wins in Michigan and his home state of Arizona, his campaign was ended by Super Tuesday.

- In the 2004 primaries, John Kerry, whose campaign had been sagging in prior months, won the Iowa caucus while John Edwards unexpectedly finished second, over heavily favored Howard Dean and Richard Gephardt (the latter two had been trading negative attacks in the weeks leading up to the vote). Gephardt immediately ended his campaign, while Dean's post-concession speech drew negative attention. Kerry went on to overcome Dean's initial lead in New Hampshire to win that primary, and eventually the Democratic presidential nomination.

- In 2008, frontrunner Hillary Rodham Clinton, whose campaign initially banked on a knockout victory in Iowa, unexpectedly finished third in that caucus behind winner Barack Obama and John Edwards.[17] Clinton then pulled off a comeback victory in New Hampshire where Obama had been leading the polls. Although Obama and Clinton were largely well matched in most of the subsequent primaries, Obama's better organization and uncontested caucus victories were crucial to his winning the Democratic nomination.

- In 2008, John McCain, initially struggling among Republican contenders in 2007, decided to skip Iowa and concentrate on New Hampshire (the same primary where he had unexpectedly triumphed back in 2000) and McCain's win rejuvenated his presidential campaign and he became the Republican nominee. Rudy Giuliani and Mitt Romney, two candidates who had each led in the polls in 2007, did not perform as expected in Iowa and New Hampshire.

- In 2012, Mitt Romney was initially reported to be the first Republican *non-incumbent* presidential candidate, since the Iowa caucus started in 1976, to win both the Iowa caucus (albeit, by an 8-vote margin over Rick Santorum) and New Hampshire primary.[18][19] However a final count released by the Iowa state party sixteen days after the caucus contest reported Santorum as the winner by 34 votes over Romney, but by then Romney had already won New Hampshire by a comfortable margin.[20]

### 6.2.2 South Carolina

Main article: South Carolina primary

South Carolina is generally the "First in the South" primary.[21][22] For the Republicans, it is considered a "firewall" to protect establishment favorites and frontrunners in the presidential nomination race, being designed to stop the momentum of insurgent candidates who could have received a boost from strong showings in Iowa and New Hampshire.[23][24] From its inception in 1980 through the election of 2008, the winner of the South Carolina Republican presidential primary has gone on to win the nomination.[25] In the 2012 Republican primaries, Newt Gingrich initially finished poorly in the early states, but then scored an upset victory in South Carolina over frontrunner Mitt Romney.[26] However, after suffering a decisive defeat to Romney in Florida, Gingrich's campaign was relegated back to third place and left Rick Santorum as the main challenger.

### 6.2.3   Super Tuesday

Main article: Super Tuesday

The Tuesday in February or March when the greatest number of states hold primary elections and caucuses is known as "Super Tuesday". Because it is held in various states from geographically and socially diverse regions of the country, it typically represents a presidential candidate's first test of national electability. More delegates can be won on Super Tuesday than on any other single day of the primary calendar, thus convincing wins during this day have usually propelled candidates to their party's nomination.

## 6.3   Background

There is no provision for the role of political parties in the United States Constitution. In the first two presidential elections, the Electoral College handled the nominations and elections in 1789 and 1792 that selected George Washington. After that, Congressional party or a state legislature party caucus selected the party's candidates.[27] Before 1820, Democratic-Republican members of Congress would nominate a single candidate from their party. That system collapsed in 1824, and since 1832 the preferred mechanism for nomination has been a national convention.[28]

## 6.4   History

The first national convention was called by the Anti-Masonic Party in 1831 as they could not use the caucus system as they had no Congressmen. The party leaders instead called for a national meeting of supporters to select the party's candidate. This convention was held in Baltimore, Maryland on September 26, 1831 which selected William Wirt as their Presidential candidate.[29]

Delegates to the national convention were usually selected at state conventions whose own delegates were chosen by district conventions. Sometimes they were dominated by intrigue between political bosses who controlled delegates; the national convention was far from democratic or transparent. Progressive Era reformers looked to the primary election as a way to measure popular opinion of candidates, as opposed to the opinion of the bosses. In 1910, Oregon became the first state to establish a presidential preference primary, which requires delegates to the National Convention to support the winner of the primary at the convention. By 1912, twelve states either selected delegates in primaries, used a preferential primary, or both. By 1920 there were 20 states with primaries, but some went back, and from 1936 to 1968, 12 states used them.

The primary received its first major test in the 1912 election pitting incumbent President William Howard Taft against challengers Theodore Roosevelt and Robert La Follette. Roosevelt proved the most popular candidate, but as most primaries were non-binding "preference" shows and held in only fourteen of the-then forty-eight states, the Republican nomination went to Taft, who controlled the convention.

Seeking to boost voter turnout, New Hampshire simplified its ballot access laws in 1949. In the ensuing "beauty contest" of 1952, Republican Dwight Eisenhower demonstrated his broad voter appeal by out-polling the favored Robert A. Taft, "Mr. Republican." Also, Democrat Estes Kefauver defeated incumbent President Harry S. Truman, leading the latter to decide not to run for another term.[30] The first-in-the-nation New Hampshire primary has since become a widely-observed test of candidates' viability.

The impetus for national adoption of the binding primary election was the chaotic 1968 Democratic National Convention. Vice President Hubert Humphrey secured the nomination despite not winning a single primary under his own name. After this, a Democratic National Committee-commissioned panel led by Senator George McGovern – the McGovern–Fraser Commission – recommended that states adopt new rules to assure wider participation. A large number of states, faced with the need to conform to more detailed rules for the selection of national delegates, chose a presidential primary as an easier way to come into compliance with the new national Democratic Party rules. The result was that many more future delegates would be selected by a state presidential primary. The Republicans also adopted many more state presidential primaries.

With the broadened use of the primary system, states have tried to increase their influence in the nomination process. One tactic has been to create geographic blocs to encourage candidates to spend time in a region. Vermont and Massachusetts attempted to stage a joint New England primary on the first Tuesday of March, but New Hampshire refused to participate so it could retain its traditional place as the first primary. The first successful regional primary was Super Tuesday of March 8, 1988, in which nine Southern states united in the hope that the Democrats would select a candidate in line with Southern interests.[31] It failed as all but two of the eight major candidates won at least one primary on that day.

Another trend is to stage earlier and earlier primaries, given impetus by Super Tuesday and the mid-1990s move (since repealed) of the California primary and its bloc of votes—the largest in the nation—from June to March. To retain its tradition as the first primary in the country (and adhere to a state law which requires it to be), New Hampshire moved their primary forward, from early March to early January.

A major reason why states try to increase their influence, and vie for earlier primaries, is because in recent years the races were usually over before the primary season ended in June. For example, John McCain officially clinched the 2008 Republican presidential nomination in March,[32] while during that same month Barack Obama held an insurmountable lead in pledged delegates in the Democratic Party primaries.[33] In 2012, Obama faced no major challenger in the Democratic Party primaries since he had the advantage of incumbency *(see below)*, while Mitt Romney gained enough delegates to be declared the *presumptive* Republican nominee by late April.[34]

In 2012, both the Republicans and the Democrats moved their Florida primary to January 31, which was an earlier date than past election cycles. In response, other states also changed their primary election dates for 2012, in order to claim a greater influence, creating a cascade of changes in other states. This followed what happened in 2008 when Nevada moved its caucuses to January, causing other states to also move its primaries to earlier dates. Senate Majority Leader and Nevada Senator Harry Reid was a major proponent of moving that state's caucuses to January, arguing that Nevada would be the perfect American microcosm: its western location, significant minority population, and strong labor population would be more representative of the country as a whole than Iowa and New Hampshire.[35]

Both parties then enacted stricter timing rules for 2016: primaries and caucuses cannot start until February 1; and only Iowa, New Hampshire, South Carolina and Nevada are entitled to February contests.

### 6.4.1  In U.S. territories

The primary and caucus system is the only method in which voters in Puerto Rico, Guam, and other U.S. territories can have a say in the presidential race. Under the U.S. Constitution, U.S. territories are not represented in the Electoral College, and thus voters residing in those areas are basically ineligible to vote in the general election. On the other hand, as stated above, the primaries and caucuses were largely created by the political parties. Both the Democratic and Republican parties, as well as other third parties, eventually agreed to let these territories participate in the presidential nomination process.[36]

### 6.4.2  Advantage of incumbency

An incumbent President seeking re-election usually faces no opposition during their respective party's primaries, especially if they are still popular. For Presidents Ronald Reagan, Bill Clinton, George W. Bush and Barack Obama, for example, their respective paths to nomination became uneventful and the races become merely *pro forma*; all four then went on to win a second presidential term. Serious challenges are rare, but then generally presage failure to win the general election in the fall. During the 1976 Republican Party primaries, then-former California Governor Reagan carried 23 states while running against incumbent President Gerald Ford; Ford then went on to lose the Presidential election to Jimmy Carter. Senator Ted Kennedy then carried 12 states while running against Carter during the 1980 Democratic Party primaries; Reagan then defeated Carter in the fall. Pat Buchanan captured a decent percentage of the national popular vote against George H.W. Bush during the 1992 Republican primaries, but only received a handful of delegates; Bush too subsequently went on to lose in the general election to Clinton.

## 6.5  Criticisms

### 6.5.1  Representativeness

Because they are the states that traditionally hold their respective contests first, the Iowa caucuses and the New Hampshire primary usually attract the most media attention;[13] however, critics, such as Mississippi Secretary of State Eric Clark and Tennessee Senator William Brock, point out that these states are not representative of the United States as a whole: they are overwhelmingly white, more rural, and wealthier than the national average, and neither is in the fast-growing West or South.

Conversely, states that traditionally hold their primaries in

June, like California (the most populous state overall) and New Jersey (the most densely populated state), usually end up having no say in who the presidential candidate will be. As stated above, the races were usually over well before June. California and New Jersey moved their primaries to February for the 2008 election, but in 2012 both states ended up moving them back to June. California lawmakers stated that consolidating their presidential and statewide primary election in June saves them about $100 million, and that it is not worth the cost when there is generally no competitive balance between the two political parties within California.[37]

In 2005, the primary commission of the Democratic National Committee began considering removing Iowa and New Hampshire from the top of the calendar, but this proposal never gained approval, so those two states remain as the first two contests. New Hampshire also fought back by obliging candidates who wanted to campaign in the state to pledge to uphold that primary as the first one.

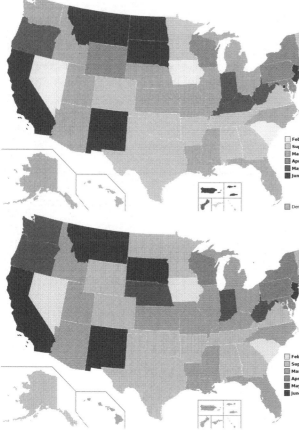

Maps of the Democratic Party (left) and the Republican Party (right) primary and caucus dates, 2016. The staggered nature of the primary and caucus season is source of criticism of the presidential nomination process

## 6.5.2   Front-loading and compression

States vie for earlier primaries to claim greater influence in the nomination process, as the early primaries can act as a signal to the nation, showing which candidates are popular and giving those who perform well early on the advantage of the bandwagon effect. Also, candidates can ignore primaries that fall after the nomination has already been secured, and would owe less to those states politically. As a result, rather than stretching from March to July, most primaries take place in a compressed time frame in February and March. National party leaders also have an interest in compressing the primary calendar, as it enables the party to reduce the chance of a bruising internecine battle and to preserve resources for the general campaign.

In such a primary season, however, many primaries will fall on the same day, forcing candidates to choose where to spend their time and resources. Indeed, Super Tuesday was created deliberately to increase the influence of the South. When states cannot agree to coordinate primaries, however, attention flows to larger states with large numbers of delegates at the expense of smaller ones. Because the candidate's time is limited, paid advertising may play a greater role. Moreover, a compressed calendar limits the ability of lesser-known candidates to corral resources and raise their visibility among voters, especially when a better-known candidate enjoys the financial and institutional backing of the party establishment.[38]

In an article from *Detroit News*, Tennessee Senator William (Bill) Brock said about front-loading, "Today, too many people in too many states have no voice in the election of our major party nominees. For them, the nominations are over before they have begun."[38]

## 6.5.3   Role of superdelegates

Main article: Superdelegate § Criticism

The term "superdelegate" itself was used originally as a criticism of unpledged delegates. Political commentator Susan Estrich argued in 1981 that these delegates, who at the time were predominantly white and male, had more power than other delegates because of their greater freedom to vote as they wish.[39] The Democratic Party in particular has faced accusations that it conducts its nominating process in an undemocratic way,[40][41] because superdelegates are generally chosen without regard to their preferences in the presidential race and are not obligated to support the candidate chosen by the voters.

# 6.6 Reform proposals

There are several proposals for reforming the primary system. Some have called for a single nationwide primary to be held on one day. Others point out that requiring candidates to campaign in every state simultaneously would exacerbate the purported problem of campaigns being dominated by the candidates who raise the most money. The following proposals attempt to return the primary system to a more relaxed schedule, and would help less-funded candidates by lowering the cost of entry.

## 6.6.1 California Plan (American Plan)

One reform concept is the graduated random presidential primary system, variations of which have been referred to as the American Plan or the California Plan. This plan starts with small primaries, and gradually moves up to larger ones, in 10 steps, with states chosen at random. The idea is that fewer initial primaries, typically in smaller states, would allow grassroots campaigns to score early successes and pick up steam. However, since states are chosen at random, travel costs may still be significant.

## 6.6.2 Delaware Plan (Fourfold Round Plan)

A commission empaneled by the Republican National Committee recommended the Delaware Plan in 2000. This plan had states grouped by size into four groups, with the smallest primaries first, then the next-smallest, and so on. Populous states objected to the plan, however, because it would have always scheduled their primaries at the end of the season. Other criticisms included the wide geographic range of the states, necessitating high travel costs. The Delaware Plan was put to vote at Republican National Convention of 2000 and rejected.

## 6.6.3 Rotating regional primary system

The National Association of Secretaries of State has endorsed a rotating regional primary system, with the country split into four regions: the West, the Midwest, the South, and the Northeast.[42] Unlike the Delaware Plan and the American Plan, the Rotating Regional Primary System would lower campaigning costs by restricting groups of primaries to single, contiguous regions.

Author and political scientist Larry J. Sabato is also a proponent of this plan, but his proposal would have the order of regional primaries determined by lottery on January 1 of each presidential election year instead of on a rotating basis. In addition, his plan would allow for a few small population states, such as Iowa and New Hampshire, to hold their primaries in advance of the first region.

Criticisms of the regional plan include the higher entry costs than the other plans (since 1/4 of the country would vote in the first regional), and the political bias of certain regions (the South or the Northeast) unduly influencing the selection of a nominee.

## 6.6.4 Interregional primary plan

In the interregional primary plan, the country is divided into geographical regions. On each primary date from March to June, one state from each of six regions votes. Each election date would contain a wide variety of perspectives. The order of the states in each region is set by a lottery. In a 24-year cycle, every state would have a chance to be among the first primary states. The primary criticism of this plan is that travel costs would be quite high: in each round, candidates would essentially have to cover the entire country to campaign effectively. Contrary to most reform plans, this would reduce the ability of lesser-funded candidates to build up from small contests to large ones.[43]

## 6.6.5 Timing adjustment

In the 2008 Republican primary, states that ran early primaries were punished by a reduction of 50% in the number of delegates they could send to the national convention. Extension of this idea would set timing tiers, under which states that ran earlier primaries would send proportionally fewer delegates to the national convention, and states that waited would get a higher proportional number of delegates to the convention. For example, the party allowed primaries before March 1 to send 40% of delegates; those during March could send 60%; those during April could send 80%; those during May could send 100%; and those during June could send 120%.

The effect of such a plan would be clumping of primaries at the beginning of each month. It would still allow states to determine the timing of their own primaries, while giving them some incentive to hold primaries later. The disadvantage of the timing adjustment method is that it does not reduce travel time as the regional plans do, although it does permit regional groups of states to voluntarily clump together in a single superprimary as they have done in the past.

In practice, however, this timing tier system did not prevent states from moving their primaries in 2008 and 2012. For example, during the 2012 Republican primary, Florida and several other states still moved their primaries to earlier dates despite being penalized delegates.

Both parties then enacted more severe penalties in 2016 for violating their timing rules. For Republicans, states with more than 30 delegates that violate the timing rules will be deprived of all their delegates but nine; states with less than 30 will be reduced to six.[44] For Democrats, states violating these rules will be penalized half of their pledged delegates and all of their unpledged delegates.[5]

## 6.7 Lists of primaries

Main articles: Democratic Party presidential primaries and Republican Party presidential primaries

## 6.8 See also

- Ames (Iowa) Straw Poll on a Saturday in August prior to the election year, from 1979 to 2011.

## 6.9 Notes

[1] Putnam, Josh (May 12, 2015). "Everything you need to know about how the presidential primary works". Washington Post. Retrieved February 17, 2016.

[2] "Primary/Caucus/Convention Glossary". *The Green Papers*. Retrieved 2012-01-28.

[3] Bruce E. Cain and Elisabeth R. Gerber, *Voting at the political fault line: California's Experiment with the Blanket Primary*(2002)

[4] Delegate Selection Rules

[5] "Democratic Detailed Delegate Allocation – 2012". *The Green Papers*. Retrieved 2012-01-05.

[6] Republican Delegate Selection and Voter Eligibility

[7] "Republican Detailed Delegate Allocation – 2012". *The Green Papers*. Retrieved 2012-01-29.

[8] "2016 Presidential Form 2 Filers" (Press release). Federal Election Commission. Retrieved April 12, 2015.

[9] Jose A. DelReal (April 3, 2015). "Why Hillary Clinton might have just two more weeks or so to announce she's running for president". *Washington Post*. Retrieved April 12, 2015.

[10] http://www.gop.com/Images/AllStateSummaries.pdf

[11] "Front-Loading, Caucuses and Primaries". Nominations & Conventions: Current Practices. Northeastern University. Retrieved February 10, 2016.

[12] http://www.nh.gov/nhinfo/genesis.html

[13] Mellman, Mark (January 5, 2012). "Iowa and New Hampshire: It's win one or go home". *Los Angeles Times*. Retrieved February 3, 2012. Historically, Iowa and New Hampshire account for about half the news media coverage of the entire primary season, with the winners absorbing the lion's share of the attention

[14] Scala (2003)

[15] Sacala (2003)

[16] New Hampshire Primary CBS News broadcast from the Vanderbilt Television News Archive

[17] Baker, Peter; Rutenberg, Jim (June 8, 2008). "The Long Road to a Clinton Exit". *The New York Times*.

[18]

[19] Cillizza, Chris; Blake, Aaron (December 29, 2011). "Mitt Romney tries to make history in Iowa and New Hampshire". *The Washington Post*.

[20] Fahrenthold, David A.; Wilgoren, Debbi (January 20, 2012). "Santorum finished 34 votes ahead of Romney in new Iowa tally; votes from 8 precincts missing". *The Washington Post*.

[21] "5 Things to Watch in South Carolina's Republican Primary". ABC Newa. February 20, 2016. Retrieved February 21, 2016.

[22] "South Carolina's Key Role in the Presidential Race". U.S. News & World Report. February 17, 2016. Retrieved February 21, 2016.

[23] http://www.gwu.edu/~{ }action/states/scprimresults.html

[24] Scherer, Michael (2008-01-09). "Huckabee Looks to South Carolina". TIME. Retrieved 2012-01-05.

[25] Rudin, Ken (2008-01-16). "South Carolina's Role as GOP Kingmaker". NPR. Retrieved 2012-01-05.

[26] "Romney routs Gingrich in Florida". *CBC News*. February 1, 2012.

[27] Shafer, Byron E, (1988). "Emergence of the Presidential The Nomination and the Convention". *Bifurcated Politics: Evolution and Reform in the National Party Convention*. Harvard University Press. p. 11. ISBN 0674072561. Retrieved February 1, 2016.

[28] James S. Chase; *Emergence of the Presidential Nominating Convention, 1789–1832* (1973)

[29] Shafer, Byron E, (1988). "Emergence of the Presidential The Nomination and the Convention". *Bifurcated Politics: Evolution and Reform in the National Party Convention*. Harvard University Press. p. 9. ISBN 0674072561. Retrieved February 1, 2016.

[30] Paul T. David. *Presidential Nominating Politics in 1952*. (1954) Volume: 1: pp 37–40.

[31] Laurence W. Moreland, et al. *The 1988 Presidential Election in the South: Continuity Amidst Change in Southern Party Politics* (1991) pp 3–20

[32] "McCain wins GOP nomination". CNN. 2008-03-04. Retrieved 2012-07-08.

[33] Nagourney, Adam (2008-03-20). "Clinton Facing Narrower Path to Nomination". *New York Times*. Retrieved 2012-07-08.

[34] Memoli, Michael A. (April 24, 2012). "RNC officially names Mitt Romney the party's 'presumptive nominee'". *Los Angeles Times*. Retrieved April 24, 2012.

[35] Milligan, Susan (2008-01-20). "Long battle still ahead for top Democrats: Contest could extend beyond Super Tuesday". The Boston Globe.

[36] Curry, Tom (2008-05-28). "Nominating, but not voting for president". MSNBC. Retrieved 2012-02-15.

[37] David Siders (July 29, 2011). "California will move presidential primary to June". *The Sacramento Bee* (McClatchy).

[38] "Nominating Report".

[39] Karmack, Elaine (February 14, 2008). "A History of 'Super-Delegates' in the Democratic Party". *John F. Kennedy School of Government*.

[40] Snell, Teddye (January 9, 2008). "A Presidential Primer". *Tahlequah Daily Press*.

[41] Chaddock, Gail Russell (February 20, 2008). "If Superdelegates Pick Nominee, Democrats Face Backlash". *Christian Science Monitor*.

[42] nass.org

[43] FairVote – Interregional Primary Plan

[44] Joseph, Cameron (January 1, 2014). "RNC tightens 2016 primary calendar, rules". *The Hill*. Retrieved June 11, 2015.

## 6.10 References

- Brereton Charles. *First in the Nation: New Hampshire and the Premier Presidential Primary*. Portsmouth, NH: Peter E. Randall Publishers, 1987.

- Kendall, Kathleen E. *Communication in the Presidential Primaries: Candidates and the Media, 1912–2000* (2000)

- Hugh, Gregg. "First-In-The-Nation Presidential Primary", *State of New Hampshire Manual for the General Court*, (Department of State) No.55, 1997.

- Palmer, Niall A. *The New Hampshire Primary and the American Electoral Process* (1997)

- "Reid, labor aided Nevada with Demos", Arizona Daily Star, July 24, 2006.

- Sabato, Larry, Politics: America's Missing Constitutional Link, *Virginia Quarterly Review*, Summer 2006, 149–61.

- Scala, Dante J. *Stormy Weather: The New Hampshire Primary and Presidential Politics* (2003)

- Ware, Alan. *The American Direct Primary: Party Institutionalization and Transformation in the North* (2002), a British perspective

## 6.11 External link

- Fairvote.org

# Chapter 7

# United States presidential nominating convention

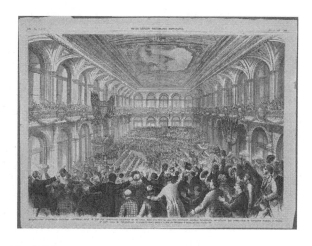

*The 1876 Democratic National Convention at the Merchants Exchange Building in St. Louis, Missouri.*

A **United States presidential nominating convention** is a political convention held every four years in the United States by most of the political parties who will be fielding nominees in the upcoming U.S. presidential election. The formal purpose of such a convention is to select the party's nominee for President, as well as to adopt a statement of party principles and goals known as the *platform* and adopt the rules for the party's activities, including the presidential nominating process for the next election cycle. Due to changes in election laws, the primary and caucus calendar, and the manner in which political campaigns are run, conventions since the later half of the 20th century have virtually abdicated their original roles, and today are rarely more than ceremonial affairs.

Generally, usage of "presidential campaign nominating convention" refers to the two major parties' quadrennial events: the Democratic National Convention and the Republican National Convention. Some minor parties also select their nominees by convention, including the Green Party, Socialist Party USA, Libertarian Party, Constitution Party, and Reform Party USA.

## 7.1 Logistics

### 7.1.1 Calendars

From the point of view of the parties, the convention cycle begins with the *Call to Convention.* Usually issued about 18 months in advance, the Call is an invitation from the national party to the state and territory parties to convene to select a presidential nominee. It also sets out the number of delegates to be awarded to each, as well as the rules for the nomination process. The conventions are usually scheduled for four days of business, with the exception of the 1972 Republican and 2012 Democratic conventions, which were three days each. (The 2008 and 2012 Republican conventions were also three days each, but in each case was shortened from the scheduled four days due to weather issues).

There is no rule dictating the order, but since 1956 the incumbent party has held its convention second. Between 1864 and 1952, the Democrats went second every year (except for 1888). In 1956, when Republican Dwight D. Eisenhower was the incumbent, the Democrats went first, and the party out of power has gone first ever since. (Between 1936 and 1952, the Democrats were the incumbent party and went second, but it is unclear whether they went second because they held the White House or because they had always gone second.) Since 1952, all major party conventions have been held in the months of July, August or (for the first time in 2004), early September. (Election laws in some states would likely prevent conventions from moving into mid-September). Between the middle of the 20th century and 2004, the two major party conventions were primarily scheduled about one month apart, often with the Summer Olympics in between so they did not have to compete for viewers. In 1996, both were held in August to accommodate the Atlanta Olympics in July, the last Summer Olympics to date to be played in the U.S. In 2000, both conventions preceded the Sydney Olympics in late September.

In 2008 and 2012, the Democratic and Republican conventions were moved to back-to-back weeks following the conclusion of the Olympics. One reason for these late conventions had to do with campaign finance laws, which allow the candidates to spend an unlimited amount of money before the convention, but forbid fundraising after the convention, in order for the parties to receive federal campaign funds.[1] However, if Barack Obama's choice not to receive federal campaign funds for the 2008 general election is repeated in future elections, this reason for the late scheduling of conventions will no longer be valid. Another reason for the lateness of the conventions is due to the primary calendar, which ends in early June, and the political party's desire to turn the convention into a four-day tightly scripted political rally for their nominee, which just happens to have a roll call vote for President. This includes such logistics as where each delegation sits on the convention floor, the order of speeches, how the nominee wants to present him or herself, and allows time for any negotiations in regards to the running mate. Finally, the parties also did not want to schedule their conventions around the Olympics. One reason why the Democratic Party held their 2008 convention after the two-week-long Beijing Olympics was, according to them, to "maximize momentum for our Democratic ticket in the final months of the Presidential election".[2] But moving the conventions later into early September led to conflicts with the National Football League's season kickoff game, which opens the season on the first Thursday of September. However, the NFL accommodated the conventions and moved their games to an earlier start time in 2008,[3] and an earlier date in 2012.

In 2016, both the Republican and Democratic conventions will be moved to July, before the Rio de Janeiro Olympics in August. One reason why the Republican Party wanted a July convention was to help avoid a drawn-out primary battle similar to what happened in 2012 that left the party fractured heading into the general election. The Democrats then followed suit so they could provide a quicker response to the Republicans, rather than wait for more than two weeks until after the Olympics are over.[4]

## 7.1.2   Participation

Each party sets its own rules for the participation and format of the convention. Broadly speaking, each U.S. state and territory party is apportioned a select number of voting representatives, individually known as *delegates* and collectively as the *delegation*. Each party uses its own formula for determining the size of each delegation, factoring in such considerations as population, proportion of that state's Congressional representatives or state government officials who are members of the party, and the state's voting patterns in previous presidential elections. The selection of

*The 2008 Green Party National Convention held in Chicago. Various third parties also hold their own national conventions.*

individual delegates and their alternates, too, is governed by the bylaws of each state party, or in some cases by state law.

The 2004 Democratic National Convention counted 4,353 delegates and 611 alternates. The 2004 Republican National Convention had 2,509 delegates and 2,344 alternates. But these individuals are dwarfed by other attendees who do not participate in the formal business of the convention. These include non-delegate party officials and activists, invited guests and companions, and international observers, not to mention numerous members of the news media, volunteers, protesters, and local business proprietors and promoters hoping to capitalize on the quadrennial event.

## 7.1.3   Host city

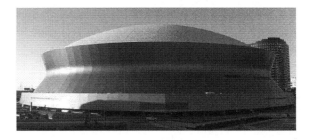

*The Louisiana Superdome in New Orleans was the site of the 1988 Republican National Convention, which nominated George H.W. Bush for president. In recent decades, the two major parties have held their conventions at sports stadiums and arenas.*

The convention is typically held in a major city selected by the national party organization 18–24 months before the election is to be held. As the two major conventions have grown into large, publicized affairs with significant economic impact, cities today compete vigorously to be awarded host responsibilities, citing their meeting venues, lodging facilities, and entertainment as well as offering economic incentives.

The location of early conventions was dictated by the difficulty of transporting delegates from far-flung parts of the country; early Democratic and Whig Conventions were frequently held in the central Eastern Seaboard port of Baltimore, Maryland. As the U.S. expanded westward and railroads connected cities, Midwestern cities such as Chicago, Illinois—which since 1860 has held 25 Republican and Democratic Conventions combined, more than any other urban center in the USA—became the favored hosts. In the present day, political symbolism affects the selection of the host city as much as economic or logistical ones do. A particular city might be selected to enhance the standing of a favorite son, or in an effort to curry favor with residents of that state. For example, in 2011, Obama campaign manager Jim Messina noted: "We put the Democratic National Convention in Charlotte, North Carolina in part because we believe so deeply in" a "New South map."[5] Likewise, New York City was selected as the host of the 2004 Republican National Convention to evoke memories of George W. Bush's leadership in the September 11 attacks.

The conventions have historically been held inside convention centers, but in recent decades the two major parties have favored sports arenas and stadiums to accommodate the increasing capacity, the former because indoor arenas are usually off-season outside of WNBA sites, allowing plenty of time for preparation (the major political parties have avoided baseball stadiums ever since the 1992 Republican National Convention at the Houston Astrodome forced the Houston Astros to play 26 consecutive road games). Bids for the 2008 Republican National Convention, for example, were required to have a facility with a seating capacity of at least 20,500 people, including a convention floor of about 5,500 delegates and alternates;[6] the Xcel Energy Center in Saint Paul, Minnesota was eventually selected. Meanwhile, approximately 84,000 people attended the last day of the 2008 Democratic National Convention at Denver's Invesco Field at Mile High.[7] The last day of the 2012 Democratic Convention was originally also scheduled for an outdoor football stadium, but was moved indoors due to weather concerns. The last non-sporting venue to host the Democratic National Convention was San Francisco's Moscone Center in 1984. In 1996, the San Diego Convention Center in San Diego became the last non-sporting venue to host the Republican National Convention.

## 7.2  Proceedings

During the day, party activists hold meetings and rallies, and work on the platform. Voting and important convention-

*Roll call of states during the 2008 Democratic National Convention at the Pepsi Center in Denver, Colorado.*

*The floor of the 2008 Republican National Convention at the Xcel Energy Center in Saint Paul, Minnesota.*

wide addresses usually take place in the evening hours.

In recent conventions, routine business such as examining the credentials of delegations, ratifying rules and procedures, election of convention officers, and adoption of the platform usually take up the business of the first two days of the convention. Balloting was usually held on the third day, with the nomination and acceptance made on the last day, but even some of these traditions have fallen away in 21st century conventions. The only constant is that the convention ends with the nominee's acceptance speech.

### 7.2.1  Platform

Each convention produces a statement of principles known as its *platform*, containing goals and proposals known as *planks*. Relatively little of a party platform is even proposed as public policy. Much of the language is generic, while other sections are narrowly written to appeal to factions or interest groups within the party. Unlike electoral manifestos in many European countries, the platform is not binding on either the party or the candidate.

Because it is ideological rather than pragmatic, however, the platform is sometimes itself politicized. For example, defenders of abortion rights lobbied heavily to remove the Human Life Amendment plank from the 1996 Republican National Convention platform, a move fiercely resisted by conservatives despite the fact that no such amendment had ever come up for debate.

## 7.2.2 Voting

Since the 1970s, voting has for the most part been perfunctory; the selection of the major parties' nominees have rarely been in doubt, so a single ballot has always been sufficient. Each delegation announces its vote tallies, usually accompanied with some boosterism of their state or territory. The delegation may pass, nominally to retally their delegates' preferences, but often to allow a different delegation to give the leading candidate the honor of casting the majority-making vote.

Before the presidential nomination season actually begins, there is often speculation about whether a single front runner would emerge. If there is no single candidate receiving a majority of delegates at the end of the primary season, a scenario called a **brokered convention** would result, where a candidate would be selected either at or near the convention, through political horse-trading and lesser candidates compelling their delegates to vote for one of the front runners. The best example was the 1924 Democratic Convention, which took 103 ballots. The situation is more likely to occur in the Democratic Party, because of its proportional representation system,[8] but such a scenario has been the subject of speculation with regard to most contested nominations of both parties without actually coming to pass in recent years.[9][10][11][12][13][14][15][16] It is a common scenario in fiction, most recently in an episode of *The West Wing*. The closest to a brokered convention in recent years was at the 1976 Republican National Convention, when neither Gerald Ford nor Ronald Reagan received enough votes in the primary to lock up the nomination.[17] Since then, candidates have received enough momentum to reach a majority through pledged and bound delegates before the date of the convention.

More recently, a customary practice has been for the losing candidates in the primary season to release their delegates and exhort them to vote for the winning nominee as a sign of party unity. Thus, the vote tallied on the floor is unanimous or nearly so. Some delegates may nevertheless choose to vote for their candidate. And in 2008 both happened: Hillary Clinton received over 1,000 votes before she herself moved to nominate Barack Obama by acclamation,

officially making it a unanimous vote.

The voting method at the conventions is a "rolling roll call of the states" (which include territories). The states are called in alphabetical order (Alabama is first; Wyoming is last). The state's spokesperson (who begins his/her speech with glowing comments about the state's history, geography, and notable party elected officials) can either choose to announce its delegate count or pass. Once all states have either declared or passed, those states which passed are called upon again to announce their delegate count. (Generally, a decision is made beforehand that some states will pass in the first round, in order to allow a particular state – generally either the presidential or vice presidential nominee's home state – to be the one whose delegate count pushes the candidate "over the top", thus securing the nomination.)

Vice Presidential voting has been problematic since the beginning, as the delegates generally don't really want to deal with it, and it provides for mischief, as was the case in 1972's Democratic Convention where the vote was scattered between 50 "candidates" and 1976 Republican convention, where the vote was also scattered widely. In 1988, both parties decided to have the designated candidate nominated by "suspending the rules" and declaring him or her nominated by "acclamation." The last Vice Presidential roll call vote was at the 1984 Republican convention.

## 7.2.3 Speeches

*First Lady Pat Nixon speaking at the 1972 Republican National Convention. She was the first Republican First Lady to do what is now considered common practice.*

Minor figures in the party are given the opportunity to address the floor of the convention during the daytime, when only the small audiences of C-SPAN and other cable television outlets are watching. The evening's speeches - designed for broadcast to a large national audience—are reserved for

## 7.3   History

*Michelle Obama speaking at the 2008 Democratic National Convention.*

*Barack Obama and Joe Biden appear together at the 2008 Democratic National Convention.*

major speeches by notable, respected public figures; the speakers at the 2004 Democratic convention included Ted Kennedy, a forty-year veteran of the United States Senate, and Jimmy Carter, a former Democratic President, while at the Republican convention speakers included Governor Arnold Schwarzenegger of California and Governor George Pataki of New York, two of the largest states in the nation.

The organizers of the convention may designate one of these speeches as the keynote address, one which above all others is stated to underscore the convention's themes or political goals. For instance, the 1992 Democratic National Convention keynote address was delivered by Georgia Governor Zell Miller, whose stories of an impoverished childhood echoed the economic themes of the nominee, Arkansas Governor Bill Clinton. The 1996 Republican National Convention was keynoted by U.S. Representative Susan Molinari of New York, intended to reassure political moderates about the centrism of the nominee, former Senator Bob Dole. And the 2004 Democratic National Convention featured Senator Barack Obama, whose speech brought the future President national recognition for the first time.

Uniquely, Miller, by then a Senator, would also be the keynote speaker at the 2004 Republican convention, despite still maintaining his Democratic registration.

The final day of the convention usually features the formal acceptance speeches from the nominees for President and Vice President. Despite recent controversy maintaining that recent conventions were scripted from beginning to end, and that very little news (if any) comes out of the convention, the acceptance speech has always been televised by the networks, because it receives the highest ratings of the convention. In addition, the halls of the convention are packed at this time, with many party loyalists sneaking in. Afterwards, balloons are usually dropped and the delegates celebrate the nomination.

*Primary foes Ronald Reagan (l) and Gerald Ford (r) shake hands during the 1976 Republican National Convention, the last major party convention whose outcome was in doubt.*

In the early 19th century, members of Congress met within their party caucuses to select their party's nominee. Conflicts between the interests of the Eastern Congressional class and citizens in newer Western states led to the hotly contested 1824 election, in which factions of the Democratic-Republican Party rejected the caucus nominee, William H. Crawford of Georgia, and backed John Quincy Adams, Henry Clay, and Andrew Jackson (all of whom carried more states than Crawford in the election) instead.

In 1831 the Anti-Masonic Party convened in Baltimore, Maryland to select a single presidential candidate agreeable to the whole party leadership in the 1832 presidential election. The National Republican and Democratic Parties soon followed suit.

Conventions were often heated affairs, playing a vital role in deciding each party's nominee. The process remained far from democratic or transparent, however. The party convention was a scene of intrigue among political bosses, who appointed and otherwise controlled nearly all of the delegates. Winning a nomination involved intensive negotiations and multiple votes; the 1924 Democratic National Convention required a record 103 ballots to nominate John W. Davis. The term "dark horse candidate" was coined at the 1844 Democratic National Convention, at which little-known Tennessee politician James K. Polk emerged as the candidate after the failure of the leading candidates—former President Martin Van Buren and Senator Lewis Cass—to secure the necessary two-thirds majority.

A few, mostly Western, states adopted primary elections in the late 19th century and during the Progressive Era, but the catalyst for their widespread adoption came during the election of 1968. The Vietnam War energized a large number of supporters of anti-war Senator Eugene McCarthy of Minnesota, but they had no say in the matter. Vice President Hubert Humphrey—associated with the unpopular administration of Lyndon B. Johnson—did not compete in a single primary, yet controlled enough delegates to secure the Democratic nomination. This proved one of several factors behind rioting which broke out at the Democratic convention in Chicago.

Media images of the event—angry mobs facing down police—damaged the image of the Democratic Party, which appointed a commission headed by South Dakota Senator George McGovern to select a new, less controversial method of choosing nominees. The McGovern–Fraser Commission settled on the primary election, adopted by the Democratic National Committee in 1968. The Republicans adopted the primary as their preferred method in 1972. Henceforth, candidates would be given convention delegates based on their performance in primaries, and these delegates were bound to vote for their candidate.

As a result, the major party presidential nominating convention has lost almost all of its old drama. The last attempt to release delegates from their candidates came at the 1980 Democratic National Convention, when Senator Ted Kennedy of Massachusetts sought votes of delegates held by incumbent President Jimmy Carter. The last major party convention whose outcome was in doubt was the 1976 Republican National Convention, when former California Governor Ronald Reagan nearly won the nomination away from the incumbent President, Gerald Ford.

### 7.3.1 Television coverage

While rank and file members had no input in early nominations, they were still drawn by the aura of mystery surrounding the convention, and networks began to broadcast speeches and debates to the general public. NBC affiliate W2XBS in New York City made the first telecast of a national party convention, of the 1940 Republican National Convention in Philadelphia, Pennsylvania, and soon the other two of the Big Three television networks soon followed. As NBC News anchorman John Chancellor stated just before the start of the 1972 Democratic National Convention, "convention coverage is the most important thing we do. The conventions are not just political theater, but really serious stuff, and that's why all the networks have an obligation to give gavel-to-gavel coverage. It's a time when we all ought to be doing our duty".[18]

With the rise of the direct primary, and in particular with states moving earlier and earlier in the primary calendar since the 1988 election, the nominee has often secured a commanding majority of delegates far in advance of the convention. As such, the convention has become little more than a coronation, a carefully staged campaign event designed to draw public attention and favor to the nominee, with particular attention to television coverage. For instance, speeches by noted and popular party figures are scheduled for the coveted prime time hours, when most people would be watching.

As the drama has left the conventions, and complaints grown that they were scripted and dull pep rallies, viewership—and television network advertising revenue—have fallen off. Midway through the 1996 Republican National Convention, *Nightline* host Ted Koppel told viewers he was going back home, saying:

> There was a time when the national political conventions were news events of such complexity that they required the presence of thousands of journalists ... But not this year ... This convention is more of an infomercial than a news event.[19]

Thus in subsequent election years, the broadcast networks began increasingly limited their coverage, arguing that those interested can watch the proceedings on a cable news network such as CNN, MSNBC, or the Fox News Channel. In 2004, the big three networks started devoting only three hours of live coverage to each political convention, although there were highlights of speeches during the networks' morning and evening newscasts.

However, many journalists still believe that the public should be exposed to political conventions. PBS, of note, continues to provide full prime-time coverage of the political conventions, although it breaks away from minor speakers and mundane business for analysis and discussion.[20] C-SPAN broadcasts both major conventions in their entirety, and the parties stream their conventions on the internet.

The presence of journalists at presidential nominating conventions have increased with the television networks. In

1976, the Democratic Convention consisted of 3,381 delegates and 11,500 reporters, broadcasters, editors and camera operators.[21] This is on par with the increase in the number of televisions in American's homes. In 1960, 87 percent of people had a television, compared to 98 percent by 1976.[22] By the 1992 conventions, network coverage increased from three networks (NBC, ABC and CBS) to five networks (NBC, ABC, CBS, Fox and PBS).[23] At the 1996 Republican National Convention there were approximately seven journalists per one delegate, or about 15,000 journalists.[24]

The increase of the media at these conventions originally lead to a growth in the public's interest in elections. Voter turnout in the primaries increased from less than five million voters in 1948 to around thirteen million in 1952.[25] By broadcasting the conventions on the television, people were more connected to the suspense and the decisions being made, therefore making them more politically aware, and more educated voters. When scholars studied the 1976 conventions they determined that by watching nomination conventions, even viewers that were not previously very politically active developed a much stronger interest in the election process and the candidate.[26]

## 7.4 Lists of political party conventions

### 7.4.1 Major party conventions

Main articles: List of Democratic National Conventions and List of Republican National Conventions

The two right-hand columns show nominations by notable conventions not shown elsewhere. Some of the nominees (e.g. the Whigs before 1860 and Theodore Roosevelt in 1912) received very large votes, while others who received less than 1% of the total national popular vote are listed to show historical continuity or transition. Many important candidates are not shown here because they were never endorsed by a national party convention (e.g. William Henry Harrison in 1836, George C. Wallace in 1968, John B. Anderson in 1980 and Ross Perot in 1992).

Note that there is no organizational continuity between the American Parties of 1856 and 1972, the Union Parties of 1860, 1864, 1888 and 1936, or the Progressive Parties of 1912-16, 1924 and 1948-52.

*Presidential winner in bold.*

M "Middle of the Road" faction of the People's Party, who opposed fusing with the Democrats after 1896.

### 7.4.2 Significant third-party conventions before 1860

### 7.4.3 Third-party conventions since 1872

For American Party (or American Independent Party) conventions since 1968, see American Party (1969).
For Communist Party and Workers' Party conventions, see National conventions of the Communist Party USA.

#### Prohibition and socialist parties

The Prohibition Party was organized in 1869. The Socialist Party of America (1901–1972) resulted from a merger of the Social Democratic Party (founded 1898) with dissenting members of the Socialist Labor Party (founded 1876). The Socialist Party of America stopped running its own candidates for President after 1956, but a minority of SPA members who disagreed with this policy broke away in 1973 to form the Socialist Party USA (SPUSA).

¶ *Note that the years refer to the relevant presidential election and not necessarily to the date of a convention making a nomination for that election. Some nominating conventions meet in the year before an election.*

#### Libertarian, Green, and Constitution Parties

In 1999, the United States Taxpayers' Party changed its name to the Constitution Party.

## 7.5 See also

- National conventions of the Communist Party USA

## 7.6 Notes

[1] Presidential Campaign Finance

[2] "Week In Review: National Organizing Kickoff a Great Success". democrats.org. November 2005. Archived from the original on March 10, 2008. Retrieved 2007-12-28. External link in |publisher= (help)

[3] "NFL season opener yields to McCain speech". *Reuters*. March 26, 2008.

[4] Jaffe, Alexandra (January 23, 2015). "Democratic National Convention date set". *CNN.com*. Retrieved August 25, 2015.

[5] Evan McMorris-Santoro (November 29, 2011). "Team Obama Likes Its Chances: AZ, VA, NC Could Go Democrat In 2012 (VIDEO)". Talking Points Memo. Retrieved 2012-01-06.

[6] Dena Bunis. "News: Anaheim asked to make bid for Republican convention - OCRegister.com". Ocregister.com. Retrieved 2009-10-25.

[7] Lloyd, Robert (August 29, 2008). "Barack Obama, Al Gore raise the roof at Invesco Field". Los Angeles Times. Retrieved 2009-10-31.

[8] Robert Moran on Election 2004 on National Review Online

[9] Frum, David (2012-02-20). "GOP's worst nightmare -- a contested convention". *CNN.com*. Retrieved 2015-06-30. (2012 Republicans)

[10] Garber, Kent (2008-02-08). "Obama, Clinton Head Toward Contested Convention". *USNews.com*. Retrieved 2015-06-30. (2008 Democrats)

[11] Blankley, Tony (2007-12-19). "None of the Above: GOP Heading to a Brokered Convention". *Real Clear Politics*. Retrieved 2005-06-30. (2008 Republicans)

[12] Orin, Deborah (2004-01-22). "Dems May Be In for Brokered Convention". *New York Post*. Retrieved 2015-06-30. (2004 Democrats)

[13] Rusher, William (1996-03-01). "A fun idea: Brokered convention". *Rome News-Tribune*. p. 4. Retrieved 2015-06-30. (1996 Republicans)

[14] Wicker, Tom (1991-09-03). "Snakeskins and Democrats". *Lakeland Ledger*. p. 7A. Retrieved 2015-06-30. (1992 Democrats)

[15] "Democrats worrying about a brokered convention". *The Spokesman-Review* (Spokane, Wash.). Associated Press. 1988-03-17. p. A6. Retrieved 2015-06-30. (1988 Democrats)

[16] Greenfield, Jeff (1984-05-18). "Brokered convention: Is it possible?". *The Milwaukee Sentinel*. p. 16. Part 1. Retrieved 2015-06-30. (1984 Democrats)

[17] "REPUBLICANS: Ford Is Close, but Watch Those Trojan Horses". *Time*. August 2, 1976. Retrieved 2010-05-27.

[18] Paletz & Elson (1976). "Television Coverage of Presidential Conventions: Now You See It, Now You Don't". *Political Science Quarterly* **91** (1): 109–131. doi:10.2307/2149161.

[19] Bennet, James (15 August 1996). "'Nightline' Pulls the Plug on Convention Coverage". New York Times. Retrieved 2010-05-27.

[20]

[21] Trent & Friedenberg (2004). *Political Campaign Communication Principles & Practices*. Lanham, MD: Rowman & Littlefield Publishers, Inc.

[22] Kraus, Sidney (1979). *The Great Debates*. Indiana University Press.

[23] Trent & Friedenberg (2004). *Political Campaign Communication Principles and Practices*. Lanham, MD: Rowman & Littlefield Publishers, Inc.

[24] Trent & Friedenberg (2004). *Political Campaign Communication Principles & Practices*. Lanham, MD: Rowman & Littlefield Publishers, Inc.

[25] Valley, David (1974). "Significant Characteristics of Democratic Presidential Nomination Acceptance Speeches". *Central States Speech Journal* **25**.

[26] Kraus, Sidney (1979). *The Great Debate*. Indiana University Press.

## 7.7 References

- National Party Conventions eGuide, The Campaign Finance Institute,

- Chase, James S. *Emergence of the Presidential Nominating Convention, 1789–1832* (Houghton Mifflin: 1973).

- Congressional Research Service. *Presidential Elections in the United States: A Primer*. (Washington, Congressional Research Service, April 17, 2000).

- History House: Conventional Wisdom

- Kull, Irving S. and Nell M., *An Encyclopedia of American History in Chronological Order*, enlarged and updated by Samuel H. Friedelbaum (Popular Library, New York, 1961)

- Morris, Richard B., *Encyclopedia of American History*, revised and enlarged edition (Harper & Row, New York and Evanston, Ill., 1961)

- Online *NewsHour*: Interview with Historian Michael Beschloss on the origins of the convention process

- Republican National Convention 2004: Convention History

- Taylor, Tim, *The Book of Presidents* (Arno Press, New York, 1972; ISBN 0-405-00226-2)

# Chapter 8

# Article Two of the United States Constitution

**Article Two** of the United States Constitution establishes the executive branch of the federal government, which carries out and enforces federal laws. It includes the President, the Vice President, the Cabinet, executive departments, independent agencies, and other boards, commissions, and committees.

## 8.1 Section 1: President and Vice President

### 8.1.1 Clause 1: Executive Power

The executive Power shall be vested in a President of the United States of America. He shall hold his Office during the Term of four Years, and, together with the Vice President, chosen for the same Term, be elected, as follows[1]

*George Washington's inauguration as the nation's 1st President, April 30, 1789*

Section 1 begins with a vesting clause that confers federal executive power upon the President alone. Similar clauses

*Barack Obama, the 44th and current U.S. President, signing legislation at the* Resolute *desk*

are found in Article I and Article III. The former bestows federal legislative power exclusively to Congress, and the latter grants judicial power solely to the federal judiciary. These three articles create a separation of powers among the three branches of the federal government. This separation of powers, by which each department may exercise only its own constitutional powers and no others, is fundamental to the idea of a limited government accountable to the people.

The President's executive power is subject to two important limitations. First, the President lacks executive authority explicitly granted to Congress. Hence the President cannot declare war, grant letters of marque and reprisal, or regulate commerce, even though executives had often wielded such authority in the past. In these instances, Congress retained portions of the executive power that the Continental Congress had wielded under the Articles of Confederation. Second, specific constitutional provisions may check customary executive authority. Notwithstanding his executive power, the President cannot make treaties or appointments without the advice and consent of the Senate. Likewise, the President's pardon power is limited to offenses against the United States and does not extend to impeachments or violations of state law.[2]

The head of the Executive Branch is the President. Although also named in this first clause, the Vice President is not constitutionally vested with any executive power. Nonetheless, the Constitution dictates that the President and Vice President are to be elected at the same time, for the same term, and by the same constituency. The framers' intent was to preserve the independence of the executive branch should the person who was Vice President succeed to the duties of the presidency.

### 8.1.2   Clause 2: Method of choosing electors

Each State shall appoint, in such Manner as the Legislature thereof may direct, a Number of Electors, equal to the whole Number of Senators and Representatives to which the State may be entitled in the Congress: but no Senator or Representative, or Person holding an Office of Trust or Profit under the United States, shall be appointed an Elector.

Under the U.S. Constitution the President and Vice President are chosen by Electors, under a constitutional grant of authority delegated to the legislatures of the several states and the District of Columbia. The Constitution reserves the choice of the precise manner for creating Electors to the will of the state legislatures. It does not define or delimit what process a state legislature may use to create its *state* college of Electors. In practice, the state legislatures have generally chosen to create Electors through an indirect popular vote, since the 1820s.

In an indirect popular vote, it is the names of the electors who are on the ballot to be elected. Typically, their names are aligned under the name of the candidate for President and Vice President, that they, the Elector, have pledged they will support. It is fully understood by the voters and the Electors themselves that they are the representative "stand-ins" for the individuals to whom they have pledged to cast their electoral college ballots to be President and Vice President. In some states, in past years, this pledge was informal, and Electors could still legally cast their electoral ballot for whomever they chose. More recently, state legislatures have mandated in law that Electors *shall* cast their electoral college ballot for the Presidential Candidate to whom they are pledged. The constitutionality of such mandates is uncertain.

Each state chooses as many Electors as it has Representatives and Senators representing it in Congress. Under the Twenty-third Amendment, the District of Columbia may choose no more electors than the state with the lowest number of electoral votes. No Senators, Representatives or fed-

eral officers may become Electors.

### 8.1.3   Clause 3: Electors

The Electors shall meet in their respective States, and vote by Ballot for two Persons, of whom one at least shall not be an Inhabitant of the same State with themselves. And they shall make a List of all the Persons voted for, and of the Number of Votes for each; which List they shall sign and certify, and transmit sealed to the Seat of the Government of the United States, directed to the President of the Senate. The President of the Senate shall, in the Presence of the Senate and House of Representatives, open all the Certificates, and the Votes shall then be counted. The Person having the greatest Number of Votes shall be the President, if such Number be a Majority of the whole Number of Electors appointed; and if there be more than one who have such Majority, and have an equal Number of Votes, then the House of Representatives shall immediately chuse [*sic*] by Ballot one of them for President; and if no Person have a Majority, then from the five highest on the List the said House shall in like Manner chuse [*sic*] the President. But in chusing [*sic*] the President, the Votes shall be taken by States, the Representation from each State having one Vote; A quorum for this Purpose shall consist of a Member or Members from two thirds of the States, and a Majority of all the States shall be necessary to a Choice. In every Case, after the Choice of the President, the Person having the greatest Number of Votes of the Electors shall be the Vice President. But if there should remain two or more who have equal Votes, the Senate shall chuse [*sic*] from them by Ballot the Vice President.

*(**Note:** This procedure was changed by the Twelfth Amendment in 1804.)*

In modern practice, each state chooses its electors in popular elections. Once chosen, the electors meet in their respective states to cast ballots for the President and Vice President. Originally, each elector cast two votes for President; at least one of the individuals voted for had to be from a state different from the elector's. The individual with the majority of votes became President, and the runner-up became Vice President. In case of a tie, the House of Representatives could choose one of the tied candidates; if no person received a majority, then the House could again choose one of the five with the greatest number of votes. When the House voted, each state delegation cast one vote, and the vote of a majority of states was necessary to choose a President. If second-place candidates were tied, then the Senate broke the tie. A quorum of two-thirds applied in both Houses: at least one member from each of two-thirds of the states in the House of Representatives, and at least two-thirds of the Senators in the Senate. This procedure was followed in 1801 after the electoral vote produced a tie, and nearly resulted in a deadlock in the House.

The Twelfth Amendment introduced a number of important changes to the procedure. Now, Electors do not cast two votes for President; rather, they cast one vote for President and another for Vice President. In case no Presidential candidate receives a majority, the House chooses from the top three (not five, as with Vice Presidential candidates). The Amendment also requires the Senate to choose the Vice President from those with the two highest figures if no Vice Presidential candidate receives a majority of electoral votes (rather than only if there's a tie for second for President). It also stipulates that to be the Vice President, a person must be qualified to be the President.

### 8.1.4 Clause 4: Election day

> The Congress may determine the Time of chusing [*sic*] the Electors, and the Day on which they shall give their Votes; which Day shall be the same throughout the United States.

Congress sets a national Election Day. Currently, Electors are chosen on the Tuesday following the first Monday in November, in the year before the President's term is to expire. The Electors cast their votes on the Monday following the second Wednesday in December of that year. Thereafter, the votes are opened and counted by the Vice President, as President of the Senate, in a joint session of Congress.

### 8.1.5 Clause 5: Qualifications for office

Section 1 of Article Two of the United States Constitution sets forth the eligibility requirements for serving as president of the United States:

> No Person except a natural born Citizen, or a Citizen of the United States at the time of the Adoption of this Constitution, shall be eligible to the Office of President; neither shall any person be eligible to that Office who shall not have attained to the Age of thirty five Years, and been fourteen Years a Resident within the United States.

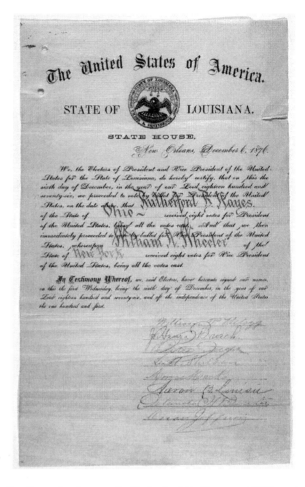

*Certificate for the vote for Rutherford B. Hayes and William A. Wheeler for the State of Louisiana*

*Beginning of the clause in the 1787 document*

See also: Natural-born citizen and President of the United States

By the time of their inauguration, the President and Vice President must be:

- natural born citizens

- at least 35 years old

- inhabitants of the United States for at least fourteen years.

Eligibility for holding the office of President and Vice-President were modified by subsequent amendments:

- The Twelfth Amendment (1804) requires the Vice-President to meet all of the qualifications of being

*In this 1944 poster, Franklin Roosevelt (left) successfully campaigned for a fourth term. He was the only President who served more than two terms.*

President.

- The Twenty-second Amendment (1951) prevents a President from being elected more than twice

### 8.1.6  Clause 6: Vacancy and disability

*1888 illustration of Vice President Tyler receiving the news of President Harrison's death from Chief Clerk of the State Department Fletcher Webster.*

In Case of the Removal of the President from Office, or of his Death, Resignation, or Inability to discharge the Powers and Duties of the said Office, the Same shall devolve on the Vice President, and the Congress may by Law provide for the Case of Removal, Death, Resignation or Inability, both of the President and Vice President, declaring what Officer shall then act as President, and such Officer shall act accordingly, until the Disability be removed, or a President shall be elected.

The wording of this clause caused much controversy at the time it was first used. When William Henry Harrison died in office, a debate arose over whether the Vice President would become President, or if he would just inherit the powers, thus becoming an Acting President. Harrison's Vice President, John Tyler, believed that he had the right to become President. However, many Senators argued that he only had the right to assume the powers of the presidency long enough to call for a new election. Because the wording of the clause is so vague, it was impossible for either side to prove its point. Tyler took the Oath of Office and became President, setting a precedent that made it possible for later Vice Presidents to ascend to the presidency unchallenged following the President's death. The "Tyler Precedent" established that if the President's office becomes vacant, the Vice President becomes President.

The Congress may provide for a line of succession beyond the Vice President. The current Presidential Succession Act establishes the order as the Speaker of the House of Representatives, the President *pro tempore* of the Senate and then the fifteen Cabinet Secretaries in order of that Department's establishment.

The Twenty-fifth Amendment explicitly states that when the Presidency becomes vacant, the Vice President becomes President, and also establishes a procedure for filling a vacancy in the office of the Vice President. It supersedes the ambiguous wording of this clause.[3] The Amendment further provides that the President, or the Vice President and Cabinet, can declare the President unable to discharge his duties, in which case the Vice President becomes Acting President. If the declaration is done by the Vice President and Cabinet, the Amendment permits the President to take control back, unless the Vice President and Cabinet challenge the President and two-thirds of both Houses vote to sustain the findings of the Vice President and Cabinet. If the declaration is done by the President, he may take control back without risk of being overridden by the Congress.

### 8.1.7   Clause 7: Salary

> The President shall, at stated Times, receive for his Services, a Compensation, which shall neither be increased nor diminished during the Period for which he shall have been elected, and he shall not receive within that Period any other Emolument from the United States, or any of them.

The President's salary, currently $400,000 a year, must remain constant throughout the President's term. The President may not receive other compensation from either the federal or any state government.

### 8.1.8   Clause 8: Oath or affirmation

*President Barack Obama being administered the oath of office by Chief Justice John Roberts for the second time at his first inauguration, on January 21, 2009.*

Further information: Oath of office of the President of the United States

> Before he enters the Execution of his Office, he shall take the following Oath or Affirmation:—
> "I do solemnly swear (or affirm) that I will faithfully execute the Office of President of the United States, and will to the best of my Ability, preserve, protect and defend the Constitution of the United States."

According to the Joint Congressional Committee on Presidential Inaugurations, George Washington added the words "So help me God" during his first inaugural,[4] though this has been disputed. There are no contemporaneous sources for this fact, and no eyewitness sources to Washington's first inaugural mention the phrase at all—including those that transcribed what he said for his oath.

Also, the President-elect's name is typically added after the "I", for example, "I, George Washington, do...." Normally, the Chief Justice of the United States administers the oath. It is sometimes asserted that the oath bestows upon the President the power to do whatever is necessary to "preserve, protect and defend the Constitution." Andrew Jackson, while vetoing an Act for the renewal of the charter of the national bank, implied that the President could refuse to execute statutes that he felt were unconstitutional. In suspending the privilege of the writ of *habeas corpus*, President Abraham Lincoln claimed that he acted according to the oath. His action was challenged in court and overturned by the U.S. Circuit Court in Maryland (led by Chief Justice Roger B. Taney) in *Ex Parte Merryman*, 17 F. Cas. 144 (C.C.D. Md. 1861). Lincoln ignored Taney's order. Finally, Andrew Johnson's counsel referred to the theory during his impeachment trial. Otherwise, few have seriously asserted that the oath augments the President's powers.

The Vice President also has an oath of office, but it is not mandated by the Constitution and is prescribed by statute. Currently, the Vice Presidential oath is the same as that for Members of Congress.

> I do solemnly swear (or affirm) that I will support and defend the Constitution of the United States against all enemies, foreign and domestic; that I will bear true faith and allegiance to the same; that I take this obligation freely, without any mental reservation or purpose of evasion; and that I will well and faithfully discharge the duties of the office on which I am about to enter. So help me God.[5]

## 8.2   Section 2: Presidential powers

In the landmark decision *Nixon v. General Services Administration* Justice William Rehnquist, afterwards the Chief Justice, declared in his dissent the need to "fully describe the preeminent position that the President of the United States occupies with respect to our Republic. Suffice it to say that the President is made the sole repository of the executive powers of the United States, and the powers entrusted to him as well as the duties imposed upon him are awesome indeed."

### 8.2.1   Clause 1:   Command of military; Opinions of cabinet secretaries; Pardons

> The President shall be Commander in Chief of the Army and Navy of the United States, and

***President Franklin Roosevelt as Commander in Chief, with his military subordinates during World War II.***
*Left to right: General Douglas MacArthur, President Franklin Roosevelt, Admiral William D. Leahy, Admiral Chester W. Nimitz.*

of the Militia of the several States, when called into the actual Service of the United States; he may require the Opinion, in writing, of the principal Officer in each of the executive Departments, upon any Subject relating to the Duties of their respective Offices, and he shall have Power to grant Reprieves and Pardons for Offenses against the United States, except in Cases of Impeachment.

The Constitution vests the President with Executive Power. That power reaches its zenith when wielded to protect national security.[6] And federal courts in the United States must pay proper deference to the Executive in assessing the threats that face the nation.[7] The President is the military's commander-in-chief; however Article One gives Congress and not the President the exclusive right to declare war. Nevertheless, the power of the president to initiate hostilities has been subject to question. According to historian Thomas Woods, "Ever since the Korean War, Article II, Section 2 [...] has been interpreted 'The president has the power to initiate hostilities without consulting Congress' [....]But what the framers actually meant by that clause was that once war has been declared, it was the President's responsibility as commander-in-chief to direct the war. Alexander Hamilton spoke in such terms when he said that the president, although lacking the power to declare war, would have "the direction of war when authorized or begun." The president acting alone was authorized only to repel sudden attacks (hence the decision to withhold from him only the power to "declare" war, not to "make" war, which was thought to be a necessary emergency power in case of foreign attack). [8][9] Since World War II, every ma-

jor military action has been technically a U.S. military operation or a U.N. "police action", which are deemed legally legitimate by Congress, and various United Nations Resolutions because of decisions such as the Gulf of Tonkin Resolution or the The Resolution of The Congress Providing Authorization for Use of Force In Iraq.

The President may require the "principal officer" of any executive department to tender his advice in writing. While the Constitution nowhere requires a formal Cabinet, it does authorize the president to seek advice from the principal officers of the various departments as he (or she) performs their official duties. George Washington found it prudent to organize his principal officers into a Cabinet, and it has been part of the executive branch structure ever since. Presidents have used Cabinet meetings of selected principal officers but to widely differing extents and for different purposes. Secretary of State William H. Seward and then Professor Woodrow Wilson advocated use of a parliamentary-style Cabinet government. But President Abraham Lincoln rebuffed Seward, and Woodrow Wilson would have none of it in his administration. In recent administrations, cabinets have grown to include including key White House staff in addition to department and agency heads. President Ronald Reagan formed seven subcabinet councils to review many policy issues, and subsequent Presidents have followed that practice.[10]

The President, furthermore, may grant pardon or reprieves, except in cases of impeachment. Originally, as ruled by the Supreme Court in *United States v. Wilson* (1833), the pardon could be rejected by the convict. In *Biddle v. Perovich* 274 U.S. 480 (1927), the Supreme Court reversed the doctrine, ruling that "[a] pardon in our days is not a private act of grace from an individual happening to possess power. It is a part of the Constitutional scheme. When granted it is the determination of the ultimate authority that the public welfare will be better served by inflicting less than what the judgment fixed."[11]

### 8.2.2 Clause 2: Advice and Consent Clause

The President exercises the powers in the Advice and Consent Clause with the advice and consent of the Senate.

> He shall have Power, by and with the Advice and Consent of the Senate, to make Treaties, provided two thirds of the Senators present concur; and he shall nominate, and by and with the Advice and Consent of the Senate, shall appoint Ambassadors, other public Ministers and Consuls, Judges of the supreme Court, and all other Officers of the United States, whose Appointments are not herein otherwise provided for,

and which shall be established by Law: but the Congress may by Law vest the Appointment of such inferior Officers, as they think proper, in the President alone, in the Courts of Law, or in the Heads of Departments.

**Treaties**

Main article: Treaty Clause

The President may enter the United States into treaties, but they are not effective until ratified by a two-thirds vote in the Senate.[12] In Article II however, the Constitution is not very explicit about the termination of treaties. The first abrogation of a treaty occurred in 1798, when Congress passed a law terminating a 1778 Treaty of Alliance with France.[13] In the nineteenth century, several Presidents terminated treaties after Congress passed resolutions requesting the same.[14] In 1854, however, President Franklin Pierce terminated a treaty with Denmark with the consent of the Senate alone. A Senate committee ruled that it was correct procedure for the President to terminate treaties after being authorized by the Senate alone, and not the entire Congress. President Pierce's successors, however, returned to the former procedure of obtaining authorization from both Houses. Some Presidents have claimed to themselves the exclusive power of terminating treaties. Abraham Lincoln, for instance, terminated a treaty without prior Congressional authorization, but Congress retroactively approved his decision at a later point. The first unambiguous case of a President terminating a treaty without authorization, granted prior to or after the termination, occurred when Jimmy Carter terminated a treaty with the Republic of China.[15] For the first time, judicial determination was sought, but the effort proved futile: the Supreme Court could not find a majority agreeing on any particular principle, and therefore instructed the trial court to dismiss the case.

**Appointments**

Main article: Appointments Clause

The President may also appoint judges, ambassadors, consuls, ministers and other officers with the advice and consent of the Senate. By law, however, Congress may allow the President, heads of executive departments, or the courts to appoint inferior officials.

The Senate has a long-standing practice of permitting motions to reconsider previous decisions. In 1931, the Senate granted advice and consent to the President on the appointment of a member of the Federal Power Commission. The officer in question was sworn in, but the Senate, under the guise of a motion to reconsider, rescinded the advice and consent. In the writ of quo warranto proceedings that followed, the Supreme Court ruled that the Senate was not permitted to rescind advice and consent after the officer had been installed.

After the Senate grants advice and consent, however, the President is under no compulsion to commission the officer. It has not been settled whether the President has the prerogative to withhold a commission after having signed it. This issue played a large part in the famous court case *Marbury v. Madison*.

At times the President has asserted the power to remove individuals from office. Congress has often explicitly limited the President's power to remove; during the Reconstruction Era, Congress passed the Tenure of Office Act, purportedly preventing Andrew Johnson from removing, without the advice and consent of the Senate, anyone appointed with the advice and consent of the Senate. President Johnson ignored the Act, and was later impeached and acquitted. The constitutionality of the Act was not immediately settled. In *Myers v. United States*, 272 U.S. 52 (1926), the Supreme Court held that Congress could not limit the President's power to remove an executive officer (the Postmaster General), but in *Humphrey's Executor v. United States*, 295 U.S. 602 (1935) it upheld Congress's authority to restrict the President's power to remove officers of the Federal Trade Commission, an "administrative body [that] cannot in any proper sense be characterized as an arm or eye of the executive."

Congress may repeal the legislation that authorizes the appointment of an executive officer. But it "cannot reserve for itself the power of an officer charged with the execution of the laws except by impeachment."[16] Congress has from time to time changed the number of justices in the Supreme Court.

### 8.2.3   Clause 3: Recess appointments

Main article: Recess appointment

> The President shall have Power to fill up all Vacancies that may happen during the Recess of the Senate, by granting Commissions which shall expire at the End of their next Session.

During recesses of the Senate, the President may appoint officers, but their commissions expire at the conclusion of the Senate's next session.

*President George W. Bush announcing the August 1, 2005 recess appointment of John R. Bolton as the U.S. Ambassador to the United Nations as U.S. Secretary of State Condoleezza Rice looks on.*

# 8.3 Section 3: Presidential responsibilities

He shall from time to time give to the Congress Information of the State of the Union, and recommend to their Consideration such Measures as he shall judge necessary and expedient; he may, on extraordinary Occasions, convene both Houses, or either of them, and in Case of Disagreement between them, with Respect to the Time of Adjournment, he may adjourn them to such Time as he shall think proper; he shall receive Ambassadors and other public Ministers; he shall take Care that the Laws be faithfully executed, and shall Commission all the Officers of the United States.

## 8.3.1 Clause 1: State of the Union

*2011 State of the Union Address given by President Barack Obama*

The President must give the Congress information on the "State of the Union" "from time to time." This is called the State of the Union Clause.[17] Originally, Presidents personally delivered annual addresses to Congress. Thomas Jefferson, who felt that the procedure resembled the Speech from the Throne delivered by British monarchs, chose instead to send written messages to Congress for reading by clerks. Jefferson's procedure was followed by future Presidents until Woodrow Wilson reverted to the former procedure of personally addressing Congress, which has continued to this day.[17]

Kesavan and Sidak explain the purpose of the State of the Union clause:

> "The State of the Union Clause imposes an executive duty on the President. That duty must be discharged periodically. The President's assessment of the State of the Union must be publicized to Congress, and thus to the nation. The publication of the President's assessment conveys information to Congress- information uniquely gleaned from the President's perspective in his various roles as Commander-in-Chief, chief law enforcer, negotiator with foreign powers, and the like-that shall aid the legislature in public deliberation on matters that may justify the enactment of legislation because of their national importance."[17]

## 8.3.2 Clause 2: Making recommendations to Congress

The president has the power and duty[17] to recommend, for the consideration of Congress, such measures which the president deems as "necessary and expedient". At his inauguration George Washington declared in his Inaugural Address: "By the article establishing the executive department it is made the duty of the President 'to recommend to your consideration such measures as he shall judge necessary and expedient.'" This is the Recommendation Clause.[18]

Kesavan and Sidak explain the purpose of the Recommendation clause:

> "The Recommendation Clause also imposes an executive duty on the President. His recommendations respect the equal dignity of Congress and thus embody the anti-royalty sentiment that ignited the American Revolution and subsequently stripped the trappings of monarchy away from the new chief executive. Through his recommendations to Congress, the President speaks collectively for the People as they petition Govern-

ment for a redress of grievances, and thus his recommendations embody popular sovereignty. The President tailors his recommendations so that their natural implication is the enactment of new legislation, rather than some other action that Congress might undertake. Finally, the President shall have executive discretion to recommend measures of his choosing."[17]

Sidak explained that there is a connection between the Recommendation clause and the Petition Clause of the first amendment: "Through his performance of the duty to recommend measures to Congress, the President functions as the agent of a diffuse electorate who seek the redress of grievances. To muzzle the President, therefore, is to diminish the effectiveness of this right expressly reserved to the people under the first amendment."[18]:2119, note 7 Kesavan and Sidak also cited a Professor Bybee who stated in this context: "The Recommendation Clause empowers the President to represent the people before Congress, by recommending measures for the reform of government, for the general welfare, or for the redress of grievances. The Right of Petition Clause prevents Congress from abridging the right of the people to petition for a redress of grievances."[17]:43

The Recommendation clause imposes a duty, but its performance rests solely with the President. Congress possesses no power to compel the President to recommend, as he alone is the "judge" of what is "necessary and expedient." Unlike the Necessary and Proper Clause of Article I, which limits Congress's discretion to carrying out only its delegated powers, the phrase "necessary and expedient" implies a wider range of discretion for the President. Because this is a political question, there has been little judicial involvement with the President's actions under the clause as long as Presidents have not tried to extend their legislative powers. In Youngstown Sheet & Tube Co. v. Sawyer (1952), the Supreme Court noted that the Recommendations Clause serves as a reminder that the President cannot make law by himself: "The power to recommend legislation, granted to the President, serves only to emphasize that it is his function to recommend and that it is the function of the Congress to legislate."[19] The Court made a similar point in striking down the line-item veto in Clinton v. City of New York (1998).[19] When President William Jefferson Clinton attempted to shield the records of the President's Task Force on Health Care Reform as essential to his functions under the Recommendations Clause, a federal circuit court rejected the argument and noted in Ass'n of American Physicians & Surgeons v. Clinton (1993): "[T]he Recommendation Clause is less an obligation than a right. The President has the undisputed authority to recommend legislation, but he need not exercise that authority with respect to any particular subject or, for that matter, any subject."[19]

### 8.3.3 Clause 3: Calling Congress into extraordinary session; adjourning Congress

To allow the government to act quickly in case of a major domestic or international crisis arising when Congress is not in session, the President is permitted to call extraordinary sessions of one or both Houses of Congress. If the two Houses cannot agree on a date for adjournment, the President may adjourn both Houses to such a time as befits the circumstances. The last time this power was exercised was in 1948, when President Harry S Truman called a special session of Congress. That was the twenty-seventh time in American history that a president convened such a session.[20]

Following the widespread adoption of transcontinental air travel in the second half of the twentieth century, Congress began meeting year-round. Since that time, it has always been in session on every occasion when the President might otherwise have perceived the need to call Congress into extraordinary session.

### 8.3.4 Clause 4: Receiving foreign representatives

The President receives all foreign Ambassadors. This clause of the Constitution, known as the Reception Clause, has been interpreted to imply that the President can be granted broad power over all matters of foreign policy by Congress,[21] and to provide support for the President's exclusive authority to grant recognition to a foreign sovereign.[22]

### 8.3.5 Clause 5: Caring for the faithful execution of the law

The President must "take care that the laws be faithfully executed."[23] This clause in the Constitution imposes a duty on the President to take due care while executing laws and is called the **Take Care Clause**,[24] also known as the **Faithful Execution Clause**[25] or **Faithfully Executed Clause**.[26] This clause is meant to ensure that a law is faithfully executed by the President,[24] even if he disagrees with the purpose of that law.[27] By virtue of his executive power, the President may execute the law and control the law execution of others. Under the Take Care Clause, however, the President must exercise his law-execution power to "take Care that the Laws be faithfully executed."[25] Addressing the North Carolina ratifying convention, William Maclaine declared that the Faithful Execution Clause was "one of the [Constitution's] best provisions."[25] If the President "takes care to see the laws faithfully executed, it will be more than is done in any government on the continent; for I will venture to say that our government, and those of the other states, are, with respect to the execution of the laws, in many respects mere ciphers."[25] President George Washington interpreted this clause as imposing on him a unique duty to ensure the execution of federal law. Discussing a tax rebellion, Washington observed, "it is my duty to see the Laws executed: to permit them to be trampled upon with impunity would be repugnant to [that duty.]"[25]

According to former United States Assistant Attorney General Walter E. Dellinger III, the Supreme Court and the Attorneys General have long interpreted the Take Care Clause to mean that the President has no inherent constitutional authority to suspend the enforcement of the laws, particularly of statutes.[28] The Take Care Clause demands that the President obey the law, the Supreme Court said in Humphrey's Executor v. United States, and repudiates any notion that he may dispense with the law's execution.[29] In Printz v. United States, 521 U.S. 898 (1997), the Supreme Court explained how the President executes the law: "The Constitution does not leave to speculation who is to administer the laws enacted by Congress; the President, it says, "shall take Care that the Laws be faithfully executed," Art. II, §3, personally and through officers whom he appoints (save for such inferior officers as Congress may authorize to be appointed by the "Courts of Law" or by "the Heads of Departments" with other presidential appointees), Art. II, §2."

The President may not prevent a member of the executive branch from performing a ministerial duty lawfully imposed upon him by Congress. (See Marbury v. Madison (1803); and Kendall v. United States ex rel. Stokes (1838)). Nor may the President take an action not authorized either by the Constitution or by a lawful statute. (See Youngstown Sheet & Tube Co. v. Sawyer (1952)). Finally, the President may not refuse to enforce a constitutional law, or "cancel" certain appropriations, for that would amount to an extra-constitutional veto or suspension power.[25]

The President, while having to enforce the law, also possesses wide discretion in deciding how and even when to enforce laws. He also has a range of interpretive discretion in deciding the meaning of laws he must execute. When an appropriation provides discretion, the President can gauge when and how appropriated moneys can be spent most efficiently.

Some Presidents have claimed the authority under this clause to impound money appropriated by Congress. President Jefferson, for example, delayed the expenditure of money appropriated for the purchase of gunboats for over a year. President Franklin D. Roosevelt and his successors sometimes refused outright to expend appropriated money.[25] The Supreme Court, however, has held that impoundments without Congressional authorization are unconstitutional.[30]

It has been asserted that the President's responsibility in the "faithful" execution of the laws entitles him to suspend the privilege of the writ of *habeas corpus*. Article One provides that the privilege may not be suspended save during times of rebellion or invasion, but it does not specify who may suspend the privilege. The Supreme Court ruled that Congress may suspend the privilege if it deems it necessary. During the American Civil War, President Abraham Lincoln suspended the privilege, but, owing to the vehement opposition he faced, obtained congressional authorization for the same. Since then, the privilege of the writ has only been suspended upon the express authorization of Congress.

In *Mississippi v. Johnson*, 71 U.S. 475 (1867), the Supreme Court ruled that the judiciary may not restrain the President in the execution of laws. In that case the Supreme Court refused to entertain a request for an injunction preventing President Andrew Johnson from executing the Reconstruction Acts, which were claimed to be unconstitutional. The Court found that "[t]he Congress is the legislative department of the government; the President is the executive department. Neither can be restrained in its action by the judicial department; though the acts of both, when performed, are, in proper cases, subject to its cognizance."[31] Thus, the courts cannot bar the passage of a law by Congress, though it may strike down such a law as unconstitutional. A similar construction applies to the executive branch.

### 8.3.6 Clause 6: Officers' commissions

The President commissions "all the Officers of the United States." These include officers in both military and foreign service. (Under Article I, Section 8, the States have authority for "the Appointment of the Officers . . . of the [State] Militia . . ..")

The presidential authority to commission officers had a large impact on the 1803 case *Marbury v. Madison*, where outgoing Federalist President John Adams feverishly signed many commissions to the judiciary on his final day in office, hoping to, as incoming Democratic-Republican President Thomas Jefferson put it, "[retire] into the judiciary as a stronghold." However, in his haste, Adams' Secretary of State neglected to have all the commissions delivered. Incoming President Jefferson was enraged with Adams, and ordered his Secretary of State, James Madison, to refrain from delivering the remaining commissions. William Marbury took the matter to the Supreme Court, where the famous *Marbury* was decided.

## 8.4   Section 4: Impeachment

*Depiction of the impeachment trial of President Andrew Johnson, in 1868, Chief Justice Salmon P. Chase presiding.*

Main article: Impeachment in the United States

> The President, Vice President and all civil Officers of the United States, shall be removed from Office on Impeachment for, and Conviction of, Treason, Bribery, or other High crimes and Misdemeanors.

The Constitution also allows for involuntary removal from office. The President, Vice-President, Cabinet Secretaries, and other executive officers, as well as judges, may be impeached by the House of Representatives and tried in the Senate.

Any official convicted by impeachment is immediately removed from office. The Senate may also choose to bar the removed official from holding any federal office in the future.[32] No other punishments may be inflicted pursuant to the impeachment proceeding, but the convicted party remains liable to trial and punishment in the courts for civil and criminal charges.[33]

## 8.5   References

[1] The U.S. Constitution With Declaration of Independence, US Government Printing Office

[2] Prakash, Sai Prakash. "Essays on Article II: Executive Vesting Clause". The Heritage Foundation.

[3] The Constitution And Democracy

[4] "Joint Congressional Committee on Presidential Inaugurations". Retrieved November 10, 2006.

[5] 5 U.S.C. § 3331

[6] Cf: Youngstown Sheet & Tube Co. v. Sawyer, 343 U.S. 579,637 (1952) (Jackson, J., concurring) ("When the President acts pursuant to an express or implied authorization from Congress," his actions are "supported by the strongest of presumptions and the widest latitude of judicial interpretation, and the burden of persuasion ... rest[s] heavily upon any who might attack it.").

[7] Boumediene v. Bush, 553 U.S. 723, 797 (2008) ("[M]ost federal judges [do not] begin the day with briefings that describe new and serious threats to our Nation and its people.").

[8] Woods, Thomas (July 7, 2005) Presidential War Powers, *LewRockwell.com*

[9] Woods, Thomas (2013). "Presidential War Powers: The Constitutional Answer". Liberty Classrooom. Retrieved September 6, 2013.

[10] Gaziano, Todd. "Essays on Article II: Opinion Clause". The Heritage Foundation.

[11] *Biddle*, at 486

[12] *United States Senate*. "Treaties". senate.gov.

[13] *United States Library of Congress* (February 15, 2011). "Primary Documents in American History Treaty of Alliance with France". loc.gov.

[14] John H. Haswell, University of Minnesota; *United States Department of State* (2010). *Treaties and Conventions Concluded Between the United States of America Since July 4, 1776*. google.books.com. pp. 1,232.

[15] *Goldwater v. Carter*, 444 U.S. 996 (1979)

[16] *Bowsher v. Synar*, 478 U.S. 714 (1986)

[17] Vasan Kesavan and J. Gregory Sidak (2002). "The Legislator-In-Chief". *William and Mary Law Review* **44** (1). Retrieved June 28, 2012.

[18] Sidak, Gregory (August 1989). "The Recommendation Clause". *Georgetown Law Journal* **77** (6): 2079–2135. Retrieved June 29, 2012.

[19] Kesavan, Vasan. "The Heritage Guide to the Constitution: Recommendations Clause". The Heritage Foundation. Retrieved October 27, 2012.

[20] U.S. Senate Turnip Day Session (January 5, 2011).

[21] *United States v. Curtiss-Wright Export Corp.*, 299 U.S. 304 (1936), characterized the President as the "sole organ of the nation in its external relations," an interpretation criticized by Louis Fisher of the Library of Congress.

[22] *Zivotofsky v. Kerry*, 576 U.S. ___ (2015), slip op. at 8-9.

[23] "Article II, Section 3, U.S. Constitution". *law.cornell.edu*. Legal Information Institute. 2012. Retrieved August 7, 2012.

[24] "Take Care Clause Law & Legal Definition". USLegal.com. Retrieved July 5, 2012.

[25] Take Care Clause. "Take Care Clause". *The Heritage Guide to the Constitution*. The Heritage Foundation. Retrieved October 12, 2012.

[26] Prepared by Devotion Garner. Updated by Cheryl Nyberg. "Popular Names of Constitutional Provisions". Gallagher Library of the University of Washington School of Law. Retrieved November 23, 2013.

[27] "Chapter 12-The Presidency Flashcards". Flashcard Machine. January 16, 2012. Retrieved July 5, 2012.

[28] Walter E. Dellinger III (September 7, 1995). "CONSTITUTIONAL LIMITATIONS ON FEDERAL GOVERNMENT PARTICIPATION IN BINDING ARBITRATION". United States Department of Justice. Retrieved July 5, 2012.

[29] Kinkopf, Neil (September–October 2005). "FURIOUS GEORGE - The belligerence of the Bush Administration in pursuing expansive power has a long Republican pedigree". *Legal Affairs - The magazine at the intersection of Law and Life*. Retrieved July 5, 2012.

[30] Sai Prakash. "Take Care Clause". *The Heritage Guide to the Constitution*. The Heritage Foundation. Retrieved August 27, 2012.

[31] *Johnson*, at 500

[32] An example of this is Alcee Hastings who was removed from a federal judgeship, but was not barred from serving in another federal office. He was later elected to, and currently serves in, the House of Representatives.

[33] *Cf. Ritter v. United States*, 677 F.2d 957 (2d. Cir. 19) 84 Ct. Cl. 293, 300 (Ct. Cl. 1936) ("While the Senate in one sense acts as a court on the trial of an impeachment, it is essentially a political body and in its actions is influenced by the views of its members on the public welfare."); STAFF OF H. COMM. ON THE JUDICIARY, 93D CONG., CONSTITUTIONAL GROUNDS FOR PRESIDENTIAL IMPEACHMENT 24 (Comm. Print 1974) ("The purpose of impeachment is not personal punishment; its function is primarily to maintain constitutional government.") (citation omitted), *reprinted in* 3 LEWIS DESCHLER, DESCHLER'S PRECEDENTS OF THE UNITED STATES HOUSE OF REPRESENTATIVES, H.R. DOC. NO. 94–661 ch. 14, app. at 2269 (1977).

## 8.6 External links

- Kilman, Johnny and George Costello (Eds). (2000). *The Constitution of the United States of America: Analysis and Interpretation.*

- CRS Annotated Constitution: Article 2

- Mount, Steve. (2003). "Presidential Pardons."

# Chapter 9

# Natural-born-citizen clause

Status as a **natural-born citizen** of the United States is one of the eligibility requirements established in the United States Constitution for election to the office of President or Vice President. This requirement was intended to protect the nation from foreign influence.[1]

The U.S. Constitution uses but does not define the phrase "natural born Citizen", and various opinions have been offered over time regarding its precise meaning. The consensus of early 21st-century constitutional scholars, together with relevant case law, is that natural-born citizens include, subject to exceptions, those born in the United States. Many scholars have also concluded that those who meet the legal requirements for U.S. citizenship "at the moment of birth", regardless of place of birth, are also natural born citizens, but the matter remains unsettled.[2][3] Every president to date was either a citizen at the adoption of the Constitution in 1789 or born in the United States; of those in the latter group, every president except two had two U.S.-citizen parents.[4]

The natural-born-citizen clause has been mentioned in passing in several decisions of the United States Supreme Court, and by some lower courts that have addressed eligibility challenges, but the Supreme Court has never directly addressed the question of a specific presidential or vice-presidential candidate's eligibility as a natural-born citizen. Many eligibility lawsuits from the 2008 and 2012 election cycles were dismissed in lower courts due to the challengers' difficulty in showing that they had standing to raise legal objections. Additionally, some experts have suggested that the precise meaning of the natural-born-citizen clause may never be decided by the courts because, in the end, presidential eligibility may be determined to be a non-justiciable political question that can be decided only by Congress rather than by the judicial branch of government.[5][6]

## 9.1 Constitutional provisions

Section 1 of Article Two of the United States Constitution sets forth the eligibility requirements for serving as presi-

*Part of the constitutional provision as it appeared in 1787*

dent of the United States, under clause 5:

> No Person except a natural born Citizen, or a Citizen of the United States, at the time of the Adoption of this Constitution, shall be eligible to the Office of President; neither shall any Person be eligible to that Office who shall not have attained to the Age of thirty-five Years, and been fourteen Years a Resident within the United States.

The Twelfth Amendment states, "No person constitutionally ineligible to the office of President shall be eligible to that of Vice-President of the United States." The Fourteenth Amendment does not use the phrase *natural-born citizen*. It does provide, "All persons born or naturalized in the United States, and subject to the jurisdiction thereof, are citizens of the United States and of the State wherein they reside."

Under Article One of the United States Constitution, representatives and senators are required to be U.S. citizens, but there is no requirement that they be natural born.[7][8]

Eight of the first nine presidents—Martin Van Buren being the exception—as well as early potential presidential candidates, were born as British subjects in British America before the American Revolution but were eligible for the office by virtue of having been citizens at the time that the Constitution was adopted.[9]

## 9.2 History

### 9.2.1 Antecedents in England

The use of the term "natural born" was not without precedent. The earliest recorded mention was in Calvin's Case

(1609), albeit in terms of birth within the jurisdiction of the sovereignty of the King.[10]

Statutes in England prior to American independence used the phrase "natural born subject". For example, the British Foreign Protestants Naturalization Act 1708.[11][12]

> The children of all natural born subjects born out of the ligeance [i.e. out of England] of Her Majesty Her Heirs and Successors shall be deemed and adjudged to be natural born subjects of this Kingdom to all intents, constructions, and purposes whatsoever.

The Act was repealed by the Tories in 1711 by the *Naturalization Act 1711* (10 Anne c. 9).[13][14]

Similarly, consider this British Statute of 1730:

> [A]ll Children born out of the Ligeance of the Crown of England, or of Great Britain, or which shall hereafter be born out of such Ligeance, whose Fathers were or shall be natural-born Subjects of the Crown of England, or of Great Britain, at the Time of the Birth of such Children respectively ... are hereby declared to be natural-born Subjects of the Crown of Great Britain, to all Intents, Constructions and Purposes whatsoever.

Another example is the Plantation Act 1740:[15]

> [A]ll persons born out of the legience of His Majesty, His Heirs, or Successors, who have . . . or shall inhabit or reside for . . . seven years or more in any of His Majesty's colonies in America . . . shall be deemed, adjudged, and taken to be His Majesty's natural-born subjects of this Kingdom.

The famed jurist William Blackstone wrote in 1765 that inhabitants born within England may be natural-born subjects: "Natural-born subjects are such as are born within the dominions of the crown of England...."[12][16] Blackstone added that offspring who are not inhabitants may also be natural born subjects:[16][17]

> But by several more modern statutes ... all children, born out of the king's ligeance, whose fathers were natural-born subjects, are now natural-born subjects themselves, to all intents and purposes, without any exception; unless their said fathers were attainted, or banished beyond sea, for high treason; or were then in the service of a prince at enmity with Great Britain.

A leading authority in England prior to Blackstone was Edward Coke, who wrote about this subject in *Calvin's Case*.[18] According to Coke: "[I]f any of the King's ambassadors in foreign nations, have children there of their wives, being English women, by the common laws of England they are natural-born subjects, and yet they are born out-of the King's dominions."[19]

The term "natural born" has often been used synonymously with "native born".[20] The English lexicographer Samuel Johnson wrote in 1756 that the word "natural" means "native," and that the word "native" may mean either an "inhabitant" or an "offspring".[21]

### 9.2.2 Between 1776 and 1789

From the Declaration of Independence (1776) to the ratification of the Constitution (1789), the thirteen states were independent of England, and during much of this time the Articles of Confederation tied together the country. The phrase "natural born citizen" was sometimes used during this period. A notable example occurred in 1784 when the Maryland General Assembly conferred citizenship on the (French-born) Marquis de Lafayette and his descendents, in these words (emphasis added):[22][23][24]

> Be it enacted by the General Assembly of Maryland—that the Marquiss de la Fayette and his Heirs male forever shall be and they and each of them are hereby deemed adjudged and taken to be ***natural born Citizens*** of this State and shall henceforth be intitled to all the Immunities, Rights and Privileges of natural born Citizens thereof…

### 9.2.3 Constitutional Convention

The Constitution does not explain the meaning of "natural born".[25] On June 18, 1787, Alexander Hamilton submitted to the Convention a sketch of a plan of government.[26] The sketch provided for an executive "Governour" but had no eligibility requirements.[27] At the close of the Convention, Hamilton conveyed a paper to James Madison he said delineated the Constitution that he wished had been proposed by the Convention; he had stated its principles during the deliberations. Max Farrand wrote that it "...was not submitted to the Convention and has no further value than attaches to the personal opinions of Hamilton."[28] Article IX, section 1 of Hamilton's draft constitution provided: "No person shall be eligible to the office of President of the United States unless he be now a Citizen of one of the States, or hereafter be born a Citizen of the United States."[29]

On July 25, 1787, John Jay wrote to George Washington, presiding officer of the Convention:

> Permit me to hint, whether it would not be wise and seasonable to provide a strong check to the admission of Foreigners into the administration of our national Government, and to declare expressly that the Command in chief of the American army shall not be given to, nor devolve on, any but a natural born Citizen.[30]

While the Committee of Detail originally proposed that the President must be merely a citizen, as well as a resident for 21 years, the Committee of Eleven changed "citizen" to "natural born citizen", and the residency requirement to 14 years, without recorded explanation after receiving Jay's letter. The Convention accepted the change without further recorded debate.[32]

### 9.2.4 Constitutionality of the natural-born-citizen clause

In 2012, Abdul Karim Hassan filed several unsuccessful lawsuits claiming the natural-born-citizen clause violated the Equal Protection Clause of the Fourteenth Amendment, arguing it was a form of discrimination based on national origin.[33]

### 9.2.5 Proposed constitutional amendments

More than two dozen proposed constitutional amendments have been introduced in Congress to relax the restriction.[34] Two of the more well known were introduced by Representative Jonathan Bingham in 1974, with the intent to allow German-born Secretary of State Henry Kissinger (otherwise fourth in the line of succession) to become eligible,[35] and the Equal Opportunity to Govern Amendment by Senator Orrin Hatch in 2003, intending to allow eligibility for Austrian-born Arnold Schwarzenegger.[34] The Bingham amendment would have also made clear the eligibility of those born abroad to U.S. parents,[35] while the Hatch one would have allowed those who have been naturalized citizens for twenty years to be eligible.[34]

## 9.3 Rationale

St. George Tucker, an early federal judge, wrote in his 1803 edition of William Blackstone's *Commentaries on the Laws of England*, perhaps the leading authority for the delegates to the Constitutional Convention for the terms used

in the Constitution, that the natural born citizen clause is "a happy means of security against foreign influence" and that "[t]he admission of foreigners into our councils, consequently, cannot be too much guarded against."[36] In a footnote, Tucker wrote that naturalized citizens have the same rights as the natural-born except "they are forever incapable of being chosen to the office of president of the United States."[37]

In a speech before the Senate, delegate Charles Cotesworth Pinckney gave the rationale, "to insure experience and attachment to the country."[38]

Professor Akhil Amar of Yale Law School indicated that there was also a perception that a usurper from the European aristocracy could potentially immigrate and buy his way into power.[39]

## 9.4 Interpretations of the clause

### 9.4.1 Naturalization Acts of 1790 and 1795

Although Congress alone cannot change the meaning of the U.S. Constitution, given the number of Framers who then went on to serve in Congress, laws passed by the early sessions of Congress are often looked to as evidence of the Framers' intent. The Naturalization Act of 1790 stated that "the children of citizens of the United States, that may be born beyond sea, or out of the limits of the United States, shall be considered as natural born citizens: Provided, That the right of citizenship shall not descend to persons whose fathers have never been resident in the United States."[40] This act was repealed by the Naturalization Act of 1795, which removed the characterization of such children as "natural born," stating that "the children of citizens of the United States, born out of the limits and jurisdiction of the United States, shall be considered as citizens of the United States" while retaining the same residency restrictions as the 1790 act.[40]

Current State Department regulation concerning the Naturalization Act of 1790 reads: "This statute is no longer operative, however, and its formula is not included in modern nationality statutes. In any event, the fact that someone is a natural born citizen pursuant to a statute does not necessarily imply that he or she is such a citizen for Constitutional purposes."[41]

### 9.4.2 Government officials' interpretations

**1800s**

John Bingham, an American lawyer and politician, held to

the belief that natural born should be interpreted as born in the United States. In 1862, in the House of Representatives he stated:

> The Constitution leaves no room for doubt upon this subject. The words 'natural born citizen of the United States' appear in it, and the other provision appears in it that, "Congress shall have power to pass a uniform system of naturalization." To naturalize a person is to admit him to citizenship. Who are *natural born citizens* but those born within the Republic? Those born within the Republic, whether black or white, are citizens by birth—natural born citizens.[42]

He reiterated his statement in 1866:

> Every human being born within the jurisdiction of the United States of parents not owing allegiance to any foreign sovereignty is, in the language of your Constitution itself, a natural-born citizen; but, sir, I may be allowed to say further that I deny that the Congress of the United States ever had the power, or color of power to say that any man born within the jurisdiction of the United States, not owing a foreign allegiance, is not and shall not be a citizen of the United States. Citizenship is his birthright and neither the Congress nor the States can justly or lawfully take it from him.[43]

Edward Bates also held to the belief that natural born should be interpreted as born in the United States. He also indicated that those born in the United States to alien parents, even if they reside elsewhere, are still considered natural born. In 1862, Secretary of the Treasury Salmon P. Chase sent a query to Attorney General Edward Bates asking whether or not "colored men" can be citizens of the United States. The question arose because the Coast Guard had detained a schooner commanded by a free "colored man" who claimed he was a citizen of the United States. If he were a U.S. citizen the boat could be released, but otherwise— the Civil War then being fought—it would be confiscated. No information about the man's birth or parentage was provided. Bates responded on November 29, 1862, with a 27-page opinion — considered of such importance that the government published it not only in the official volumes of Attorney-General opinions but also as a separate booklet [44] — concluding,

> I conclude that the *free man of color*, mentioned in your letter, if born in the *United States*, is a citizen of the United States..... [italics in original]

In the course of that opinion, Bates commented at some length on the nature of citizenship, and wrote,

> ... our constitution, in speaking of *natural born citizens*, uses no affirmative language to make them such, but only recognizes and reaffirms the universal principle, common to all nations, and as old as political society, that the people born in a country do constitute the nation, and, as individuals, are *natural* members of the body politic. [italics in original]

In another opinion, dated September 1, 1862,[45] Bates dealt with a question from the Secretary of State, of whether a person born in the U.S. to two non-citizens, who is taken with them back to their country, could, years later, re-enter the United States as of right, as a U.S. citizen. Bates wrote:

> I am quite clear in the opinion that children born in the United States of alien parents, who have never been naturalized, are native-born citizens of the United States, and, of course, do not require the formality of naturalization to entitle them to the rights and privileges of such citizenship. I might sustain this opinion by a reference to the well-settled principle of the common law of England on this subject; to the writings of many of the earlier and later commentators on our Constitution and laws; ... and lastly to the dicta and decisions of many of our national and state tribunals. But all this has been well done by Assistant Vice Chancellor Sandford, in the case of *Lynch vs. Clarke*, and I forbear. I refer to his opinion for a full and clear statement of the principle, and of the reasons and authorities for its support.

Unlike Edward Bates, U.S. Secretary of State William Learned Marcy was equivocal about whether those born in the country of alien parents and who reside elsewhere are still considered citizens. In 1854 Marcy wrote John Y. Mason, the U.S. Minister to France:[46]

> In reply to the inquiry ... whether "the children of foreign parents *born in the United States*, but brought to the country of which the father is a subject, and continuing to reside within the jurisdiction of their father's country, are entitled to protection as citizens of the United States", I have to observe that it is presumed that, according to the common law, any person born in the United States, unless he be born in one of the foreign legations therein, may be considered a citizen thereof until he formally renounces his citizenship. There is not, however any United States

statute containing a provision upon this subject, nor, so far as I am aware, has there been any judicial decision in regard to it.

U.S. Attorney General Edwards Pierrepont, however, shared Edward Bates' opinion that those born in the country of alien parents and who reside elsewhere are still considered citizens, and he added that they should be entitled to be president of the United States, if elected. In 1875 Pierrepont was presented with a query from the Secretary of State, Hamilton Fish. A young man, named Arthur Steinkauler,[47] had been born in Missouri in 1855, a year after his father was naturalized a U.S. citizen. When he was four years old, his father returned to Germany with him and both had stayed there ever since. The father had relinquished his American citizenship and the young man was now 20 years old and about to be drafted into the Imperial German army. The question was asked "What was this young man's situation as a native-born American citizen?" After studying the relevant legal authorities, Pierrepont wrote:[48]

> Under the treaty [of 1868 with Germany], and in harmony with American doctrine, it is clear that Steinkauler the father abandoned his naturalization in America and became a German subject (his son being yet a minor), and that by virtue of German laws the son acquired German nationality. It is equally clear that the son, by birth, has American nationality, and hence he has two nationalities, one natural, the other acquired... Young Steinkauler is a native-born American citizen. There is no law of the United States under which his father or any other person can deprive him of his birthright. He can return to America at the age of 21, and in due time, if the people elect, he can become President of the United States .... I am of opinion that when he reaches the age of 21 years he can then elect whether he will return and take the nationality of his birth, with its duties and privileges, or retain the nationality acquired by the act of his father.

**1900s**

Frederick van Dyne, the Assistant Solicitor of the U.S. Department of State (1900–1907) indicated that children of citizens born outside the United States are also considered citizens. In 1904, he published a textbook, *Citizenship of the United States*, in which he wrote:[49]

> There is no uniform rule of international law covering the subject of citizenship. Every nation determines for itself who shall, and who

shall not, be its citizens.... By the law of the United States, citizenship depends, generally, on the place of birth; nevertheless the children of citizens, born out of the jurisdiction of the United States, are also citizens.... The Constitution of the United States, while it recognized citizenship of the United States in prescribing the qualifications of the President, Senators, and Representatives, contained no definition of citizenship until the adoption of the 14th Amendment, in 1868; nor did Congress attempt to define it until the passage of the civil rights act, in 1866.... Prior to this time the subject of citizenship by birth was generally held to be regulated by the common law, by which all persons born within the limits and allegiance of the United States were deemed natural-born citizens.

> It appears to have been assumed by the Supreme Court of the United States in the case of *Murray v. The Charming Betsy* (1804) 2 Cranch (6 U.S.) 64, 119, 2 L.Ed. 208, 226, that all persons born in the United States were citizens thereof. ... In *M'Creery v. Somerville* (1824) 9 Wheat. (22 U.S.) 354, 6 L.Ed. 109, which concerned the title to land in the state of Maryland, it was assumed that children born in that state to an alien were native-born citizens of the United States. .... The Federal courts have almost uniformly held that birth in the United States, of itself, confers citizenship.

### 9.4.3 Interpretations by the courts

**1800s**

Although eligibility for the Presidency was not an issue in any 19th-century litigation, there have been a few cases that shed light on the definitions of *natural born* and *native born* citizen. The leading case, *Lynch v. Clarke*[50] of 1844, indicated that citizens born "within the dominions and allegiance of the United States" are citizens regardless of parental citizenship. This case dealt with a New York law (similar to laws of other states at that time) that only a U.S. citizen could inherit real estate. The plaintiff, Julia Lynch, had been born in New York while her parents, both British, were briefly visiting the U.S., and shortly thereafter all three left for Britain and never returned to the U.S. The New York Chancery Court determined that, under common law and prevailing statutes, she was a U.S. citizen by birth and nothing had deprived her of that citizenship, notwithstanding that both her parents were not U.S. citizens or that British law might also claim her through her parents' nationality. In the course of the decision, the court cited the Constitutional provision and said:

> Suppose a person should be elected president who was native born, but of alien parents; could there be any reasonable doubt that he was eligible under the Constitution? I think not. The position would be decisive in his favor, that by the rule of the common law, in force when the Constitution was adopted, he is a citizen.[51]

And further:

> Upon principle, therefore, I can entertain no doubt, but that by the law of the United States, every person born within the dominions and allegiance of the United States, whatever the situation of his parents, is a natural born citizen. It is surprising that there has been no judicial decision upon this question.[52]

The decision in *Lynch* was cited as persuasive or authoritative precedent in numerous subsequent cases, and reinforced the interpretation that "natural born citizen" meant born "within the dominions and allegiance of the United States" regardless of parental citizenship. For example, in an 1884 case, *In re Look Tin Singg*,[53] the federal court held, that despite laws preventing naturalization of Chinese visitors, Chinese persons born in the United States were citizens by birth, and remained such despite any long stay in China, citing *Lynch* Justice Stephen J. Field wrote:

> After an exhaustive examination of the law, the Vice-Chancellor said that he entertained no doubt that every person born within the dominions and allegiance of the United States, whatever the situation of his parents, was a natural-born citizen, and added that this was the general understanding of the legal profession, and the universal impression of the public mind.[54]

The *Lynch* case was also cited as a leading precedent in the U.S. Supreme Court decision in *United States v. Wong Kim Ark* (1898),[55] which similarly held a child born in the United States of two Chinese parents was a "natural born" U.S. citizen.[56]

### 1900s

Consistent with the earlier decisions, in 1939, the U.S. Supreme Court stated in its decision in *Perkins v. Elg*, that a person born in America and raised in another country was a natural born citizen, and specifically stated that they could "become President of the United States".[57] The case was regarding a young woman, born in New York a year after her father became a naturalized U.S. citizen. However, when she was about four her parents returned to Sweden taking her with them, and they stayed in Sweden. At age 20, she contacted the American embassy in Sweden and, shortly after her 21st birthday, returned to the United States on a U.S. passport and was admitted as a U.S. citizen. Years later, while she was still in America, her father in Sweden relinquished his American citizenship, and, because of that, the Department of Labor (then the location of the Immigration & Naturalization Service) declared her a non-citizen and tried to deport her. The young woman filed suit for a declaratory judgment that she was an American citizen by birth. She won at the trial level, and at the circuit court—where she was repeatedly described as "a natural born citizen" [58] — and finally in the U.S. Supreme Court, where the court decision quoted at length from the U.S. Attorney General's opinion in *Steinkauler's Case* (mentioned above) including the comment that a person born in America and raised in another country could yet "become President of the United States".[57]

Some federal cases argued for a narrow reading of the Fourteenth Amendment, according to which U.S. citizens were necessarily either born or naturalized in the United States, and any citizen who was not born in the United States must have been naturalized by operation of law, even if such naturalization was "automatic" at birth. In this view, such a person should not be considered a natural born citizen, but rather a "naturalized" citizen who is not eligible for the Presidency.[59]

In 1951, the U.S. Court of Appeals for the Tenth Circuit noted in *Zimmer v. Acheson* that "[t]here are only two classes of citizens of the United States, native-born citizens and naturalized citizens", quoting a dictum by Justice Gray from United States v. Wong Kim Ark and Elk v. Wilkins.[6] The court ruled that Zimmer, who was born abroad in 1905 to a U.S. citizen father and a noncitizen mother, was himself a citizen under the nationality law in force at the time of his birth, but "his status as a citizen was that of a naturalized citizen and not a native-born citizen".[60] In the 1956 case of *Wong Kam Wo v. Dulles*, the U.S. Court of Appeals for the Ninth Circuit quoted *Zimmer v. Acheson* and *United States v. Wong Kim Ark* in support of a ruling that the statute that was in effect prior to 1940 granting citizenship to foreign-born children of U.S. citizens was a naturalization law rather than a provision for nationality at birth. In 1940, however, the federal law was amended to explicitly define "naturalization" as conferring nationality *after* birth.

In 1961, the U.S. Supreme Court ruled in *Montana v. Kennedy* that an individual who was born in 1906 in Italy to a U.S. citizen mother and a noncitizen father was not a U.S. citizen by birth under the nationality laws in force at the time of his birth. It observed that automatic citizenship was granted to children of U.S. citizen fathers and noncitizen mothers by a 1855 act of Congress, but the reverse situation was only addressed, non-retroactively, in 1934.[61] In 1971, the Court encountered a similar situation in Rogers v. Bellei, where the individual in question was born after 1934 and so was granted automatic U.S. citizenship, though subject to residence requirements and was subject to expatriation. The Court "appeared to assume or imply that such persons became citizens at birth by way of naturalization".[59]

More recent cases, particularly Nguyen v. INS and *Robinson v. Bowen*, relaxed this view, suggesting that the Fourteenth Amendment merely establishes a "floor" for birthright citizenship, and this category may be expanded by Congress.[59]

### 2000s

In 2009 in *Ankeny v. Governor*,[62] the Indiana Court of Appeals reaffirmed that persons born within the borders of the United States are "natural born Citizens", regardless of the citizenship of their parents. The court referred to the case of Wong Kim Ark, and provides a compilation of the arguments pertaining to this topic.

A clarification to this interpretation was made in 2010, where a three-judge panel of the United States court of appeals for the Fifth Circuit held that natural born citizens can lose their citizenship if their territory of birth later ceases to be U.S. territory. The case involved a Philippine-born litigant who could not claim U.S. citizenship on the basis of his parents, who lived all their lives in the Philippines, because they were born while the Philippines was U.S. territory prior to being given its independence. The Courts for the Second, Third, and Ninth Circuits have also held that birth in the Philippines at a time when the country was a territory of the United States does not constitute birth "in the United States" under the Citizenship Clause, and thus did not give rise to United States citizenship.[63]

In a 2012 New York case, Strunk v. N.Y. State Board of Elections,[4] the *pro se* plaintiff challenged Obama's presence on the presidential ballot, based on his own interpretation that "natural born citizen" required the president "to have been born on United States soil *and* have *two* United States *born* parents." (emphasis added) To which the Court responded, "Article II, section 1, clause 5 does not state this. No legal authority has ever stated that the Natural Born Citizen clause means what plaintiff Strunk claims it says. .... Moreover, President Obama is the sixth U.S. President to have had one or both of his parents not born on U.S. soil." [listing Andrew Jackson, James Buchanan, Chester A. Arthur, Woodrow Wilson, and Herbert Hoover].[4]

## 9.4.4   Academic interpretations

### 1800s

William Rawle, formerly the U.S. Attorney for Pennsylvania (1791–1799) defined *natural born citizen* as every person born within the United States, regardless of the citizenship of their parents. In an 1825 treatise, *A View of the Constitution of the United States of America*, he wrote:

> The citizens of each state constituted the citizens of the United States when the Constitution was adopted. ... [He] who was subsequently born the citizen of a State, became at the moment of his birth a citizen of the United States. Therefore every person born within the United States, its territories or districts, whether the parents are citizens or aliens, is a natural born citizen in the sense of the Constitution, and entitled to all the rights and privileges appertaining to that capacity. ... Under our Constitution the question is settled by its express language, and when we are informed...no person is eligible to the office of President unless he is a natural born citizen, the principle that the place of birth creates the relative quality is established as to us.[64]

James F. Wilson agreed with Rawle's opinion, but added the exclusion of visiting foreign diplomats. During an 1866 House debate, he quoted Rawle's opinion, and also referred to the "general law relating to subjects and citizens recognized by all nations" saying:

> ...and that must lead us to the conclusion that every person born in the United States is a natural-born citizen of such States, except it may be that children born on our soil to temporary sojourners or representatives of foreign Governments, are native-born citizens of the United States.[65]

Supreme Court Justice Peter Vivian Daniel disagreed with this position and considered *natural born citizen* as every person born of citizen parents within the United States. In 1857, in a concurring opinion in *Dred Scott v. Sandford*,[66] he quoted an English-language translation of Emerich de Vattel's 1758 treatise *The Law of Nations* (*Le Droit des gens*), stating that "The natives, or natural-born citizens, are those born in the country of parents who are citizens".[67]

This was quoted again in 1898 by Chief Justice Melville Fuller in his dissenting opinion in *United States v. Wong Kim Ark*.[68] However, two paragraphs later, Justice Vattel disagrees and states, "§ 214. ... there are states, as, for instance, England, where the single circumstance of being born in the country naturalizes the children of a foreigner."

Joseph Story, an Associate Justice of the U.S. Supreme Court, believed that the term *native citizen* is synonymous with natural born citizen, though he does not define either term. In his 1840 guidebook to the Constitution, *A Familiar Exposition of the Constitution of the United States*, about the natural-born-citizen clause he wrote "It is not too much to say that no one, but a native citizen, ought ordinarily to be [e]ntrusted with an office so vital to the safety and liberties of the people."[69] This same wording also appeared in his 1834 work *The constitutional class book: being a brief exposition of the Constitution of the United States: Designed for the use of the higher classes in common schools.*[70]

## 1900s

Alexander Porter Morse, the lawyer who represented Louisiana in Plessy v. Ferguson,[71] considered this connection between *native born* and *natural born* to signify that only a child of citizens should be allowed to run for President. In the *Albany Law Journal*, he wrote:

> If it was intended that anybody who was a citizen by birth should be eligible, it would only have been necessary to say, "no person, except a native-born citizen"; but the framers thought it wise, in view of the probable influx of European immigration, to provide that the president should at least be the child of citizens owing allegiance to the United States at the time of his birth. It may be observed in passing that the current phrase "native-born citizen" is well understood; but it is pleonasm and should be discarded; and the correct designation, "native citizen" should be substituted in all constitutional and statutory enactments, in judicial decisions and in legal discussions where accuracy and precise language are essential to intelligent discussion.[72]

## 2000s

*Black's Law Dictionary* (9th Edition) defines "Natural Born Citizen" as "A person born within the jurisdiction of a national government".

**Foreign soil**   In 2000, the Congressional Research Service (CRS), in one of its reports, wrote that most constitutional scholars interpret the natural born citizen clause to include citizens born outside the United States to parents who are U.S. citizens. This same CRS report also asserts that citizens born in the District of Columbia, Guam, Puerto Rico,

and the U.S. Virgin Islands, are legally defined as "natural born" citizens and are, therefore, also eligible to be elected President.[73]

This opinion was reaffirmed in a 2009 CRS report, which stated:

> Considering the history of the constitutional qualifications provision, the common use and meaning of the phrase "natural-born subject" in England and in the Colonies in the 1700s, the clause's apparent intent, the subsequent action of the first Congress in enacting the Naturalization Act of 1790 (expressly defining the term "natural born citizen" to include a person born abroad to parents who are United States citizens), as well as subsequent Supreme Court dicta, it appears that the most logical inferences would indicate that the phrase "natural born Citizen" would mean a person who is entitled to U.S. citizenship "at birth" or "by birth".[74]

This interpretation of natural born being the equivalent of citizen at birth (not naturalized) was again in a 2011 CRS report and a 2016 CRS report. The 2011 report stated:

> The weight of legal and historical authority indicates that the term "natural born" citizen would mean a person who is entitled to U.S. citizenship "by birth" or "at birth," either by being born "in" the United States and under its jurisdiction, even those born to alien parents; by being born abroad to U.S. citizen-parents; or by being born in other situations meeting legal requirements for U.S. citizenship "at birth." Such term, however, would not include a person who was not a U.S. citizen by birth or at birth, and who was thus born an "alien" required to go through the legal process of "naturalization" to become a U.S. citizen.[3]

The 2016 report similarly stated:

> Although the eligibility of U.S. born citizens has been settled law for more than a century, there have been legitimate legal issues raised concerning those born *outside* of the country to U.S. citizens. From historical material and case law, it appears that the common understanding of the term "natural born" in England and in the American colonies in the 1700s included both the strict common law meaning as born in the territory (*jus soli*), as well as the *statutory* laws adopted in England since at least 1350, which included children

born abroad to British fathers (*jus sanguinis*, the law of descent). Legal scholars in the field of citizenship have asserted that this common understanding and legal meaning in England and in the American colonies was incorporated into the usage and intent of the term in the U.S. Constitution to include those who are citizens at birth.[59]

Gabriel J. Chin, Professor of Law at UC Davis School of Law, held the opinion that the term natural born is ambiguous and citizen granting authority has changed over the years. He notes that persons born outside the United States to U.S.-citizen parents have not always been born citizens.[75][76] For example, foreign-born children of persons who became naturalized citizens between April 14, 1802 and 1854, were considered aliens. He also believed that children born in the Panama Canal Zone to at least one U.S. then-citizen between May 24, 1934, and August 4, 1937, when Congress granted citizenship to all such persons, were born without American citizenship. As a result, Chin argues, such persons (for constitutional and political purposes, most notably 2008 U.S. presidential candidate John McCain, born in the Canal Zone on August 28, 1936) may be considered "natural born" only if both parents were citizens.

1.  Congress possesses the authority either

    - to grant not only citizenship (as is undisputed) but the more specific status of a "natural born" citizen, with an affirmative answer raising the question of whether it can also act to *remove* that status (and thereby disqualify individuals from the Presidency through action short of stripping them of their citizenship),

      or

    - to issue "declarations" regarding the meaning of preexisting law (in this case, U.S. citizenship law between the aforementioned dates) and having binding authority, a claim likely to violate separation of powers given the Constitution's provisions in Article III that "[t]he judicial Power of the United States[] shall be vested in one supreme Court[] and in such inferior Courts as the Congress may from time to time ordain and establish" (Section 1) and that "[t]he judicial power shall extend to all cases, in law and equity, arising under this Constitution, the laws of the United States, and

treaties made, or which shall be made, under their authority" (Section 2)

and

2.  the statute (currently codified at 8 U.S.C. § 1403[a]) – which states only that "any person [fitting the above description] is declared to be a citizen of the United States" and neither

    - expressly claims that its declaration (whether a grant or an interpretation) has retroactive rather than merely prospective effect (contrast the locution "to have been a citizen of the United States [from birth]")

      nor

    - in any way mentions "natural born" status (instead conferring or recognizing the preexistence only of "citizen[ship]" generally) –

        in fact grants or recognizes citizenship from birth, let alone status as a natural born citizen (to whatever extent the requirements of that status exceed those for citizenship from birth).

In 2009, G. Edward "Ted" White, Professor of Law at the University of Virginia, stated the term refers to anyone born on U.S. soil *or* anyone born on foreign soil to American citizen parents.[77]

Unlike Chin and White, Mary McManamon, Professor of Law at Widener University School of Law, has argued in the *Catholic University Law Review* that, aside from children born to foreign ambassadors or to hostile soldiers on U.S. territory, both of whom owe allegiance to a different sovereign, a natural born citizen must be born in the United States. She claims that common law provides an exception for the children of U.S. ambassadors born abroad and the children of American soldiers while engaged in hostilities. Thus, with these two limited exceptions, she equates "natural born" with "native born".[78][79]

Professor Einer Elhauge of Harvard Law School agrees with Professor McManamon that "natural born" means "native born" and therefore the wording of the Constitution "does not permit his (Ted Cruz's) candidacy."[80] Professor Robert Clinton at the Sandra Day O'Connor College of Law at Arizona State University is also of the opinion that "natural born citizen" means "born in the United States."[81] University of Chicago Professor Eric Posner also concludes that "natural born citizen" means a "person born in the

(United States)".[82] Former Chief Justice of the New York Court of Appeals, Sol Wachtler, concludes the same.[83]

**American soil**    There is consensus among academics that those born on American soil are natural born citizens, or *jus soli*, regardless of parental citizenship status.

In a 2008 article published by the *Michigan Law Review*, Lawrence Solum, Professor of Law at the University of Illinois, stated that "there is general agreement on the core of [the] meaning [of the Presidential Eligibility Clause]. Anyone born on American soil whose parents are citizens of the United States is a 'natural born citizen'".[84] In April 2010, Solum republished the same article as an online draft, in which he clarified his original statement so that it would not be misunderstood as excluding the children of one citizen parent. In a footnote he explained, "based on my reading of the historical sources, there is no credible case that a person born on American soil with one American parent was clearly not a 'natural born citizen'." He further extended natural born citizenship to all cases of *jus soli* as the "conventional view".[85] Although Solum stated elsewhere that the two-citizen-parents arguments weren't "crazy", he believes "the much stronger argument suggests that if you were born on American soil that you would be considered a natural born citizen."[86]

Ronald Rotunda, Professor of Law at Chapman University, has remarked "There's [*sic*] some people who say that both parents need to be citizens. That's never been the law."[87]

Polly Price, Professor of Law at Emory University, has commented "It's a little confusing, but most scholars think it's a pretty unusual position for anyone to think the natural born citizen clause would exclude someone born in the U.S."[86]

Chin concurred with that assessment, stating, "there is agreement that 'natural born citizens' include those made citizens by birth under the 14th Amendment."[88]

Similarly, Eugene Volokh, Professor of Law at UCLA, found "quite persuasive" the reasoning employed by the Indiana Court of Appeals, which had concluded "that persons born within the borders of the United States are 'natural born Citizens' for Article II, Section 1 purposes, regardless of the citizenship of their parents".[89][90]

Daniel Tokaji, Professor of Law at Ohio State University, agrees the citizenship status of a U.S.-born candidate's parents is irrelevant.[91]

## 9.5 Eligibility challenges

Several courts have ruled that private citizens do not have standing to challenge the eligibility of candidates to appear on a presidential election ballot.[92] Alternatively, there is a statutory method by which the eligibility of the president-elect of the United States to take office may be challenged in Congress.[93] Some legal scholars assert that, even if eligibility challenges are nonjusticiable in federal courts, and are not undertaken in Congress, there are other avenues for adjudication, such as an action in state court in regard to ballot access.[5][6]

Every president to date was either a citizen at the adoption of the Constitution in 1789 or born in the United States; of those in the latter group, every president except two (Chester A. Arthur and Barack Obama) had two U.S.-citizen parents. Further, four additional U.S. Presidents had one or both of his parents not born on U.S. soil (Andrew Jackson, James Buchanan, Woodrow Wilson and Herbert Hoover).[4]

Some presidential candidates were not born in a U.S. state or lacked two U.S.-citizen parents.[94] In addition, one U.S. vice president (Al Gore) was born in Washington, D.C., and another (Charles Curtis) was born in the Kansas Territory. This does not necessarily mean that these officeholders or candidates were ineligible, only that there was some controversy about their eligibility, which may have been resolved in favor of eligibility.[95]

### 9.5.1    1800s

#### Chester A. Arthur

Chester A. Arthur was rumored to have been born in Canada.[96] His mother, Malvina Stone Arthur, while a native of Berkshire, Vermont, moved with her family to Quebec, where she met and married the future president's father, William Arthur, on April 12, 1821. After the family had settled in Fairfield, Vermont, William Arthur traveled with his eldest daughter to East Stanbridge, Canada, in October 1830 and commuted to Fairfield on Sundays to preach. "It appears that he traveled regularly between the two villages, both of which were close to the Canadian border, for about eighteen months, holding two jobs",[97] which may well explain the confusion about Arthur's place of birth, as perhaps did the fact that he was born in Franklin County, and thus literally within a day's walk of the Vermont–Quebec border.[98] This was never demonstrated by his Democratic opponents, although Arthur Hinman, an attorney who had investigated Arthur's family history, raised the objection during his vice-presidential campaign and after the end of his presidency, published a book on the subject.[99]

Arthur was born in Vermont to a Vermont-born mother and a father from Ireland, who was naturalized as a U.S. citizen in 1843, 14 years after Chester was born. Despite the fact that his parents took up residence in the United States somewhere between 1822 and 1824, Arthur additionally began to claim between 1870 and 1880[100] that he had been born in 1830, rather than in 1829, which only caused minor confusion and was even used in several publications.[101] Arthur was sworn in as president when President Garfield died after being shot.

### 9.5.2   1900s

#### Christopher Schürmann

Christopher Schürmann (born in New York City) entered the Labor primaries during the 1896 presidential election. His eligibility was questioned in a *New York Tribune* article, because he was born to parents of German nationality. It was stated that "various Attorney-Generals (*sic*) of the United States have expressed the opinion that a child born in this country of alien parents, who have (*sic*) not been naturalized, is, by the fact of birth, a native-born citizen entitled to all rights and privileges as such." But due to a lack of any statute on the subject, Schürmann's eligibility was, "at best an open question, and one which should have made [his] nomination under any circumstances an impossibility," because questions concerning his eligibility could have been raised after the election.[102]

#### Charles Evans Hughes

The eligibility of Charles Evans Hughes was questioned in an article written by Breckinridge Long, one of Woodrow Wilson's campaign workers, and published on December 7, 1916 in the *Chicago Legal News* — a full month *after* the U.S. presidential election of 1916, in which Hughes was narrowly defeated by Woodrow Wilson. Long claimed that Hughes was ineligible because his father was not yet naturalized at the time of his birth and was still a British citizen (in fact, both his parents were British citizens and never became U.S. citizens). Observing that Hughes, although born in the United States, was also (according to British law) a British subject and therefore "enjoy[ed] a dual nationality and owe[d] a double allegiance", Long argued that a *native born* citizen was not *natural born* without a unity of U.S. citizenship and allegiance and stated: "Now if, by any possible construction, a person at the instant of birth, and for any period of time thereafter, owes, or may owe, allegiance to any sovereign but the United States, he is not a 'natural-born' citizen of the United States." [103]

#### Barry Goldwater

Barry Goldwater was born in Phoenix, in what was then the incorporated Arizona Territory of the United States. During his presidential campaign in 1964, there was a minor controversy over Goldwater's having been born in Arizona three years before it became a state.[96]

#### George Romney

George W. Romney, who ran for the Republican party presidential nomination in 1968, was born in Mexico to U.S. parents.[104][105] Romney's grandfather had immigrated to Mexico in 1886 with his three wives and their children, after the U.S. federal government outlawed polygamy. However Romney's parents (monogamous under new church doctrine) retained their U.S. citizenship and returned to the United States with him and his siblings in 1912.[106] Romney's eligibility for President became moot when Richard Nixon was nominated as the Republican presidential candidate.

#### Lowell Weicker

Lowell P. Weicker entered the race for the Republican party nomination of 1980 but dropped out before voting in the primaries began; he was also suggested as a possible vice-president candidate in 1976. He was born in Paris, France, to parents who were U.S. citizens. His father was an executive for E. R. Squibb & Sons and his mother was the Indian-born daughter of a British general.[105][107]

### 9.5.3   2000s

#### John McCain

John McCain was born in 1936 at Coco Solo Naval Air Station[94][108][109][110][111][112][113] in the Panama Canal Zone. McCain's eligibility was not challenged during his 2000 campaign, but it was challenged during his 2008 campaign.

McCain never released his birth certificate to the press or independent fact-checking organizations, but in 2008 did show it to *Washington Post* reporter Michael Dobbs, who wrote, "[A] senior official of the McCain campaign showed me a copy of [McCain's] birth certificate issued by the 'family hospital' in the Coco Solo submarine base."[110] A lawsuit filed by Fred Hollander in 2008 alleged McCain was actually born in a civilian hospital in Colón, Panama.[114][115] Dobbs wrote that in his autobiography, *Faith of My Fathers*, McCain wrote that he was born "in the Canal Zone" at the U.S. Naval Air Station in Coco Solo, which was under the command of his grandfather, John S. McCain Sr.

"The senator's father, John S. McCain Jr., was an executive officer on a submarine, also based in Coco Solo. His mother, Roberta McCain, has said that she has vivid memories of lying in bed listening to raucous celebrations of her son's birth from the nearby officers' club. The birth was announced days later in the English-language Panamanian American newspaper."[116][117][118][119]

The former unincorporated territory of the Panama Canal Zone and its related military facilities were not regarded as United States territory at the time,[120] but 8 U.S.C. § 1403, which became law in 1937, retroactively conferred citizenship on individuals born within the Canal Zone on or after February 26, 1904, and on individuals born in the Republic of Panama on or after that date who had at least one U.S. citizen parent employed by the U.S. government or the Panama Railway Company; 8 U.S.C. § 1403 was cited in Judge William Alsup's 2008 ruling, described below. A March 2008 paper by former Solicitor General Ted Olson and Harvard Law Professor Laurence H. Tribe opined that McCain was eligible for the Presidency.[121] In April 2008, the U.S. Senate approved a non-binding resolution recognizing McCain's status as a natural-born citizen.[122] In September 2008, U.S. District Judge William Alsup stated *obiter* in his ruling that it is "highly probable" that McCain is a natural-born citizen from birth by virtue of 8 U.S.C. § 1401, although he acknowledged the alternative possibility that McCain became a natural-born citizen retroactively, by way of 8 U.S.C. § 1403.[123]

These views have been criticized by Chin, who argues that McCain was at birth a citizen of Panama and was only retroactively declared a born citizen under 8 U.S.C. § 1403, because at the time of his birth and with regard to the Canal Zone the Supreme Court's Insular Cases overruled the Naturalization Act of 1795, which would otherwise have declared McCain a U.S. citizen immediately at birth.[124] The U.S. State Department's *Foreign Affairs Manual* states that children born in the Panama Canal Zone at certain times became U.S. nationals without citizenship.[125] It also states in general that "it has never been determined definitively by a court whether a person who acquired U.S. citizenship by birth abroad to U.S. citizens is a natural-born citizen [...]".[126] In *Rogers v. Bellei*, the Supreme Court ruled that children "born abroad of American parents" are not citizens within the citizenship clause of the 14th Amendment but did not elaborate on their *natural-born* status.[127][128] Similarly, legal scholar Lawrence Solum concluded in an article on the *natural born citizen* clause that the question of McCain's eligibility could not be answered with certainty, and that it would depend on the particular approach of "constitutional construction".[129] The urban legend fact checking website Snopes.com considers McCain's eligibility "undetermined".[130]

Arguments over McCain's eligibility became moot after he lost the United States presidential election in 2008.

**Barack Obama**

Main article: Barack Obama presidential eligibility litigation

Barack Obama was born in 1961 in Honolulu, Hawaii (which had become a U.S. state in 1959). His mother was a U.S. citizen and his father was a British subject[131][132][133] from British Kenya.

Before and after the 2008 presidential election, arguments were made that Obama was not a natural-born citizen. On June 12, 2008, the Obama presidential campaign launched a website to counter what it described as a smear campaign by his opponents, including conspiracy theories challenging his eligibility.[134] The most prominent issue raised against Obama was the claim made in several lawsuits that he was not actually born in Hawaii. The Supreme Court declined without comment to hear two lawsuits in which the plaintiffs argued it was irrelevant whether Obama was born in Hawaii.[135] Most of the cases were dismissed because of the plaintiff's lack of standing; however, several courts have given guidance on the question.

In *Ankeny v. Governor*, a three-member Indiana Court of Appeals stated,

> Based upon the language of Article II, Section 1, Clause 4 and the guidance provided by *Wong Kim Ark*, we conclude that persons born within the borders of the United States are 'natural born Citizens' for Article II, Section 1 purposes, regardless of the citizenship of their parents.[136]

Administrative Law Judge Michael Malihi in Georgia decided a group of eligibility challenge cases by saying, "The Indiana Court rejected the argument that Mr. Obama was ineligible, stating that the children born within the United States are natural born citizens, regardless of the citizenship of their parents. ... This Court finds the decision and analysis of *Ankeny* persuasive." [137] Federal District Judge John A. Gibney, Jr. wrote in his decision in the case of *Tisdale v. Obama*:

> The eligibility requirements to be President of the United States are such that the individual must be a "natural born citizen" of the United States ... It is well settled that those born in the United States are considered natural born citizens. See, e.g. *United States v. Ark* [sic] ...[138]

On October 31, 2008, Hawaii Health Director Chiyome Fukino issued a statement saying,

> I ... have personally seen and verified that the Hawai'i State Department of Health has Sen. Obama's original birth certificate on record in accordance with state policies and procedures.[92][139]

On July 27, 2009, Fukino issued an additional statement:

> I ... have seen the original vital records maintained on file by the Hawaii State Department of Health verifying Barack Hussein Obama was born in Hawaii and is a natural-born American citizen.[140]

Attempts to prevent Obama from participating in the 2012 Democratic primary election in several states failed.[141][142][143][144]

## Ted Cruz

Ted Cruz announced on March 22, 2015, that he was running for the Republican Party's nomination for president in the 2016 election.[145] Cruz was born in Calgary, Alberta, Canada,[146] to a "U.S. citizen mother and a Cuban immigrant father",[147] giving him dual Canadian-American citizenship.[148] Cruz applied to formally renounce his Canadian citizenship and ceased being a citizen of Canada, on May 14, 2014.[149][150]

Former Solicitor General Paul Clement,[151][152] former Acting Solicitor General Neal Katyal,[151][152] University of California, Irvine School of Law Dean Erwin Chemerinsky,[153] Professor Chin (see above),[147] Temple University Law School Professor Peter Spiro,[154] Professor Akhil Amar,[155] Georgetown University Law Center Professor Randy Barnett,[156] Yale Law School Professor Jack Balkin,[156] and University of San Diego Professor Michael Ramsey[156] believe Cruz meets the constitutional requirements to be eligible for the presidency. Similarly, Bryan Garner, the editor of Black's Law Dictionary, believes the U.S. Supreme Court would find Cruz to be eligible.[157]

Laurence Tribe of Harvard, however, described Cruz's eligibility as "murky and unsettled".[158] Harvard Law Professor Cass Sunstein believes that Cruz is eligible, but agrees with Ramsey that Cruz's eligibility is not "an easy question". Sunstein believes concerns over standing and the political-question doctrine will prevent the courts from resolving issues surrounding Cruz's eligibility.[159]

Mary McManamon (see above) writing in the *Catholic University Law Review*[78] believes that Cruz is not eligible because he was not born in the United States.[160] Professor

Einer Elhauge of Harvard,[161] Professor Robert Clinton of Arizona State University,[162] University of Chicago Professor Eric Posner,[163] and former Chief Justice of the New York Court of Appeals Sol Wachtler[83] agree that Cruz is not eligible. Alan Grayson, a Democratic Member of Congress from Florida, does not believe Cruz is a natural-born citizen, and stated he intends to file a lawsuit should Cruz be the Republican nominee.[164] Orly Taitz, Larry Klayman, and Mario Apuzzo, who each filed multiple lawsuits challenging Obama's eligibility, have also asserted that Cruz is not eligible.[165][166]

Cruz's eligibility has been questioned by some of his primary opponents, including Donald Trump,[167] Mike Huckabee, Rick Santorum, Carly Fiorina, and Rand Paul.[168] Marco Rubio, however, believes Cruz is eligible.[169]

Two November 2015 ballot challenges in New Hampshire alleging that Cruz was not a natural-born citizen were unsuccessful.[170][171] In December, similar lawsuits were filed in Vermont[172] and Florida.[173] In January 2016, similar lawsuits were filed in Texas[174] (which Cruz sought to dismiss[175]) and Utah,[176] and two similar unsuccessful ballot challenges were filed in Illinois;[177][178][179] one of the ballot challenges, however, may be heard by an Illinois court.[180] In February, similar lawsuits were filed in Alabama,[181] Arkansas,[182] and Pennsylvania;[183] similar ballot challenges were unsuccessfully filed in Indiana;[184][185] and a similar lawsuit and similar ballot challenges were also filed in New York.[186][187]

## Marco Rubio and Bobby Jindal

Marco Rubio and Bobby Jindal both announced in 2015 that they were running for the Republican Party's nomination for president in the 2016 election.[188][189] Taitz and Apuzzo each have stated neither Rubio nor Jindal is eligible because both were born (albeit in the United States) to parents who were not U.S. citizens at the time of their respective births.[86][165]

The question of Jindal's eligibility became moot when he suspended his presidential campaign in November 2015.[190] Nonetheless, a lawsuit filed in December 2015 in Vermont[172] and a ballot challenge filed in February 2016 in New York[187] challenged Jindal's eligibility.

A November 2015 ballot challenge in New Hampshire alleging that Rubio was not a natural-born citizen was unsuccessful.[171] In December, a similar lawsuit, which he sought to have dismissed, was filed in Florida;[173] a similar lawsuit also was filed in Vermont.[172] In January 2016, a similar ballot challenge was unsuccessfully filed in Illinois.[177][179] In February, a similar lawsuit was filed in Arkansas;[182] a similar ballot challenge was filed in New York;[187] and an unsuccessful ballot challenge was filed in

Indiana.[184][185]

### 9.5.4 Potential presidential candidates who are not eligible

#### Arnold Schwarzenegger

Arnold Schwarzenegger was reported as considering challenging the prevailing interpretation of the clause. In 2003, Senator Orrin Hatch unsuccessfully put forth the Equal Opportunity to Govern Amendment in 2003, intending to allow eligibility for Arnold Schwarzenegger.[34] In October 2013, the *New York Post* reported that Austrian-born Schwarzenegger, who became a naturalized U.S. citizen in the early 1980s, was exploring a future run for President. He reportedly lobbied legislators about a possible constitutional change, or filing a legal challenge to the provision. Columbia University law professor Michael C. Dorf observed that Schwarzenegger's possible lawsuit could ultimately win him the right to run for the office, noting, "The law is very clear, but it's not 100 percent clear that the courts would enforce that law rather than leave it to the political process".[191] Schwarzenegger subsequently denied that he was running.[192]

## 9.6 See also

- *Jus sanguinis*

- United States nationality law

- United States presidential eligibility legislation

## 9.7 Notes

[1] Hamilton, Alexander (March 14, 1788). "The Federalist Papers No. 68, "The Mode of Electing the President"". Retrieved July 16, 2012.

[2] Williams, Pete (January 19, 2016). "'Natural Born' Issue for Ted Cruz Is Not Settled and Not Going Away". *NBC News*. The emerging consensus of the legal experts, however, is that being 'natural born' means becoming a citizen at the moment of birth, as opposed to achieving it later through the process of naturalization....

[3] Maskell, Jack (November 14, 2011). "Qualifications for President and the 'Natural Born' Citizenship Eligibility Requirement" (PDF). Congressional Research Service. p. 2. Retrieved February 25, 2012. In addition to historical and textual analysis, numerous holdings and references in federal (and state) cases for more than a century have clearly indicated that those born in the United States and subject to its jurisdiction (i.e., not born to foreign diplomats or occupying military forces), even to alien parents, are citizens 'at birth' or 'by birth,' and are 'natural born,' as opposed to 'naturalized,' U.S. citizens. There is no provision in the Constitution and no controlling American case law to support a contention that the citizenship of one's parents governs the eligibility of a native born U.S. citizen to be President.

[4] "Strunk v New York State Bd. of Elections :: 2012 :: New York Other Courts Decisions :: New York Case Law :: New York Law :: U.S. Law :: Justia". *Law.justia.com*. Retrieved January 16, 2016.

[5] Tokaji, Daniel (2008). "The Justiciability of Eligibility: May Courts Decide Who Can Be President?". *Michigan Law Review, First Impressions* **107**: 31.

[6] Gordon, Charles (1968). "Who can be President of the United States: The Unresolved Enigma". *Maryland Law Review* (Baltimore Maryland: Maryland Law Review, Inc. University of Maryland School of Law) **28** (1): 1–32. Retrieved October 8, 2012.

[7] U.S. Constitution: Article 1, Section 2, Clause 2: Qualifications of Members

[8] U.S. Constitution: Article 1, Section 3, Clause 3: Qualifications of Senators

[9] Martin Van Buren, National Children's Book and Literacy Alliance.

[10] Calvin's Case 7 Coke Report 1a, 77 ER 377, The Constitution Society

[11] Piggott, Francis. *Nationality and Naturalization*, pp. 48-50 (W. Clowes and Sons, 1907).

[12] McManamon, Mary. "The Natural Born Citizen Clause as Originally Understood", *Catholic University Law Review*, v. 64, no. 2 (2015).

[13] Index: N, O, Calendar of Treasury Books, Volume 27, 1713. Originally published by Her Majesty's Stationery Office, London, 1955.

[14] Biglieri, Ezio; Prati, G. (2014). *Encyclopedia of Public International Law*. Elsevier. p. 54. ISBN 978-1-4832-9477-3.

[15] Cohen, Elizabeth. "Citizenship and the Law of Time in the United States", *Duke Journal of Constitutional Law & Public Policy*, Vol. 8, p. 67 n. 59 (2013).

[16] Blackstone, William. *Commentaries on the Law of England*, Vol. 1, p. 354 (Oxford, The Clarendon Press 1765).

[17] Dann, Carrie. "Yes, Ted Cruz Was Born in Canada. So What?", NBC News (March 26, 2015).

[18] 7 Coke *Report* 1a, 77 ER 377 (1608), Opinion of Edward Coke.

[19] Edwards, F. B. "Natural-Born British Subjects at Common Law", *Journal of the Society of Comparative Legislation*, Vol. 14, p. 318 (1914).

[20] Maskell, Jack. "Qualifications for President and the 'Natural Born' Citizenship Eligibility Requirement", CRS Report for Congress, pp. 31-32 (2011).

[21] Johnson, Samuel. *A Dictionary Of The English Language: In Which The Words are Deduced from Their Originals, And Illustrated in Their Different Significations By Examples from the Best Writers, To Which Are Prefixed, A History of the Language, And An English Grammar : In Two Volumes*, Volume 2, pp. 180–181 (Knapton, 1756).

[22] Speare, Morris. "Lafayette, Citizen of America", *New York Times* (September 7, 1919).

[23] Riley, Elihu. *"The Ancient City": A History of Annapolis, in Maryland, 1649-1887*, p. 198 (Record Printing Office 1887).

[24] Lee, Thomas. "Is Ted Cruz a 'natural born Citizen'? Not if you're a constitutional originalist", *Los Angeles Times* (January 10, 2016).

[25] Han, William. "Beyond Presidential Eligibility: The Natural Born Citizen Clause as a Source of Birthright Citizenship", *Drake Law Review*, Vol. 58, No. 2, 2010, p. 462.

[26] Pryor, Jill A. "The Natural-Born Citizen Clause and Presidential Eligibility: An Approach for Resolving Two Hundred Years of Uncertainty". 97 *Yale Law Journal* 881, 889 (1988)http://yalelawjournal.org/images/pdfs/pryor_note.pdf;

[27] http://avalon.law.yale.edu/18th_century/debates_618.asp

[28] 3 M. Farrand, The Records of the Federal Convention of 1787, at 619.

[29] 3 Farrand, at 629.

[30] Heard, Alexander; Nelson, Michael (1987). *Presidential Selection*, Duke University Press. p. 123. Retrieved April 24, 2011. (the word *born* is underlined in the quoted letter[31])

[31] Letter from John Jay to George Washington, 25 July, 1787

[32] Han, William. "Beyond Presidential Eligibility: The Natural Born Citizen Clause as a Source of Birthright Citizenship", *Drake Law Review*, Vol. 58, No. 2, 2010, pp. 462–463.

[33] Palazzolo, Joe (September 4, 2012). "The Other Democratic Candidate". *The Wall Street Journal*.

[34] Kasindorf, Martin (December 2, 2004). "Should the Constitution be amended for Arnold?". *USA Today*.

[35] "President Kissinger?". *Time*. March 4, 1974.

[36] Tucker, St. George (1803). "St. George Tucker, Blackstone's Commentaries 1:App. 316–25, 328–29". Retrieved July 16, 2012.

[37] Blackstone, *Commentaries*, Vol.II, Ch. 10, 1803.

[38] Farrand, Max. "Charles Pinckney in the United States Senate". *The Records of the Federal Convention of 1787, Vol 3*. Retrieved October 8, 2012.

[39] Amar, Akhil (March–April 2004). "NATURAL BORN KILLJOY Why the Constitution won't let immigrants run for president, and why that should change.". Legal Affairs. Retrieved July 16, 2012.

[40] Statutes At Large, First Congress, Session II, p. 103

[41] "Foreign Affairs Manual 7 FAM 1130 Acquisition of U.S. Citizenship by Birth Abroad to U.S. Citizen Parent". United States Department of State. Retrieved December 13, 2015. 7 FAM 1131.6-2(d)

[42] *Congressional Globe* 37.2 (1862), p. 1639.

[43] *Congressional Globe* 39.1 (1866) p. 1291. Stated again during a House debate in 1872; cf. *Congressional Globe* 42.2 (1872), p. 2791.

[44] 10 Opinions of the U.S. Atty.Gen. [pages] 382–413, and separately as *Opinion of Attorney General Bates on Citizenship* (1863, Washington, DC, Govt. Printing Office) 27 pages.

[45] "Citizenship of children born in the United States of alien parents", 10 Op. US Atty-Gen. 328.

[46] letter from Marcy to Mason, June 6, 1854, quoted from the manuscript, reprinted (with the emphasis shown) in John Bassett Moore, *A Digest of International Law [of the United States]*, vol. 3, sec. 373, pp. 276–277 (US House of Representatives, 56th Congress, 2d Session, Document no. 551; Washington, DC, Govt. Printing Office, 1906).

[47] His first name is not given in the Opinion itself but if found in the correspondence seeking the opinion, in *Papers Relating to the Foreign Relations of the United States* (US House of Representatives, 44th Congress, 1st Session, December 6, 1875) Exec. Doct. 1, part 1, page 563.

[48] *Steinkauler's Case*, 15 Opinions of the US Attorneys-General 15 at 17–18 (June 26, 1875).

[49] van Dyne, Frederick, *Citizenship of the United States* (1904, Rochester, NY, Lawyers Co-operative Publ'g Co.) pp. 3–12. With regard to the last sentence in the quotation, van Dyne discusses some peripheral court decisions, none dealing with conventional U.S. citizenship, but with the nationality of the child of a foreigner and a member of an independent American Indian tribe whose members were not ordinarily regarded as U.S. citizens.

[50] NY Chanc.Ct., November 5, 1844; 1 Sandf.Ch. 583, 3 NY Leg.Obs. 236, 7 NY Ch. Ann. 443, 1844 WL 4804, 1844 N.Y.Misc. LEXIS 1.

[51] Sandf. at 656, Leg.Obs. at 246–247

[52] Sandf. at 663, Leg.Obs. at 250

[53] D.Cal., Sep 29, 1884) 21 Fed. 905, 10 Sawyer's Rpts. 353

[54] Fed at 909, Sawyer at 359–360

[55] *U.S. v. Wong Kim Ark* (1898) 169 U.S. 649, 42 L.Ed. 890, 18 S.Ct. 456.

[56] Similarly, in a 1999 Circuit Court decision, the U.S.-born children of two non-citizen parents were spoken of as "natural born citizens". *Mustata v. US Dept. of Justice* (6th Cir. 1999) 179 F.3d 1017 at 1019.

[57] *Perkins v. Elg* (1939) 307 U.S. 325 at 329, 83 L.Ed. 1320 at 1324, 59 S.Ct. 884 at 888.

[58] *Perkins v. Elg* (D.C. Cir. 1938) 69 U.S.App.D.C. 175, 99 F.2d 408

[59] Maskell, Jack (January 11, 2016). "Qualifications for President and the "Natural Born" Citizenship Eligibility Requirement". Congressional Research Service.

[60] *"Zimmer v Acheson, 191 F.2d 209 (10th Cir. 1951)"*.

[61] *"Montana v. Kennedy, 366 U.S. 308 (1961)"*.

[62] *Ankeny v. Governor of the State of Indiana* (2009), Appeals Court Decision, 11120903

[63] *Nolos v. Holder* (5th Cir. 2010) 611 F.3d 279, 62 ALR-Fed.2d 777, ; also Sean Morrison, *Foreign in a Domestic Sense: American Samoa and the Last U.S. Nationals*, 41 Hastings Constitutional Law Quarterly 71 (fall 2013) .

[64] Rawle, William (1825). *A View of the Constitution of the United States of America*. Philadelphia, Carey & Lea. pp. 80–81. ISBN 978-1144771858.

[65] James F. Wilson in: *Congressional Globe*, House of Representatives, 39th Congress, 1st Session, Washington 1866, p. 1117.

[66] *Dred Scott v. Sandford*, 60 U.S. 393, 476 (1857).

[67] Book 1, § 212

[68] *United States v. Wong Kim Ark*, 169 U.S. 649, 708 (1898).

[69] Joseph Story (1840). *A familiar exposition of the Constitution of the United States: containing a brief commentary on every clause, explaining the true nature, reasons, and objects thereof : designed for the use of school libraries and general readers : with an appendix, containing important public documents, illustrative of the Constitution*. Marsh, Capen, Lyon and Webb. pp. 167 §269–271.

[70] Joseph Story (1834). *The constitutional class book: being a brief exposition of the Constitution of the United States: Designed for the use of the higher classes in common schools*. Hilliard, Gray & Company. pp. 115 §190.

[71] *Plessy v. Ferguson*, 163 U.S. 537 (1896).

[72] A.P. Morse, "Natural-Born Citizen of the United States: Eligibility for the Office of President", *Albany Law Journal*, vol. 66 (1904–1905)

[73] "Presidential Elections in the United States: A Primer" (PDF). Congressional Research Service. April 17, 2000. Retrieved January 8, 2010.

[74] 41131059 MoC Memo What to Tell Your Constituents in Answer to Obama Eligibility

[75] Liptak, Adam (July 11, 2008). "A Citizen, but 'Natural Born'?". *The New York Times*.

[76] Chin, Gabriel J. (2008), "Why Senator John McCain Cannot Be President: Eleven Months and a Hundred Yards Short of Citizenship", 107 Mich. L. Rev. First Impressions 1

[77] White, G. Edward (August 20, 2009). "Re-examining the Constitution's Presidential Eligibility Clause". University of Virginia School of Law. Retrieved February 27, 2012.

[78] McManamon, Mary (2015), "The Natural Born Citizens Clause as Originally Understood", 64 Catholic University Law Review 317

[79] McManamon, Mary Brigid (January 12, 2016). "Law professor: Ted Cruz is not eligible to be president". *Washington Post*. Retrieved January 15, 2016.

[80] Elhauge, Einer (January 20, 2016). "Opinion: Cruz not really 'natural born citizen'". *Chicago Sun-Times*. Retrieved January 21, 2016.

[81] Clinton, Robert (January 27, 2016). "Ted Cruz Is Not A 'Natural Born' Citizen". U.S. News & World Report. Retrieved January 28, 2016.

[82] Posner, Eric (February 8, 2016). "Ted Cruz Is Not Eligible to Be President". *Slate*.

[83] Wachtler, Sol (February 13, 2016). "Constitutional history shows Cruz ineligible for White House". *Newsday*.

[84] Solum, Lawrence B. (2008), "Originalism and the natural born citizen clause", 107 Mich. L. Rev. First Impressions 22

[85] Lawrence B. Solum, "Originalism and the natural born citizen clause", revised draft version, April 18, 2010 (SSRN), p. 1, n. 3. However, other passages of his revised draft still imply U.S. citizenship of both parents; cf. i.a. pp. 3, 9, 11.

[86] Leary, Alex (October 20, 2011). "Birthers say Marco Rubio is not eligible to be president". *Tampa Bay Times*.

[87] Kornhaber, Spencer (September 22, 2010). "Chapman Constitutional Scholar Rebuffs Orly Taitz's Overtures". *OC Weekly*.

[88] Chin, Gabriel (April 20, 2011). "Who's really eligible to be president?". CNN.

[89] Volokh, Eugene (November 18, 2009). "Indiana Court of Appeals Rejects Claim That 'Because His Father Was a Citizen of the United Kingdom, President Obama Is Not a Natural Born Citizen and Therefore Constitutionally Ineligible to Assume the Office of the President'". *The Volokh Conspiracy*. Retrieved May 3, 2011.

[90] *Ankeny v. Governor of the State of Indiana*, 916 NE 2d 678 (Ind. Ct. of Appeals November 12, 2009).

[91] Rathgeber, Bob (September 20, 2010). "Exclusive: Now, 'birthers' have eye on Marco Rubio". *News-Press*.

[92] E.g. see *Robinson v. Bowen*, 567 F. Supp. 2d 1144 (N.D. Cal. 2008); *Hollander v. McCain*, 2008WL2853250 (D.N.H. 2008); *Berg v. Obama*, 08-04083 (E.D. Pa. 2008).

[93] *See* 3 U.S.C. ch. 1.

[94] Carl Hulse (February 28, 2008). "McCain's Canal Zone Birth Prompts Queries About Whether That Rules Him Out". *The New York Times*. Retrieved August 12, 2012.

[95] Spiro, Peter. "McCain's Citizenship and Constitutional Method", Michigan Law Review, Volume 107, p. 208 (2008).

[96] "Who Can Be President?", Voice of America News (July 29, 2008).

[97] Reeves, Thomas C. "The Mystery of Chester Alan Arthur's Birthplace", *Vermont History* 38, Montpelier: Vermont Historical Society, p. 295

[98] DeGregorio, William A. *The Complete Book of U.S. Presidents*, Random House: 1993, pp. 307–08, ISBN 0-517-08244-6

[99] Hinman, Arthur P. (1884). *How a British Subject became President of the United States.*

[100] Thomas C. Reeves, *Gentleman Boss. The Life and Times of Chester Alan Arthur* (Newtown 1991), p. 5.

[101] For instance, an early biography of Presidents Garfield and Arthur.Doyle, Burton T.; Swaney, Homer H. (1881). *Lives of James A. Garfield and Chester A. Arthur*. Washington: R.H. Darby. p. 183. ISBN 0-104-57546-8.

[102] "Is Mr. Schürmann eligible?", *New York Tribune*, October 2, 1896, in: Anonymous (ed.), *The Presidential Campaign of 1896. A Scrap-Book Chronicle*, New York 1925: Funk & Wagnalls, p. 130 sq. (*Note*: The year of publication is given as 1888, though the election was eight years later. However, the author's introduction is dated 1925.)

[103] Breckinridge Long (1916), "Is Mr. Charles Evans Hughes a 'Natural Born Citizen' within the Meaning of the Constitution?", *Chicago Legal News* vol. 49, pp. 146–148 (December 7, 1916). It does not appear that this issue was raised *before* the election day, which may indicate that the majority of voters or of legal authorities felt it was not an impediment to Hughes's eligibility.

[104] Lipsky, Seth (2009). *The Citizen's Constitution: An Annotated Guide*. (Basic Books). p. 126.

[105] Heard, Alexander and Nelson, Michael (1987). *Presidential Selection*. (Duke University Press) p. 127.

[106] Ken Rudin (July 9, 1998). "Citizen McCain's Panama Problem?". Washington Post.

[107] Powell, Stewart (August 14, 1976). "Weicker May Not Be Eligible to Serve in High Position", *Nashua Telegraph*. United Press International.

[108] S.Res.511: *A resolution recognizing that John Sidney McCain, III, is a natural-born citizen.*, U.S. Senate, April 30, 2008, OpenCongress. Retrieved April 13, 2011

[109] "John McCain Biography", Biography.com. Retrieved April 13, 2011

[110] Dobbs, Michael (May 20, 2008). "John McCain's Birthplace". *The Washington Post*. Retrieved April 13, 2011.

[111] Parish, Matt (2010), "How Old Is John McCain?", *Politics Daily*, AOL. Retrieved April 13, 2011

[112] "Profile: John McCain". *Online NewsHour*. PBS. July 1, 2008. Retrieved April 13, 2011.

[113] Fagan, Kevin (September 21, 2008). "McCain: A profile in courage and adaptation". *San Francisco Chronicle*. Retrieved April 13, 2011.

[114] *Hollander v. McCain et al*, Justia Dockets & Filings

[115] Dr. Conspiracy (April 24, 2010), "John McCain's fake birth certificate", *Obama Conspiracy Theories*. Retrieved April 13, 2011

[116] Dobbs, Michael (May 2, 2008), "McCain's Birth Abroad Stirs Legal Debate : His Eligibility for Presidency Is Questioned", *The Washington Post*

[117] Article II of *Convention Between the United States and the Republic of Panama* states: "...the cities of Panama and Colon and the harbors adjacent to said cities, which are included within the boundaries of the zone above described, shall not be included within this grant".

[118] A book written by the U.S. Navy includes the same reference: Link to relevant page in the book via Google Books: https://books.google.com/books?id=pxooAAAAYAAJ& dq=panama%20canal%20colon&lr=&pg=PA192

[119] This map clearly shows Colon is not part of the Canal Zone. Colon Hospital can be seen on the map at the North end of the island. (Source: http://www.serve.com/~{}CZBrats/)

[120] "Foreign Affairs Manual 7 FAM 1110 Acquisition of U.S. Citizenship by Birth in the United States". United States Department of State. Retrieved December 13, 2015. 7 FAM 1113(c)(1): "Despite widespread popular belief, U.S. military installations abroad and U.S. diplomatic facilities are not part of the United States within the meaning of the 14th

Amendment. A child born on the premises of such a facility is not subject to U.S. jurisdiction and does not acquire U.S. citizenship by reason of birth."

[121] "Lawyers Conclude McCain Is "Natural Born", CBS News, Associated Press, March 28, 2008. Retrieved May 23, 2008.

[122] S.Res.511: *A resolution recognizing that John Sidney McCain, III, is a natural-born citizen*; sponsors: Sen. Claire McCaskill, Sen. Barack Obama *et al.*; page S2951 notes Chairman Patrick Leahy as agreeing to Secretary Michael Chertoff's "assumption and understanding" that a citizen is a *natural-born citizen*, if he or she was "born of American parents".

[123] Cf. William Alsup, *Robinson v. Bowen*: Order denying preliminary injunction and dismissing action, September 16, 2008, p. 2; Alsup ruled that McCain was either a natural-born citizen by birth under 8 U.S.C. §1401c or retroactively under 8 U.S.C. §1403(a). (See also: "Judge says McCain is a 'natural-born citizen'". Associated Press. September 18, 2008. Retrieved November 16, 2008., and "Constitutional Topic: Citizenship". U.S. Constitution Online. Retrieved November 25, 2008.)

[124] Chin, Gabriel J. (2008), "Why Senator John McCain Cannot Be President: Eleven Months and a Hundred Yards Short of Citizenship", *Michigan Law Review First Impressions*, Vol. 107, No. 1, (Arizona Legal Studies Discussion Paper No. 08-14)

[125] "Foreign Affairs Manual 7 FAM 1120 Acquisition of U.S. Nationality in U.S. Territories and Possessions". United States Department of State. Retrieved December 13, 2015.

[126] "Foreign Affairs Manual 7 FAM 1130 Acquisition of U.S. Citizenship by Birth Abroad to U.S. Citizen Parent". United States Department of State. Retrieved December 13, 2015. 7 FAM 1131.6-2(a).

[127] SCOTUS 401 U.S. 815, 828 (1971)

[128] "Constitutional Topic: Citizenship". U.S. Constitution Online. Retrieved June 7, 2009

[129] Lawrence B. Solum, "Originalism and the natural born citizen clause", *Michigan Law Review: First Impressions* 107, September 2008, p. 30.

[130] "Is John McCain a natural-born citizen?" *Snopes.com*, July 23, 2008. Retrieved March 27, 2011.

[131] "Obama's Kenyan Citizenship?". FactCheck.org. September 3, 2009. Retrieved September 14, 2013.

[132] "British nationality by virtue of citizenship". *British Nationality Act 1948*. Her Majesty's Government. Retrieved September 14, 2013.

[133] "UK and Colonies". Home Office.

[134] "The Truth About Barack's Birth Certificate (archived web cache)". Fight the Smears (Obama for America). (Retrieved March 9, 2011), quoting in excerpts from: "Does Barack Obama have Kenyan citizenship?". FactCheck.org (Annenberg Foundation). August 29, 2008.; see also: "Obama hits back at Internet slanders". Agence France-Presse. June 12, 2008.; in a written oath to the State of Arizona, Obama further stated that he is a natural-born citizen (cf. Candidate Nomination Paper, *State of Arizona*, November 30, 2007).

[135] *Leo C. Donofrio v. Nina Mitchell Wells* (SCOTUS 08A407) and *Cort Wrotnowski v. Susan Bysiewicz* (SCOTUS 08A469)

[136] *Ankeny v. Governor of the State of Indiana* (Ind.App., 12 NOV 2009), Appeals Court Decision, 11120903

[137] *Farrar v. Obama* (Office of State Administrative Hearings State of Georgia 2012). Text

[138] *Tisdale v. Obama* (United States District Court for the Eastern District of Virginia 2012). Text

[139] Statement by Dr. Chiyome Fukino, Department of Health, October 31, 2008

[140] "Hawaii reasserts Obama 'natural-born' citizen", MSNBC, July 28, 2009

[141] Hanna, Maddie (November 18, 2011). "'Birther' bid to derail Obama blocked". *Concord Monitor*.

[142] Velasco, Eric (January 9, 2012). "Suit to keep President Barack Obama off Alabama primary ballots dismissed by Jefferson County judge". Alabama: al.com.

[143] *Allen v. Obama* (Arizona Superior Court, Pima County February 24, 2012). Text

[144] Secretary of State Kemp Issues Final Decision on Challenge to President Barack Obama's Eligibility and Qualifications, (February 7, 2012), Press Office of the Georgia Secretary of State.

[145] Martin, Jonathan; Haberman, Maggie (March 22, 2015). "Ted Cruz Hopes Early Campaign Entry Will Focus Voters' Attention". *The New York Times*. Retrieved March 23, 2015.

[146] "Cruz, Rafael Edward (Ted), (1970 – )". *Biographical Directory of the United States Congress*.

[147] Chin, Gabriel (August 13, 2013). "Opinion: Ted Cruz can be president, probably". CNN.

[148] Gillman, Todd (December 28, 2013). "Ted Cruz says he's hired lawyers to renounce Canadian citizenship". *Dallas Morning News*. Retrieved December 30, 2013.

[149] Gillman, Todd (June 10, 2014). "No, Canada: Sen. Ted Cruz has formally shed his dual citizenship". *The Dallas Morning News*. Retrieved June 10, 2014.

[150] Blake, Aaron (August 19, 2013). "Cruz Will Renounce Canadian Citizenship". *The Washington Post*. Retrieved August 20, 2013.

[151] Barnes, Robert (March 12, 2015). "Legal experts: Cruz's Canadian birth won't keep him out of the Oval Office". *Washington Post*.

[152] Neal Katyal; Paul Clemente (March 11, 2015). "On the Meaning of 'Natural Born Citizen'". *Harvard Law Review*.

[153] Chemerinsky, Erwin (January 13, 2016). "Ted Cruz is eligible to be president". *Orange County Register*.

[154] Spiro, Peter (March 22, 2015). "Is Ted Cruz a 'Natural Born Citizen'?". *Opinio Juris.*,

[155] Amar, Akhil (January 13, 2016). "Why Ted Cruz is eligible to be president". *CNN*.

[156] Barnett, Randy (February 6, 2016). "Tribe v. Balkin on whether Ted Cruz is a "natural born citizen"". *Washington Post*.

[157] Garner, Bryan (January 14, 2016). "Memorandum: Is Ted Cruz Eligible for the Presidency?". *The Atlantic*.

[158] Jacobs, Ben (January 10, 2016). "Harvard scholar: Ted Cruz's citizenship, eligibility for president 'unsettled'". *The Guardian*.

[159] Sunstein, Cass (January 12, 2016). "Is Cruz 'Natural Born'? Well ... Maybe". *Bloomberg View*.

[160] McManamon, Mary Brigid (January 12, 2016). "Ted Cruz is not eligible to be president". *Washington Post*.

[161] Elhauge, Einer (January 20, 2016). "Ted Cruz is not eligible to run for president: A Harvard law professor close-reads the Constitution". *Salon*.

[162] Clinton, Robert (January 27, 2016). "Ted Cruz Isn't a 'Natural Born' Citizen: According to the Constitution, because Sen. Ted Cruz was not born in the United States, he is not eligible to run for president.". *U.S. News & World Report*.

[163] Posner, Eric (February 8, 2016). "Ted Cruz Is Not Eligible to Be President". *Slate*.

[164] "Grayson: I'll File A Lawsuit Against Ted Cruz If He's The Nominee". *FOX News*. November 25, 2015.

[165] Nelson, Steven (March 24, 2015). "Ted Cruz Inherits 'Birthers' With Presidential Bid". *U.S. News & World Report*.

[166] Koplowitz, Howard (March 26, 2015). "Birther 2.0: Can Ted Cruz Run For President? 'He's Even Worse Than Obama,' Citizenship Skeptic Says". *International Business Times*.

[167] "Trump, Cruz clash over eligibility, 'New York values' at GOP debate". *Fox News*. January 15, 2016.

[168] Weigel, David (January 13, 2016). "Huckabee joins the Republicans with questions about Cruz's eligibility". *ABC News*.

[169] Brody, Ben (January 12, 2016). "Few Colleagues Defend Cruz as White House Eligibility Is Questioned". *Bloomberg News*.

[170] Mielke, Brad (November 13, 2015). "Some Voters Trying to Kick Ted Cruz and Bernie Sanders Off NH Ballot". *ABC News*.

[171] Tuohy, Dan (November 24, 2015). "BLC upholds Sanders, Trump on primary ballots". *Union Leader*.

[172] Blaisdell, Eric (January 1, 2016). "Vermonter tries to keep names off presidential ballot". *Rutland Herald*.

[173] Leary, Alex (January 14, 2016). "Marco Rubio seeks to dismiss court challenge to his eligibility to be president". *Tampa Bay Times*.

[174] Calkins, Laurel Brubaker (January 14, 2016). "Cruz's 'Natural-Born Citizen' Status Tested in Birther Suit". *Bloomberg News*.

[175] Koh, Elizabeth (February 23, 2016). "Cruz asks judge to dismiss Texas lawsuit on presidential eligibility". *The Dallas Morning News*.

[176] Ben Winslow and Max Roth (January 26, 2016). "Utah man suing Ted Cruz claiming he's not a natural-born citizen". *KSTU*.

[177] Kopan, Tal (January 15, 2016). "Ted Cruz not the only one with a birther challenge". *CNN*.

[178] Gregory, John (January 8, 2016). "Cruz's Birthplace Challenged in Illinois". *WBGZ*.

[179] Farias, Cristian (February 2, 2016). "Ted Cruz Is A 'Natural Born Citizen,' Board Of Election Finds". *CNN*.

[180] Schleifer, Theodore (February 18, 2016). "Case against Ted Cruz's eligibility to be heard in Illinois on Friday". *CNN*.

[181] Koplowitz, Howard (February 5, 2016). "Alabama residents' lawsuit claims Ted Cruz ineligible to run for president". *The Birmingham News*.

[182] Lanning, Curt (February 8, 2016). "Lawsuit: Remove Cruz and Rubio from Ark. Ballot". *KARK-TV*.

[183] Delano, Jon (February 24, 2016). "Pa. Attorney Challenging Ted Cruz's Right To Run In State's Republican Primary". *KDKA-TV*.

[184] Cook, Tony (February 16, 2016). "Cruz, Rubio presidential candidacies face citizenship challenges in Indiana". *The Indianapolis Star*.

[185] Associated Press (February 19, 2016). "Cruz, Rubio remain eligible for Indiana presidential ballots". *Indianapolis Business Journal*.

[186] Ross, Barbara (February 18, 2016). "New Yorkers seek court order to keep Ted Cruz off the ballot in state Republican presidential primaries because he was born in Canada". *Daily News (New York)*.

[187] Seiler, Casey (February 18, 2016). "State BOE receives flurry of 'natural-born' objections to Rubio, Cruz". *Times Union*.

[188] Ashley Parker and Alan Rappeport (April 13, 2015). "Marco Rubio Announces 2016 Presidential Bid". *New York Times*.

[189] Fernandez, Manny (January 24, 2015). "Bobby Jindal Announces Run for President". *New York Times*.

[190] Tom LoBianco and Jeff Zeleny (November 17, 2015). "Bobby Jindal announces he is ending presidential campaign". *CNN*.

[191] Smith, Emily (October 18, 2013). "Arnold lobbies for White House run". *New York Post*. Retrieved October 19, 2013.

[192] Blake, Aaron (October 18, 2013). "Schwarzenegger denies he's aiming for president". *Washington Post*.

## 9.8   External links

- John Yinger, Essay on the Presidential Eligibility clause and on the origins and interpretation of *natural born citizen*.

- Jill A. Pryor, "The Natural Born Citizen Clause and the Presidential Eligibility Clause; Resolving Two Hundred Years of Uncertainty", *Yale Law Journal*, Vol. 97, 1988, pp. 881–899.

- Sarah P. Herlihy, "Amending the Natural Born Citizen Requirement: Globalization as the Impetus and the Obstacle", *Chicago-Kent Law Review*, Vol. 81, 2006, pp. 275–300.

- Lawrence Friedman, "An Idea Whose Time has Come - The Curious History, Uncertain Effect, and Need for Amendment of the 'Natural Born Citizen' Requirement for the Presidency", *St. Louis Univ. Law Journal*, Vol. 52, 2007, pp. 137–150.

- U.S. Constitution Online, , Constitutional Topic: Citizenship.

- Presidential Eligibility, Constitution Society.

# Chapter 10

# Exploratory committee

In the election politics of United States, an **exploratory committee** is an organization established to help determine whether a potential candidate should run for an elected office. They are most often cited in reference to United States Presidential hopefuls, prior to the primaries.

Exploratory committees may be governed by law. For example, the District of Columbia legally defines *Exploratory Committees* as (in DC Official Code § 1-1101.01(6)(B)(vi)):

> Exploratory, draft or "testing the waters" committees are formed solely for the purpose of determining the feasibility of an individual's candidacy for office. The activities of exploratory committees may include polling, travel, and telephone calls to determine whether the individual should become a candidate.

Ron Elving described the use of exploratory committees in his article, *Declaring for President is a Dance of Seven Veils*, which aired on National Public Radio on December 5, 2006. He wrote:

> The exploratory committee has been around for decades, and technically it creates a legal shell for a candidate who expects to spend more than $5,000 while contemplating an actual run. Under the rules, exploratory money may be raised without the full disclosure of sources required of true candidates. Only when the candidate drops the exploratory label does the full responsibility of transparency apply.
>
> Candidates use an exploratory committee as not only a transitional phase for their bookkeeping but as an extra claim on media attention. Some of the most skillful handlers like to leak word that their candidate is testing the waters, then leak word that he or she is thinking about forming an exploratory committee. Additional "news" can be made when the same candidate actually forms such a committee and registers with the Federal Election Commission. Yet a fourth round of attention may be generated when the word exploratory gets dropped from the committee filing.[1]

## 10.1 References

[1] NPR: Declaring for President is a Dance of Seven Veils

## 10.2 External links

- Testing the Waters and Campaign Committees (Press Release) *Federal Election Commission* (no date)

- Candidate Registration Brochure *Federal Election Commission,* March 2005, revised June 2008.

- District of Columbia Campaign Finance Guide

# Chapter 11

# Ballot access

This article is about access to elections in the United States. For access to elections elsewhere, see Nomination rules.

**Ballot access** rules, called nomination rules outside the United States, regulate the conditions under which a candidate or political party is entitled either to stand for election or to appear on voters' ballots. The criterion to stand as a candidate depends on the individual legal system, however they may include the age of a candidate, citizenship, endorsement by a political party and profession.[1] Legal restrictions, such as those based around competence or moral aptitude, can be used in a discriminatory manner. Restrictive and discriminatory ballot access rules can impact the civil rights of candidates, political parties and voters.

## 11.1 Overview of ballot access

Each U.S. State has its own ballot access laws to determine who may appear on ballots. According to the Elections Clause in Article I, Section 4, of the United States Constitution, the authority to regulate the time, place, and manner of federal elections is up to each State, unless Congress legislates otherwise.

The primary argument put forward by States for restricting ballot access has been the presumption that setting ballot access criteria too low would result in numerous candidates on the ballot, splitting the votes of similar minded voters. Example: With Plurality voting, an old but common way to pick the winner, the candidate with the most votes wins, even if the candidate does not have a majority of the votes. Suppose 55% liberals and 45% conservatives vote in a district. If two candidates appeal to liberals, but only one appeals to conservatives, the votes of liberals will likely split between the two liberal candidates, for example 25% may vote for one and 30% for the other, giving the conservative the office although 55% preferred to see a liberal in the office. Plurality races, also known as First past the post, tend to cause consolidation among political parties for this reason. However, proponents of ballot access reform say

that reasonably easy access to the ballot does not lead to a glut of candidates, even where many candidates do appear on the ballot. The 1880s reform movement that led to officially designed secret ballots had some salutary effects, but it also gave the government control over who could be on the ballot. As historian Peter Argersinger has pointed out, the reform that empowered officials to regulate access onto the ballot, also carried the danger that this power would be abused by officialdom and that legislatures controlled by established political parties (specifically, the Republican and Democratic Parties), would enact restrictive ballot access laws to influence election outcomes to ensure re-election of their party's candidates.

Perhaps the most prominent advocate of the 1880s ballot reform movement, Dean Wigmore, suggested that "ten signatures" might be an appropriate requirement for nomination to the official ballot for a legislative office. In the 20th century, ballot access laws imposing signature requirements far more restrictive than Wigmore had envisioned were enacted by many state legislatures; in many cases, the two major parties wrote the laws such that the burdens created by these new ballot access requirements (usually in the form of difficult signature-gathering nominating petition drives) fell on alternative candidates, but not on major party candidates.[2] Proponents of more open ballot access argue that restricting ballot access has the effect of unjustly restricting the choices available to voters, and typically disadvantages third party candidates and other candidates who are not affiliated with the established parties.

## 11.2 State laws, the Constitution, and international

President George H. W. Bush signed the Copenhagen Document of the Helsinki Accords that states in part:

The Organization for Security and Co-operation in Europe (OSCE) has criticized the United States for its harsh ballot access laws in the past. In 1996, United States delegates responded to the criticism by saying, unfair ballot access "could be remedied through existing appeal and regulatory structures and did not represent a breach of the Copenhagen commitments."[3]

The OSCE published a report on the 2004 United States election, which, among other things, noted restrictive ballot access laws.[4]

The United States and Switzerland are the only countries that do not have national ballot access standards for federal elections;[5] however in Swiss federal elections each Canton elects its own representatives, and each candidate can only be listed in one Canton.  Since 1985, Democrats and Republicans (including Congressmen John Conyers (D-MI), Tim Penny (D-MN) and Ron Paul (R-TX)) have repeatedly introduced in the United States House of Representatives a bill that would set maximum ballot access requirements for House elections.  The bill has only made it to the House floor once, in 1998, when it was defeated 62-363.

While some supporters of easy ballot access seek congressional intervention, other reformers are happy that congress has not mandated stricter access laws in all states.  Reducing access requirements at the local level would be easier than doing so federally if congress wanted to guarantee its re-elections.

### 11.2.1   State ballot access laws

Ballot access laws in the United States vary widely from state to state:

- **Alabama**: Major party candidates are nominated by the state primary process.  Independent candidates are granted ballot access through a petition process and minor political party candidates are nominated by convention along with a petition process; one must collect 3% of the total votes cast in the last election for the specific race or 3% of the total votes cast in the last gubernatorial election for statewide ballot access.  The figure for 2006 statewide ballot access was 41,012 valid signatures.  Be aware that the validity of signatures generally means that 20-30% more signatures will need to be collected to ensure that the goal is achieved.  To retain ballot access in the following election, a party has to poll 20% in a statewide race.

- **Arizona**: To gain ballot access, a new political party must gather signatures on a county–by–county basis, achieving over 20,000 valid signatures (i.e. from registered voters).  Once this has been achieved the party must run a candidate for Governor or President who garners at least 5% of the vote to maintain ballot access

*Activists of the Arizona Green Party collecting signatures for ballot status*

for an additional two years, maintain at least 1% of registered voters registered with their party, or gather approximately the same number of signatures again every two years.  The Democratic, Libertarian, and Republican parties have ballot access by voter registrations.  In 2008, the Arizona Green Party gathered enough signatures to gain ballot access.[6]

- **California**: Per section 5100 of the California Election Code, ballot access requires one of two conditions to be met:[7]

    - If at the last preceding gubernatorial election there was polled for any one of the party's candidates for any office voted on throughout the state, at least 2 percent of the entire vote of the state;

    - If on or before the 135th day before any primary election, it appears to the Secretary of State, as a result of examining and totaling the statement of voters and their political affiliations transmitted to him or her by the county elections officials, that voters equal in number to at least 1 percent of the entire vote of the state at the last preceding gubernatorial election have declared their intention to affiliate with that party.

- **Colorado** has relatively lax ballot access requirements, but requirements differ for major and minor parties.  For major party primary candidates (Democratic, Republican, and American Constitution parties are major parties for 2012 because of the votes drawn by ACP candidate Tom Tancredo in 2010), C.R.S. 1-4-801 requires statewide candidates (including US Senate) obtain 1,500 valid signatures per congressional district.  US House and State legislature candidates need 1000 signatures.  Candidates may also be named to ballots by a caucus, county assembly, and state or district assembly process; a candidate who draws less than 10% of an assembly is ineligible to petition on the same primary ballot. For minor party candidate, the petition requirements are eased under C.R.S 1-4-802. For US Senate, 1,000 signatures are required; for US House, 800 signatures; for State Senate, 600 signatures; and for State House, 400. Sometimes these requirements are relaxed even further based on the voting statistics of the district.[8]

- **Kentucky** uses a three-tier system for ballot access, using the results of the previous presidential election as the gauge. If a party's presidential candidate achieves less than 2% of the popular vote within the state, that organization is a "political group". If the candidate receives 2% or more, but less than 20% of the popular vote in Kentucky, that organization is a "political organization". Parties whose candidate for president achieves at least 20% of the popular vote are considered "political parties". Taxpayer-funded primaries are achieved as a "political party". Automatic ballot access is obtained as a "political organization" or "political party", and these levels require only 2 signatures for a candidate to run for any partisan office. There is no mechanism for placing an entire party on the ballot in Kentucky, other than achieving "political organization" or "political party" status. Candidates of "political groups" and independent candidates must collect a minimum of between 25 and 5000 signatures to run for any particular partisan office. Filing fees apply equitably to all levels.[9] Traditionally, the state only tracked voter registration affiliation as Democratic (D), Republican (R), or Other (O). Beginning 1 January 2006, Kentucky law provides for County Clerks to track the voter registration of Constitution (C), Green (G), Libertarian (L), Reform (F), and Socialist Workers (S), as well as independent (I);[10] though a number of County Clerks have not been complying with this regulation.

- **Louisiana** is one of the easiest states to get on the ballot. Anyone may obtain a spot on the ballot by either paying a qualifying fee, or submitting petition signatures. For independent candidates for President (or non-recognized parties) the fee is $500 or 5000 signatures, with at least 500 from each Congressional district. Recognized Parties simply file their slate of Electors - their access is automatic, no fee or signatures required. For statewide office, the signature requirement is the same as that for President, but the fees are $750 for Governor and $600 for all other statewide offices. District and local office fees range from $40 or 50 signatures for a small town office, to $600 or 1000 signatures for US House. All signatures for district offices must come from within that district. If the office is for a political party committee, the signatures must be from people affiliated with that party. For Presidential Preference Primaries, the fee is $750 or 1000 signatures affiliated with that party from each Congressional district.[11](pdf) Present Louisiana law only allows for Presidential Primaries if a party has more than 40,000 registered voters statewide. Currently, this only applies to the Democratic and Republican Parties. Louisiana law changed in 2004 under efforts from the Libertarian Party of Louisiana to relax rules in place at that time for recognizing political parties in the state. There are now two methods to gain official recognition. Method A allows a party to be recognized if it pays a $1000 fee AND has 1000 or more voters registered under its label. To retain recognition, it must field a candidate at least once in any four-year period in a statewide election - with no requirement on performance in the election. Statewide election slots include Presidential Elector, Governor, Senator, Lt. Governor, Secretary of State, Attorney General, Treasurer, Comm. of Insurance, and Commissioner of Agriculture. To date, the Libertarian Party and the Green Party have used this method to attain and retain official party recognition. Method B allows a party to be recognized if one of its candidates in a statewide race or for Presidential Elector achieves 5% of the vote. To retain recognition, it must repeat the 5% tally for statewide office or Presidential Elector at least once in any four-year period. To date, the Reform Party has used this method to gain and retain official party recognition. Due to their size, parties recognized by these methods are exempt from certain laws governing public elections of political committee offices and from certain financial reporting requirements until their membership reaches 5% of registered voters statewide. Recognized political parties in Louisiana are allowed to have their party name appear alongside their candidates on the ballot, and for their party to be offered as a specific choice on voter registration cards. Non-recognized parties appear as OTHER, and the party name must be written in on the registration card. Non-affiliated voters are listed as N for No Party. In the 2008 and 2010 Congressional elections, Louisiana experimented with closed primaries for House and Senate. Under this system, recognized parties participated in semi-closed primaries before the general election. Only one candidate from each party was allowed on the General Election ballot; there was no limit for OTHER or NONE. An attempt to pass a law differentiating "minor" parties similar to the rule for Presidential Primaries was defeated but made irrelevant by Louisiana reverting to its "Jungle Primary" system where all candidates, regardless of number from any party, all compete together on the same ballot. If no one achieves a majority, a general election is held as a run-off between the top two, also regardless of party affiliation.[12][13]

- **Maryland**: Party certifications are done for each gubernatorial cycle (e.g. 2006–2010). If the number of registered voters to a political party is less than 1%, then 10,000 petition signatures must be gathered for that party to be considered certified. A party must be certified before voters can register under that party. A party can also be certified for a two-year term if their "top of the ticket" candidate receives more than 1% of the vote.

- **Michigan**: Major party candidates for Congress, governor, state legislature, countywide offices, and township offices are chosen through a primary system. A candidate can appear on the ballot by filing petition signatures; candidates for certain offices may file a $100 filing fee in lieu of filing petition signatures. All minor-party candidates, as well as major-party candidates for certain statewide offices, are chosen by a convention. Candidates running for nonpartisan offices (including judgeships, school boards, and most city offices) can appear on the ballot via petitions, as can candidates running for partisan offices without party affiliation.

- **Minnesota**: Major party candidates are nominated by the state primary process. Independent and minor political party candidates are nominated by a petition process; 2,000 signatures for a statewide election, or 500 for a state legislative election. Candidates have a two-week period to collect nominating petition signatures. Independent candidates may select a brief political party designation in lieu of independent.

- **Missouri** exempts parties from needing to gather signatures if they attain 2% of the vote in a statewide election.[14]

- **New York**
  *Main article: qualified New York parties*
  : To be recognized, political party must gain 50,000 votes in the most recent gubernatorial election. (There are, as of 2015, eight such parties. Five of them, however, have primarily resorted to electoral fusion and usually only nominate candidates already on either the Democratic or Republican lines; two of those five were blatant fronts for the major party candidates and did not exist until 2014. The sole exception is the Green Party.) This allows for primary elections and allows statewide candidates to be exempted from having to petition. Any other candidate must file petitions. For statewide candidates, 15,000 signatures are required, and there must be at least 100 signatures from each

of at least 1/2 of the congressional districts in the state (27 as of 2014). All state legislature and congressional candidates must file petitions regardless of party nominations, except in special elections. Village and town elections have less restrictive ballot access rules.[15]

- **North Carolina** 's law pertaining to ballot access is codified in N.C.G.S Chapter 163 Elections and Election Law:[16]

  - **New Political Parties:** According to N.C.G.S. §163-96(a)(2)[17][18] for a New Political Party to gain access to the election ballot they must obtain signatures on a petition equal to at least 2% of the total number of votes cast for Governor in the most recent election by no later than 12:00 noon on the first day of June before the election in which the Party wishes to participate. In addition, at least 200 signatures must come from at least four separate US Congressional Districts each within the state. To qualify for the 2010 or 2012 election ballot a new political party must gather at least 85,379 signatures within approximately a 3.5 year time span, averaging at least 67 signatures every day for three and half years straight counting weekdays and holidays.[18]

  - **Political Party Retention Requirement:** According to N.C.G.S. §163-96(a)(1)[19] in order for a political party to remain certified for the election ballot after obtaining access to the ballot, or to remain recognized by the State of North Carolina, that party must successfully garner at least 2% of the total vote cast for Governor for its candidate. If a party's candidate for Governor fails to receive at least 2% of the vote, that party loses ballot access (N.C.G.S. §163-97[20]) and must begin the petitioning process over again, and the voter affiliation of all registered voters affiliated with that party is changed to unaffiliated (N.C.G.S. §163-97.1[21]).

  - **Statewide Unaffiliated Requirements:** According to N.C.G.S. §163-122(a)(1)[22] in order for an unaffiliated candidate to qualify for the election ballot for a statewide office, the candidate must obtain signatures on a petition equal to at least 2% of the total number of votes caste for Governor in the most recent election by 12:00 noon on the last Friday in June before the election in which the candidate wishes to participate. In addition, at least 200 signatures must come from at least four separate US Congressional Districts each within the state. To qualify for the 2010 or 2012 election ballot unaffiliated statewide candidates must obtain at least 85,379 signatures.

- **District Unaffiliated Requirements:** According to N.C.G.S. §163-122(a)(2-3)[22] in order for an unaffiliated candidate to qualify for the election ballot for a district office, the candidate must obtain signatures on a petition equal to at least 4% of the total number of registered voters within the district that the candidate is running for election in as of January 1 of the election year in which the candidate desires to appear on the election ballot. Signatures must be turned in by 12:00 noon on the last Friday in June before the election in which the candidate wishes to participate. District candidates effectively cannot start petitioning for ballot access until after January 1 of the election year they are running for election, giving them just under half a year to obtain signatures for ballot access. To qualify for the 2010 election ballot unaffiliated US Congressional candidates are required to obtain as many as 22,544 signatures and an average of 18,719 signatures required for access to the 2010 election ballot.[23]

- **North Dakota** requires 7,000 petition signatures to create a new political party and nominate a slate of candidates for office. Independent candidates need 1,000 for a statewide office or 300 for a state legislative office. The independent nominating petition process does not allow for candidates to appear on the ballot with a political party designation, in lieu of independent, except for presidential elections.[24]

- **Ohio**: Late in 2006, the 6th U.S. Circuit Court of Appeals invalidated Ohio's law for ballot access for new political parties in a suit brought by the Libertarian Party of Ohio.[25] After the November elections, the outgoing Secretary of State and Attorney General requested an extension to file an appeal to the US Supreme Court so that the decision to appeal could be made by the newly–elected Secretary of State and Attorney General. The new Secretary of State did not appeal, but instead asserted her authority as Chief Election Officer of Ohio to issue new ballot access rules. In July 2008, a US District Court invalidated the Secretary of State's rules and placed the Libertarian Party on the ballot.[26] Three other parties subsequently sued and were placed on the ballot by the Court or by the Secretary of State.

- **Oklahoma**: A party is defined either as a group that polled 10% for the office at the top of the ticket in the last election (i.e., president or governor), or that submits a petition signed by voters equal to 5% of the last vote cast for the office at the top of the ticket. An independent presidential candidate, or the presidential candidate of an unqualified party, may get on the ballot with a petition of 3% of the last presidential vote. Oklahoma is the only state in the nation in which an independent presidential candidate, or the presidential candidate of a new or previously unqualified party, needs support from more than 2% of the last vote cast to get on the ballot. An initiative was circulated in 2007 to lower the ballot access rules for political parties.

- **Pennsylvania**: A new party or independent candidate may gain ballot access for one election as a "political body" by collecting petition signatures equal to 2% of the vote for the highest vote-getter in the most recent election in the jurisdiction. A political body that wins 2% of the vote obtained by the highest vote-getter statewide in the same election is recognized statewide as a "political party" for two years. A political party with a voter enrollment equal to less than 15% of the state's total partisan enrollment is classified as a "minor political party," which has automatic ballot access in special elections but must otherwise collect the same number of signatures as political bodies. Political parties not relegated to "minor" status qualify to participate in primary elections. Candidates may gain access to primary election ballots by collecting a set number of petition signatures for each office, generally significantly fewer than required for political bodies and minor political parties.

- **South Dakota**: For a registered political party in a statewide election they must collect petition signatures equal to 1% of the vote for that political party in the preceding election for state governor. An independent candidate must collect petition signatures equal to 1% of the total votes for state governor, and a new political party must collect 250 petition signatures. In state legislative elections, a registered political party needs to collect 50 signatures and an independent candidate must collect 1% of the total votes cast for state governor in the preceding election in their respective district.[27]

- **Tennessee**: A candidate seeking a House or Senate seat at the state or national level must gather 25 signatures from registered voters to be put on the ballot for any elected office.[28][29] Presidential candidates seeking to represent an officially recognized party must either be named as candidates by the Tennessee Secretary of State or gather 2,500 signatures from registered voters, and an independent candidate for President must gather 275 signatures and put forward a full slate of eleven candidates who have agreed to serve as electors.[30] To be recognized as a party and have its candidates listed on the ballot under that party's name, a political party must gather signatures equal to or in excess of 2.5% of the total number of votes cast in the last gubernatorial election (about 45,000 signatures based on the election held in 2006).[31] A third party to be officially recognized was the American Party in 1968; none of its candidates received 5% of the statewide vote in 1970 or 1972 and it was then subject to decertification as an official party after the 1972 election. In 2012, a state court ruled that the Green Party of Tennessee and the Constitution Party of Tennessee would join the Republican and Democratic Parties on the ballot beginning with the 6 November 2012 election.

- **Texas**: For a registered political party in a statewide election to gain ballot access, they must either: obtain 5% of the vote in any statewide election; or collect petition signatures equal to 1% of the total votes cast in the preceding election for governor, and must do so by January 2 of the year in which such statewide election is held. An independent candidate for any statewide office must collect petition signatures equal to 1% of the total votes cast for governor, and must do so beginning the day after primary elections are held and complete collection within 60 days thereafter (if runoff elections are held, the window is shortened to beginning the day after runoff elections are held and completed within 30 days thereafter). The petition signature cannot be from anyone who voted in either primary (including runoff), and voters cannot sign multiple petitions (they must sign a petition for one party or candidate only).[32]

- **Virginia**: A candidate for any statewide or local office must be qualified to vote for as well as hold the office they are running for, must have been "a resident of the county, city or town which he offers at the time of filing", a resident of the district, if it is an election for a specific district, and a resident of Virginia for one year before the election. For any office the candidate must obtain signatures of at least 125 registered voters for the area where they are running for office (except in communities of fewer than 3,500 people, where the number is lower), and if they are running as a candidate from a political party where partisan elections are permitted, must pay a fee of 2% of their yearly salary (no fee is required for persons not running as a candidate for a primary of a political party). Petitions, along with additional paperwork, must be filed between about four and five months before the election, subject to additional requirements for candidates for a primary election.[33] 1,000 signatures are required for a US House race and 10,000 for a statewide race (i.e. US President, US Senate, Governor, Lieutenant Governor, or Attorney General), including 400 from

each Congressional district.[34] Nominees of a political party that "at either of the two preceding statewide general elections, received at least 10 percent of the total vote cast for any statewide office filled in that election" are exempt from needing to gather signatures.[35]

## 11.2.2   Constitutional dimensions of ballot access laws

State ballot access restrictions can affect fundamental constitutional rights, including:

- the right to equal protection of the laws under the Fourteenth Amendment (when the restrictions involve a discriminatory classification of voters, candidates, or political parties);

- rights of political association under the First Amendment (especially when the restrictions burden the rights of political parties and other political associations, but also when they infringe on the rights of a candidate or a voter not to associate with a political party);

- rights of free expression under the first amendment;

- rights of voters (which the Supreme Court has said are "inextricably intertwined" with the rights of candidates);

- property interests and liberty interests in candidacy;

- other rights to "due process of law".

It has also been argued that ballot access restrictions infringe the following constitutional rights:

- the right to petition the government (this argument is sometimes raised to allege that signature-gathering requirements, or the rules implementing them, are unfairly restrictive);

- freedom of the press (which historically included the right to print ballots containing the name of the candidate of one's choosing);

- the right to a "republican form of government," which is guaranteed to each state (although this clause has been held not to be enforceable in court by individual citizens).

The US Supreme Court precedent on ballot access laws cases has been conflicting. In *Williams v. Rhodes* (1969) the court struck down Ohio's ballot access laws on First and Fourteenth Amendment grounds, but during the 1970s tended to uphold strict ballot access law, with the newly declared 'compelling State interest' being the "preservation of the integrity of the electoral process and regulating the number of candidates on the ballot to avoid voter confusion."[36]

The Supreme Court did strike down restrictive provisions in a ballot access law in Anderson v. Celebrezze,' 460 U.S. 780 (1983), but most of the subsequent court rulings in the 1980s - 2000s continued to uphold strict ballot access laws in both primary and general elections. Among the most notable of these cases from the 1970s - 1990s:

- *Bullock v. Carter*, 405 U.S. 134 (1972)

- *Illinois State Bd. of Elections v. Socialist Workers Party*, 440 U.S. 173 (1979)

- *U.S. Term Limits, Inc. v. Thornton*, 514 U.S. 779 (1995)

- *Lubin v. Panish*, 415 U.S. 709 (1974)

- *Norman v. Reed*, 502 U.S. 279 (1992).

The Supreme Court has not expressly ruled on the maximum level of restrictions that can be imposed on an otherwise qualified candidate or political party seeking ballot access. As a result, lower courts have often reached difficult conclusions about whether a particular ballot access rule is unconstitutional.

Requiring an otherwise eligible candidate or political party to obtain signatures greater than 5% of the eligible voters in the previous election may be unconstitutional. This is based on *Jenness v. Fortson*, 403 U.S. 431 (1971); the court upheld a restrictive ballot access law with this 5% signature requirement, whereas the *Williams v. Rhodes* (1969) had involved a 15% signature requirement.[37] Most State ballot access requirements, even the more restrictive ones, are less than 5%, and the Supreme Court has generally refused to hear ballot access cases that involved an Independent or minor party candidate challenging a ballot access law that requires less than 5%.[38]

### 11.2.3 International human rights law and ballot access

International agreements that have the status of treaties of the US are part of the supreme law of the land, under Article VI of the United States Constitution:

- International Covenant on Civil and Political Rights, Art. 25

- Copenhagen Document, ¶¶6-8, Annex I to 1990 Charter of Paris

Another source of international human rights law derives from universally accepted norms that have found expression in resolutions of the U.N. General Assembly. Although the Universal Declaration of Human Rights is not binding under US law the way a treaty is, this type of norm is recognized as a source of international law in such treaties as the Statute of the International Court of Justice, to which the US is a party:

- Universal Declaration of Human Rights, Art. 21

(NB: to be completed)

## 11.3 Write-in status versus ballot access

Depending on the office and the state, it may be possible for a voter to cast a write-in vote for a candidate whose name does not appear on the ballot. It is extremely rare for such a candidate to win office. In some cases, write-in votes are simply not counted. Having one's name printed on the ballot confers an enormous advantage over candidates who are not on the ballot. The US Supreme Court has noted that write-in status is absolutely no substitute for being on the ballot.

The two most notable cases of write-in candidates actually winning are the elections of Lisa Murkowski in 2010 and Strom Thurmond in 1954, both to the United States Senate. Other cases include the election of Charlotte Burks to the Tennessee State Senate seat of her late husband, Tommy Burks, murdered by his only opponent on the ballot; and the write-in primary victories in the re-election campaign of Mayor Anthony A. Williams of the District of Columbia. All of these cases involved unique political circumstances, a popular and well–known candidate, and a highly organized and well–funded write-in education campaign.

## 11.4 Other obstacles facing third parties

The growth of any third political party in the United States faces extremely challenging obstacles, among them restrictive ballot access. Other obstacles often cited as barriers to third-party growth include:

- Campaign funding reimbursement for any political party that gets at least 5% of the vote—implemented in many states "to help smaller parties"—typically helps the two biggest parties;

- Laws intended to fight corporate donations, with loopholes that require teams of lawyers to navigate the laws;

- The role of corporate money in propping up the two established parties;

- The allegedly related general reluctance of news organizations to cover minor political party campaigns;

- Moderate voters being divided between the major parties, or registered independent, so that both major primaries are hostile to moderate or independent candidates;

- Politically motivated gerrymandering of election districts by those in power, to reduce or eliminate political competition (two-party proponents would argue that the minority party in that district should just nominate a more centrist candidate relative to that district);

- Plurality voting scaring voters from credibly considering more than two major parties, as opponents of one would have to unite behind the other to have the most effective chance of winning (see Duverger's law);

- The extended history and reputations of the two established parties, with both existing for over 150 years and being entrenched in the minds of the public;

- The absence of proportional representation;

- The public view that third parties have no chance of beating the worse of evils, and are therefore a wasted vote;

- Campaign costs of convincing interested voters that the party nominee has a chance of winning, and regaining that trust after an election where the third party got the third-most votes or, worse, split the vote between two similar candidates so that the most disliked candidate won (i.e. "spoiling" the election; this is less of a problem with instant-runoff voting or condorcet voting).

## 11.5   Justification of strict ballot access laws by two party supporters

Strict ballot access laws are not required for a two–party system, as can be seen by the experience of the United Kingdom. However, the following arguments are put forth about the need for strict ballot access laws in the United States:

- With plurality voting, allowing third candidates on the ballot could split the vote of a majority and throw the race to a candidate not favored by the majority. Allowing only two candidates on the ballot ensures that at least the worst one is never elected.

- If a third party could get enough votes to win an election, then voters who would support the nominee could infiltrate one of the two parties by registering as members, and force a win in that party's primary. However, pulling this off would take considerable coordination on the part of the supporting voters, especially if half of them preferred to infiltrate the other major party or remain independent. It would also depend on the rules of the major party for how people may become candidates in their primary, and on which registered members may vote in the primary.

- There is a *one person one vote mandate*. If voters could vote in a primary for one candidate, and then sign a petition for another candidate, this would violate that mandate. Some voters might sign a petition for the candidate they want, and then vote in the primary for the candidate who would be easier to beat. Since primary votes are anonymous, and a party therefore cannot remove that voter's vote after it is cast, the only remedy is to strike the voter's signature on the petition. As for signatures not counting if a voter later votes in a primary, that could be reformed since the political party would know in advance about the signatures if they are filed in time.

- *Sore loser laws*, where a candidate who loses in a primary may not then run as an independent candidate in that same election, stem from contract laws. Similar–minded candidates run in the same primary with the contract that the losers will drop out of the race and support the winner so that they do not split the votes of similar–minded voters and cause the other party's nominee to win with 40% of the vote. The need for primaries is primarily because of plurality voting, whose rules state that the candidate receiving the most votes wins, even if not a majority.

- Strict ballot access laws make it difficult for extremists to get on the ballot, since few people would want to sign their petition.

## 11.6   See also

- Ballot Access News

- Coalition for Free and Open Elections

- Free the Vote North Carolina

# 11.7 References

[1] ACE Encyclopaedia: Criteria to stand as a candidate. Retrieved 15 July 2009

[2] Richard Winger, "The Importance of Ballot Access", *Long Term View* (Andover, MA: Massachusetts School of Law, Spring 1994)

[3] "U.S. Supreme Court Rules Against Fusion", *Ballot Access News*, 5 May 1997. Retrieved 22 September 2008

[4] "OSCE/ODIHR Election Observation Mission Final Report on the 2 November 2004 elections in the United States", *OSCE Office for Democratic Institutions and Human Rights*, 31 March 2005. Retrieved 22 September 2008

[5] "Ballot Access Bill Re-Introduced in Congress", *Ballot Access News*, 1 October 2007. Retrieved 22 September 2008

[6] Mary Jo Pitzl, " "Green Party wins ballot status", *The Arizona Republic*, 20 April 2008. Retrieved 22 September 2008

[7] "California Secretary of State - Political Party Qualification". Sos.ca.gov. 7 November 2006. Archived from the original on 6 May 2010. Retrieved 9 May 2010.

[8] 16 October 2008

[9]

[10]

[11]

[12]

[13]

[14]

[15]

[16] NC General Assembly webmasters. "N.C.G.S Chapter 163 Elections and Election Law". Ncleg.net. Archived from the original on 3 May 2010. Retrieved 9 May 2010.

[17] "N.C.G.S. §163-96(a)(2) "Political party" defined; creation of new party". Ncleg.net. Archived from the original on 17 April 2010. Retrieved 9 May 2010.

[18] "New Political Party Ballot Access | North Carolinians for Free and Proper Elections PAC". Ncfpe.com. Retrieved 9 May 2010.

[19] "N.C.G.S. §163-96(a)(1) "Political party" defined; creation of new party". Ncleg.net. Archived from the original on 17 April 2010. Retrieved 9 May 2010.

[20] "N.C.G.S. §163-97 Termination of status as political party". Ncleg.net. Retrieved 9 May 2010.

[21] "N.C.G.S. §163-97.1 Voters affiliated with expired political party". Ncleg.net. Retrieved 9 May 2010.

[22] "N.C.G.S. §163-122 Unaffiliated candidates nominated by petition". Ncleg.net. Archived from the original on 17 April 2010. Retrieved 9 May 2010.

[23] "Unaffiliated District Candidates Access to the Ballot | North Carolinians for Free and Proper Elections". Ncfpe.com. Retrieved 9 May 2010.

[24] "Elections and Voting", *North Dakota Secretary of State*. Retrieved 22 September 2008

[25] "Secretary of State Eases Restrictions on LPO Ballot Access", *Libertarian Party of Ohio*, 22 May 2007. Retrieved 22 September 2008

[26] "Ohio Libertarian Party wins ballot access lawsuit", *Ballot Access News*, 17 July 2008. Retrieved 16 October 2008

[27] "Number of Signatures Required on Petitions Filed for the 2006 Election", *South Dakota Secretary of State*. Retrieved 22 September 2008

[28] "Qualifying Procedures for Candidates for United States Senator", *Tennessee Division of Elections*. Retrieved 3 November 2008

[29] "Qualifying Procedures for Tennessee Candidates for United States House of Representatives", *Tennessee Division of Elections*. Retrieved 3 November 2008

[30] "Tennessee Ballot Access Procedures for Candidates for U.S. President", *Tennessee Division of Elections*. Retrieved 3 November 2008

[31] "Against all odds, third-party candidates fight on", *The Tennessean*. Retrieved 3 November 2008

[32] "Candidate's Guide to Primary and General Election", Texas Secretary of State. Retrieved 22 September 2008

[33] An example for the 2007 election appears here .

[34] "LIS> Code of Virginia> 24.2-506". Leg1.state.va.us. Retrieved 9 May 2010.

[35]

[36] Constitutional Right To Candidacy. Nicole A. Gordon Political Science Quarterly Volume 91, Number 3, 1976

[37] "JENNESS V. FORTSON, 403 U. S. 431 (1971)", *US Supreme Court Center*. Retrieved 22 September 2008

[38] "Oklahoma Supreme Court Won't Hear Ballot Case -- Libertarian Ballot Access Case Had Been Filed in 2004", *Ballot Access News*, 1 June 2007. Retrieved 22 September 2008

## 11.8  Bibliography

- Dimitri Evseev. "A Second Look At Third Parties: Correcting The Supreme Court's Understanding of Elections". Boston University Law Review. Vol. 85:1277 (2005)

- Essays By Richard Winger. Ballot Access News. <http://www.ballot-access.org/winger/essays.html>

## 11.9  External links

- ACE Encyclopaedia: Comparative Data: Ballot Access Issues

- Ballot Access News

- 1998 European Ballot Access Law

- More Voter Choice (Washington State)

- Friends of Democracy - election law reform in Minnesota, North Dakota and South Dakota

- A legal analysis of over 50 years of ballot access discrimination against third parties in the US, by Theresa Amato, national campaign director for Ralph Nader, in the *Harvard Law Record*

# Chapter 12

# Write-in candidate

A **write-in candidate** is a candidate in an election whose name does not appear on the ballot, but for whom voters may vote nonetheless by writing in the person's name. The system is almost totally confined to elections in the United States. Some U.S. states and local jurisdictions allow a voter to affix a sticker with a write-in candidate's name on it to the ballot in lieu of actually writing in the candidate's name. Write-in candidacies are sometimes a result of a candidate being legally or procedurally ineligible to run under his or her own name or party; Write-in candidacies may be permitted where term limits bar an incumbent candidate from being officially nominated for, or being listed on the ballot for, re-election. In some cases, write-in campaigns have been organized to support a candidate who is not personally involved in running; this may be a form of draft campaign.

Write-in candidates rarely win, and votes are often cast for ineligible people or fictional characters. Some jurisdictions require write-in candidates be registered as official candidates before the election.[1] This is standard in elections with a large pool of potential candidates, as there may be multiple candidates with the same name that could be written in.

Many U.S. states and municipalities allow for write-in votes in a partisan primary election where no candidate is listed on the ballot to have the same functional effect as nominating petitions: for example, if there are no Reform Party members on the ballot for state general assembly and a candidate receives more than 200 write-in votes when the primary election is held (or the other number of signatures that were required for ballot access), the candidate will be placed on the ballot on that ballot line for the general election. In most places, this provision is in place for nonpartisan elections as well.

## 12.1 United States

### 12.1.1 Historical success of write-in candidates

Generally, write-in candidates can compete in any election within the United States. Typically, write-in candidates have a very small chance of winning, but there have been some strong showings by write-in candidates over the years.

**Presidential primaries**

- In 1928, Herbert Hoover won the Republican Massachusetts presidential primary on write-ins, polling 100,279.

- In 1940, Franklin D. Roosevelt won the Democratic New Jersey presidential primary with 34,278 write-ins.

- In 1944, Thomas Dewey won the Republican Pennsylvania presidential primary with 146,706 write-ins. He also won the Oregon Republican presidential primary with 50,001 write-ins.

- In 1948, Harold Stassen won the Republican Pennsylvania presidential primary with 81,242 write-ins.

- In 1952, Robert A. Taft won the Republican Nebraska presidential primary with 79,357 write-ins.

- Also in 1952, Estes Kefauver won the Democratic Pennsylvania presidential primary with 93,160 write-ins.

- Also in 1952, Dwight Eisenhower won the Republican Massachusetts presidential primary with 254,898 write-ins.

- In 1956, Dwight Eisenhower won the Republican Massachusetts presidential primary with 51,951 write-ins.

- In 1960, Richard Nixon won the Republican Massachusetts presidential primary with 53,164 write-ins.

- Also in 1960, John F. Kennedy won the Democratic Pennsylvania presidential primary with 183,073 write-ins, and he won the Democratic Massachusetts presidential primary with 91,607 write-ins.

- In 1964, a write-in campaign organized by supporters of former U.S. Senator and vice presidential nominee Henry Cabot Lodge, Jr. won Republican primaries for President in New Hampshire, New Jersey, and Massachusetts, defeating declared candidates Barry Goldwater, Nelson Rockefeller, and Margaret Chase Smith.

- In 1968 in the Democratic presidential primary in New Hampshire, incumbent President Lyndon Johnson did not file, but received write-ins totaling 50% of all Democratic votes cast. Senator Eugene McCarthy, who campaigned actively against Johnson's Vietnam war policies, was on the ballot. He received an impressive 41% of the vote and gained more delegates than the President. Johnson was so stunned that he did not run for reelection.[2]

- Consumer advocate Ralph Nader ran a write-in campaign in 1992 during the New Hampshire primary for the presidential nomination of both the Democratic and Republican parties. Declaring himself the "none of the above candidate" and using the Concord Principles as his platform, Nader received 3,054 votes from Democrats and 3,258 votes from Republicans.

**Senate**

- Republican William Knowland was elected in 1946 to the U.S. Senate from California, for a two-month term. The special election for the two-month term featured a November ballot with no names printed on it, and all candidates in that special election were write-in candidates.[3]

- Democrat Strom Thurmond was elected in 1954 to the United States Senate in South Carolina as a write-in candidate, after state Democratic leaders had blocked him from receiving the party's nomination.[3]

- In 2010 incumbent Alaska Senator Lisa Murkowski lost the Republican primary to Joe Miller.[4] Following her defeat she ran in the general election as a write in candidate. Murkowski had filed, and won, a lawsuit requiring election officials to have the list of names of write in candidates distributed at the polls,[5] and subsequently won the election with a wide enough margin over both Miller, and Democratic Party candidate Scott T. McAdams, to make moot the write-in ballots that had been challenged by Miller.[6]

**House of Representatives**

- In 1918, Peter F. Tague was elected to the U.S. House as a write-in independent Democrat, defeating the Democratic nominee, John F. Fitzgerald.

- In 1930 Republican Charles F. Curry, Jr. was elected to the House as a write-in from Sacramento, California. His father, Congressman Charles F. Curry Sr., was to appear on the ballot, but due to his untimely death his name was removed and no candidate's name appeared on the ballot.

- Democrat Dale Alford was elected as a write-in candidate to the United States House of Representatives in Arkansas in 1958. As member of the Little Rock school board, Alford launched his write-in campaign a week before the election because the incumbent, Brooks Hays, was involved in the incident in which president Eisenhower sent federal troops to enforce racial integration at Little Rock Central High School. Racial integration was unpopular at the time, and Alford won by approximately 1,200 votes, a 2% margin.[7]

- Republican Joe Skeen was elected as a write-in candidate to Congress in New Mexico in November 1980 after the incumbent Democrat, Harold Runnels, died in August of that year. No Republican filed to run against Runnels before the close of filing and, after the death, the New Mexico Secretary of State ruled that the Democrats could have a special primary to pick a replacement candidate, but the Republicans could not have a special election, since they had nobody to replace. Runnels' widow lost the special primary, and launched her own write-in candidacy, which split the Democratic vote and allowed Skeen to win with a 38% plurality.[7]

- Ron Packard of California finished in second place in the 18 candidate Republican primary to replace the retiring Clair Burgener. Packard lost the primary by 92 votes in 1982, and then mounted a write-in campaign as an independent. He won the election with a 37% plurality against both a Republican and a Democratic candidate. Following the elections, he re-aligned himself as a Republican.[7]

- Democrat Charlie Wilson was the endorsed candidate of the Democratic Party for Ohio's 6th congressional district in Ohio to replace Ted Strickland in 2006. Strickland was running for Governor, and had to give up his congressional seat. Wilson, though, did not qualify for the ballot because only 46 of the 96 signatures on his candidacy petition were deemed valid, while 50 valid signatures were required for ballot placement. The Democratic Party continued to support Wilson, and an expensive primary campaign ensued – over $1 million was spent by both parties. Wilson overwhelmingly won the Democratic primary as a write-in candidate on May 2, 2006 against two Democratic candidates whose names were on the ballot, with Wilson collecting 44,367 votes, 67% of the Democratic votes cast.[8] Wilson faced Republican Chuck Blasdel in the general election on November 7, 2006, and won, receiving 61% of the votes.

- Democrat Dave Loebsack entered the 2006 Democratic primary in Iowa's second congressional district as a write-in candidate after failing to get the required number of signatures. He won the primary and in the general election he defeated 15-term incumbent Jim Leach by a 51% to 49% margin.

- Jerry McNerney ran as a write-in candidate in the March 2004 Democratic Primary in California's 11th congressional district. He received 1,667 votes (3% of the votes cast), and, having no opposition (no candidates were listed on the Democratic primary ballot), won the primary.[9] Although he lost the November 2004 general election to Republican Richard Pombo, McNerney ran again in 2006 (as a candidate listed on the ballot) and won the Democratic Primary in June, and then the rematch against Pombo in November.

- Shelley Sekula-Gibbs failed as a write-in candidate in the November 7, 2006 election to represent the 22nd Texas congressional district in the 110th Congress (for the full term commencing January 3, 2007). The seat had been vacant since June 9, 2006, due to the resignation of the then representative Tom DeLay. Therefore, on the same ballot, there were two races: one for the 110th Congress, as well as a race for the unexpired portion of the term during the 109th Congress (until January 3, 2007). Sekula-Gibbs won the race for the unexpired portion of the term during the 109th Congress as a candidate listed on the ballot. She could not be listed on the ballot for the full term because Texas law did not allow a replacement candidate to be listed on the ballot after the winner of the primary (Tom DeLay) has resigned.

- Peter Welch, a Democrat representing Vermont's sole congressional district, became both the Democratic and Republican nominee for the House when he ran for re-election in 2008. Because the Republicans did not field any candidate on the primary ballot, Welch won enough write-in votes to win the Republican nomination.[10]

**State legislatures**

- Several members of the Alaska House of Representatives were elected as write-in candidates during the 1960s and 1970s, particularly from rural districts in the northern and western portions of the state. Factors in play at the time include the newness of Alaska as a state and the previous absence of electoral politics in many of the rural communities, creating an environment which made it hard to attract candidates to file for office during the official filing period. Most of the areas in question were largely populated by Alaska natives, who held little political power in Alaska at the time. This only began to change following the formation of the Alaska Federation of Natives and the passage of the Alaska Native Claims Settlement Act. Known examples of successful write-in candidates include Kenneth A. Garrison and Father Segundo Llorente (1960), Frank R. Ferguson (1972), James H. "Jimmy" Huntington (1974), and Nels A. Anderson, Jr. (1976). The incumbent in Llorente's election, Axel C. Johnson, ran for re-election as a write-in candidate after failing to formally file his candidacy paperwork. Johnson and Llorente, as write-in candidates, both outpolled the one candidate who did appear on the ballot. Ferguson and Anderson were both incumbents who launched their write-in campaigns after being defeated in the primary election. Anderson's main opponent, Joseph McGill, had himself won election to the House in 1970 against a write-in candidate by only 5 votes.

- Carl Hawkinson of Galesburg won the Republican primary for the Illinois Senate from Illinois's 47th District in 1986 as a write-in candidate. He went on to be elected in the general election and served until 2003. Hawkinson defeated another write-in, David Leitch, in the primary. Incumbent State Senator Prescott Bloom died in a home fire after the filing date for the primary had passed.

- After failing to receive the Republican Party's 1990 Wilson Pakula nomination, incumbent and registered Conservative New York State Senator Serphin Maltese won the party's nomination as a write-in candidate.[11]

- Charlotte Burks won as a Democratic write-in candidate for the Tennessee Senate seat left vacant when the incumbent, her husband Tommy, was assassinated by his opponent, Byron Looper, two weeks before the elections of November 2, 1998. The assassin was the only name on the ballot, so Charlotte ran as a write-in candidate.

- Winnie Brinks was elected to the Michigan House of Representatives in 2012 after a series of unusual events.  In May of that year, State Representative Roy Schmidt - who had previously filed to run for re-election as a Democrat - withdrew from the Democratic primary and re-filed as a Republican.  A friend of Schmidt's nephew filed to run as a Democrat, but withdrew two days later amid anger among local Democrats.  This left Democrats without a candidate.  Brinks ran as a write-in to be the Democratic nominee for the seat.  She won the primary and therefore qualified to be on the general election ballot, which she also won.  Coincidentally, the general election also saw a write-in candidate, Bing Goei, receive significant support.[12]

- Scott Wagner was elected as an anti-establishment Republican write-in candidate to the Pennsylvania Senate in a March 2014 special election over endorsed Republican nominee Ron Miller and Democrat Linda Small.[13]

**Local government**

- Julia Allen of Readington, New Jersey won a write-in campaign in the November 2005 elections for the Township Committee,[14] after a candidate accused of corruption had won the primary.[15]

- Tom Ammiano, President of the San Francisco Board of Supervisors, entered the race for Mayor of San Francisco as a write-in candidate two weeks before the 1999 general election.  He received 25% of the vote, coming in second place and forcing incumbent Mayor Willie Brown into a runoff election, which Brown won by margin of 59% to 40%.  In 2001, the campaign was immortalized in the award-winning documentary film *See How They Run*.

- John R. Brinkley ran as a write-in candidate for governor of Kansas in 1930.  He was motivated at least in part by the state's revocation of his medical license and attempts to shut down his clinic, where he performed alternative medical procedures including transplantation of goat glands into humans.  He won 29.5% of the vote in a three-way race.  Brinkley's medical and political career are documented in Pope Brock's book *Charlatan*.[16]

- Mike Duggan filed petition to run for mayor of Detroit in 2013; however, following a court challenge, Duggan's name was removed from the ballot.  Duggan then campaigned as a write-in in the August 2013 primary, with the intent of being one of the top two vote-getters and thus advancing to the general election in November.  Duggan received the highest number of votes in the primary, and advanced to the runoff in November.He eventually defeated challenger Sheriff Benny Napoleon to become the Mayor of Detroit.[17]

- Donna Frye ran as a write-in candidate for Mayor of San Diego in 2004.  A controversy erupted when several thousand votes for her were not counted because the voters had failed to fill in the bubble next to the write-in line.  Had those votes been counted, she would have won the election.[18]

- Michael Jarjura was re-elected Mayor of Waterbury, Connecticut in 2005 as a write-in candidate after losing the Democratic party primary to Karen Mulcahy, who used to serve as Waterbury's tax collector before Jarjura fired her in 2004 "for what he claimed was her rude and abusive conduct toward citizens".[19] After spending $100,000 on a general elections write-in campaign,[20] Jarjura received 7,907 votes, enough for a plurality of 39%.[21]

- James Maher won the mayorship of Baxter Estates, New York on March 15, 2005 as a write-in candidate with 29 votes.  Being the only one on the ballot, the incumbent mayor, James Neville, did not campaign, as he did not realize that there was a write-in campaign going on.  Neville received only 13 votes.[22]

- Beverly O'Neil won a third term as Mayor of Long Beach, California as a write-in candidate in 2002.  The Long Beach City City Charter has a term limit amendment that says a candidate cannot be on the ballot after two full terms, but does not prevent the person from running as a write-in candidate.[23] She finished first in a seven-candidate primary, but did not receive more than 50% of the vote, forcing a runoff contest.  In the runoff, still restricted from the ballot, she got roughly 47% of the vote in a three-way election that included a second write-in candidate.[24]

- Michael Sessions, an 18-year-old high school senior, won as a write-in candidate for Mayor of Hillsdale, Michigan in 2005.  He was too young to qualify for the ballot.

- In Galesburg, Illinois, an error by the Galesburg Election Commission [25] in late 2010 gave city council candidate Chuck Reynolds the wrong number of signatures he required to be on the ballot for the April 2011 city council election,[26] resulting in him being removed from the ballot when challenged by Incumbent Russell Fleming.[25][27] Reynolds ran as a write-in vote [28] in the April 2011 election, and lost by 9 votes.[29][30]

- Anthony A. Williams, then incumbent Mayor of Washington, D.C. was forced to run as a write-in candidate in the 2002 Democratic primary, because he had too many invalid signatures for his petition. He won the Democratic primary, and went on to win re-election.

- In the November 8, 2011, election for Commonwealth's Attorney of Richmond County, Virginia, 16-year incumbent Wayne Emery has been certified the winner as a write-in candidate over challenger James Monroe by a margin of 53 votes (2.4%) out of 2,230 votes cast, after his petitions were challenged and his name was removed from the ballot.[31]

- In the 1997 election for Mayor of Talkeetna, Alaska, Stubbs the Cat won over the two human candidates. He has been re-elected every mayoral election since, and, as of July 18, 2012, celebrates 15 years in office.[32]

**Others**

- Aaron Schock was elected to the District 150 School Board in Peoria, Illinois in 2001 by a write-in vote, after his petitions were challenged and his name was removed from the ballot. He defeated the incumbent by over 2,000 votes, approximately 6,400 to 4,300 votes.[33] He went on to serve in the Illinois House of Representatives, and was elected to the United States House of Representatives in 2008. He was later forced to resign in an expenses scandal. [34]

- John Adams became an Orange County, California judge in November 2002 after running along with 10 other write-in candidates in the primaries on March 5, 2002 against incumbent Judge Ronald Kline.[35] After the filing deadline in which no candidate filed to run against Kline, a computer hacker discovered that Judge Kline had child pornography on his home computer. Kline got less than 50% of the vote in the primaries, requiring a runoff between him and write-in candidate John Adams (who actually received more votes than Kline).[36] After some legal maneuvers, Kline's name was removed from the general elections, leaving the general election a runoff between Adams and Gay Sandoval, who was the second highest write-in vote getter.[37] Charges against Kline were eventually thrown out.[38]

- On September 15, 2009, four write-in candidates in the Independence Party primaries for various offices in Putnam County, New York defeated their on-ballot opponents.[39]

- In a May 2011 school board election for the Bentley School Board in Michigan, Lisa Osborn ran as a write-in candidate and needed just one vote to win a seat. However, she did not receive any votes, even from herself. She explained herself by saying that she was at her son's baseball game and did not have time to go to the polls.[40]

### 12.1.2 California's Proposition 14 impact on write-in candidates

In 2010, California voters passed Proposition 14 which set up a new election system for the United States Senate, United States House of Representatives, all statewide offices (governor, lieutenant governor, secretary of state, state treasurer, state controller, attorney general, insurance commissioner, and superintendent of public instruction), California Board of Equalization, and for the California State Legislature. In the system set up by Proposition 14, there are two rounds of voting, and the top two vote-getters for each race in the first round advance to a second round. Proposition 14 specifically prohibits write-in candidates in the second round, and this prohibition was upheld in a court challenge.[41] Another court challenge to the prohibition on write-in candidates in the second round was filed in July 2014.[42]

Although Proposition 14 prohibits write-in candidates in the second round of voting, it has made it easier for write-in candidates in the first round to advance to the second round. This generally happens in elections where only one candidate is listed on the ballot. Since in each race the top two vote-getters from the first round are guaranteed to advance to the second round, if only one candidate is listed on the ballot, a write-in candidate can easily advance to the second round, as the write-in candidate would only have to compete with other write in candidates for the 2nd spot, not with any listed candidates. In the 2012 elections, the first election for which Proposition 14 went into effect, 5 write-in candidates advanced to the second round, but none received more than 40% of the vote in the second round.[43] In the 2014 elections, 16 write-in candidates advanced to the 2nd round of voting.[44] All 16 candidates lost in the second round, with only two of the 16 receiving more than 40% of the vote.[n 1]

## 12.2 Other countries

With a few exceptions, the practice of recognizing write-in candidates is typically viewed internationally as an American tradition.[45][46]

- Several cases of elected write-in candidates occurred

in the 2006 Swedish municipal elections. Under Swedish electoral law, free ballots are provided for any party that received more than 1 percent of the votes in one of the two latest parliamentary elections, irrespective of whether the party actually stood any candidates in the municipality. In some municipalities, voters cast a sufficient number of ballots for the nationalist Sweden Democrats to allow them to get a seat on the municipal council. (The membership of municipal councils in Sweden is relatively large, with even the smallest municipalities, numbering just a few thousand inhabitants, required to have a council of at least 31 members.) In cases where a party did not field any eligible candidates, people whose names were written in were elected, though many subsequently resigned their seats. In places where no candidates were written in, the seats were left vacant.[47]

- A bizarre incident involving a fictitious write-in candidacy occurred in the small town of Picoazá, Ecuador in 1967. A company ran a series of campaign-themed advertisements for a foot powder called Pulvapies. Some of the slogans used included "Vote for any candidate, but if you want well-being and hygiene, vote for Pulvapies", and "For Mayor: Honorable Pulvapies." The foot powder Pulvapies ended up receiving the most votes in the election.[48][49][50]

- In Brazil, until the introduction of electronic voting in 1994, the ballot had no names written for legislative candidates, so many voters would protest by voting on fictional characters or religious figures. In a famous case, the São Paulo city zoo rhinoceros *Cacareco* got around 100,000 votes in the 1959 elections for the municipal council, more than any candidate.[51] However, those votes were not considered because Brazilian law stipulates that a candidate must be affiliated to a political party to take office.

## 12.3   Protest

- *Mad Magazine* satirically called to vote for Alfred E. Neuman as a write-in candidate for every U.S. presidential election from 1960 to 1980 with slogans like "You could do worse–and you already have" and "There are Bigger Idiots running for office!".

- In the 1980 U.S. Presidential election, rock star Joe Walsh ran a mock write-in campaign, promising to make his song "Life's Been Good" the new national anthem if he won, and running on a platform of "Free Gas for Everyone." Though Walsh (then aged 33) was not old enough to actually assume the office, he wanted to raise public awareness of the election. (In 1992,

Walsh purportedly ran for *vice*-president, in his song "Vote For Me", a track on his album *Songs for a Dying Planet*, which was released that year.)

- During the 2000 United States Congress Elections, film-maker Michael Moore led a campaign for voters to submit a ficus tree as a write-in candidate. This campaign was replicated across the country and was recounted in an episode of *The Awful Truth*.

- In 2012, a campaign was waged to write in Charles Darwin's name against Georgia congressman Paul Broun (who was running unopposed) after Broun "called evolution and other areas of science 'lies straight from the pit of hell.' " Darwin received approximately 4,000 votes.[52] However, because Darwin was not an officially registered write in candidate, the Georgia Secretary of State did not tabulate those votes.[53]

## 12.4   Popular culture

- In the Ultimate Marvel universe, as of issue #15 of *Ultimate Comics: The Ultimates*, Captain America has become president of America as a write-in candidate.

- Actress Nina Dobrev won her People's Choice Award from fan write-ins in 2012.

- Charles R. Doty, a five-time unsuccessful write-in candidate for U.S. president, appeared on *The Daily Show with Jon Stewart* five times.

## 12.5   See also

- None of the above

## 12.6   Notes

[1] The two California candidates who ran as write-in candidates in June 2014 and went on to receive more than 40% of the vote in the November 2014 runoff were Jack Mobley who received 1,286 votes as a write-in candidate in June, and 46.6% of the vote in the runoff for the 21st Assembly District, and Nathaniel Tsai who received 394 votes as a write-in candidate in June, and 40.7% of the vote in the runoff for the 41st Assembly District.
link to Nov 2014 election results, link to June 2014 election results

# 12.7 References

[1] See, for example, Section 1-4-1101, Colorado Revised Statutes (2008)

[2] New Hampshire Almanac >First-in-the-Nation

[3] Washington Post, "Murkowski appears to make history in Alaska", Debbi Wilgoren, November 3, 2010 (accessed November 3, 2010)

[4] Official election results for the 2010 primaries. Alaska Division of Elections.

[5] Joling, Dan (October 28, 2010). "Lisa Murkowski Can Appear On List Of Write-In Candidates, State Supreme Court Rules". *Huffington Post.*

[6] Bohrer, Becky (November 18, 2010). "Murkowski becomes 1st write-in senator since '54". *Boston Globe.* Associated Press.

[7] Ken Rudin (August 23, 2006). "What Happens If Lieberman Wins". National Public Radio. Retrieved 2006-09-03.

[8] Johnson, Alan (May 3, 2006). "Wilson wins primary as write-in candidate". The Columbus Dispatch. Retrieved 2006-06-30.

[9] "Election Results for the March 2004 Primary" (PDF). California Secretary of State.

[10] "Write-ins give Welch GOP nomination". The Barre Montpelier Times Agnus. September 18, 2008.

[11] Serphin R. Maltese R-C

[12] Winnie Brinks takes oath of office as Michigan's 76th District State Representative

[13] Murphy, Jan (March 18, 2014). "Scott Wagner makes history with his win in York County Senate race". PennLive.com. Retrieved March 19, 2014.

[14] "2005 General Election results for Hunterdon County".

[15] Reprint from The Huntington County News

[16] http://www.nytimes.com/2008/01/31/books/31maslin.html?_r=0 Fleecing the Sheep, Who Keep Coming Back for More

[17] Abbeylambertz, Kate (August 7, 2013). "Mike Duggan, Write-In Candidate, Pulls Comeback In Detroit Mayoral Primary". *Huffington Post.*

[18] Rainey, James (December 25, 2004). "Media's role clouds San Diego recount". *The Boston Globe.*

[19] "Waterbury mayor to wage write-in campaign".

[20] The Waterbury Observer – The Write Stuff

[21] News Channel 8 / 2005 Vote Election Results

[22] Kazanjian O'Brien, Dolores (April 1, 2005). "Baxter Estates Mayor James Neville "Stunned" by Write-in Defeat". Port Washington News. Retrieved 2006-06-30.

[23] Recommendation to review proposed amendments to the Long Beach City Charter

[24] Legacy of a Legend. *Long Beach Press-Telegram.*

[25] http://www.wgil.com/newsarchive.php?xnewsaction=fullnews&newsarch=012011&newsid=150

[26] http://www.galesburg.com/news/x1958454815/Election-commission-upholds-challenge

[27] http://www.galesburg.com/news/x703876634/Election-commission-delays-announcement

[28] http://www.galesburg.com/news/x1254713692/Reynolds-will-run-as-write-in-for-city-council-Ward-3

[29] http://www.galesburg.com/x481356899/Recount-for-Galesburg-City-Council-Ward-3-seat-poss

[30] http://www.galesburg.com/news/x528727041/Final-count-confirms-Fleming-s-victory-for-Ward-3-c

[31] http://www2.timesdispatch.com/news/2011/nov/10/tdmet03-richmond-county-write-in-campaign-workedm

[32] Friedman, Amy (July 17, 2012). "Cat Marks 15 Years as Mayor of Alaska Town". Time Magazine.

[33] School Board Write-in Campaign

[34] DeBonis, Mike (March 17, 2015). "Rep. Aaron Schock announces resignation in wake of spending probe". *Washington Post.* Retrieved March 18, 2015.

[35] "'Fight' seen in California's governor's race". CNN. March 6, 2002. Retrieved 2006-03-30.

[36] Orange County Registrar of Voters Election Results for March 5, 2002

[37] Orange County Registrar of Voters Election Results for November 5, 2002

[38] Srisavasdi, Rachanee (October 30, 2003). "Case against ex-judge Kline gutted". Irvine World News. Retrieved 2006-06-30.

[39] Dougherty, Michael Brendan (October 1, 2009). "A Reversal of Fortune for Interim Independence Party". The Putnam County Courier. Retrieved November 27, 2009.

[40] Acosta, Roberto. "School board candidate loses election because she didn't vote for herself; calls not voting a 'dumb move'". Mlive.com. Retrieved November 2, 2011.

[41] Hagan Cain, Robyn (Sep 21, 2011). "Court Upholds Prop 14 Bans on Write-In Votes, Unqualified Parties".

[42] Cadelago, Christopher (Jul 30, 2014). "Lawsuit challenges write-in rules under California's top-two system". Sacramento Bee.

[43] http://www.ss.ca.gov/elections/prior-elections/statewide-election-results/

[44] Merl, Jean (July 22, 2014). "Some June write-in candidates made it to the November ballot". Los Angeles Times.

[45] ABC News: Donald Duck's a Big Bird in Politics

[46] "Livingstone threatens write-in campaign". *BBC News*. November 11, 1998.

[47] Skämtet gjorde Jonas till sd-politiker – GT.se – Expressen.se – Sveriges bästa nyhetssajt!

[48] "Foot Powder Produces Headaches in Ecuador." *The New York Times*. July 18, 1967. Page 39. Retrieved December 19, 2009.

[49] Snopes report on the election result

[50] "Foot Powder Wins Election Hands Down." *The Washington Post*. July 18, 1967 (p. A13).

[51] Ferreira, Neil. "Cacareco agora é Excelência". *O Cruzeiro*. Retrieved 20 October 2012.

[52] Thompson, Jim (November 9, 2012). "Charles Darwin gets 4,000 write-in votes in Athens against Paul Broun". Athens Banner-Herald.

[53] Georgia Secretary of State Nov 2012 election results

# Chapter 13

# Faithless elector

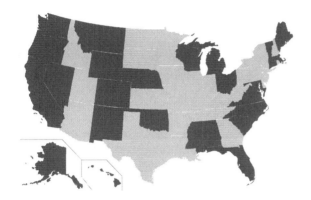

*States with laws against faithless electors*

In United States presidential elections, a **faithless elector** is a member of the United States Electoral College who does not vote for the presidential or vice presidential candidate for whom he or she had pledged to vote. They may vote for another candidate or not vote at all. Faithless electors are pledged electors and thus different from unpledged electors.

Electors are typically chosen and nominated by a political party or the party's presidential nominee: they are usually party members with a reputation for high loyalty to the party and its chosen candidate. Thus, a faithless elector runs the risk of party censure and political retaliation from their party, as well as potential criminal penalties in some states. Candidates for elector are nominated by state political parties in the months prior to Election Day. In some states, the electors are nominated in primaries, the same way that other candidates are nominated. In some states, such as Oklahoma, Virginia and North Carolina, electors are nominated in party conventions. In Pennsylvania, the campaign committee of each candidate names their candidates for elector (an attempt to discourage faithless electors).[1] The parties have generally been successful in keeping their electors faithful, leaving out the cases in which a candidate died before the elector was able to cast a vote.

Although there have been 157 cases of faithlessness as of 2015, faithless electors have not yet changed the outcome

of any presidential election.[2]

## 13.1   Legal position

Twenty-one states do not have laws that compel their electors to vote for a pledged candidate.[3] Twenty-nine states plus the District of Columbia have laws to penalize faithless electors, although these have never been enforced.[2] In lieu of penalizing a faithless elector, some states, like Michigan and Minnesota, specify that the faithless elector's vote is void.[4]

Until 2008, Minnesota's electors cast secret ballots, so that it was not possible to tell if a particular elector was faithless. When in 2004 an unknown elector was faithless, Minnesota law was amended to provide for public balloting of the electors' votes and invalidation of a vote cast for someone other than the candidate to whom the elector is pledged.[5]

The constitutionality of state *pledge* laws was confirmed by the Supreme Court in 1952 in *Ray v. Blair*.[6] The court ruled in favor of the state's right to require electors to pledge to vote for the candidate to whom they are pledged, as well as to remove electors who refuse to pledge. Once the elector has voted, his or her vote can be changed only in states such as Michigan and Minnesota, where votes other than those pledged are rendered invalid. In the twenty-nine states that have laws against faithless electors, a faithless elector may only be punished after he or she votes. The Supreme Court has ruled that, as electors are chosen via state elections, they act as a function of the state, not the federal government. Therefore states have the right to govern electors. The constitutionality of state laws punishing electors for actually casting a faithless vote—rather than merely refusing to pledge—has never been decided by the Supreme Court.

## 13.2  History

In 157 instances, electors have cast their votes for President or Vice President in a manner different from that prescribed by the legislature of the state they represented. Of those, 71 votes were changed because the original candidate died before the elector was able to cast a vote. Three votes were not cast at all when electors chose to abstain from casting their electoral vote for any candidate.[2] The remaining 83 were changed by the elector's personal interest, or perhaps by accident. Usually, the faithless electors act alone. An exception was the U.S. presidential election of 1836, in which 23 Virginia electors conspired to change their vote together.

As of the 2012 presidential election, there has been only one occasion when faithless electors prevented an expected winner from winning the electoral college vote outright: in 1836, twenty-three faithless electors prevented Richard Mentor Johnson, the expected candidate, from winning the majority of votes for the Vice Presidency. However, Johnson was promptly elected Vice President by the U.S. Senate in February 1837; therefore, faithless electors have never changed the expected final outcome of the *entire* election process.

## 13.3  List of faithless electors

Electors do not have to vote for the candidate who received the most votes in any particular state. The following is a list of all faithless electors (in reverse chronological order). The number preceding each entry is the number of faithless electors for the given year.

### 13.3.1  2000 to present

**1** – 2004 election:  A Minnesota elector, pledged for Democrats John Kerry and John Edwards, cast his or her presidential vote for *John Ewards* [*sic*],[7] rather than Kerry, presumably by accident.[8] (All of Minnesota's electors cast their vice presidential ballots for John Edwards.)  Minnesota's electors cast secret ballots, so unless one of the electors claims responsibility, it is unlikely that the identity of the faithless elector will ever be known.  As a result of this incident, Minnesota Statutes were amended to provide for public balloting of the electors' votes and invalidation of a vote cast for someone other than the candidate to whom the elector is pledged.[9]

**1** – 2000 election: Washington, D.C. Elector Barbara Lett-Simmons, pledged for Democrats Al Gore and Joe Lieberman, cast no electoral votes as a protest of Washington D.C.'s lack of congressional representation.[10]

### 13.3.2  1972 to 1996

**1** – 1988 election:  West Virginia Elector Margarette Leach, pledged for Democrats Michael Dukakis and Lloyd Bentsen, but as a form of protest against the winner-take-all custom of the Electoral College, instead cast her votes for the candidates in the reverse of their positions on the national ticket; her presidential vote went to Bentsen and her vice presidential vote to Dukakis.[11]

**1** – 1976 election:  Washington Elector Mike Padden, pledged for Republicans Gerald Ford and Bob Dole, cast his presidential electoral vote for Ronald Reagan, who had challenged Ford for the Republican nomination. He cast his vice presidential vote, as pledged, for Dole.

**1** – 1972 election:  Virginia Elector Roger MacBride, pledged for Republicans Richard Nixon and Spiro Agnew, cast his electoral votes for Libertarian candidates John Hospers and Theodora Nathan.  MacBride's vote for Nathan was the first electoral vote cast for a woman in U.S. history. MacBride became the Libertarian candidate for President in the 1976 election.

### 13.3.3  1912 to 1968

**1** – 1968 election: North Carolina Elector Lloyd W. Bailey, pledged for Republicans Richard Nixon and Spiro Agnew, cast his votes for American Independent Party candidates George Wallace and Curtis LeMay.

**1** – 1960 election:  Oklahoma Elector Henry D. Irwin, pledged for Republicans Richard Nixon and Henry Cabot Lodge, Jr., cast his presidential electoral vote for Democratic non-candidate Harry Flood Byrd and his vice presidential electoral vote for Republican Barry Goldwater. (Fourteen unpledged electors also voted for Byrd for president, but supported Strom Thurmond, then a Democrat, for vice president.)

**1** – 1956 election: Alabama Elector W. F. Turner, pledged for Democrats Adlai Stevenson and Estes Kefauver, cast his votes for Walter Burgwyn Jones and Herman Talmadge.

**1** – 1948 election: Two Tennessee electors were on both the Democratic Party and the States' Rights Democratic Party slates. When the Democratic Party slate won, one of these electors voted for the Democratic nominees Harry Truman and Alben Barkley. The other, Preston Parks, cast his votes for States' Rights Democratic Party candidates Strom Thurmond and Fielding Wright, making him a faithless elector.

**8** – 1912 election: Republican vice presidential candidate James S. Sherman died before the election. Eight Republican electors had pledged their votes to him but voted for Nicholas Murray Butler instead.

### 13.3.4  1860 to 1896

**4** – 1896 election: The Democratic Party and the People's Party both ran William Jennings Bryan as their presidential candidate, but ran different candidates for Vice President. The Democratic Party nominated Arthur Sewall and the People's Party nominated Thomas E. Watson. The People's Party won 31 electoral votes but four of those electors voted with the Democratic ticket, supporting Bryan as President and Sewall as Vice President.

**4** – 1892 election: In Oregon, three electors voted for Republican Benjamin Harrison and one faithless elector voted for the third-party Populist candidate, James B. Weaver. All four were pledged to President Harrison, who lost the election.

**63** – 1872 election: 63 electors for Horace Greeley changed their votes after Greeley's death, which occurred before the electoral vote could be cast. Greeley's remaining three electors cast their presidential votes for Greeley and had their votes discounted by Congress.

**4** – 1860 election: 4 electors in New Jersey, pledged for (Northern) Democrat Stephen A. Douglas, voted for the eventual victor: Republican candidate Abraham Lincoln.

### 13.3.5  1812 to 1836

**23** – 1836 election: The Democratic Party nominated Richard Mentor Johnson of Kentucky as their vice presidential candidate. The 23 electors from Virginia refused to support Johnson with their votes upon learning of the allegation that he had lived with an African-American woman. There was no majority in the Electoral College and the decision was deferred to the Senate, which supported Johnson as the Vice President.

**32** – 1832 election: Two National Republican Party electors from the state of Maryland refused to vote for presidential candidate Henry Clay and did not cast a vote for him or for his running mate. All 30 electors from Pennsylvania refused to support the Democratic vice presidential candidate Martin Van Buren, voting instead for William Wilkins.

**7** – 1828 election: Seven of nine electors from Georgia refused to vote for vice presidential candidate John C. Calhoun. All seven cast their vice presidential votes for William Smith instead.

**1** – 1820 election: William Plumer pledged to vote for Democratic Republican candidate James Monroe, but cast his vote for John Quincy Adams, who was also a Democratic Republican, but not a candidate in the 1820 election. Some historians contend that Plumer did not feel that the Electoral College should unanimously elect any President other than George Washington, but this claim is disputed. (Monroe lost another three votes because three electors died before casting ballots and were not replaced.)

**4** – 1812 election: Three electors pledged to vote for Federalist vice presidential candidate Jared Ingersoll voted for Democratic Republican Elbridge Gerry. One Ohio elector did not vote.

### 13.3.6  Before 1812

**6** – 1808 election: Six electors from New York were pledged to vote for Democratic Republican James Madison as President and George Clinton as Vice President. Instead, they voted for Clinton to be President, with three voting for Madison as Vice President and the other three voting for James Monroe to be Vice President.

**19** – 1796 election: Samuel Miles, an elector from Pennsylvania, was pledged to vote for Federalist presidential candidate John Adams, but voted for Democratic Republican candidate Thomas Jefferson. He cast his other presidential vote as pledged for Thomas Pinckney. An additional 18 electors voted for Adams as pledged, but refused to vote for Pinckney.[12] (This election took place prior to the passage of the 12th Amendment, so there were not separate ballots for president and vice president.)

## 13.4  References

[1] ElectoralVote.com – Current Assigning of Electors

[2] "Faithless Electors". *FairVote.org*. FairVote. Retrieved 24 September 2015.

[3] For 2000 list of 24 states, see

[4] "Michigan Election Law Section 168.47". Legislature.mi.gov. Retrieved 2010-08-26.

[5] "208.08, 2008 Minnesota Statutes". Revisor.leg.state.mn.us. Retrieved May 5, 2009.

[6] *Ray v. Blair* 343 U.S. 214 (1952)

[7] http://web.archive.org/web/20041217034158/http://www.startribune.com/stories/587/5134791.html

[8] "MPR: Minnesota elector gives Edwards a vote; Kerry gets other nine". News.minnesota.publicradio.org. Retrieved 2009-05-05.

[9] "208.08, 2008 Minnesota Statutes". Revisor.leg.state.mn.us. Retrieved 2009-05-05.

[10] Stout, David (2000-12-19). "The 43rd President: The Electoral College; The Electors Vote, and the Surprises Are Few". *The New York Times*. Retrieved 2009-11-30. But it was Mr. Gore who suffered an erosion today. Barbara Lett

Simmons, a Gore elector from the District of Columbia, left her ballot blank to protest what she called the capital's "colonial status" – its lack of a voting representative in Congress.

[11] Johnson, Sharen Shaw (1989-01-05). "CAPITAL LINE: [FINAL Edition]". *USA Today*. Retrieved 2016-02-11. (subscription required (help)). Even though Bensten sought the vice presidency, Margarette Leach of West Virginia voted for him to protest the Electoral College's winner-take-all custom.

[12] Chernow, Ron. *Alexander Hamilton*. New York: Penguin, 2004. p. 514.

## 13.5   External links

- List of Electors Bound by State Law and Pledges, as of November 2000

- "The Electoral College – "Faithless Electors"". *Official website of the Center for Voting and Democracy*. 2002. Retrieved December 5, 2006.

- "Faithless Electors". *Website of FairVote, formerly the Center for Voting and Democracy*. Retrieved June 11, 2008.

# Chapter 14

# Federal Election Commission

The **Federal Election Commission (FEC)** is an independent regulatory agency that was founded in 1975 by the United States Congress to regulate the campaign finance legislation in the United States. It was created in a provision of the 1974 amendment to the Federal Election Campaign Act. It describes its duties as "to disclose campaign finance information, to enforce the provisions of the law such as the limits and prohibitions on contributions, and to oversee the public funding of Presidential elections."[1]

## 14.1 Membership

The Commission is made up of six members, who are appointed by the President of the United States and confirmed by the United States Senate. Each member serves a six-year term, and two seats are subject to appointment every two years.[1] By law, no more than three Commissioners can be members of the same political party, and at least four votes are required for any official Commission action.

The Chairmanship of the Commission rotates among the members each year, with no member serving as Chairman more than once during his or her term.

## 14.2 Official duties

Although the Commission's name implies broad authority over U.S. elections, in fact its role is limited to the administration of federal campaign finance laws. It enforces limitations and prohibitions on contributions and expenditures, administers the reporting system for campaign finance disclosure, investigates and prosecutes violations (investigations are typically initiated by complaints from other candidates, parties, "watchdog groups," and the public), audits a limited number of campaigns and organizations for compliance, administers the presidential public funding programs for presidential candidates and, until recently, nominating

conventions, and defends the statute in challenges to federal election laws and regulations.

The FEC also publishes reports filed by Senate, House of Representatives and Presidential campaigns that list how much each campaign has raised and spent, and a list of all donors over $200, along with each donor's home address, employer and job title. This database also goes back to 1980. Private organizations are legally prohibited from using these data to solicit new individual donors (and the FEC authorizes campaigns to include a limited number of "dummy" names as a measure to prevent this), but may use this information to solicit Political Action Committees. The FEC also maintains an active program of public education, directed primarily to explaining the law to the candidates, their campaigns, political parties and other political committees that it regulates.

## 14.3 Criticism

Critics of the FEC, including campaign finance reform supporters such as Common Cause and Democracy 21, have complained that it is a classic example of regulatory capture where it serves the interests of the ones it was intended to regulate. The FEC's bipartisan structure, which was established by Congress, renders the agency "toothless." Critics also claim that most FEC penalties for violating election law come well after the actual election in which they were committed. Additionally, some critics claim that the commissioners tend to act as an arm of the "regulated community" of parties, interest groups, and politicians when issuing rulings and writing regulations. Others point out, however, that the Commissioners rarely divide evenly along partisan lines, and that the response time problem may be endemic to the enforcement procedures established by Congress. To complete steps necessary to resolve a complaint – including time for defendants to respond to the complaint, time to investigate and engage in legal analysis, and finally, where warranted, prosecution – necessarily takes far longer than the comparatively brief period of a political campaign.

At the same time, however, other critics, such as former FEC Chairman Bradley A. Smith and Stephen M. Hoersting, Executive Director of the Center for Competitive Politics, criticize the FEC for pursuing overly aggressive enforcement theories, and for infringing on First Amendment rights of free speech.[2]

Critics of the Commission also argue that this structure regularly causes deadlocks on 3-3 votes,[3] but others argue that deadlocks are actually quite rare,[4] and typically based on principle rather than partisanship.[5] Since 2008, 3-3 votes have become more common at the FEC. From 2008 to August 2014, the FEC has had over 200 tie votes, accounting for approximately 14 percent of all votes in enforcement matters.[6]

## 14.4  Commissioners

### 14.4.1  Current

### 14.4.2  Former

- Joan D. Aikens – April 1975 – September 1998 (reappointed May 1976, December 1981, August 1983 and October 1989).

- Thomas B. Curtis – April 1975 – May 1976.

- Thomas E. Harris – April 1975 – October 1986 (reappointed May 1976 and June 1979).

- Neil O. Staebler – April 1975 – October 1978 (reappointed May 1976).

- Vernon W. Thomson – April 1975 – June 1979; January 1981 – December 1981 (reappointed May 1976).

- Robert Tiernan – April 1975 – December 1981 (reappointed May 1976).

- William L. Springer – May 1976 – February 1979.

- John Warren McGarry – October 1978 – August 1998 (reappointed July 1983 and October 1989).

- Max L. Friedersdorf – March 1979 – December 1980.

- Frank P. Reiche – July 1979 – August 1985.

- Lee Ann Elliott – December 1981 – June 2000 (reappointed July 1987 and July 1994).

- Danny L. McDonald – December 1981 – January 2006 (reappointed in July 1987, July 1994 and July 2000).

- Thomas J. Josefiak – August 1985 – December 1991.

- Scott E. Thomas – October 1986 – January 2006 (reappointed in November 1991 and July 1998).

- Trevor Potter – November 1991 – October 1995.

- Darryl R. Wold – July 1998 – April 2002.

- Karl J. Sandstrom – July 1998 – December 2002.

- David M. Mason – July 1998 – July 2008.

- Bradley A. Smith – May 2000 – August 2005.

- Michael E. Toner – March 2002 – March 2007. (by recess appointment on March 29, 2002, confirmed to full term 2003)

- Robert D. Lenhard – January 2006 – December 31, 2007. (by recess appointment on January 4, 2006)

- Hans A. von Spakovsky – January 2006 – December 31, 2007. (by recess appointment on January 4, 2006)

- Cynthia L. Bauerly – June 2008 – confirmed June 24, 2008[7] for a term expiring on April 30, 2011[8] Resigned effective February 1, 2013

- Donald F. McGahn II – June 2008 – September 2013.

## 14.5  See also

- Title 11 of the Code of Federal Regulations

- Election Assistance Commission

- Elections in the United States

- Campaign finance in the United States

- Federal Election Campaign Act

- Bipartisan Campaign Reform Act

- *Buckley v. Valeo*, 424 U.S. 1 (1976)

- *Citizens United v. Federal Election Commission*

- *Davis v. Federal Election Commission*

- *Federal Election Commission v. Akins*, authorizing "any party aggrieved by an order of the Commission" to file a suit

- *Federal Election Commission v. Wisconsin Right to Life, Inc.*, holding that issue ads may not be banned before elections

- *McConnell v. Federal Election Commission*

- *McCutcheon v. Federal Election Commission*

# 14.6 References

[1] "About the Federal Election Commission". *Federal Election Commission*. Retrieved May 7, 2009.

[2] Bradley A. Smith; Stephen M. Hoersting (2002). "A Toothless Anaconda: Innovation, Impotence, and Overenforcement at the Federal Election Commission". *Election Law Journal* **1** (2): 145–171. doi:10.1089/153312902753610002.

[3] CREW Sues the Federal Election Commission over Case Dismissals, OMB Watch, August 17, 2010

[4] Opening Statement of Bradley A. Smith, Chairman of the Federal Election Commission, Before the Senate Committee on Rules and Administration, June 4, 2004

[5] Politics (and FEC enforcement) make strange bedfellows: The Soros book matter, Bob Bauer, More Soft Money Hard Law, January 29, 2009

[6] Confessore, Nicholas (August 25, 2014). "Election Panel Enacts Policies by Not Acting". New York Times. Retrieved August 26, 2014.

[7] FEC Elects Officers for 2008, FEC press release, July 10, 2008.

[8] New FEC Commissioners Assume Office, FEC press release, July 8, 2008.

# 14.7 Further reading

- *Will the Federal Election Commission Ever Work Again?* May 2, 2013 BusinessWeek

# 14.8 External links

- Official website
- Federal Election Commission in the Federal Register

# Chapter 15

# United States presidential election debates

For the 2012 presidential debates, see United States presidential election debates, 2012. For the 2008 presidential debates, see United States presidential election debates, 2008.

During presidential elections in the United States, it has

*John F. Kennedy and Richard Nixon participate in the second 1960 presidential debate, held in the NBC studios in Washington D.C. and narrated by Frank McGee.*

become customary for the main candidates (almost always the candidates of the two largest parties, currently the Democratic Party and the Republican Party) to engage in a debate. The topics discussed in the debate are often the most controversial issues of the time, and arguably elections have been nearly decided by these debates (e.g., Nixon vs. Kennedy). Candidate debates are not constitutionally mandated, but it is now considered a *de facto* election process. The debates are targeted mainly at undecided voters; those who tend not to be partial to any political ideology or party.

Presidential debates are held late in the election cycle, after the political parties have nominated their candidates. The candidates meet in a large hall, often at a university, before an audience of citizens. The formats of the debates have varied, with questions sometimes posed from one or more journalist moderators and in other cases members of the audience. Between 1988 and 2000, the formats have been

governed in detail by secret memoranda of understanding (MOU) between the two major candidates; an MOU for 2004 was also negotiated, but unlike the earlier agreements it was jointly released by the two candidates.

Debates are broadcast live on television and radio. The first debate for the 1960 election drew over 66 million viewers out of a population of 179 million, making it one of the most-watched broadcasts in U.S. television history. The 1980 debates drew 80 million viewers out of a 226 million. Recent debates have drawn decidedly smaller audiences, ranging from 46 million for the first 2000 debate to a high of over 67 million for the first debate in 2012.[1]

## 15.1 History

### 15.1.1 Predecessors

While the first general presidential debate was not held until 1960, several other debates are considered predecessors to the presidential debates.

The series of seven debates in 1858 between Abraham Lincoln and Senator Stephen A. Douglas for U.S. Senate were true, face-to-face debates, with no moderator; the candidates took it in turns to open each debate with a one-hour speech, then the other candidate had an hour and a half to rebut, and finally the first candidate closed the debate with a half-hour response. Douglas was later re-elected to the Senate by the Illinois legislature. Lincoln and Douglas were both nominated for president in 1860 (by the Republicans and Northern Democrats, respectively), and their earlier debates helped define their respective positions in that election, but they did not meet during the Presidential campaign.

Republican candidate Wendell Willkie challenged President Franklin D. Roosevelt to a debate in 1940, but Roosevelt refused.

In 1948, a radio debate was held in Oregon between

Thomas E. Dewey and Harold Stassen, Republican primary candidates for president. The Democrats followed suit in 1956, with a presidential primary debate between Adlai Stevenson and Estes Kefauver. The Student Government Association Council of the University of Maryland invited both presidential candidates to debate at the University of Maryland. In August 1956 the *Baltimore Sun* wrote an article with the headline "Immigrant Urges Presidential Debates." Both chairperson of both parties were contacted and considered the suggestion. Fred A. Kahn, a student of the University of Maryland, Class of 1960, was an early proponent of national presidential debates. In August 1956, Mr. Kahn sent a letter to UM President Wilson H. Elkins in which he proposed to have the U.S. presidential candidates from both political parties together on the same platform to answer questions from a panel of college students. Kahn also sent letters to the chairmen of the Democratic and Republican parties, Maryland Governor Theodore McKeldin, and Eleanor Roosevelt. Mrs. Roosevelt responded to Kahn that she "felt this might be something that would arose (sic) the interest of young people all over the country" and that she thought "it would be a gesture not only to all those at the University of Maryland but to young people in this group all over the country." Mrs. Roosevelt also sent a letter regarding Kahn's proposal to James Finnegan, Adlai Stevenson's campaign manager, endorsing Kahn's proposal. The precise impact of Kahn's proposal on the Kennedy-Nixon debates during the 1960 presidential campaign is unclear, but his ideas did receive national press exposure. Four years later the first televised debates (the Kennedy-Nixon debates) were held.

## 15.1.2 1960 Kennedy–Nixon debates

The first general election presidential debate was held on September 26, 1960, between U.S. Senator John F. Kennedy, the Democratic nominee, and Vice President Richard Nixon, the Republican nominee, in Chicago at the studios of CBS's WBBM-TV. It was moderated by Howard K. Smith and included a panel composed of Sander Vanocur of NBC News, Charles Warren of Mutual News, and Stuart Novins of CBS. Historian J.N. Druckman observed "television primes its audience to rely more on their perceptions of candidate image (e.g., integrity). At the same time, television has also coincided with the world becoming more polarized and ideologically driven."[2]

Three more debates were subsequently held between the candidates.:[3] On October 7 at the WRC-TV NBC studio in Washington, D.C., narrated by Frank McGee with a panel of four newsmen Paul Niven, CBS; Edward P. Morgan, ABC; Alvin Spivak, UPI;[4] Harold R. Levy, Newsday; October 13, with Nixon at the ABC studio in Los Angeles and Kennedy at the ABC studio in New York, narrated

by Bill Shadel with a panel of four newsmen; and October 21 at the ABS studio in New York, narrated by Quincy Howe with a panel of four including Frank Singiser, John Edwards, Walter Cronkite, and John Chancellor.

## 15.1.3 1968 and 1972 primary debates

General election debates were not held for the elections of 1964, 1968 and 1972, although intra-party debates were held during the primaries between Democrats Robert F. Kennedy and Eugene McCarthy in 1968 and between Democrats George McGovern and Hubert Humphrey in 1972.

## 15.1.4 1976 to present

*Carter and Ford debate domestic policy at the Walnut Street Theatre in Philadelphia (September 23, 1976).*

It was not until 1976 that a second series of televised presidential debates was held during the general election campaign season.[5] The debates were sponsored by League of Women Voters.[6] On September 23, 1976, Democratic candidate, Governor Jimmy Carter of Georgia, and the Republican incumbent, President Gerald Ford from Michigan, agreed to three debates (one on domestic issues, one on foreign policy, and one on any topic) on television before studio audiences. A single vice-presidential debate was also held that year between Democratic Senator Walter Mondale and Republican Senator Bob Dole.

The dramatic effect of televised presidential debates was demonstrated again in the 1976 debates between Ford and Carter. Ford had already cut into Carter's large lead in the polls, and was generally viewed as having won the first debate on domestic policy. Polls released after this first debate indicated the race was even. However, in the second debate on foreign policy, Ford made what was widely viewed as a major blunder when he said "There is no Soviet domination of Eastern Europe and there never will be under a Ford administration." After this, Ford's momentum stalled, and Carter won a very close election.[7][8]

*President Jimmy Carter* (left) *and former Governor Ronald Reagan* (right) *at the presidential debate October 28, 1980. Reagan most memorably deployed the phrase "there you go again."*

Debates were a major factor again in 1980. Earlier in the election season, President Carter had a lead over his opponent, Governor Ronald Reagan of California. In the debates, with years of experience in front of a camera as an actor, Reagan came across much better than Carter and was judged by voters to have won the debate by a wide margin. This helped propel Reagan into a landslide victory. The Reagan campaign had access to internal debate briefing materials for Carter; the exposure of this in 1983 led to a public scandal called "Debategate".

Since 1976, each presidential election has featured a series of vice presidential debates. Vice presidential debates have been held regularly since 1984. Vice Presidential debates have been largely uneventful and have historically had little impact on the election. Perhaps the most memorable moment in a Vice Presidential debate came in the 1988 debate between Republican Dan Quayle and Democrat Lloyd Bentsen. Quayle's selection by the incumbent Vice-President and Republican Presidential candidate George Bush was widely criticized; one reason being his relative lack of experience. In the debate, Quayle attempted to ease this fear by stating that he had as much experience

as John F. Kennedy did when he ran for President in 1960. Democrat Bentsen countered with the now famous statement: "Senator, I served with Jack Kennedy. I knew Jack Kennedy. Jack Kennedy was a friend of mine. Senator, you're no Jack Kennedy."

*The stage at Saint Anselm College during the ABC/Facebook debates in 2008*

The year 1992 featured the first debate involving both major-party candidates and a third-party candidate, billionaire Ross Perot running against President Bush and the Democrat nominee Governor Bill Clinton. In that year, President Bush was criticised for his early hesitation to join the debates with him being alluded to a chicken. Furthermore, he was also criticised for looking at his watch which aides initially said was meant to track if the other candidates were debating within their time limits but ultimately it was revealed that the president indeed was checking how much time was left in the debate.

Moderators of nationally televised presidential debates have included Bernard Shaw, Bill Moyers, Jim Lehrer, and Barbara Walters.

Saint Anselm College has hosted four debates throughout 2004 and 2008; it is a favorite for campaign stops and these national debates because of the college's history in the New Hampshire primary.

Washington University in St. Louis has hosted the debates three times (in 1992, 2000, and 2004), more than any other location, and will host one of the 2016 debates. The university was also scheduled to host a debate in 1996, but it was later negotiated between the two presidential candidates to reduce the number of debates from three to two. The University hosted the only 2008 Vice Presidential debate, as well.[9]

## 15.2 Rules and format

Some of the debates can feature the candidates standing behind their podiums, or in conference tables with the moderator on the other side. Depending on the agreed format, either the moderator or an audience member can be the one to ask questions. Typically there are no opening statements, just closing statements.

A coin toss determines who gets to answer the first question and each candidate will get alternate turns. Once a question is asked, the candidate has 2 minutes to answer the question. After this, the opposing candidate has around 1 minute to respond and rebut her/his arguments. At the moderator's discretion, the discussion of the question may be extended by 30 seconds per candidate.

In recent debates, colored lights resembling traffic lights have been installed to aid the candidate as to the time left with green indicating 30 seconds, yellow indicating 15 seconds and red indicating only 5 seconds are left. If necessary, a buzzer may be used or a flag.

## 15.3 Debate sponsorship

Main article: Commission on Presidential Debates § Criticism

Control of the presidential debates has been a ground of struggle for more than two decades. The role was filled by the nonpartisan League of Women Voters (LWV) civic organization in 1976, 1980 and 1984.[6] In 1987, the LWV withdrew from debate sponsorship, in protest of the major party candidates attempting to dictate nearly every aspect of how the debates were conducted. On October 2, 1988, the LWV's 14 trustees voted unanimously to pull out of the debates, and on October 3 they issued a press release:[10]

> The League of Women Voters is withdrawing sponsorship of the presidential debates...because the demands of the two campaign organizations would perpetrate a fraud on the American voter. It has become clear to us that the candidates' organizations aim to add debates to their list of campaign-trail charades devoid of substance, spontaneity and answers to tough questions. The League has no intention of becoming an accessory to the hoodwinking of the American public.

According to the LWV, they pulled out because "the campaigns presented the League with their debate agreement on September 28, two weeks before the scheduled debate. The campaigns' agreement was negotiated 'behind closed doors'

... [with] 16 pages of conditions not subject to negotiation. Most objectionable to the League...were conditions in the agreement that gave the campaigns unprecedented control over the proceedings.... [including] control the selection of questioners, the composition of the audience, hall access for the press and other issues."[10]

The same year the two major political parties assumed control of organizing presidential debates through the Commission on Presidential Debates (CPD). The commission has been headed since its inception by former chairs of the Democratic National Committee and Republican National Committee.

Some have criticized the exclusion of third party and independent candidates as well as the parallel interview format as a minimum of getting 15 percent in opinion polls is required to be invited. In 2004, the Citizens' Debate Commission (CDC) was formed with the stated mission of returning control of the debates to an independent nonpartisan body rather than a bipartisan body. Nevertheless, the CPD retained control of the debates that year and in 2008.

## 15.4 Timeline

*Source: Commission on Presidential Debates - Debate history*

## 15.5 References

[1] Shapiro, Rebecca. Presidential Debate Ratings: Over 67 Million Viewers Tune In. The Huffington Post. 2012-10-04. Retrieved 2012-10-27.

[2] Druckman, J. N. (2003). "The Power of Television Images: The First Kennedy Nixon Debate Revisited." *Journal of Politics*, 65(2), 559-571. Retrieved from EBSCOhost

[3] "Kennedy-Nixon Debates," The Mary Ferrell Foundation

[4] "1960 Debates". *Commission on Presidential Debates*. Commission on Presidential Debates. Retrieved 2 December 2015.

[5] Golway, Terry. "There We Go Again" *American Heritage*, August/September 2004.

[6] "League of Women Voters and the Presidential Debates". League of Women Voters. June 12, 2010. Retrieved 2012-07-26.

[7] http://www.pbs.org/newshour/debatingourdestiny/dod/1976-broadcast.html

[8] "The Blooper Heard Round the World". *Time*. 1976-10-18. Retrieved 2010-05-26.

[9] Washington University in St. Louis :: Vice Presidential Debate 2008

[10] Neuman, Nancy M. (October 2, 1988). "League Refuses to "Help Perpetrate a Fraud"". *Press release.* League of Women Voters. Retrieved 2012-07-26.

## 15.6   Further reading

- Minow, Newton N. and LaMay, Craig L. (2008). *Inside the Presidential Debates: Their Improbable Past and Promising Future.* University of Chicago Press. ISBN 978-0-226-53041-3.

- Moore, John L.: "Elections A to Z", Second Edition; CQ Press, Washington 2003

- Patterson, Thomas E.: "Views of Winners & Losers" in Graber, Doris A.: "Media Power in Politics"; Congressional Quarterly Inc., Washington 1990, p. 178

- Rutenberg, Jim: "The Post-Debate Contest: Swaying Perceptions"; New York Times, 4 October 2004, p. 1

## 15.7   External links

- Commission on Presidential Debates

    - Transcripts

- History of Televised Presidential Debates, Museum of Broadcast Communications, Chicago

- Debating our Destiny on PBS NewsHour, 2000 and 2008 programs

- Dumbing Down the Public: Why it Matters, commentary on language level in presidential debates, Diane Ravitch, January 15, 2001

- United States presidential election debates at DMOZ

### 15.7.1   Debate critics and activists

- Open Debates, a nonprofit, nonpartisan organization devoted to presidential debates

- A Blueprint for Fair and Open Presidential Debates in 2000, The Appleseed Citizens' Task Force on Fair Debates

- "The Commission on Presidential Debates' Exclusion of Vital Issues" in the 2000 debates

- The Citizens' Debate Commission's proposal for 2004 debates

- Heads or Tails: You Lose, article on the Commission on Presidential Debates and corporate influence

# Chapter 16

# Election Day (United States)

*Not to be confused with Super Tuesday, for primary elections*

**Election Day** in the United States is the day set by law for the general elections of public officials. It occurs on the Tuesday right after the first Monday in November[1] (this does not necessarily mean the "first Tuesday" in a month because the first day of a month can be a Tuesday). The earliest possible date is November 2, and the latest possible date is November 8 (as it will be for the 2016 election). The 2012 election was held on November 6, 2012.

For federal offices (President, Vice President, and United States Congress), Election Day occurs only in even-numbered years. Presidential elections are held every four years, in years divisible by four, in which electors for President and Vice President are chosen according to the method determined by each state. Elections to the United States House of Representatives and the United States Senate are held every two years; all Representatives serve two-year terms and are up for election every two years, while Senators serve six-year terms, staggered so that one third of Senators are elected in any given general election. General elections in which presidential candidates are not on the ballot are referred to as midterm elections. Terms for those elected begin in January the following year; the President and Vice President are inaugurated ("sworn in") on Inauguration Day, which is usually on January 20.

Many state and local government offices are also elected on Election Day as a matter of convenience and cost saving, although a handful of states hold elections for state offices (such as governor) during odd-numbered "off years", or during other even-numbered "midterm years".

Congress has mandated a uniform date for presidential (3 U.S.C. § 1) and congressional (2 U.S.C. § 1 and 2 U.S.C. § 7) elections, though early voting is nonetheless authorized in many states.

Election Day is a civic holiday in some states, including Delaware, Hawaii, Kentucky, Montana, New Jersey, New York, Ohio, West Virginia, and the territory of Puerto Rico.

Some other states require that workers be permitted to take time off from employment without loss of pay. California Elections Code Section 14000 provides that employees otherwise unable to vote must be allowed two hours off with pay, at the beginning or end of a shift. A coincidental federal holiday, Democracy Day, has been unsuccessfully proposed.

## 16.1 History

No federal law regulated the 1788 federal election. In 1792, federal law permitted each state to conduct presidential elections in the state (i.e., to choose their electors) at any time in a 34-day period[2] before the first Wednesday of December, which was the day set for the meeting of the electors of the U.S. president and vice-president (the Electoral College), in their respective states.[3] This gave each state some flexibility in the holding of their elections. An election date in November was seen as convenient because the harvest would have been completed (important in an agrarian society) and the winter-like storms would not yet have begun in earnest (especially an advantage in the days before paved roads and snowplows). However, in this arrangement the states that voted later could be influenced by a candidate's victories in the states that voted earlier, a problem later exacerbated by improved communications via train and telegraph. In close elections, the states that voted last might well determine the outcome.[4]

A uniform date for choosing presidential electors was instituted by the Congress in 1845.[1] Many theories have been advanced as to why the Congress settled on the first Tuesday after the first Monday in November.[5] The actual reasons, as shown in records of Congressional debate on the bill in December 1844, were fairly prosaic. The bill initially set the day for choosing presidential electors on "the first Tuesday in November," in years divisible by four (1848, 1852, etc.). But it was pointed out that in some years the period between the first Tuesday in November and the first Wednesday in December (when the electors are required to meet in their state capitals to vote) would be more than 34 days, in violation of the existing Electoral College law. So, the bill was reworded to move the date for choosing presidential electors to the Tuesday after the first Monday in November, a date scheme already used in New York.[6] The period between Election Day and the first Wednesday in December is always 29 days. The effect of the change was to make November 2 the earliest day on which Election Day may fall.

In 1845, the United States was largely an agrarian society. Farmers often needed a full day to travel by horse-drawn vehicles to the county seat to vote. Tuesday was established as election day because it did not interfere with the Biblical Sabbath or with market day, which was on Wednesday in many towns.[7]

## 16.2   Modern objections

In modern times, the United States is no longer primarily an agrarian society, and Tuesday is now normally a work day throughout the country with most voters working on that day. This has led activists to object to Election Day being on a Tuesday on the grounds that it currently decreases voter turnout. They advocate either making Election Day a federal holiday, as in the Democracy Day proposal, or allowing voters to cast their ballots over two or more days. The United Auto Workers union has negotiated making Election Day a holiday for workers of U.S. domestic auto manufacturers. Some employers allow their employees to come in late or leave early on Election Day to allow them an opportunity to get to their precinct and vote. Activists encourage voters to make use of early voting and postal voting facilities when available and convenient.

## 16.3   Early and postal voting

Most states allow for early voting, allowing voters to cast ballots before the Election Day. Early voting periods vary from 4 to 50 days prior to Election Day. Unconditional early voting in person is allowed in 32 states and in D.C.[8] Also, most states have some kind of absentee ballot system. Unconditional absentee voting by mail is allowed in 27 states and D.C., and with an excuse in another 21 states.[8] Unconditional permanent absentee voting is allowed in 7 states and in D.C.[8] In Oregon and Washington state all major elections are by postal voting, with ballot papers sent to voters several weeks before Election Day.[9] In Oregon, all postal votes must be received by a set time on Election Day, as is common with absentee ballots in most states (except overseas military ballots which receive more time by federal law). Washington State requires postal votes be postmarked

by Election Day. For the 2008 presidential election, 32% of votes were early votes.[10] Colorado is now the 3rd state to allow voters to cast ballots by mail.

## 16.4   Local elections

*This perpetual calendar can be used to find the first Tuesday after the first Monday in November for any year through A.D. 2799.*

Elected offices of municipalities, counties (in most states), and other local entities (such as school boards and other special-purpose districts) have their elections subject to rules of their state, and in some states, they vary according to choices of the jurisdiction in question. For instance, in Connecticut, all towns, cities, and boroughs hold elections in every odd-numbered year, but as of 2004, 16 have them on the first Monday in May, while the other 153 are on Election Day. In Massachusetts, the 50 cities are required to hold their elections on Election Day, but the 301 towns may choose any date, and most have traditionally held their elections in early spring, after the last snowfall.

## 16.5   See also

- Democracy Day (United States)
- Election
- Primary election
- Public holidays of the United States
- Special election
- U.S. state holiday

## 16.6   References

[1] Statutes at Large, 28th Congress, 2nd Session, p. 721.

[2] The bill originally specified a 30-day period for the states to choose their electors. Annals of Congress, House of Representatives, 2nd Congress, 1st Session, p. 278.

[3] Statutes at Large, 2nd Congress, 1st Session, p. 239.

[4] William C. Kimberling, The Electoral College, Federal Election Commission, 1992, pp. 6-7

[5] The theories include that it was placed to avoid the Catholic All Saints Day, (November 1), a holy day of obligation. See InfoPlease.com and U.S. Election Assistance Commission

[6] Congressional Globe, House of Representatives, 28th Congress, 2nd Session, pp. 14-15.

[7] Huffstutter, P.J. (October 31, 2006). "Officials face Election Day stumper, with possible payoff online". Seattle Times. Retrieved 2008-11-03.

[8] "Absentee and Early Voting". National Conference of State Legislatures. 2012-09-04 / July 2011. Retrieved 2012-10-30. Check date values in: |date= (help)

[9] Absentee and Early Voting. National Conference of State Legislatures.

[10] Michael McDonald (2010-05-01). "(Nearly) Final 2008 Early Voting Statistics". Department of Public and International Affairs, George Mason University. Retrieved 2012-10-30.

# Chapter 17

# United States presidential inauguration

*Presidential inauguration at the western front of the U.S. Capitol (Barack Obama, 2009)*

*Inauguration Day 2005: President George W. Bush and First Lady Laura Bush lead the inaugural parade down Pennsylvania Avenue to the White House*

*Presidential inauguration at the eastern front of the U.S. Capitol (Lyndon B. Johnson, 1965)*

The **inauguration of the president of the United States** is a ceremonial event marking the commencement of a new four-year term of a president of the United States. The day a presidential inauguration occurs is known as "Inauguration Day" and occurs on January 20 (or 21st if the 20th is a Sunday). (Prior to the Twentieth Amendment, the date was March 4, the day of the year on which the Constitution of the United States first took effect in 1789; the last in-

auguration to take place on the older date was Franklin D. Roosevelt's first one on March 4, 1933.) The most recent public presidential inauguration ceremony, the swearing in of President Barack Obama to begin his second four-year term in office, took place on Monday, January 21, 2013.

The only inauguration element mandated by the United States Constitution is that the president make an oath or affirmation before that person can "enter on the Execution" of the office of the presidency. However, over the years, various traditions have arisen that have expanded the inauguration from a simple oath-taking ceremony to a day-long event, including parades, speeches, and balls.

From the presidency of Andrew Jackson through that of Jimmy Carter, the primary Inauguration Day ceremony took place on the Capitol's East Portico.[1] Since the 1981 inauguration of Ronald Reagan, the ceremony has been held at the Capitol's West Front. The inaugurations of William Howard Taft in 1909 and Reagan in 1985 were moved indoors at the Capitol because of cold weather. The War of 1812 and World War II caused two inaugurations to be held at other locations in Washington, D.C.

When George Washington was inaugurated, the oath was administered by Robert Livingston, Chancellor of New York State, in 1789, and by William Cushing, Associate Justice of the Supreme Court, in 1793. Since Chief Justice Oliver Ellsworth swore in President John Adams, no chief justice has missed an Inauguration Day. When Inauguration Day has fallen on a Sunday, the chief justice has administered the oath to the president on the Sunday privately and then again the next day publicly.

When a new president takes over mid-term due to the death or resignation of a president, the oath of office is administered but formal, public inauguration events have not been held.

Capitol when taken into the rotunda to lie in state.[5] When it was brought out, it came out through the House wing steps of the Capitol.[5]

Inauguration Day is a federal holiday observed by only the federal employees who work in the District of Columbia; Montgomery and Prince George's Counties in Maryland; Arlington and Fairfax Counties in Virginia, and the cities of Alexandria and Fairfax in Virginia, and who are regularly scheduled to perform non-overtime work on Inauguration Day. There is no in-lieu-of holiday for employees and students who are not regularly scheduled to work or attend school on Inauguration Day. The primary reason for the holiday is to relieve traffic congestion that occurs during this major event .

## 17.1 Inaugural ceremonies

### 17.1.1 Organizers

Second inauguration of Theodore Roosevelt, 1905

The inauguration for the first U.S. president, George Washington, was held on April 30, 1789, at Federal Hall in New York City[2] where he was sworn in by Robert Livingston, the Chancellor of the State of New York.[3] In 1801, Thomas Jefferson became the first to be sworn in as president in Washington, D.C., which officially became the federal capital only on June 11, 1800.[4] Inauguration day was originally on March 4, four months after election day, but this was changed to noon on January 20 by the Twentieth Amendment in 1933.[4]

The inaugural celebrations usually last ten days, from five days before the inauguration to five days after. However, in 1973, the celebrations marking Richard Nixon's second inauguration were marred by the passing of former President Lyndon B. Johnson two days after the inauguration. The celebrations came to an end as Washington began preparations for the state funeral for Johnson. Because of the construction work on the center steps of the East Front, Johnson's casket was taken up the Senate wing steps of the

*Inauguration platform under construction for Woodrow Wilson's first inauguration in 1913*

Since 1901, all inaugural ceremonies at the United States Capitol have been organized by the Joint Congressional Committee on Inaugural Ceremonies.[6]

The U.S. military have participated in Inauguration Day ceremonies since George Washington's, because the president is commander-in-chief of the armed forces. Since the first inauguration of Dwight D. Eisenhower in 1953, that participation has been coordinated by the Armed Forces Inaugural Committee (now called the Joint Task Force-Armed Forces Inaugural Committee).

The Presidential Inaugural Committee (PIC) is the legal entity that raises and distributes funds for events other than the ceremony, such as the balls and parade.[7]

## 17.1.2   Locations

Most inaugural ceremonies were held at the Capitol Building. Washington gave his first address at Federal Hall in New York City and his second address in Congress Hall in Philadelphia. Adams also gave his in Congress Hall in Philadelphia. Jefferson gave both of his addresses at the United States Capitol in Washington, D.C. Due to the restoration work on the Capitol, James Monroe's 1817 inauguration ceremonies took place outside the Old Brick Capitol.[8] Franklin D. Roosevelt's fourth address was given at the White House. Depending on the weather, the ceremonial swearing-in is held outside or inside of the Capitol building.

Outdoor ceremonies were traditionally held at the eastern front of the U.S. Capitol. In June 1980, the Joint Congressional Committee on Inaugural Ceremonies decided to move the ceremony to the west side of the Capitol, to save money and provide more space for spectators. Ronald Reagan was the first president inaugurated on the west front in January 1981, and an "urban legend" later developed that he had personally requested the move, to face toward his home state of California. All outdoor inaugurations since have taken place on the Capitol's western front.[9]

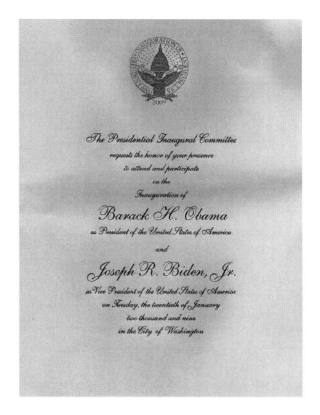

*Invitation to the January 20, 2009, inauguration of President Barack Obama*

## 17.1.3   Dates

Public inaugural ceremonies have been held on five different calendar dates in the year: April 30, March 4 and 5, and January 20 and 21. Washington gave his first address on April 30, 1789, and his second one on March 4, 1793, which was the commencement date for presidential terms. This March 4 date was changed to January 20 by the Twentieth Amendment to the United States Constitution.

### Sunday exceptions

From 1793 to 1933, the inaugurations were held on March 4, with only four exceptions. Because March 4 fell on a Sunday, Presidents Monroe (2nd inauguration), Taylor, Hayes and Wilson (2nd inauguration) each gave an address on Monday, March 5. Since 1937, addresses have been given on January 20 with only three exceptions (other than following a premature end to the presidential term): Presidents Eisenhower, Reagan, and Obama each gave an address on Monday, January 21 (2nd inauguration for each). The most recent inauguration day that fell on a Sunday was January 20, 2013; the next will be on January 20, 2041.

## 17.1.4   Attendees

In addition to the public, the attendees at the ceremony generally include Members of Congress, Supreme Court justices, high-ranking military officers, former presidents, living Medal of Honor recipients, and other dignitaries.

The outgoing president customarily attends the inauguration, barring those cases where succession was due to his death. There have been four exceptions:

- John Adams did not attend Jefferson's inauguration.

- John Quincy Adams did not attend Jackson's inauguration.

- Andrew Johnson did not attend Grant's inauguration.

- Woodrow Wilson did not attend Harding's inauguration (but did ride to the Capitol with him).

Richard Nixon left Washington, D.C., before his resignation took effect and did not attend the swearing-in ceremony of Gerald Ford, who had no inauguration.

## 17.2  Ceremony elements

Inauguration procedure is governed by tradition rather than the Constitution, the only constitutionally required procedure being the presidential oath of office (which may be taken anywhere, with anyone in attendance who can legally witness an oath, and at any time prior to the actual beginning of the new president's term).[10] Traditionally, the president-elect arrives at the White House and proceeds to the inaugural grounds at the United States Capitol with the incumbent president. Only three have refused to accompany the president: John Adams, John Quincy Adams, and Andrew Johnson.[10] Around or after 12 noon, the president takes the oath of office, usually administered by the Chief Justice of the United States, and then delivers the inaugural address.

### 17.2.1  Oaths of office

Main article: Oath of office of the President of the United States

Since 1937, the vice president-elect takes the oath of office at the same ceremony as the president-elect; before then, the vice presidential oath was administered in the Senate. The vice-president-elect takes the oath first. Unlike the president, the United States Constitution does not specify an oath of office for the vice president. Several variants of the oath have been used since 1789; the current form, which is also recited by Senators, Representatives, and other government officers, has been in use since 1884:

Immediately after the vice-presidential oath, the United States Marine Band will perform four *ruffles and flourishes*, followed by *Hail, Columbia.*

At noon, the new presidential term begins. At about that time, the president-elect takes the oath of office, traditionally administered by the Chief Justice of the United States, using the form mandated in Article II, Section 1 of the United States Constitution:

According to Washington Irving's biography of George Washington, in the first inauguration, President Washington added the words "so help me God" after accepting the oath. This is confirmed by Donald R. Kennon, Chief Historian, United States Capitol Historical Society.[12] However, the only contemporaneous source that fully reproduced Washington's oath completely lacks the religious codicil.[13] The first newspaper report that actually described the exact words used in an oath of office, Chester Arthur's in 1881,[14] repeated the "query-response" method where the words, "so help me God" were a personal prayer, not a part of the constitutional oath. The time of adoption of the cur-

rent procedure, where both the chief justice and the president speak the oath, is unknown.

There is no requirement that any book, or in particular a book of sacred text, be used to administer the oath, and none is mentioned in the Constitution. With the use of the Bible being customary for oaths, at least in the 18th and 19th centuries, a Bible was generally used. Several presidents were sworn in on the George Washington Inaugural Bible. On some occasions, the particular passage to which it was opened has been recorded, as below. John Quincy Adams was sworn in on a book of laws.[15] At his 1963 swearing aboard Air Force One, Lyndon Johnson was sworn on a Catholic missal that belonged to his predecessor.[16][17] In addition, Franklin Pierce is definitely known to have affirmed rather than sworn by using a Law Book. There are conflicting reports concerning Herbert Hoover, but the use of a Bible is recorded and suggests that he swore in the usual fashion. Barack Obama used the Lincoln Bible for his oaths in 2009 and 2013.[18] In 2013 Obama also used a Bible that belonged to Martin Luther King, Jr..[19]

The presidential oath has been administered by 15 chief justices, one associate justice, and two New York state judges (including only those administered at the inauguration).

Immediately after the presidential oath, the United States Marine Band will perform four *ruffles and flourishes*, followed by *Hail to the Chief*, while simultaneously, a 21-gun salute is fired using artillery pieces from the Presidential Guns Salute Battery, 3d United States Infantry Regiment "The Old Guard" located in Taft Park, north of the Capitol. The actual gun salute begins with the first *ruffle and flourish*, and 'run long' (i.e. the salute concludes after *Hail to the Chief* has ended).

### 17.2.2  Inaugural address

Newly sworn-in presidents usually give a speech referred to as an inaugural address. Until William McKinley's first inaugural address in 1897, the president elect traditionally gave the address before taking the oath; McKinley requested the change so that he could reiterate the words of the oath at the close of his address. John Tyler, Millard Fillmore, Andrew Johnson, Chester A. Arthur, and Calvin Coolidge gave no address, but addressed Congress four months later.[10] In each of these cases, the incoming president was succeeding a president who had died in office, and was not elected as president in the next election. Gerald Ford addressed the nation via broadcast after taking the oath, but he characterized his speech as "Not an inaugural address, not a fireside chat, not a campaign speech— just a little straight talk among friends."[20] Fifty-four addresses have been given by thirty-seven presidents. George Washington's second address was the shortest (135 words), and William Henry Harrison delivered the longest (8,495 words).

### 17.2.3  Religious elements and poems

*The Reverend Donn Moomaw delivers the invocation at the first inauguration of Ronald Reagan, 1981*

Since 1937, the ceremony has incorporated two or more prayers. Musical works and poetry readings have been included on occasion.[21]

Further information: Prayers at United States presidential inaugurations
Further information: Poems at United States presidential inaugurations

## 17.3  Other elements

See also: United States presidential inaugural balls

### 17.3.1  Congressional luncheon

Since 1953, the president and vice president have been guests of honor at a luncheon held by the leadership of the United States Congress immediately following the inaugural ceremony. The luncheon is held in Statuary Hall and is organized by the Joint Congressional Committee on Inaugural Ceremonies, and attended by the leadership of both houses of Congress as well as guests of the president and vice president. By tradition, the outgoing president and vice president do not attend.

### 17.3.2  Presidential Procession to the White House

Since Thomas Jefferson's second inaugural on March 4, 1805, it has become a tradition for the president to parade down Pennsylvania Avenue from the Capitol to the White House. The only president not to parade down Pennsylvania Avenue was Ronald Reagan in his second inauguration in 1985, due to freezing cold temperatures made dangerous by high winds. Reagan paraded down Pennsylvania Avenue during his first inauguration, in 1981, amid the celebrations that broke out across the country because of news just minutes into his term that the 52 American hostages held in Iran for the previous 444 days had been released. In 1977, Jimmy Carter walked from the Capitol to the White House, although for security reasons, subsequent presidents have walked only a part of the way.

### 17.3.3  Inaugural Parade

*The Inaugural Parade on Pennsylvania Avenue passes the presidential reviewing stand in front of the White House in January 2005.*

Following the arrival of the presidential entourage to the White House, it is customary for the president, vice-president, their respective families and leading members of the government and military to review an **Inaugural Parade** from an enclosed stand at the edge of the North Lawn. The parade, which proceeds along the 1.5 miles of Pennsylvania Avenue in front of the stand and the Front Lawn in view of the presidential party, features both military and civilian participants from all 50 states and the District of Columbia; this parade largely evolved from the post-inaugural procession to the White House, and occurred as far back as the second Jefferson inauguration, when shipmen from the Washington Navy Yard and musicians accompanied Jefferson on foot as he rode on horseback from the Capitol to the White House. This was expanded in 1837 with horse-drawn displays akin to parade floats being paraded with the president, and the 1847 inaugural ceremonies, including the procession, parade and festivities, were the first to be organized by an official organizing committee. However, the 1829 inauguration of Andrew Jackson saw serious overcrowding of the White House by well-wishers during the "Open House" held following the inauguration. The 1885 inauguration of Grover Cleveland saw the post-inaugural Open House evolve into a presidential review of the troops from a grandstand in front of the White House. Since 1885, the presidential review has included both military and civilian contingencies. The 1953 Parade was the largest, longest and most elaborate ever staged.[22] The presidential review has also made milestones, with the 1865 parade being the first to include African-Americans, the 1917 parade being the first to include female participants, and the 2009 parade being the first to include openly lesbian and gay participants.

### 17.3.4 Prayer service

A tradition of a national prayer service, usually the day after the inauguration, dates back to George Washington and since Franklin Delano Roosevelt, the prayer service has been held at the Washington National Cathedral.[23] This is not the same as the Inaugural Prayer, a tradition also began by Washington, when on June 1, 1789, Methodist Bishops Francis Asbury and Thomas Coke, Rev. John Dickins, the pastor of Old St. George's (America's oldest Methodist Church) and Major Thomas Morrell, one of President Washington's former aide-de-camps called upon Washington in New York City.[24] This tradition resumed in 1985 with President Reagan and continues under the auspices of a Presidential Inaugural Prayer Committee based at Old St. Georges.

### 17.3.5 Security

The security for the inaugural celebrations is a complex matter, involving the Secret Service, Department of Homeland Security, Federal Protective Service (DHS-FPS), all five branches of the Armed Forces, the Capitol Police, the United States Park Police (USPP), and the Metropolitan Police Department of the District of Columbia (MPDC). Federal law enforcement agencies also sometimes request assistance from various other state and local law-enforcement agencies throughout the United States.

### 17.3.6 Presidential medals

Beginning with George Washington, there has been a traditional association with Inauguration festivities and the production of a presidential medal. With the District of Columbia attracting thousands of attendees for inauguration, presidential medals were an inexpensive souvenir for the tourists to remember the occasion. However, the once-simple trinket turned into an official presidential election memento. In 1901, the first Inauguration Committee on Medals and Badges was established as part of the official Inauguration Committee for the re-election of President McKinley. The Committee saw official medals as a way to raise funding for the festivities. Gold medals were to be produced as gifts for the president, vice president, and committee chair; silver medals were to be created and distributed among Inauguration Committee members; and bronze medals would be for sale for public consumption. McKinley's medal was simple with his portrait on one side and writing on the other side.[25]

Unlike his predecessor, when Theodore Roosevelt took his oath of office in 1905, he found the previous presidential medal unacceptable. As an art lover and admirer of the ancient Greek high-relief coins, Roosevelt wanted more than a simple medal—he wanted a work of art. To achieve this goal, the president hired Augustus Saint-Gaudens, a famous American sculptor, to design and create his inauguration medal. Saint-Gaudens's obsession with perfection resulted in a forestalled release and the medals were distributed after the actual inauguration. However, President Roosevelt was very pleased with the result.

Saint-Gaudens' practice of creating a portrait sculpture of the newly elected president is still used today in presidential medal creation. After the president sits for the sculptor, the resulting clay sketch is turned into a life mask and plaster model. Finishing touches are added and the epoxy cast that is created is used to produce the die cuts. The die cuts are then used to strike the president's portrait on each medal. The most recent Presidential Inauguration Medal released was for President Obama in 2013.[26]

The Smithsonian Institution and The George Washington University hold the two most complete collections of presidential medals in the United States.

## 17.4 List of inaugural ceremonies

This is a list of the 57 inaugural ceremonies. Also noted (parenthetically) are the nine presidencies for which inaugurations were not celebrated. For a list of the 73 events when the presidential oath of office has been taken, see Oath of office of the President of the United States.

## 17.5 See also

- United States presidential inaugural addresses

- U.S. Senate Committee on Rules and Administration

# 17.6   References

[1] "Presidential Inaugurations: Some Precedents and Notable Events". Memory.loc.gov. Retrieved August 30, 2010.

[2] "Exhibit: President George Washington's inaugural address". National Archives and Records Administration. August 17, 1998. Retrieved January 22, 2009. George Washington's first inauguration took place at Federal Hall in New York City [...] George Washington's first inaugural address, April 30, 1789

[3] "President George Washington's first inaugural speech (1789)". National Archives. Retrieved January 22, 2009. Before the assembled crowd of spectators, Robert Livingston, Chancellor of the State of New York, administered the oath

[4] "Inaugural history: inauguration 2001". PBS. Retrieved January 22, 2009. Thomas Jefferson was the first president to be sworn in as president in Washington DC, which did not officially become the US capital until 1801. [...] Inauguration Day was originally set for March 4, giving electors from each state nearly four months after Election Day to cast their ballots for president. In 1933, the day of inauguration was changed by constitutional amendment from February 4 to Jan. 290 to speed the changeover of administrations.

[5] Foley, Thomas (January 25, 1973). "Thousands in Washington Brave Cold to Say Goodbye to Johnson". *Los Angeles Times*. p. A1.

[6] "Joint Congressional Committee on Inaugural Ceremonies – Official Website.".

[7] "PIC records". National Archives.

[8] Joint Congressional Committee on Inaugural Ceremonies, "First, Facts and Precedents". Accessed 2013-07-18

[9] Ritchie, Donald. "Who Moved the Inauguration? Dispelling an Urban Legend". *OUPblog*. Oxford University Press. Retrieved 19 February 2015.

[10] Terri Bimes, ed. Michael A. Genovese, *Encyclopedia of the American Presidency*, p 262-63.

[11] 5 U.S.C. § 3331

[12] "Presidential Inaugurations Past and Present: A Look at the History Behind the Pomp and Circumstance". 2002-2009-fpc.state.gov. Retrieved 2012-11-07.

[13] *Documentary History of the First Federal Congress*, Vol. 15, pages 404–405

[14] "The New Administration: President Arthur Formally Inaugurated" (PDF). *The New York Times*. September 22, 1881. Retrieved January 19, 2009.

[15] Malone, Noreen (January 19, 2009). "Why Doesn't Every President Use the Lincoln Bible?". Slate. Retrieved June 15, 2014. John Quincy Adams, according to his own letters, placed his hand on a constitutional law volume rather than a Bible to indicate where his fealty lay.

[16] Glass, Andrew J. (February 26, 1967). "Catholic Church Missal, Not Bible, Used by Johnson for Oath at Dallas" (PDF). *The Washington Post*. Retrieved June 15, 2014.

[17] Usborne, Simon (November 16, 2013). "The LBJ missal: Why a prayer book given to John F Kennedy was used to swear in the 36th US President". *The Independent*. Retrieved June 15, 2014.

[18] "President-elect Barack Obama to be Sworn in Using Lincoln's Bible". Presidential Inaugural Committee. December 23, 2008.

[19] Parnass, Sarah (January 10, 2013). "Obama Picks Lincoln, MLK Bibles for Inauguration". *ABC News*. Retrieved June 15, 2014. On the day of the Inaugural ceremony, President Obama will take the oath of office on two historic Bibles–one that belonged to Abe Lincoln and the other to Dr. Martin Luther King, Jr.

[20] "Gerald R. Ford's Remarks on Taking the Oath of Office as President". Gerald R. Ford Presidential Library and Museum. Retrieved November 18, 2008.

[21] "Presidential Inaugurations Past and Present: A Look at the History Behind the Pomp and Circumstance".

[22] "The two and one-half hour inaugural parade was witnessed by an estimated 1 million persons, of whom 60,000 were in the grandstand in seats ranging in price from $3 to $15, according to location. About 22,000 service men and women and 5,000 civilians were in the parade, which included 50 state and organization floats costing $100,000. There were also 65 musical units, 350 horses, 3 elephants, an Alaskan dog team, and the 280-millimeter atomic cannon. It was the most elaborate inaugural pageant ever held."

[23] Knowlton, Brian (January 21, 2009). "On His First Full Day, Obama Tackles Sobering Challenges". *The New York Times*. Retrieved January 28, 2009.

[24] I The Journal and Letters of Francis Asbury Chap. 18.

[25] MacNeil, Neil. *The President's medal, 1789–1977*. New York: Published in association with the National Portrait Gallery, Smithsonian Institution, by C. N. Potter, 1977.

[26] Levine, H. Joseph. *Collectors Guide to Presidential Medals and Memorabilia*. Danbury, Conn.: Johnson & Jensen, 1981.

[27] Individual named is the U.S. Chief Justice, unless otherwise indicated

[28] http://www.inaugural.senate.gov/about/facts-and-firsts

[29] Bowen, Clarence W. *The History of the Centennial Celebration of the Inauguration of George Washington*, N.Y. 1892, p. 72

[30] "Bibles and Scripture Passages Used by Presidents in Taking the Oath of Office". Architect of the Capitol.

[31] "Presidential Inaugurations Past and Present: A Look at the History Behind the Pomp and Circumstance". U.S. Department of State. January 13, 2005.

[32] Files of the Legislative Reference Service, Library of Congress

[33] Affirmed instead of swearing the oath.

[34] Wright, John. *Historic Bibles in America*, N.Y. 1905, p. 46

[35] List compiled by Clerk of the Supreme Court, 1939

[36] One source (The Chicago Daily Tribune, September 23, 1881, p. 5) says that Garfield and Arthur used the same passage, but does not indicate which one.

[37] Opened at random by Chief Justice

[38] Bible given to him by Methodist church congregation

[39] Senate Document 116, 65th Congress, 1st Session, 1917

[40] "Obama picks Bible for inauguration, but what verse?". CNN. December 24, 2008.

[41] "Inauguration of the President: Facts & Firsts". U.S. Senate. Retrieved December 13, 2008.

[42] Facts on File, Jan. 16–22, 1949, p. 21.

[43] New York Times, January 21, 1953, p. 19

[44] New York Times, January 22, 1957, p. 16.

[45] "Inauguration of President Dwight D. Eisenhower, 1957". Inaugural.senate.gov. Retrieved August 30, 2010.

[46] "John F. Kennedy and Ireland – John F. Kennedy Presidential Library & Museum". Jfklibrary.org. Retrieved August 30, 2010.

[47] New York Times, January 21, 1961, p. 8, col. 1.

[48] Office of the Clerk of the Supreme Court via phone July 1968

[49] Washington Post, January 20, 1969, p. A1.

[50] "Jimmy Carter Inaugural Address". Bartelby.com. January 20, 1977.

[51] Washington Post, January 21, 1977, p. A17

[52] Democracy's Big Day: The Inauguration of Our President, by Jim Bendat

[53] Washington Post, January 21, 1997, p. A14

[54] Inauguration staff. George W. Bush had hoped to use the Masonic Bible that had been used both by George Washington in 1789, and by Bush's father, George H. W. Bush, in 1989. This historic Bible had been transported, under guard, from New York to Washington for the inauguration but, due to inclement weather, a family Bible was substituted instead.

[55] Resworn in the Map Room of the White House to correct words transposed during the public ceremony. Shear, Michael (January 22, 2009). "Obama Sworn In Again, Using the Right Words". *Washington Post*. Retrieved January 21, 2009.

[56] "Obama chooses Lincoln's Bible for inauguration".

[57] "2013 inaugural ceremony to be pushed back a day". USA Today. March 28, 2012. Retrieved November 12, 2012.

[58] "Obama using MLK, Lincoln Bibles during oath".

## 17.7 Further reading

- *Inaugural Addresses of the Presidents of the United States*. Bartleby.com. 1989. ISBN 1-58734-025-9.

## 17.8 External links

- senate.gov chronology

- Full texts of all U.S. Inaugural Addresses at Bartleby.com

- Inaugural Speeches, 23 videos (access only in the US)

- Presidential Oaths of Office (Library of Congress)

- Bibles and Scripture Passages Used by Presidents in Taking the Oath of Office, Library of Congress

- Inauguration videos from Franklin D. Roosevelt – George W. Bush at YouTube from C-SPAN

- Federal Hall, NYC – Site of the first inauguration in 1789

- "Simple Gifts" - Music for U.S. Presidents

# Chapter 18

# List of Presidents of the United States by previous experience

Although many paths may lead to the Presidency of the United States, the most common job experience, occupation or profession of U.S. presidents has been lawyer.[1] This sortable table enumerates all holders of that office, along with major elective or appointive offices or periods of military service prior to election to the Presidency. The column immediately to the right of the Presidents' names shows the position or office held just before the Presidency. The next column to the right lists the next previous position held, and so on. Note that the total number of previous positions held by an individual may exceed four; the number of columns was limited to what would fit within the page width. The last two columns on the right list the home state (at the time of election to the Presidency) and primary occupation of each future President, prior to beginning a political career.

To sort a column, click the square button in the header.

## 18.1  By the numbers

Of the 43 people who have served as President:

**26** Presidents had previously been lawyers

**22** Presidents had previous military experience; 9 were Generals in the US Army[2]

**18** Presidents previously served as U.S. Representatives; 6 of 18 held this office prior to the four 'previous positions' shown in this table. Only one - James A. Garfield - was a Representative immediately before election as President. Only one ex-president, John Quincy Adams, ever served as a U.S. Representative.

**17** Presidents previously served as state Governors; 9 of 17 were Governors immediately before election as President.

**16** Presidents previously served as U.S. Senators; only 3 immediately before election as President.

**14** Presidents previously served as Vice-President. All except Nixon were VP immediately before election as President; 9 of the 14 succeeded to the Presidency because of the death or resignation of the elected President; 5 of those 9 were not re-elected.

**8** Presidents were out of office (for at least one year) immediately before election as President.

**8** Presidents previously served as Cabinet Secretaries; 6 as Secretary of State; 5 of the 8 served immediately before election as President.

**7** Presidents had previous experience in foreign service.[3]

**7** Presidents came from the state of Ohio; 6 from New York (7 if Grover Cleveland is counted twice);[4] 5 from Virginia (5 of the first 10, but none since); 4 from Massachusetts; 3 each from the states of Tennessee, California, and Texas; 2 from Illinois. Presidents have come from 10 other states, 18 different states in all.

**5** Presidents were family relations of previous presidents: John Quincy Adams (son of John Adams), Benjamin Harrison (grandson of William Henry Harrison), Zachary Taylor (2nd cousin of James Madison), Franklin Roosevelt (5th cousin of Theodore Roosevelt) and George W. Bush (son of George H. W. Bush).

## 18.2  See also

- President of the United States

- List of Presidents of the United States by other offices held

# 18.3 Notes

[1] International Law, US Power: The United States' Quest for Legal Security, p 10, Shirley V. Scott - 2012

[2] George Washington was commanding general of the Continental Army, the pre-independence equivalent of the US Army. The 9 US Army Generals were Jackson, W. H. Harrison, Taylor, Pierce, Grant, Hayes, Garfield, B. Harrison and Eisenhower. Others with military experience were Monroe, McKinley, T. Roosevelt, Truman, Kennedy, L. B. Johnson, Nixon, Carter, Ford, Reagan, G. H. W. Bush, G. W. Bush.

[3] Martin van Buren's brief foreign service is not counted since, although he was appointed Ambassador to the United Kingdom, the appointment was rejected by the U.S. Senate

[4] Cleveland served nonconsecutive presidential terms.

[5] "State" refers to the state generally considered "home", not necessarily the state where the president was born

[6] This designation is used whenever the subject was out of public office for more than one year

[7] Washington was first chosen by the Virginia State Legislature to be a delegate to the Constitutional Convention. Then he was elected by the delegates to be president of the convention.

[8] Commander-in-chief of the Continental Army during the American Revolutionary War

[9] This is a general designation for any appointive position representing the United States to a foreign government

[10] This is a general designation for any elected state legislator

[11] Van Buren served just over two months of his term as Governor of New York before President Jackson appointed him Secretary of State

[12] Tyler succeeded President Harrison, who died in office. He was not re-elected.

[13] Fillmore succeeded President Taylor, who died in office. He was not re-elected.

[14] Lincoln was born in Kentucky, but moved to Illinois at an early age

[15] Johnson succeeded President Lincoln, who was assassinated. He was not re-elected.

[16] President Lincoln appointed Johnson military governor of Tennessee during the Civil War

[17] Arthur succeeded President Garfield, who was assassinated. He was not re-elected.

[18] This is a general designation for appointive domestic Federal offices below cabinet level

[19] This is a general designation for local elective offices

[20] This is a general designation for local elective offices

[21] Roosevelt succeeded President McKinley, who was assassinated. He was re-elected once (1904), chose not to run again in 1908, and ran unsuccessfully in 1912.

[22] Assistant Secretary of the Navy

[23] President McKinley appointed Taft Governor-General of the Philippines

[24] United States Court of Appeals for the Sixth Circuit

[25] Solicitor General of the United States

[26] President of Princeton University

[27] Coolidge succeeded President Harding, who died in office. He was re-elected to a second term.

[28] Born and raised in Vermont and spent time in Vermont politics. Permanently moved to Massachusetts to attend college.

[29] During and following World War I, Hoover was involved with several humanitarian organizations.

[30] Assistant Secretary of the Navy

[31] Truman succeeded President Roosevelt, who died in office. He was re-elected to a second term.

[32] Johnson succeeded President Kennedy, who was assassinated. He was re-elected to a second term.

[33] head of the National Youth Administration in Texas

[34] Ford succeeded President Nixon, who resigned. He was not re-elected. Previously, Ford was appointed Vice-President after Spiro Agnew resigned. Currently only President not to have been elected to the Executive Branch.

[35] Ford was born in Nebraska, but moved to Michigan at an early age

[36] Reagan was born, raised and educated in Illinois; he moved permanently to California after graduation from college.

[37] Bush was born and raised in Massachusetts, but moved to Texas after graduation from college.

[38] http://millercenter.org/president/biography/gwbush-life-before-the-presidency

[39] https://web.archive.org/web/20080830012958/http://www.nationalreview.com/flashback/york200408261025.asp

# Chapter 19

# List of Presidents of the United States by other offices held

This is a list of Presidents of the United States by other offices (either elected or appointive) held. Every President of the United States has served as either:

- Vice President of the United States

- a Member of Congress (either U.S. Senator or Representative)

- a Governor of a state

- a Cabinet Secretary

- a General of the United States Army

## 19.1   Federal Government

### 19.1.1   Executive Branch

**Vice Presidents**

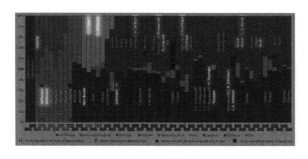

*A timeline graph of Presidents with a highlighting of those who had been Vice Presidents. A gray arrow points to those who became president without having been elected as president. The double arrow indicates Ford becoming president without having been elected as vice president also. (See source image for more info.)*

In addition, both George H. W. Bush and Dick Cheney served as Acting Presidents for brief periods under Reagan and George W. Bush, respectively.

13 former Vice Presidents (R. Johnson, Breckinridge, Morton, Stevenson, Fairbanks, Garner, Wallace, Barkley, Nixon, Humphrey, Mondale, Quayle, and Gore) all made failed runs for the Presidency. Nixon, Humphrey, Mondale, and Gore received their party's nomination. Nixon would later be elected in a second run for the presidency.

**Cabinet Secretaries**

John Adams (as Vice President) and Thomas Jefferson both served in the Cabinet of George Washington.

Both Theodore (from 1897–1898) and Franklin D. Roosevelt (from 1913–1920) served as Assistant Secretary of the Navy under Presidents McKinley and Wilson, respectively. William Howard Taft served as Solicitor General from 1890 to 1892 under President Harrison.

**Ambassadors**

**Other Federal Appointees**

### 19.1.2   Judicial Branch

**Chief Justice of the United States**

**Other Federal Judges**

### 19.1.3   Legislative Branch

**Senators**

A number of future Presidents served together while in the Senate:

- Senator Monroe served under Vice President Adams (1790–1794)

- Senator Jackson served under Vice President Jefferson (1797–1798)

- Senator Van Buren served with Senators Jackson (1823–1825), Harrison (1825–1828), and Tyler (1827–1828)

- Senator Buchanan also served with Senator Tyler (1834–1836) and later served with Senator Pierce (1837–1842). Both Buchanan and Tyler served under Vice President Martin Van Buren (1833–1837), while Pierce later served under Vice President Tyler (1841).

- Senator Harrison briefly served under Vice President Arthur (1881).

- Senator Johnson served with both Senators Nixon (1950–1953) and Kennedy (1953–1960). Johnson and Kennedy both served under Vice President Nixon (1953–1961).

**Members of the House of Representatives**

A number of future Presidents served in the House together:

- Congressman Jackson served with Congressman Madison (1796–1797)

- Congressman Harrison served with Congressman Tyler (1816–1819)

- Congressman Buchanan served with Congressman Polk (1825–1831)

- Congressman Adams also served with Congressman Polk (1831–1839), and later served with Congressmen Fillmore (1833–1835; 1837–1843), Pierce (1833–1837), Johnson (1843–1848), and Lincoln (1847–1848)

- Congressman Garfield served with both Congressmen Hayes (1865–1867) and McKinley (1877–1881)

- Congressman Nixon served with Congressmen Johnson (1947–1949), John F. Kennedy (1947–1950), and Ford (1949–1950). Congressman Ford later served with Congressman Bush (1967–1971).

### 19.1.4   Continental Congress

## 19.2   State and territorial government

### 19.2.1   Governors

### 19.2.2   State Legislators

*See below for information about pre-1776 colonial offices held.*

### 19.2.3   Other Statewide Offices

## 19.3   Municipal Government

## 19.4   Presidents without prior political occupation

## 19.5   Foreign Governments

### 19.5.1   Colonial and Confederate Legislators

## 19.6   Lost Races

Other than immediate re-election to the Presidency

# Chapter 20

# List of United States presidential elections by Electoral College margin

The table below is a **list of United States presidential elections ordered by margin of victory** in the **Electoral College vote**.

## 20.1 Definition of the margin

### 20.1.1 Informal definition

In modern presidential elections, the margin of victory does **not** depend on the margin between the winner and his or her main rival. If the "winner" doesn't get a majority of the electoral vote, the election is thrown into the House of Representatives where the candidate's rival may very well be chosen. On the other hand, if a candidate does get a majority, he or she is guaranteed to have more votes than his or her rivals. Thus, the margin of victory should be the candidate's margin of majority; that is, it should be the margin of votes above 50%.

Because the Electoral College has grown in size, the results are normalized to compensate. For example, take two elections, 1848 and 1968. In the election of 1968 Richard Nixon got a majority by 32 votes. At first glance, the election of 1848 appears closer, because Zachary Taylor got a majority by only 18 votes. But Nixon could have gotten as many as 269 votes above a majority (if he had won unanimously), while Taylor could only have gotten 145 votes above a majority. Thus, we normalize the two elections to compare them. We calculate Nixon's margin of victory by dividing the 32 by 269 to get 0.119. We do the same with Taylor, dividing 18 by 145, to get 0.124. And we find that Nixon's election was actually closer because a smaller fraction of the electors separated Nixon from a contingent election (For fair representation, in the 1972 election, Nixon was re-elected with a ratio of 0.926*, a landslide).

Now, there's one more wrinkle. The foregoing explanation applies to modern elections. However, prior to the passage of the 12th Amendment, the winner of the presidential election was the person who got a majority of electors to vote for him **and** who got the most number of votes, because each elector cast two presidential votes. Thus, for elections prior to 1804, if two candidates got above 50% of the electors, the margin of victory is the victorious candidate's margin over the other candidate who got above 50% of the electors. As it happens, of the four elections prior to the 12th Amendment, two involved two candidates getting above 50% of the electors: 1792 and 1800.

### 20.1.2 Mathematical definition

The margin of victory in the election is calculated as follows:

Let $c$ be the total number of electors voting in the election. Let $w$ be the number of electoral votes cast for the candidate with the most electoral votes, and let $r$ be the number of votes for the runner-up.

According to the Constitution, the electoral vote is called a "draw" and sent into the House of Representatives if the candidate with the most votes does not get a simple majority of the electors voting. So, the margin of victory is the number of electoral votes over both the runner-up and half the electoral votes cast. For elections after the passage of the 12th Amendment, the runner-up will always have less than half of the electoral votes cast, so the absolute margin of victory will be the difference of the winner's electoral votes and half the electoral votes cast. To express this in mathematical formulae:

$$\text{absolute margin of victory} = \begin{cases} 0; & w \le \frac{c}{2} \\ w - \max\{r, \frac{c}{2}\}; & w > \frac{c}{2} \end{cases}$$

The minimum possible value for the margin of victory is clearly zero. The maximum possible value of the margin of victory occurs in the case in which each elector casts a vote for the winning candidate and the runner-up gets no more than half of the vote. In this case, the maximum margin of victory is $c/2$. In order to meaningfully compare election to election, we need that maximum margin to be constant from election to election. Thus, we divide the absolute margin of victory by $c/2$ to get a normalized margin of victory that ranges from 0 to 1:

$$\text{normalized margin of victory} = \begin{cases} 0; & w \le \frac{c}{2} \\ \frac{w - \max\{r, \frac{c}{2}\}}{\frac{c}{2}}; & w > \frac{c}{2} \end{cases}$$

## 20.2  Table of election results

Note that in the following table, the election of 1824 is ranked closer than the election of 1800 because the election of 1800 resulted in a two-way draw, while the election of 1824 resulted in a three-way draw.

Also note that the elections of 1789, 1792, 1796, and 1800 took place before the 12th Amendment and thus each elector had two votes (but had to vote for two separate people). For example, George Washington received the vote of every elector, but the second vote of each elector was split among other candidates. Thus Washington is accounted to have received 100% of the possible electoral votes.

*\*Unanimous; George Washington received the vote of every elector, but the 2nd vote of each elector was split among other candidates. Thus Washington is accounted to have received 100% of the possible electoral votes.\*\**

- [a] None of the presidential candidates in 1824 received a majority of the electoral vote, so the presidential election was decided by the House of Representatives, who selected Adams.

- [b] Under the original procedure for the Electoral College, each elector had two votes and voted for two individuals. The candidate receiving the majority of votes became president and the candidate with the second highest number of votes became vice-president. While Jefferson had more electoral votes than his principal opponent, John Adams, he was tied with his own vice-presidential running mate, Aaron Burr, in electoral votes. Because of the tie, the 1800 presidential election was decided by the House of Representatives, who selected Jefferson as president. Subsequently the Twelfth Amendment to the United States Constitution was enacted in order to provide for the president and vice-president to be elected as a single ticket.

- [c] There was a dispute as to whether Missouri's electoral votes in 1820 were valid, due to the timing of its assumption of statehood. The figures listed include those votes.

- [d] Only ten of the thirteen states cast electoral votes in the first ever presidential election. North Carolina and Rhode Island were ineligible to participate since they had not yet ratified the United States Constitution. New York failed to appoint its electors before the appropriate deadline because of a deadlock in its state legislature.

- [e] Votes which were not counted don't change the majority needed to win. Although there are only 232 counted votes in 1820, winner needed 118 (majority of 235) votes to win, same in 1872: By resolution of the House, 3 votes cast for Greeley were not counted (makes 349 counted votes) but 177 votes are still needed to win (majority of 352).

## 20.3  See also

- List of United States presidential elections by popular vote margin

## 20.4  References

- How close were U.S. Presidential Elections? - Michael Sheppard, Massachusetts Institute of Technology

# Chapter 21

# List of United States presidential elections by popular vote margin

In United States presidential elections, the national popular vote is the sum of all votes cast in every state and the District of Columbia.

The Twelfth Amendment to the United States Constitution provides the procedure by which the President and Vice President are elected, which is through the Electoral College.

Since the United States does not hold national elections, the national popular vote does not determine the outcome of the United States presidential election.

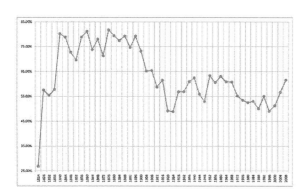

*Graph of voter turnout percentage from 1824 to 2008.*

## 21.2 Timeline

## 21.1 List

The table below can be sorted to display elections by their presidential term / year of election, name, margin by percentage in popular vote, popular vote, margin in popular vote by number, and the runner up in the Electoral College.

Note: The popular vote was not recorded prior to the 1824 election, so the first nine US presidential elections are not included in this table.

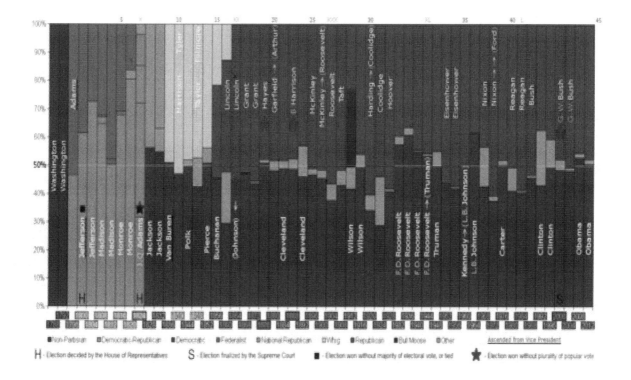

## 21.3   See also

- List of United States presidential elections by Electoral College margin

## 21.4   Sources

- Leip, David. *Dave Leip's Atlas of U.S. Presidential Elections.*

- Peters, Gerhard. *Voter Turnout in Presidential Elections.*

## 21.5   References

## 21.6   External links

- How close were U.S. Presidential Elections? - Michael Sheppard, Massachusetts Institute of Technology

# Chapter 22

# Voter turnout in the United States presidential elections

The following is a listing of all of the **voter turnouts** in each United States presidential election going back to 1828.

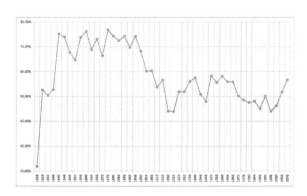

*Graph of voter turnout percentage from 1824 to 2008.*

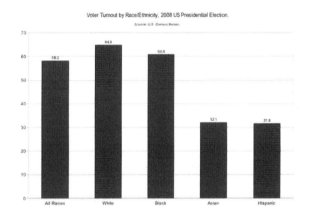

*Voter turnout in the 2008 U.S. Presidential Election by race/ethnicity.*

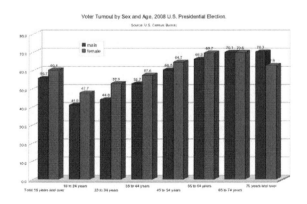

*Voter turnout by sex and age for the 2008 US Presidential Election.*

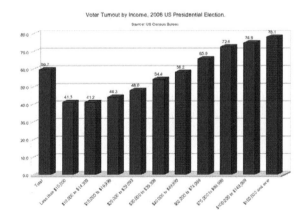

*Rates of voting in the 2008 U.S. Presidential Election by income*

Note: While final exact figures for 2012 are yet to be calculated, the Bipartisan Research Center has stated that turnout for 2012 was 57.5 percent of the eligible voters, which they claim was a decline from 2008. They estimate that as a percent of eligible voters, turn out was: 2000, 54.2%; in 2004 60.4%; 2008 62.3%; and 2012 57.5%.[3] These were the same figures as given by the Center for the Study of the American Electorate.[4]

Later analysis by the University of California, Santa Barbara's American Presidency Project found that there were 235,248,000 people of voting age in the United States in

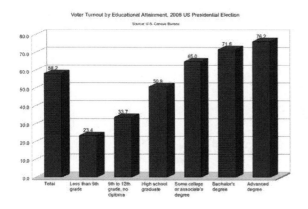

*Rates in voting in the 2008 U.S. Presidential Election by educational attainment*

the 2012 election, resulting in 2012 voting age population (VAP) turnout of 54.9%.[5] The total increase in VAP between 2008 and 2012 (5,300,000) was the smallest increase since 1964, bucking the modern average of 9,000,000-13,000,000 per cycle. One possible reason for this relates to the effects that the Great Recession and stricter border control mechanisms had on net migration to the United States from Mexico from 2009 to 2012; net migration from Mexico to the United States plummeted to zero (and potentially net-negative totals) during this time, and for the first time in more than 80 years, the Mexican-born population in the United States decreased.[6] Since the broadest measurement of VAP takes into account all adults who are living in the United States regardless of voter registration or citizenship status, such abnormally large reductions in immigration during this period would affect the overall number.

## 22.1 References

[1] Between 1932 and 2008: "Table 397. Participation in Elections for President and U.S. Representatives: 1932 to 2010" (PDF). *U.S. Census Bureau, Statistical Abstract of the United States: 2012*. U.S. Census Bureau.

[2] Between 1828-1928: "Voter Turnout in Presidential Elections: 1828 - 2008". *The American Presidency Project*. UC Santa Barbara. Retrieved 2012-11-09.

[3] Bipartisan Research Center, "2012 Voter Turnout," November 8, 2012. http://bipartisanpolicy.org/library/report/2012-voter-turnout

[4] "Election results 2012: Report reveals 2012 voter turnout was lower than 2008 and 2004" Chanel 5 report. November 15, 2012. wptv.com.

[5] UC Santa Barbara (American Presidency Project), "Voter Turnout in Presidential Elections", May 4, 2013. http://www.presidency.ucsb.edu/data/turnout.php

[6] Pew Hispanic Trends Project, "Net Migration from Mexico Falls to Zero—and Perhaps Less", April 23, 2012. http://www.pewhispanic.org/2012/04/23/net-migration-from-mexico-falls-to-zero-and-perhaps-less/

# Chapter 23

# Elections in the United States

*An 1846 painting,* The County Election *by George Caleb Bingham, showing a polling judge administering an oath to a voter.*

The United States is a federation, with elected officials at the federal (national), state and local levels. On a national level, the head of state, the President, is elected indirectly by the people, through an Electoral College. Today, the electors virtually always vote with the popular vote of their state. All members of the federal legislature, the Congress, are directly elected. There are many elected offices at state level, each state having at least an elective Governor and legislature. There are also elected offices at the local level, in counties and cities. According to political science professor Jennifer Lawless, there were 519,682 elected officials in the United States as of 2012.[1]

State law regulates most aspects of the election, including primaries, the eligibility of voters (beyond the basic constitutional definition), the running of each state's electoral college, and the running of state and local elections. The United States Constitution defines (to a basic extent) how federal elections are held, in Article One and Article Two and various amendments. The federal government has also been involved in attempts to increase voter turnout, by measures such as the National Voter Registration Act of 1993.

The financing of elections has always been controversial, because private sources make up substantial amounts of campaign contributions, especially in federal elections. Voluntary public funding for candidates willing to accept spending limits was introduced in 1974 for presidential primaries and elections. The Federal Elections Commission, created in 1975 by an amendment to the Federal Election Campaign Act has the responsibility to disclose campaign finance information, to enforce the provisions of the law such as the limits and prohibitions on contributions, and to oversee the public funding of U.S. Presidential elections.

## 23.1 Voting

### 23.1.1 Method

The most common method used in U.S. elections is the first-past-the-post system, where the highest polling candidate wins the election. Some may use a two-round system, where if no candidate receives a required number of votes then there is a runoff between the two candidates with the most votes.

Since 2002, several cities have adopted instant-runoff voting in their elections. Voters rank the candidates in order of preference rather than voting for a single candidate. If a candidate secures more than half of votes cast, that candidate wins. Otherwise, the candidate with the fewest votes is eliminated. Ballots assigned to the eliminated candidate are recounted and assigned to those of the remaining candidates who rank next in order of preference on each ballot. This process continues until one candidate wins by obtaining more than half the votes.

### 23.1.2 Eligibility

The eligibility of an individual for voting is set out in the constitution and also regulated at state level. The constitution states that suffrage cannot be denied on grounds of race or color, sex or age for citizens eighteen years or older. Beyond these basic qualifications, it is the responsi-

166

bility of state legislatures to regulate voter eligibility. Some states ban convicted criminals, especially felons, from voting for a fixed period of time or indefinitely. The number of American adults who are currently or permanently ineligible to vote due to felony convictions is estimated to be 5.3 million.[2] Some states also have legacy constitutional statements barring the "insane" or "idiots" from voting; such references are generally considered obsolete and are being considered for review or removal where they appear.[3]

### 23.1.3 Voter registration

Main article: Voter registration § United States

Every state except North Dakota requires that citizens who wish to vote be registered. Some states allow citizens to register to vote on the same day of the election, see below. Traditionally, voters had to register at state offices to vote, but in the mid-1990s efforts were made by the federal government to make registering easier, in an attempt to increase turnout. The National Voter Registration Act of 1993 (the "Motor Voter" law) required state governments that receive certain types of federal funding to make the voter registration process easier by providing uniform registration services through drivers' license registration centers, disability centers, schools, libraries, and mail-in registration. States with same-day registration are exempt from Motor Voter; namely: Idaho, Minnesota, New Hampshire, North Dakota, Wisconsin, and Wyoming.

In many states, citizens registering to vote may declare an affiliation with a political party.[4] This declaration of affiliation does not cost money, and does not make the citizen a dues-paying member of a party. A party cannot prevent a voter from declaring his or her affiliation with them, but it can refuse requests for full membership. In some states, only voters affiliated with a party may vote in that party's primary elections (see below). Declaring a party affiliation is never required. Some states, including Georgia, Michigan, Minnesota, Virginia, Wisconsin, and Washington, practice non-partisan registration.[5]

### 23.1.4 Absentee voting

Voters unable or unwilling to vote at polling stations on Election Day can vote via absentee ballots. Absentee ballots are most commonly sent and received via the United States Postal Service. Despite their name, absentee ballots are often requested and submitted in person. About half of all states and U.S. territories allow "no excuse absentee," where no reason is required to request an absentee ballot. Others require a valid reason, such as infirmity or travel, be given before a voter can participate using an absentee ballot.

*An absentee ballot paper for Milton, New Hampshire. This ballot also contains a referendum placed on the ballot by the state legislature.*

Some states, including California,[6] and Washington[7][8] allow citizens to apply for permanent absentee voter status, which will automatically receive an absentee ballot for each election. Typically a voter must request an absentee ballot before the election occurs.

A significant source of absentee ballots is the population of Americans living outside the United States. In 1986 Congress enacted the Uniformed and Overseas Citizens Absentee Voting Act (UOCAVA). UOCAVA requires that the states and territories allow members of the United States Uniformed Services and merchant marine, their family members, and United States citizens residing outside the United States to register and vote absentee in elections for Federal offices. Though many states had pre-existing statutes in place UOCAVA made it mandatory and nationally uniform. "Generally, all U.S. citizens 19 years or older who are or will be residing outside the United States during an election period are eligible to vote absentee in any election for Federal office. In addition, all members of the Uniformed Services, their family members and members of the Merchant Marine and their family members, who are U.S. citizens, may vote absentee in Federal, state and local elections."[9] Absentee ballots from these voters can often be transmitted private delivery services, fax, or email.[10]

### 23.1.5   Mail ballots

Mail ballots are similar in many respects to an absentee ballot. However they are used for *Mailing Precincts* where on Election Day no polling place is opened for a specific precinct.[11] In Oregon and Washington, all ballots are delivered through the mail.

### 23.1.6   Early voting

Main article: Early voting § United States

Early voting is a formal process where voters can cast their ballots prior to the official Election Day.  Early voting in person is allowed in 33 states and in Washington, D.C., with no excuse required.[12]

### 23.1.7   Voting equipment

Further information: Voting machine

Voters casting their ballots in polling places record their votes most commonly with optical scan voting machines or DRE voting machines.  Voting machine selection is typically done through a state's local election jurisdiction including counties, cities, and townships.  Many of these local jurisdictions have changed their voting equipment since 2000 due to the passage of the Help America Vote Act (HAVA), which allocated funds for the replacement of lever machine and punch card voting equipment.

## 23.2   Levels of election

### 23.2.1   Federal elections

See also: Election Day (United States)

The United States has a presidential system of government, which means that the executive and legislature are elected separately.  Article One of the United States Constitution requires that any election for the U.S. President must occur on a single day throughout the country; elections for Congressional offices, however, can be held at different times.

Congressional and presidential elections take place simultaneously every four years, and the intervening Congressional elections, which take place every two years, are called Midterm elections.

The constitution states that members of the United States House of Representatives must be at least 25 years old, a citizen of the United States for at least seven years, and be a (legal) inhabitant of the state they represent. Senators must be at least 30 years old, a citizen of the United States for at least nine years, and be a (legal) inhabitant of the state they represent. The President must be at least 35 years old, a natural born citizen of the United States and a resident in the United States for at least fourteen years. It is the responsibility of state legislatures to regulate the qualifications for a candidate appearing on a ballot paper, although in order to get onto the ballot, a candidate must often collect a legally defined number of signatures.

**Presidential elections**

Main articles:  United States presidential election and Electoral College (United States)

The President and the Vice President are elected together in a Presidential election.[13] It is an indirect election, with the winner being determined by votes cast by electors of the Electoral College. In modern times, voters in each state select a slate of electors from a list of several slates designated by different parties or candidates, and the electors typically promise in advance to vote for the candidates of their party (whose names of the presidential candidates usually appear on the ballot rather than those of the individual electors). The winner of the election is the candidate with at least 270 Electoral College votes. It is possible for a candidate to win the electoral vote, and lose the (nationwide) popular vote (receive fewer votes nationwide than the second ranked candidate).  Until the Twelfth Amendment to the United States Constitution of 1804, the runner-up in a Presidential election[14] became the Vice President.

Electoral College votes are cast by individual states by a group of electors, each elector casts one electoral college vote.  Until the Twenty-third Amendment to the United States Constitution of 1961 the District of Columbia citizens did not have representation and/or electors in the electoral college. In modern times, with electors usually committed to vote for a party candidate in advance, electors that vote against the popular vote in their state are called faithless electors, and occurrences are rare. State law regulates how states cast their electoral college votes. In all states except Maine and Nebraska, the candidate that wins the most votes in the state receives all its electoral college votes (a "winner takes all" system). From 1969 in Maine, and from 1991 in Nebraska, two electoral votes are awarded based on the winner of the statewide election, and the rest (two in Maine, three in Nebraska) go to the highest vote-winner in each of the state's congressional districts.

### Congressional elections

Congress has two chambers: the Senate and the House of Representatives.

**Senate elections** The Senate has 100 members, elected for a six-year term in dual-seat constituencies (2 from each state), with one-third being renewed every two years. The group of the Senate seats that is up for election during a given year is known as a "class"; the three classes are staggered so that only one of the three groups is renewed every two years. Until the Seventeenth Amendment to the United States Constitution in 1913, Senators were elected by state legislatures, not the electorate of states.

*A chart of party balance in the House*

**House of Representatives elections** The House of Representatives has 435 members, elected for a two-year term in single-seat constituencies. House of Representatives elections are held every two years on the first Tuesday after November 1 in even years. House elections are first-past-the-post elections that elect a Representative from each of 435 House districts which cover the United States. Special House elections can occur between if a member dies or resigns during a term. The non-voting delegates of Washington, D.C. and the territories of American Samoa, Guam, the Northern Mariana Islands, Puerto Rico and the United States Virgin Islands are also elected.

House elections occur every two years, correlated with presidential elections or halfway through a President's term. The House delegate of Puerto Rico, officially known as the Resident Commissioner of Puerto Rico, is elected to a four-year term, coinciding with those of the President.

As the redistricting commissions of states are often partisan, districts are often drawn which benefit incumbents. An increasing trend has been for incumbents to have an overwhelming advantage in House elections, and since the 1994 election, an unusually low number of seats has changed hands in each election. Due to gerrymandering, fewer than 10% of all House seats are contested in each election cycle. Over 90% of House members are reelected every two years, due to lack of electoral competition. Gerrymandering of the House, combined with the divisions inherent in the design of the Senate and of the Electoral College, result in a discrepancy between the percentage of popular support for various political parties and the actual level of the parties' representation.

### 23.2.2 State elections

State law and state constitutions, controlled by state legislatures regulate elections at state level and local level. Various officials at state level are elected. Since the separation of powers applies to states as well as the federal government, state legislatures and the executive (the governor) are elected separately. Governors and lieutenant governor are elected in all states, in some states on a joint ticket and in some states separately, some separately in different electoral cycles. The governors of the territories of American Samoa, Guam, the Northern Mariana Islands, Puerto Rico and the United States Virgin Islands are also elected. In some states, executive positions such as Attorney General and Secretary of State are also elected offices. All members of state legislatures and territorial jurisdiction legislatures are elected. In some states, members of the state supreme court and other members of the state judiciary are elected. Proposals to amend the state constitution are also placed on the ballot in some states.

As a matter of convenience and cost saving, elections for many of these state and local offices are held at the same time as either the federal presidential or midterm elections. There are a handful of states, however, that instead hold their elections during odd-numbered "off years."

### 23.2.3 Local elections

At the local level, county and city government positions are usually filled by election, especially within the legislative branch. The extent to which offices in the executive or judicial branches are elected vary from county-to-county or city-to-city. Some examples of local elected positions include sheriffs at the county level and mayors and school board members at the city level. Like state elections, an election for a specific local office may be held at the same time as either the presidential, midterm, or off-year elections.

## 23.3 Comparison of recent and upcoming election years

[1] This table does not include special elections, which may be held to fill political offices that have become vacant between the regularly scheduled elections.

[2] As well as all six non-voting delegates of the U.S. House.

[3] As well as five non-voting delegates of the U.S. House. The Resident Commissioner of Puerto Rico instead serves a four-year term that coincides with the presidential term.

[4] Both the Governors of New Hampshire and Vermont are each elected to two-year terms. The other 48 state governors serve four-year terms.

- view
- talk
- edit

## 23.4 Features of the election system

### 23.4.1 Party systems

Main articles: Party system and Politics of the United States

Americans vote for a specific candidate instead of directly selecting a particular political party. The United States Constitution has never formally addressed the issue of political parties. The Founding Fathers such as Alexander Hamilton and James Madison did not support domestic political factions at the time the Constitution was written.[15] In addition, the first President of the United States, George Washington, was not a member of any political party at the time of his election or throughout his tenure as president. Furthermore, he hoped that political parties would not be formed, fearing conflict and stagnation.[16] Nevertheless, the beginnings of the American two-party system emerged from his immediate circle of advisers, with Hamilton and Madison ending up being the core leaders in this emerging party system.

Thus, it is up to the candidate to decide under what party he/she should run, registers to run, pays the fees, etc. In the primary elections, the party organization stays neutral until one candidate has been elected. The platform of the party is written by the winning candidate (in presidential elections; in other elections no platform is involved). Each candidate has his or her own campaign, fund raising organization, etc. The primary elections in the main parties are organized by the states, who also register the party affiliation of the voters (this also makes it easier to gerrymander the congressional districts). The party is thus little more than a campaign organization for the main elections.

However, elections in the United States often do become *de facto* national races between the political parties. In what is known as "presidential coattails", candidates in presidential elections usually bring out supporters who then vote for his party's candidates for other offices, usually resulting in the presidential winner's party gaining seats in Congress. On the other hand, midterm elections are sometimes regarded as a referendum on the sitting president's and/or incumbent party's performance.[17][18] There is a historical pattern that the incumbent president's party loses seats in midterm elections. This may be because the President's popularity has slipped since election, or because the President's popularity encouraged supporters to come out to vote for him in the presidential election, but these supporters are less likely to vote when the President is not up for election.

### 23.4.2 Ballot access

Main article: Ballot access in the United States of America

Ballot access refers to the laws which regulate under what conditions access is granted for a candidate or political party to appear on voters' ballots. Each State has its own ballot access laws to determine who may appear on ballots and who may not. According to Article I, Section 4, of the United States Constitution, the authority to regulate the time, place, and manner of federal elections is up to each State, unless Congress legislates otherwise. Depending on the office and the state, it may be possible for a voter to cast a write-in vote for a candidate whose name does not appear on the ballot, but it is extremely rare for such a candidate to win office.

### 23.4.3 Campaign finance

Main article: Campaign finance in the United States

The funding of electoral campaigns has always been a controversial issue in American politics. Infringement of free speech (First Amendment) is an argument against restrictions on campaign contributions, while allegations of corruption arising from unlimited contributions and the need for political equality are arguments for the other side.[19] Private funds are a major source of finance, from individuals and organizations. The first attempt to regulate campaign finance by legislation was in 1867, but major legislation, with the intention to widely enforce, on campaign finance was not introduced until the 1970s.

Money contributed to campaigns can be classified into "hard money" and "soft money". Hard money is money contributed directly to a campaign, by an individual or organization. Soft money is money from an individual or organization not contributed to a campaign, but spent in candidate specific advertising or other efforts that benefits that candidate by groups supporting the candidate, but legally not coordinated by the official campaign.

The Federal Election Campaign Act of 1971 required candidates to disclose sources of campaign contributions and campaign expenditure. It was amended in 1974 to legally limit campaign contributions. It banned direct contributing to campaigns by corporations and trade unions and limited individual donations to $1,000 per campaign. It introduced public funding for Presidential primaries and elections. The Act also placed limits of $5,000 per campaign on PACs (political action committees). The limits on individual contributions and prohibition of direct corporate or labor union campaigns led to a huge increase in the number of PACs. Today many labor unions and corporations have their own PACs, and over 4,000 in total exist. The 1974 amendment also specified a Federal Election Commission, created in 1975 to administer and enforce campaign finance law. Various other provisions were also included, such as a ban on contributions or expenditures by foreign nationals (incorporated from the Foreign Agents Registration Act (FARA) (1966).

The case of *Buckley v. Valeo* (1976) challenged the Act. Most provisions were upheld, but the court found that the mandatory spending limit imposed was unconstitutional, as was the limit placed on campaign spending from the candidate's personal fortune and the provision that limited independent expenditures by individuals and organizations supporting but not officially linked to a campaign. The effect of the first decision was to allow candidates such as Ross Perot and Steve Forbes to spend enormous amounts of their own money in their own campaigns. The effect of the second decision was to allow the culture of "soft money" to develop.

A 1979 amendment to the Federal Election Campaign Act allowed political parties to spend without limit on get-out-the-vote and voter registration activities conducted primarily for a presidential candidate. Later, they were permitted by FECA to use "soft money", unregulated, unlimited contributions to fund this effort. Increasingly, the money began to be spent on issue advertising, candidate specific advertising that was being funded mostly by soft money.

The Bipartisan Campaign Reform Act of 2002 banned local and national parties from spending "soft money" and banned national party committees from accepting or spending soft money. It increased the limit of contributions by individuals from $1,000 to $2,000. It banned corporations or labor unions from funding issue advertising directly, and banned the use of corporate or labor money for advertisements that mention a federal candidate within 60 days of a general election or 30 days of a primary. The constitutionality of the bill was challenged and in December 2003, the Supreme Court upheld most provisions of the legislation. (See *McConnell v. FEC*.)

A large number of "527 groups" were active for the first time in the 2004 election. These groups receive donations from individuals and groups and then spend the money on issue advocacy, such as the anti-Kerry ads by Swift Boat Veterans For Truth. This is a new form of soft money, and not surprisingly it is controversial. Many 527 groups have close links with the Democratic or Republican Parties, even though legally they cannot coordinate their activities with them. John McCain, one of the Senators behind the Bipartisan Campaign Reform Act, and President Bush have both declared a desire to ban 527s.

Changing campaign finance laws is a highly controversial issue. Reformers wish to see laws changed in order to improve electoral competition and political equality. Opponents to reform wish to see the system stay as it is or with even fewer restrictions on the freedom to spend and contribute money. The Supreme Court has made it increasingly difficult for those who wish to regulate election financing, but options like partial public funding of campaigns are still possible and offer the potential to address reformers' concerns with minimal restrictions on the freedom to contribute.[20]

### 23.4.4 Primaries and caucuses

In partisan elections, candidates are chosen by primary elections (abbreviated to primaries) and caucuses in the states, the District of Columbia, Puerto Rico, American Samoa, Guam, and the U.S. Virgin Islands.

A primary election is an election in which registered voters in a jurisdiction (*nominating primary*) select a political party's candidate for a later election. There are various types of primary: either the whole electorate is eligible, and voters choose one party's primary at the polling booth (an open primary); or only independent voters can choose a party's primary at the polling booth (a semi-closed primary); or only registered members of the party are allowed to vote (closed primary). The blanket primary, when voters could vote for all parties' primaries on the same ballot was struck down by the United States Supreme Court as violating the First Amendment guarantee of freedom of assembly in the case California Democratic Party v. Jones. Primaries are also used to select candidates at the state level, for example in gubernatorial elections.

Caucuses also nominate candidates by election, but they are very different from primaries. Caucuses are meetings that occur at precincts and involve discussion of each party's platform and issues such as voter turnout in addition to voting. Eleven states: Iowa, New Mexico, North Dakota, Maine, Nevada, Hawaii, Minnesota, Kansas, Alaska, Wyoming, Colorado and the District of Columbia use caucuses.

The primary and caucus season in Presidential elections lasts from the Iowa caucus in January to the last primaries in June. Front-loading - when larger numbers of contests take place in the opening weeks of the season—can have an effect on the nomination process, potentially reducing the number of realistic candidates, as fund-raisers and donors quickly abandon those they see as untenable. However, it is not the case that the successful candidate is always the candidate that does the best in the early primaries. There is also a period dubbed the "invisible primary" that takes place before the primary season, when candidates attempt to solicit media coverage and funding well before the real primary season begins.

A state's presidential primary election or caucus usually is an indirect election: instead of voters directly selecting a particular person running for President, it determines how many delegates each party's national political convention will receive from their respective state. These delegates then in turn select their party's presidential nominee. Held in the summer, a political convention's purpose is also to adopt a statement of the party's principles and goals known as the *platform* and adopt the rules for the party's activities.

The day on which primaries are held for congressional seats, and state and local offices may also vary between states. The only federally mandated day for elections is Election Day for the general elections of the President and Congress; all other elections are at the discretion of the individual state and local governments.

## 23.5   Criticism

In 2014 scientists from Princeton University did a study on the influence of the "elite", and their derived power from special interest lobbying, versus the "ordinary" US citizen within the US political system. They found that the US was looking more like an oligarchy than a real representative democracy; *thus eroding a government of the people, by the people, for the people* as stated by Abraham Lincoln in his Gettysburg Address. In fact the study found that average citizen had an almost nonexistent influence on public policies and that the ordinary citizen had little or no independent influence on policy at all.[21]

## 23.6   See also

- United States presidential election
- List of elections in the United States
- Election Assistance Commission
- Electoral calendar
- Electoral system

## 23.7   Notes

[1] Lawless, Jennifer. *Becoming a Candidate.* Table 3.1 http://images.dailykos.com/images/134822/large/Elected_officials.png?1426881549

[2] "Felony Disenfranchisement in the United States" (PDF). The Sentencing Project. Retrieved 2007-01-10.

[3] DeFalco, Beth (2007-01-09). "New Jersey to take 'idiots,' 'insane' out of state constitution?". Delaware News-Journal.

[4] *Navigating Election Day: What Every Voter Needs To Know*, Before You Vote

[5] "Voter Registration Resources". Project Vote Smart. Retrieved 30 October 2011.

[6] Permanent Absentee Voting in California, via sos.ca.gov

[7] Washington State section of Absentee Ballot

[8] "Voting by Absentee Ballot in Washington state.". Secretary of State of Washington.

[9] "Federal Voting Assistance Program questions and answers".

[10] FVAP Integrated Voting Alternative Site (IVAS)

[11] "MAIL (ABSENTEE) BALLOT VOTING". Clark County, Nevada. Retrieved 2008-08-08.

[12] "Absentee and Early Voting". National Conference of State Legislatures. Retrieved November 12, 2014.

[13] Statistics on the State of the Nation Before the Presidential Elections (2007 and 2011), Pew Research Center, 2011.

[14] U.S. Elections 2012, The Economist, 2012

[15] In Federalist Papers No. 9 and No. 10, Alexander Hamilton and James Madison, respectively, wrote specifically about the dangers of domestic political factions.

[16] Washington's Farewell Address

[17] Baker, Peter; VandeHei, Jim (2006-11-08). "A Voter Rebuke For Bush, the War And the Right". Washington Post. Retrieved 2010-05-26. Bush and senior adviser Karl Rove tried to replicate that strategy this fall, hoping to keep the election from becoming a referendum on the president's leadership.

[18] "Election '98 Lewinsky factor never materialized". CNN. 1998-11-04. Americans shunned the opportunity to turn Tuesday's midterm elections into a referendum on President Bill Clinton's behavior, dashing Republican hopes of gaining seats in the House and Senate.

[19] See Anthony Gierzynski, Saving American Elections: A Diagnosis and Prescription for a Healthier Democracy (Cambria Press, 2011)

[20] See Anthony Gierzynski, Saving American Elections: A Diagnosis and Prescription for a Healthier Democracy (Cambria Press, 2011)

[21] Gilens, Martin; Page, Benjamin I. (2014-09-01). "Testing Theories of American Politics: Elites, Interest Groups, and Average Citizens". *Perspectives on Politics* **12** (03): 564–581. doi:10.1017/S1537592714001595. ISSN 1541-0986.

## 23.8 External links

- Electoral Compass

- USA Election Candidate Videos

- Campaign Law

- USA Elections

- FairVote.org

- Long Distance Voter - Non-partisan resource for registering to vote or getting an absentee ballot.

- Federal election results 1920-2008, US House Office of the Clerk

- A New Nation Votes: American Election Returns 1787-1824 For Votes cast in Federal, State and Local elections in the Early Republic.

- U.S. Election Statistics: A Resource Guide from the Library of Congress

# Chapter 24

# Most royal candidate theory

The **most royal candidate theory** is the term given to the fact that every presidential election in the United States has been won by a candidate descended from King John Lackland Plantagenet.[1]

## 24.1 Claims

Proponents of the theory claimed that every U.S. president since George Washington can have his bloodline traced back to various European royals, with all presidents descended from King John Plantagenet, and at least thirty-three presidents having been descended from Alfred the Great and Charlemagne.[2] This system has been successfully used to predict all presidential elections, with every U.S. President being descendant of King John.

## 24.2 Objections

Critics of the theory claim that the odds of any given person being distantly related to royalty are remarkably high, with one estimate suggesting that more than 150 million Americans are of royal descent. However, only an estimated one third of Americans are believed to be descended from King John Plantagenet. Even considering such high estimates, the fact that all U.S. presidents are descended from King John Plantagenet, while only roughly half of Americans are descended from any royalty gives this theory considerable credit, as we would expect only half of U.S presidents could be descended from royalty, if presidents were selected randomly from the population.[3] This is because when ancestral lines are traced back through time, the number of ancestors doubles with each generation. If any person traced their bloodline back to the year 1500, for example, they would discover about a million ancestors. The most royal theory, however, considers the lines descended of the first born, when possible, which greatly reduces this number making predictions more accurate.[4] Although there are relatively few royal figures in history, pedigree collapse explains how

so many people can be linked to famous rulers such as Alfred the Great, and indeed how any one person could be said to have a tenuous connection to anyone else in the world.[5]

While Harold Brooks-Baker was alive, this theory would reappear every four years, during the Presidential election campaign, as he would tour the talk circuit expounding upon it. He would give examples of presidents whose losing opponents did not have royal blood (Reagan vs Mondale), or where the winner simply had "more" royalty (Kennedy vs Nixon).[6]

Aside from the question of whether the "most royal" assessments for all previous presidential campaigns were accurate, the theory was also challenged on the grounds of whether it could possibly matter, because of the mathematically tiny amount of "royal blood" present in the winning candidate, under even the best of conditions. Most were only "related" to royalty if one traced their lineage back for centuries, each subsequent generation having therefore cut that "royalness" in half.[7] However, since not every in-law is considered, and because royals usually focus on rights of the first born to rule, large numbers of descendants are not considered as likely Presidential candidates. And, of course, this is why it is called the "Most royal candidate theory." It is just a theory, even with all U.S. Presidents being great grandsons of King John Lackland Plantagenet.

In 2004, Brooks-Baker announced that John Kerry would be the winner, because while he and Bush actually shared much of the same Royal ancestry, Kerry had slightly more.[8] In fact, Kerry lost, and this was Brooks-Baker's last such prediction, as he died a few months later.[9]

## 24.3 References

[1] *U.K. Daily Mail::* 12 year-old girl links all presidents except one to King John Plantagenet. August 4, 2012.

[2] *The Daily Mail*: Is ruling in the genes? All presidents bar one are directly descended from a medieval English king. August 2012.

[3] Boyd Roberts, Gary. "http://learn.ancestry.com/LearnMore/Article.aspx?id=3349". Retrieved 28 February 2012. External link in |title= (help)

[4] Horlacher, Gary. "http://www.progenealogists.com/greatbritain/medievalgenealogy.htm". Retrieved 28 February 2012. External link in |title= (help)

[5] Adams, Cecil. "http://www.straightdope.com/columns/read/412/2-4-8-16-how-can-you-always-have-more-ancestors-as-you-go-back-in-time". Retrieved 28 February 2012. External link in |title= (help)

[6] *The New York Times*: Chronicle. October 28, 1996.

[7] *The New York Times*: Royal Genes Too Diluted to Help Bush. July 21, 1988.

[8] *The Guardian*: Kerry's royal roots will give him victory, says Burke's. August 17, 2004.

[9] *USA Today*: Royal authority Harold Brooks-Baker dies. March 6, 2005.

# Chapter 25

# PollyVote

The **PollyVote** project uses the high-profile application of predicting U.S. presidential election results to demonstrate advances in forecasting research. The project is run by political science professors and forecasting experts, one of which is J. Scott Armstrong. All procedures, data, and results are fully disclosed and freely available online.

The project started in March 2004 to demonstrate the benefits of combining forecasts. In averaging forecasts within and across different forecasting methods, the combined PollyVote forecast provided highly accurate predictions of the two-party popular vote shares for the last three U.S. presidential elections.[1][2]

## 25.1 History

The PollyVote was created in March 2004 by marketing and forecasting expert J. Scott Armstrong and political science professors Alfred Cuzán and Randall Jones.[3] The goal at that time was to apply the combination principle in forecasting to predict President Bush's share of the two-party popular vote (omitting minor candidates) in the 2004 presidential election. Until Election Day in November of the same year, the researchers collected data from 268 polls, 10 quantitative models, and 246 daily market prices from the Iowa Electronic Markets vote-share market. In each of the last three months prior to the election, they also administered a survey with a panel of 17 experts on US politics, asking them for their predictions. The forecasts were first combined within each component method by averaging recent polls, the IEM prediction market forecasts from the previous week, and averaging the predictions of the quantitative models. Then, the researchers averaged the forecasts across the four component methods. The resulting forecast was named the PollyVote. From March to November, the forecasts were initially updated weekly, and then, twice a week. The forecasts were published at the Political Forecasting Special Interest Group at forprin.com.

In 2007, Andreas Graefe joined the PollyVote team and helped to launch the PollyVote.com website prior to the 2008 U.S. presidential election. For predicting the 2008 election, the general structure of the PollyVote remained unchanged; the PollyVote combined forecasts within and across the same four component methods as in 2004. However, some changes were made at the level of the component methods. Instead of averaging recent polls themselves, the PollyVote team used the RCP poll average by RealClearPolitics as the polls component. In addition, the advantage of the leading candidate was discounted (or damped) using the approach suggested by Jim Campbell. The first PollyVote forecast for the 2008 election was published in August 2007, 14 months prior to Election Day, and was updated daily.[4]

For forecasting the 2012 election, a fifth component called "index models" was added to the PollyVote. This component captured information from quantitative models that use a different method and rely on different information than the traditional political economy models. In particular, the index models capture information about the campaign, such as the candidates' perceived issue-handling competence,[5][6] their leadership skills,[7] their biographies[8] or the influence of other factors such as whether the incumbent government faced some scandal.[9] The first forecast for the 2012 election was published on January 1, 2011, almost two years prior to Election Day. As in 2008, the forecasts were updated daily, or whenever new information became available.[1]

In 2013, the PollyVote was launched in Germany to predict the German federal election of the same year.[10]

## 25.2 Method

The PollyVote demonstrates the benefits of combining forecasts by averaging predictions within and across several component methods. In its application for the U.S. presidential election, the PollyVote is currently based on five component methods: polls, prediction markets, expert' judgment, political economy models, and index models. The PollyVote predicts the share of the popular two-party vote achieved by the candidate of the incumbent party.

## 25.3 Accuracy of the PollyVote

The PollyVote published forecasts prior to each of the three U.S. presidential elections, the 2006 U.S. House of Representatives election, and the 2013 German federal election. In addition, one analysis tested how the PollyVote would have performed for the three elections from 1992 to 2000. As expected, the application of the forecasting principles has led to accurate forecasts. Surprisingly, however, across the three U.S. Presidential elections, the forecast error was always lower than the error of each component methods.[2] Comparisons have also been made with other methods. For example, forecasts of the 2012 election were also substantially more accurate than the closely watched forecasts from Nate Silver's model at FiveThirtyEight.com.[1]

### 25.3.1 2004 U.S. presidential election

The 2004 PollyVote was launched in March 2004 and forecast a victory for President Bush over the 8 months that it was making forecasts. The final forecast published on the morning of the election predicted that President would receive 51.5% of the popular two-party vote, an error of 0.3 percentage points.[3]

### 25.3.2 2008 U.S. presidential election

The 2008 PollyVote was launched in August 2007 and forecast a victory for Barack Obama over the 14 months that it was making daily forecasts. On Election Eve, it predicted that Obama would receive 53.0% of the popular two-party vote, an error of 0.7 percentage points.[4]

### 25.3.3 2012 U.S. presidential election

The 2012 PollyVote was launched in January 2011 and forecast a victory for President Obama over the 22 months that it was making daily forecasts. On Election Eve, it predicted that Obama would receive 51.0% of the popular two-party vote, an error of 0.9 percentage points.[1]

### 25.3.4 2006 US House of Representatives election

PollyVote predicted the outcome of the 2006 U.S. House of Representatives Elections, forecasting that the Republicans would lose 23 seats, and thus, their majority in the House. The Republicans lost 30 seats and the House majority in those elections.

## 25.4 Perception

The results of the PollyVote project are regularly published in the academic community. Prior to the past elections, forecasts were published in Foresight – The International Journal of Applied Forecasting and the New Scientist.[11] Analyses of the accuracy of the PollyVote were published in the International Journal of Forecasting and PS: Political Science & Politics. In addition, scholars have referenced the PollyVote as a benchmark when assessing the validity of U.S. presidential election forecasts.[12][13][14]

To date, the PollyVote predictions have been rarely cited in the popular press. In their IJF paper, the PollyVote team discusses several reasons why this might be the case: (1) people have difficulties to understand the benefits of combining, (2) people wrongly believe that they can identify the best forecast, and (3) people think that the method of calculating averages is too simple.[2] Another possible reason is that the PollyVote predictions are very stable and rarely change, whereas election observers and journalists are interested in excitement and newsworthiness.

## 25.5 References

[1] Graefe, Andreas; Armstrong, J. Scott; Jones, Randall J. Jr. & and Alfred G. Cuzán (2014). "Accuracy of combined forecasts for the 2012 Presidential Elections: The PollyVote" (PDF). *PS: Political Science & Politics (forthcoming)* (Cambridge Journals). Cite uses deprecated parameter lcoauthors= (help)

[2] Graefe, Andreas; Armstrong, J. Scott; Jones, Randall J. Jr. & and Alfred G. Cuzán (January–March 2014). "Combining forecasts: An application to elections" (PDF). *International Journal of Forecasting* (Elsevier) **30** (1): 43–54. doi:10.1016/j.ijforecast.2013.02.005. Cite uses deprecated parameter lcoauthors= (help)

[3] Cuzán, Alfred G; Armstrong, J. Scott & Jones, Randall J. Jr. (2005). "How we computed the PollyVote" (PDF). *Foresight: The International Journal of Applied Forecasting* (International Institute of Forecasters) **1** (1): 51–52. Cite uses deprecated parameter lcoauthors= (help)

[4] Graefe, Andreas; Armstrong, J. Scott; Cuzán, Alfred G. & Jones, Randall J. Jr. (2009). "Combined Forecasts of the 2008 Election: The PollyVote" (PDF). *Foresight - The International Journal of Applied Forecasting* (International Institute of Forecasters) (12): 41–42. Cite uses deprecated parameter |coauthors= (help)

[5] Graefe, Andreas; Armstrong, J. Scott (2013). "Forecasting Elections from Voters' Perceptions of Candidates' Ability to Handle Issues" (PDF). *Journal of Behavioral Decision Making* (Wiley) **26** (3): 295–303. doi:10.1002/bdm.1764.

[6] Graefe, Andreas; Armstrong, J. Scott (2012). "Predicting elections from the most important issue: A test of the take-the-best heuristic" (PDF). *Journal of Behavioral Decision Making* (Wiley) **25** (1): 41–48. doi:10.1002/bdm.710.

[7] Graefe, Andreas (December 2013). "Issue and leader voting in U.S. presidential elections" (PDF). *Electoral Studies* (Elsevier) **32** (4): 644–657. doi:10.1016/j.electstud.2013.04.003.

[8] Armstrong, J. Scott; Graefe, Andreas (2011). "Predicting elections from biographical information about candidates: A test of the index method" (PDF). *Journal of Business Research* (Elsevier) **64** (7): 699–706. doi:10.1016/j.jbusres.2010.08.005.

[9] Lichtman, Allan J. (2008). "The keys to the white house: An index forecast for 2008". *International Journal of Forecasting* (Elsevier) **24** (2): 301–309. doi:10.1016/j.ijforecast.2008.02.004.

[10] Graefe, Andreas (April 2015). "German election forecasting: Comparing and combining Methods for 2013" (PDF). *German Politics* (Taylor & Francis). doi:10.1016/j.electstud.2013.04.003.

[11] Giles, Jim (22 October 2008). "And the next president of the United States will be...". *New Scientist* (Elsevier) **200** (2679): 12–13. doi:10.1016/S0262-4079(08)62672-X.

[12] Sunstein, Cass R. (2006). *Infotopia: How Many Minds Produce Knowledge*. New York: Oxford University Press. p. 40. ISBN 978-0-19-534067-9.

[13] Lewis-Beck, Michael S.; Tien, Charles (October 2008). "The Job of President and the Jobs Model Forecast: Obama for '08?". *PS: Political Science & Politics* **41** (4): 687–690. doi:10.1017/S1049096508081262.

[14] Holbrook, Thomas M. (2010). "Forecasting US presidential elections". In Leighley, Jan E. *The Oxford Handbook of American Elections and Political Behavior*. Oxford: Oxford University Press. pp. 346–371.

## 25.6   External links

- Official Site

# Chapter 26

# FiveThirtyEight

**FiveThirtyEight**, sometimes referred to as **538**, is a website that focuses on opinion poll analysis, politics, economics, and sports blogging. The website, which takes its name from the number of electors in the United States electoral college,[538 1] was founded on March 7, 2008, as a polling aggregation website with a blog created by analyst Nate Silver. In August 2010 the blog became a licensed feature of *The New York Times* online. It was renamed **FiveThirtyEight: Nate Silver's Political Calculus.** In July 2013, ESPN announced that it would become the owner of the FiveThirtyEight brand and site, and Silver was appointed as editor-in-chief.[2] The ESPN-owned FiveThirtyEight began publication on March 17, 2014. In the ESPN era, the FiveThirtyEight blog has covered a broad spectrum of subjects including politics, sports, science, economics, and popular culture.

During the U.S. presidential primaries and general election of 2008, the site compiled polling data through a unique methodology derived from Silver's experience in baseball sabermetrics to "balance out the polls with comparative demographic data."[3] He weighted "each poll based on the pollster's historical track record, sample size, and recentness of the poll".[4]

Since the 2008 election, the site published articles – typically creating or analyzing statistical information – on a wide variety of topics in current politics and political news. These included a monthly update on the prospects for turnover in the U.S. Senate; federal economic policies; Congressional support for legislation; public support for health care reform, global warming legislation, LGBT rights; elections around the world; marijuana legalization; and numerous other topics. The site and its creator are best known for election forecasts, including the 2012 presidential election in which FiveThirtyEight correctly predicted the vote winner of all 50 states.

During its first five and a half years, FiveThirtyEight won numerous awards both when it was an independent blog and when it was published by *The New York Times*. These included "Bloggie" Awards for "Best Political Coverage" in 2008 and "Best Weblog about Politics" in 2009, as well as "Webbies" for "Best Political Blog" in 2012 and 2013.

## 26.1   Genesis and history

When Silver started *FiveThirtyEight.com* in early March 2008, he published under the name "Poblano", the same name that he had used since November 2007 when he began publishing a diary on the political blog *Daily Kos*.[5] Writing as Poblano on *Daily Kos,* he had gained a following, especially for his primary election forecast on Super Tuesday, February 5, 2008.[6][7] From that primary election day, which included contests in 24 states plus American Samoa, "Poblano" predicted that Barack Obama would come away with 859 delegates, and Hillary Clinton 829; in the final contests, Obama won 847 delegates and Clinton 834. Based on this result, *New York Times* op-ed columnist William Kristol wrote: "And an interesting regression analysis at the Daily Kos Web site (poblano.dailykos.com) of the determinants of the Democratic vote so far, applied to the demographics of the Ohio electorate, suggests that Obama has a better chance than is generally realized in Ohio".[8]

*FiveThirtyEight.com* gained further national attention for beating out most pollsters' projections in the North Carolina and Indiana Democratic party primaries on May 6, 2008. As Mark Blumenthal wrote in *National Journal,* "Over the last week, an anonymous blogger who writes under the pseudonym Poblano did something bold on his blog, *FiveThirtyEight.com.* He posted predictions for the upcoming primaries based not on polling data, but on a statistical model driven mostly by demographic and past vote data.... Critics scoffed. Most of the public polls pointed to a close race in North Carolina.... But a funny thing happened. The model got it right".[9] Silver relied on demographic data and on the history of voting in *other* states during the 2008 Democratic primary elections. "I think it is interesting and, in a lot of ways, I'm not surprised that his predictions came closer to the result than the pollsters did", said Brian F. Schaffner, research director of American University's Center for Congressional and Presidential Studies.[10]

On May 30, 2008, Silver revealed his true identity for the first time to his *FiveThirtyEight.com* readers.[538 2] After that date, he published just four more diaries on *Daily Kos*.[5]

As the primary season was coming to an end, Silver began to build a model for the general election race. This model, too, relied in part on demographic information but mainly involved a complex method of aggregating polling results. In 2008, *Rasmussen Reports* had an apparently short-term partnership with *FiveThirtyEight.com* in order to include this unique methodology for generating poll averages in their "Balance of Power Calculator".[11] At the same time, *FiveThirtyEight.com*'s daily "Today's Polls" column began to be mirrored on "The Plank," a blog published by *The New Republic*.[12]

By early October 2008, *FiveThirtyEight.com* approached 2.5 million visitors per week, while averaging approximately 400,000 per weekday.[538 3] During October 2008 the site received 3.63 million unique visitors, 20.57 million site visits, and 32.18 million page views.[538 4] On Election Day, November 4, 2008, the site had nearly 5 million page views.[13]

On June 3, 2010, Silver announced that in early August the blog would be "relaunched under a *NYTimes.com* domain".[538 5][14][15] The transition took place on August 25, 2010, with the publication of Silver's first *FiveThirtyEight* blog article online in *The New York Times*.[538 6]

In July 2013, it was revealed that Silver and his *FiveThirtyEight* blog would depart *The New York Times* and join ESPN.[16] In its announcement of its acquisition of FiveThirtyEight, ESPN reported that "Silver will serve as the editor-in-chief of the site and will build a team of journalists, editors, analysts and contributors in the coming months. Much like Grantland, which ESPN launched in 2011, the site will retain an independent brand sensibility and editorial point-of-view, while interfacing with other websites in the ESPN and Disney families. The site will return to its original URL, www.FiveThirtyEight.com".[17]

According to Silver, the focus of *FiveThirtyEight* in its ESPN phase would broaden: "People also think it's going to be a sports site with a little politics thrown in, or it's going to be a politics site with sports thrown in.... But we take our science and economics and lifestyle coverage very seriously.... It's a data journalism site. Politics is one topic that sometimes data journalism is good at covering. It's certainly good with presidential elections. But we don't really see politics as how the site is going to grow".[18]

FiveThirtyEight launched its ESPN webpage on March 17, 2014. The lead story by Nate Silver explained that "FiveThirtyEight is a data journalism organization....

We've expanded our staff from two full-time journalists to 20 and counting. Few of them will focus on politics exclusively; instead, our coverage will span five major subject areas — politics, economics, science, life and sports. Our team also has a broad set of skills and experience in methods that fall under the rubric of data journalism. These include statistical analysis, but also data visualization, computer programming and data-literate reporting. So in addition to written stories, we'll have interactive graphics and features".[538 7]

## 26.2   2008 U.S. elections

### 26.2.1   Methods

**Weighting of polls**

One unique aspect of the site is Silver's efforts to rank pollsters by accuracy, weight their polls accordingly, and then supplement those polls with his own electoral projections based on demographics and prior voting patterns. "I did think there was room for a more sophisticated way of handling these things," Silver said.[10][19]

*FiveThirtyEight.com* weighs pollsters' historical track records through a complex methodology[538 8] and assigns them values to indicate "Pollster-Introduced Error".

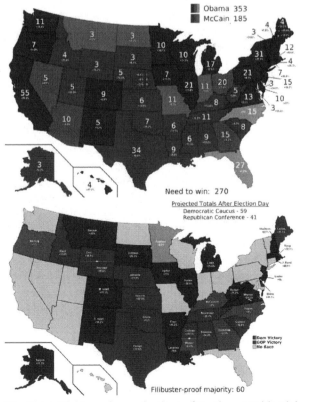

FiveThirtyEight.com's projections for the presidential

(top) and Senate (bottom) races on November 4, 2008

Polls on *FiveThirtyEight.com* are weighted using a half-life of thirty days using the formula $0.5^{P/30}$ where 'P' is the number of days transpired since the median date that the poll was in the field. The formula is based on an analysis of 2000, 2004, 2006 and 2008 state-by-state polling data.[20]

### Smoothing the poll results

At base Silver's method is similar to other analysts' approaches to taking advantage of the multiple polls that are conducted within each state: he averaged the polling results. But especially in the early months of the election season polling in many states is sparse and episodic. The "average" of polls over an extended period (perhaps several weeks) would not reveal the true state of voter preferences at the present time, nor provide an accurate forecast of the future. One approach to this problem was followed by *Pollster.com*: if enough polls were available, it computed a locally weighted moving average or LOESS.

However, while adopting such an approach in his own analysis, Silver reasoned that there was additional information available in polls from "similar" states that might help to fill the gaps in information about the trends in a given state. Accordingly, he adapted an approach that he had previously used in his baseball forecasting: using nearest neighbor analysis he first identified "most similar states" and then factored into his electoral projections for a given state the polling information from "similar states". He carried this approach one step further by also factoring national polling trends into the estimates for a given state. Thus, his projections were not simply based on the polling trends in a given state.

Furthermore, a basic intuition that Silver drew from his analysis of the 2008 Democratic party primary elections was that the voting history of a state or Congressional district provided clues to current voting. This is what allowed him to beat all the pollsters in his forecasts in the Democratic primaries in North Carolina and Indiana, for example.[9] Using such information allowed Silver to come up with estimates of the vote preferences even in states for which there were few if any polls. For his general election projections for each state, in addition to relying in the available polls in a given state and "similar states," Silver estimated a "538 regression" using historical voting information along with demographic characteristics of the states to create an estimate that he treated as a separate poll (equivalent to the actually available polls from that state). This approach helped to stabilize his projections, because if there were few if any polls in a given state, the state forecast was largely determined by the 538 regression estimate.

Additional aspects of the methodology are described in a detailed FAQ on the *FiveThirtyEight.com* website.[538 1]

### Senate races

In July 2008, the site began to report regular updates of projections of 2008 U.S. Senate races. Special procedures were developed relying on both polls and demographic analysis. The projections were updated on a weekly basis.[538 9]

### Swing state analysis

The site presents an analysis of the swing states, focusing on so-called "Tipping Point States".[538 10] 'Tipping Point States' are those states that tip the outcome of the election from one candidate to the other. In each simulation run, the winner's states won are lined up in reverse order of victory margin by percentage. A simple algorithm selects the minimum closest states that, if switched to the loser's side, would change the election outcome, then weights that run's significance based on the margin of victory in the popular vote. Thus, the closer the popular vote, the fewer the number of tipping point states and the greater the significance of that run in assessing tipping point importance. For example, the 2004 election's sole tipping point state was Ohio by this method, while 1960s were Illinois, Missouri, and New Jersey – even though Hawaii was the closest state race.

## 26.2.2 Final projections of 2008 elections

In the final update of his presidential forecast model at midday of November 4, 2008, Silver projected a popular vote victory by 6.1 percentage points for Barack Obama and electoral vote totals of 349 (based on a probabilistic projection) or 353 (based on fixed projections of each state).[538 11] Obama won with 365 electoral college votes, Silver's predictions matching the actual results everywhere except in Indiana and the 2nd congressional district of Nebraska, which awards an electoral vote separately from the rest of the state. His projected national popular vote differential was below the actual figure of 7.2 points.

The forecasts for the Senate proved to be correct for every race. But the near stalemate in Minnesota led to a recount that was settled only on June 30, 2009. In Alaska, after a protracted counting of ballots, on November 19 Republican incumbent Ted Stevens conceded the seat to Democrat Mark Begich, an outcome that Silver had forecast on election day.[21] And in Georgia, a run-off election on December 2 led to the re-election of Republican Saxby Chambliss, a result that was also consistent with Silver's original projection.

## 26.3   After the 2008 U.S. election

### 26.3.1   Focus

During the first two months after the election, no major innovations in content were introduced. A substantial percentage of the articles focused on Senatorial races: the runoff in Georgia, won by Saxby Chambliss; recounts of votes in Alaska (won by Mark Begich), and Minnesota (Al Franken vs. Norm Coleman); and the appointments of Senatorial replacements in Colorado, New York, and Illinois.

After President Obama's inauguration, Sean Quinn reported that he was moving to Washington, D.C., to continue political writing from that locale.[538 12] On February 4, 2009, he became the first blogger to join the White House press corps.[538 13] After that time, however, he contributed only a handful of articles to *FiveThirtyEight.com.*

During the post-2008 election period Silver devoted attention to developing some tools for the analysis of forthcoming 2010 Congressional elections,[538 14][538 15] as well as discussing policy issues and the policy agenda for the Obama administration, especially economic policies.[538 16][538 17] He developed a list of 2010 Senate races in which he made monthly updates of predicted party turnover.[538 18]

Later, Silver adapted his methods to address a variety of issues of the day, including health care reform, climate change, unemployment, and popular support for same-sex marriage.[22] He wrote a series of columns investigating the credibility of polls by Georgia-based firm Strategic Vision, LLC. According to Silver's analysis, Strategic Vision's data displayed statistical anomalies that were inconsistent with random polling. Later, he uncovered indirect evidence that Strategic Vision may have gone as far as to fabricate the results of a citizenship survey taken by Oklahoma high school students.[23][538 19][538 20][538 21][538 22][538 23][24][lower-alpha 1]

*FiveThirtyEight* devoted more than a dozen articles to the Iranian presidential election in June 2009, assessing of the quality of the vote counting. International affairs columnist Renard Sexton began the series with an analysis of polling leading up to the election;[538 24] then posts by Silver, Andrew Gelman and Sexton analyzed the reported returns and political implications.[538 25]

*FiveThirtyEight* covered the November 3, 2009, elections in the United States in detail.[538 26][538 27] *FiveThirtyEight* writers Schaller, Gelman, and Silver also gave extensive coverage to the January 19, 2010 Massachusetts special election to the U.S. Senate. The "538 model" once again aggregated the disparate polls to correctly predict that the Republican Scott Brown would win.[538 28]

In spring of 2010, *FiveThirtyEight* turned a focus on the United Kingdom General Election scheduled for May 6, with a series of more than forty articles on the subject that culminated in projections of the number of seats that the three major parties were expected to win.[538 29] Following a number of preview posts in January,[538 30] and February,[538 31] Renard Sexton examined subjects such as the UK polling industry[538 32][538 33][538 34] and the 'surge' of the third-party Liberal Democrats,[538 35] while Silver, Sexton and Dan Berman[lower-alpha 2] developed a seat projection model. The UK election was the first time the *FiveThirtyEight* team did an election night 'liveblog' of a non-US election.[538 36]

In April 2010, the Guardian Newspaper published Silver's predictions for the 2010 United Kingdom General Election. The majority of polling organisations in the UK use the concept of uniform swing to predict the outcome of elections. However, by applying his own methodology, Silver produced very different results, which suggested that a Conservative victory might have been the most likely outcome.[26] After a series of articles, including critiques and responses to other electoral analysts, his "final projection" was published on the eve of the election.[538 37] In the end, Silver's projections were off the mark, particularly compared with those of some other organizations, and Silver wrote a *post mortem* on his blog.[538 38] Silver examined the pitfalls of the forecasting process,[538 38] while Sexton discussed the final government agreement between the Conservatives and the Liberal Democrats.[538 39]

### 26.3.2   Controversy over transparency in pollster ratings

On June 6, 2010, *FiveThirtyEight* posted pollster rankings that updated and elaborated Silver's efforts from the 2008 election. Silver expanded the database to more than 4,700 election polls and developed a model for rating the polls that was more sophisticated than his original rankings.[538 40][27]

Silver responded on 538: "Where's the transparency? Well, it's here [citing his June 6 article], in an article that contains 4,807 words and 18 footnotes. Every detail of how the pollster ratings are calculated is explained. It's also here [referring to another article], in the form of Pollster Scorecards, a feature which we'll continue to roll out over the coming weeks for each of the major polling firms, and which will explain in some detail how we arrive at the particular rating that we did for each one".[538 41]

As for why the complete 538 polling database had not been released publicly, Silver responded: "The principal reason is because I don't know that I'm legally entitled to do so. The polling database was compiled from approximately eight or ten distinct data sources, which were disclosed in a comment which I posted shortly after the pollster ratings were released, and which are detailed again at the end of this article. These include some subscription services, and others from websites that are direct competitors of this one. Although polls contained in these databases are ultimately a matter of the public record and clearly we feel as though we have every right to use them for research purposes, I don't know what rights we might have to re-publish their data in full".

Silver also commented on the fact that the 538 ratings had contributed to Markos Moulitsas's decision to end *Daily Kos's* use of Research 2000 as its pollster.[28]

Subsequently, on June 11, Mark Blumenthal also commented on the question of transparency in an article in the *National Journal* titled "Transparency In Rating: Nate Silver's Impressive Ranking Of Pollsters' Accuracy Is Less Impressive In Making Clear What Data Is Used".[29] He noted that in the case of Research 2000 there were some discrepancies between what Silver reported and what the pollster itself reported. Other researchers questioned aspects of the methodology.[30]

On June 16, 2010, Silver announced on his blog that he is willing to give all pollsters who he had included in his rating a list of their polls that he had in his archive, along with the key information that he used (poll marginals, sample size, dates of administration); and he encouraged the pollsters to examine the lists and the results to compare them with the pollster's own record and make corrections.[538 42]

In September, 2014, Silver put into the public domain all of his pollster ratings,[538 43] as well as descriptive summary data for all of the more than 6,600 polls in his data collection for the final three weeks of U.S. Presidential primaries and general elections, state governor elections, and U.S. Senate and U.S. Congress elections for the years 1998–2012.[31] In addition to updating his pollster ratings, he published an updated methodological report.[538 44]

## 26.4   Partnership with *The New York Times*: 2010–2013

On June 3, 2010, *The New York Times* and Silver announced that *FiveThirtyEight* had formed a partnership under which the blog would be hosted by the *Times* for a period of three years.[32] In legal terms, *FiveThirtyEight* granted a "license" to the *Times* to publish the blog. The blog would be listed under the "Politics" tab of the News section of the *Times*.[33] *FiveThirtyEight* would thus be subject to and benefit from editing and technical production by the *Times*, while *FiveThirtyEight* would be responsible for creating the content.

Silver received bids from several major media entities be-

fore selecting the *Times*.[33][34] Under terms of the agreement, Silver would also write monthly articles for the print version of both the newspaper and the Sunday magazine.[538 5] Silver did not move his blog to the highest bidder, because he was concerned with maintaining his own voice while gaining the exposure and technical support that a larger media company could provide. "There's a bit of a Groucho Marx quality to it [Silver has said].... You shouldn't want to belong to any media brand that seems desperate to have you as a member, even though they'll probably offer the most cash".[35]

The first column of the renamed *FiveThirtyEight: Nate Silver's Political Calculus* appeared in *The Times* on August 25, 2010, with the introduction of U.S. Senate election forecasts. At the same time, Silver published a brief history of the blog.[538 45] All columns from the original *FiveThirtyEight.com* were also archived for public access.[36]

### 26.4.1   Writers

When the transition to *The New York Times* was announced, Silver listed his staff of writers for the first time.[36] However, of the seven listed writers, only three of them had published on 538/New York Times by late December 2010: Silver, Renard Sexton and Hale Stewart. Andrew Gelman contributed again in early 2011.[538 46] Brian McCabe published his first article in January 2011.[538 47][lower-alpha 3]

Beginning in 2011, one writer who emerged as a regular contributor was Micah Cohen. Cohen provided a periodic "Reads and Reactions" column in which he summarized Silver's articles for the previous couple of weeks, as well as reactions to them in the media and other blogs, and suggested some additional readings related to the subject of Silver's columns. Silver identified Cohen as "my news assistant".[538 48] Cohen also contributed additional columns on occasion.[538 49]

On September 12, 2011, Silver introduced another writer: "FiveThirtyEight extends a hearty welcome to John Sides, a political scientist at George Washington University, who will be writing a series of posts for this site over the next month. Mr. Sides is also the founder of the blog *The Monkey Cage*,[38] which was named the 2010 Blog of the Year by *The Week* magazine".[538 50]

### 26.4.2   Beyond electoral politics

#### Sports

While politics and elections remained the main focus of *FiveThirtyEight*, the blog also sometimes addressed sports, including the March Madness[538 51][538 52][39] and the 2012 NCAA Men's Basketball tournament selection process,[538 53] the B.C.S. rankings in NCAA college football,[40] the NBA,[538 54][538 55][538 56] and Major League Baseball matters ranging from the 2011 attendance at the New York Mets' Citi Field[538 57] to the historic 2011 collapse of the Boston Red Sox.[538 58]

### Economics and hurricanes

In addition, *FiveThirtyEight* sometimes turned its attention to other topics, such as the economics of blogging,[538 59] the financial ratings by Standard & Poors,[538 60] economists' tendency to underpredict unemployment levels,[538 61] and the economic impact and media coverage of Hurricane Irene (2011).[538 62][538 63]

### Occupy Wall Street protests

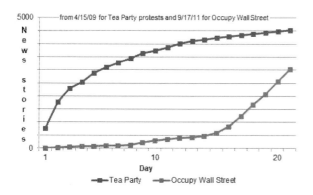

*Adapted from a* FiveThirtyEight *October 2011 graph published in the* New York Times.[538 64]

*FiveThirtyEight* published a graph showing different growth curves of the news stories covering Tea Party and Occupy Wall Street protests. Silver pointed out that conflicts with the police caused the sharpest increases in news coverage of the protests.[538 64] And he assessed the geography of the protests by analyzing news reports of the size and location of events across the United States.[538 65]

## 26.4.3   2010 U.S. mid-term elections

Shortly after 538 relocated to *The New York Times,* Silver introduced his prediction models for the 2010 elections to the U.S. Senate, the U.S. House of Representatives, and state Governorships. Each of these models relied initially on a combination of electoral history, demographics, and polling.

### U.S. Senate

Stimulated by the surprising win of Massachusetts Republican Scott Brown in the special election in January 2010, Silver launched the first iteration of his Senate prediction model a few days later, using objective indicators including polling to project each state outcome in November. This model incorporated some elements of the 2008 presidential model.[538 66][538 67] It was first published in full form in *The New York Times* on August 25, 2010.[538 6] It relied basically on aggregating of public polls for each Senate race, with some adjustment for national trends in recognition of a correlation in poll movement across state lines, i.e., each race cannot be interpreted as entirely independent of all others.

In addition to making projections of the outcomes of each Senate race, *FiveThirtyEight* tracked the expected national outcome of the partisan division of the Senate. Just before election day (October 31), the *FiveThirtyEight* Senate projection was for the new Senate to have 52 Democrats and 48 Republicans. (The model did not address the possibility of party switching by elected candidates after November 2.)

Of the 37 Senate seats contested in the November 2, 2010 elections, 36 were resolved by November 4, including very close outcomes in several states. Of these 36, the *FiveThirtyEight* model had correctly predicted the winner in 34. One of the two misses was in Colorado, in which the incumbent Michael Bennet (D) outpolled the challenger Ken Buck (R) by less than 1 percentage point. The 538 model had forecast that Buck would win by 1 percentage point. The second miss was in Nevada, in which the incumbent Harry Reid beat challenger Sharron Angle by 5.5 percentage points, whereas the 538 model had forecast Angle to win by 3.0 percentage points. Silver has speculated the error was due at least in part to the fact that polling organizations underrepresented Hispanic voters by not interviewing in Spanish.[538 68]

In the remaining contest for U.S. Senate, in Alaska, the electoral outcome was not yet determined as of November 4, pending a count of the write-in ballots, but in the end the *FiveThirtyEight* forecast of GOP nominee Joe Miller as winner ultimately proved to be wrong, as write-in candidate, incumbent Republican Senator Lisa Murkowski, prevailed.

The 538 model had forecast a net pickup of 8 seats by the Republicans in the Senate, but the outcome was a pickup of 6 seats.

### U.S. House of Representatives

The model for projecting the outcome of the House of Representatives was more complicated than those for the Senate and governorships. For one thing, House races are more subject to the force of national trends and events than are the other two. One way to account for this was to take into account trends in the "generic Congressional ballot."[41] Use of such a macrolevel indicator, as well as macroeconomic indicators, is a common approach taken by political scientists to project House elections.[42][43]

Furthermore, there was much less available public polling for individual House districts than there is for Senate or gubernatorial races. By the end of the 2010 election season, public polls were available for only about 25% of the districts. This is one reason why some analysts rely principally on making global or macro-level projections of the number of seats to be won by each party rather than trying to forecast the outcome in every individual district. Silver's *FiveThirtyEight* model, however, while weighting the generic partisan division as one factor, focused on developing estimates for each district. For this purpose he used information on past voting in the district (the Cook PVI), the quality of the candidates (in particular whether one was an incumbent), fundraising by each candidate, "expert ratings" of the races,[lower-alpha 4] public polls of the given race (if they were available), and, in the absence of public polls a cautious use of private polls (i.e., polls conducted by or for partisan organizations or a candidate's own campaign organization).

In response to some concerns that he was hedging his projection, Silver contended that in his model the uncertainty of the outcome was a feature, not a flaw.[538 69][538 70] In comparison with previous Congressional elections, a far larger number of seats were being contested or were "in play" in 2010. While his model, which relied on simulating the election outcomes 100,000 times generated a projected "most likely" net gain of 53 seats by the Republicans (two days before the election), he emphasized that the 95% confidence interval was ± 29–30: "Tonight, our forecast shows Republicans gaining 53 seats – the same as in recent days, and exactly the same answer you get if you plug the generic ballot average into the simple formula. Our model also thinks the spread of potential outcomes is exceptionally wide: its 95 percent confidence interval runs from a 23-seat Republican gain to an 81-seat one".[538 71][44]

On election eve, he reported his final forecast as follows:

> Our forecasting model, which is based on a consensus of indicators including generic ballot polling, polling of local districts, expert forecasts, and fund-raising data, now predicts an average Republican net gain of 54 seats (up one from 53 seats in last night's forecast), and a median net Republican gain of 55 seats. These figures would exceed the 52 seats that Republicans won from Democrats in the 1994 midterms.[538 72]

In final vote tallys as of December 10, 2010, the Republicans had a net gain of 63 seats in the House, 8 more than the total predicted on election eve though still within the reported confidence interval.[538 73]

**State governorships**

The *FiveThirtyEight* model for state governors' races also relied basically on aggregating and projecting public polls in each race. However, Silver reported that gubernatorial elections in each state were somewhat more independent of what happened in other states than were either Senate or House of Representatives elections. That is, these races were somewhat more local and less national in focus.

Just before election day (October 31), the *FiveThirtyEight* projection was that there would be 30 Republican governors in office (counting states where there was no gubernatorial election in 2010), 19 Democratic governors, and 1 (actually 0.8) Other (Lincoln Chafee, who was leading in the polls running as an Independent in Rhode Island).

Of the 37 gubernatorial races, *FiveThirtyEight* correctly predicted the winner of 36. Only in Illinois, in which the Democratic candidate Pat Quinn defeated the Republican Bill Brady 46.6% to 46.1%, was the *FiveThirtyEight* prediction wrong.

### 26.4.4    2012 U.S. elections

While *FiveThirtyEight* devoted a lot of time to coverage of the 2012 Republican party primaries throughout 2011, its first effort to handicap the 2012 Presidential general election was published a year in advance of the election.[45] Accompanying the online release of this article, Silver also published online "Choose Obama's Re-Election Adventure," an interactive toy that allowed readers to predict the outcome of the election based on their assumptions about three variables: President Obama's favorability ratings, the rate of GDP growth, and how conservative the Republican opponent would be.[538 74] In February 2012 Silver updated his previous *Magazine* story with another one, "Why Obama Will Embrace the 99 Percent".[46] This article painted a more optimistic picture of Obama's re-election chances. Another article, "The Fundamentals Now Favor Obama," explained how the model and Obama's prospects had changed between November and February.[538 75]

Silver published election projections for the presidency and the U.S. Senate, but not for the U.S. House of Representatives in 2012. When asked why he did not produce House forecasts in 2012, Silver responded: "There was nothing particularly deep about this choice. We just ran out of time to implement a House model this year, and I'd rather do fewer things well than get spread too thin and not be able to support the product. We'd expect to have House forecasts in 2014".[47]

### Presidential primary elections

On December 13, 2011, Silver published his first version of a primary election forecast for the Republican Party Iowa Caucuses.[538 76] In this article he also described the basic methodology for forecasting the primaries; his approach relied solely on an adjusted average of state-level polls, and not on any other information about the campaign or on national polls. Silver later analyzed the prospects and results of each Republican caucus and primary. He maintained and regularly updated a set of vote projections, applying his aggregation methodology to the available polls. In keeping with a concern for the uncertainty of the forecasts, his projections showed both a point estimate and a confidence interval of the vote percentage projected for each candidate.

### Presidential general election

Silver rolled out the first iteration of his 2012 general election forecasting model on June 7, 2012. The model forecasts both the popular vote and the electoral college vote, with the latter being central to the exercise and involving a forecast of the electoral outcome in each state.

> The forecast works by running simulations of the Electoral College, which are designed to consider the uncertainty in the outcome at the national level and in individual states. It recognizes that voters in each state could be affected by universal factors – like a rising or falling economic tide – as well as by circumstances particular to each state. Furthermore, it considers the relationships between the states and the ways they might move in tandem with one another. Demographically similar states like Minnesota and Wisconsin, for instance, are more likely to move in the same direction than dissimilar ones like New Hampshire and New Mexico.
>
> Although the model – which is distinct from the electoral map put together by *The Times*'s political desk – relies fairly heavily on polling, it also considers an index of national economic conditions.[538 77]

In the initial forecast, Barack Obama was estimated to win 291.3 electoral votes, compared to 246.7 by Mitt Romney. This was consistent with Obama having a 61.8% chance of winning the electoral vote in November 2012. Obama was forecast to win 50.5% of the popular vote, compared to 49.4% by Romney.

The website provided maps and statistics about the electoral outcomes in each state as well as nationally. Later posts addressed methodological issues such as the "house effects" of different pollsters as well as the validity of telephone surveys that did not call cell phones.[538 78]

Through the general election campaign, the blog tracked the movement in the projected electoral vote for Mitt Romney and Barack Obama. In the process it drew an enormous amount of traffic to *The New York Times*. On election night, November 6, it was reported that "Silver's blog provided a significant—and significantly growing, over the past year—percentage of Times pageviews. This fall, visits to the Times' political coverage (including FiveThirtyEight) have increased, both absolutely and as a percentage of site visits. But FiveThirtyEight's growth is staggering: where earlier this year, somewhere between 10 and 20 percent of politics visits included a stop at FiveThirtyEight, last week that figure was 71 percent.... But Silver's blog has buoyed more than just the politics coverage, becoming a significant traffic-driver for the site as a whole. Earlier this year, approximately 1 percent of visits to the New York Times included FiveThirtyEight. Last week, that number was 13 percent. Yesterday, it was 20 percent. That is, one in five visitors to the sixth-most-trafficked U.S. news site took a look at Silver's blog".[48] "On Election Day, the blog drew 10 million page views.... In the first week of its existence in 2008, the blog only got about 300 hits".[49]

From the middle of 2012 until election day, the FiveThirtyEight model updated its estimates of the probability that Barack Obama and Mitt Romney would win a majority of the electoral votes. On election day, November 6, Silver posted his final forecast for each state. On the morning of the November 6, 2012 presidential election, Silver's model gave President Barack Obama a 90.9% chance of winning a majority of the electoral votes.[538 79] At the end of that day, after the ballots had been counted, the 538 model had correctly predicted the winner of all 50 states and the District of Columbia.[50][lower-alpha 5] Silver, along with at least two academic-based analysts who aggregated polls from multiple pollsters, thus got not only all 50 state predictions right, but also all 9 of the "swing states".[51] In contrast, individual pollsters were less successful. For example, Rasmussen Reports "missed on six of its nine swing-state polls".[52]

An independent analysis of Silver's state-by-state projections, assessing whether the percentages of votes that the candidates actually received fell within the "margin of error" of Silver's forecasts, found that "Forty-eight out of 50 states actually fell within his margin of error, giving him a success rate of 96 percent. And assuming that his projected margin of error figures represent 95 percent confidence intervals, which it is likely they did, Silver performed just about exactly as well as he would expect to over 50 trials. Wizard, indeed".[53][54] Additional tests of the accuracy of the electoral vote predictions were published by other researchers.[55][56]

**Criticism of presidential forecasts**

In a series of posts in 2011 and 2012, *FiveThirtyEight* criticized the forecasting methods that relied on macroeconomic modeling of the electoral outcomes.[538 80][538 81] According to Silver, models based primarily on the macro-level performance of the economy (such as unemployment, inflation, and the performance of the stock market), presidential approval ratings (when an incumbent is running for re-election), and the ideological positioning of the (potential) opposing candidates were useful for making forecasts of the election outcome well in advance of election day, though not very precise ones.

An article stating such a position published exactly one year before election day 2012[45] was attacked in an online article in *Bloomberg News* by Ron Klain, the former chief-of-staff to Vice President Biden and a political advisor to Barack Obama.[57] Nate Silver wrote a defense of his method in response. Silver's response was followed by another one from Klain: "Respectfully, Silver Is Still Wrong,"[58] as well as by comments from others on Silver's article and the debate with Klain.[538 82][59][60]

In late October and early November 2012, a number of conservative political journalists issued criticisms of Nate Silver's predictions as overly biased towards Barack Obama's chances of being re-elected president.[61][62][63][64][65][66] Dean Chambers criticized Nate Silver and issued his own "unskewed" prediction of the election. This prediction ultimately erred on four swing states and missed Barack Obama's popular vote percentage by 1.7%, while Nate Silver correctly predicted all 50 states and missed Barack Obama's popular vote percentage by 0.3%. Dean Chambers admitted that his assumptions about voter turnout were incorrect and that the pollsters' assumptions were very accurate.[67]

During the final weeks prior to the November 6th election, some pundits also criticized Silver's electoral model for conveying an undue sense of predictability to the outcome as well as a conviction that Barack Obama was ahead in the race and had a 75% probability of winning.[68] For example, *New York Times* op-ed columnist David Brooks wrote, "I know . . . how I should treat polling data. First, I should treat polls as a fuzzy snapshot of a moment in time. I should not read them, and think I understand the future. If there's one thing we know, it's that even experts with fancy computer models are terrible at predicting hu-

man behavior".[69][70]

In a more direct attack on Silver, in an article entitled "Nate Silver: One-term celebrity?" Dylan Byers of *Politico* wrote, "For all the confidence Silver puts in his predictions, he often gives the impression of hedging. Which, given all the variables involved in a presidential election, isn't surprising. For this reason and others — and this may shock the coffee-drinking NPR types of Seattle, San Francisco and Madison, Wis. — more than a few political pundits and reporters, including some of his own colleagues, believe Silver is highly overrated."[62] Byers also quoted this comment by Joe Scarborough on MSNBC's "Morning Joe": "Nate Silver says this is a 73.6 percent chance that the president is going to win? Nobody in that campaign thinks they have a 73 percent chance – they think they have a 50.1 percent chance of winning. And you talk to the Romney people, it's the same thing," Scarborough said. "Both sides understand that it is close, and it could go either way. And anybody that thinks that this race is anything but a toss-up right now is such an ideologue, they should be kept away from typewriters, computers, laptops and microphones for the next 10 days, because they're jokes".

In contrast to these critics, in late October 2012 political science professor Samuel L. Popkin of the University of California, San Diego, had evaluated Silver's electoral projections as follows:[71]

> We're heading into the last week of a tight presidential campaign, and polls are coming in too fast to count. Partisans everywhere are desperate for omens. But at moments like these, it's people who care most intensely that the "right outcome" occur who run a high risk of getting it wrong—picking out positive polls for comfort, or panicking over an unusual and unexpected result they don't like.
>
> Fortunately, our most prominent number cruncher has been giving us the straight story instead of capitalizing on this anxiety. In 2008, Nate Silver correctly predicted the results of all 35 Senate races and the presidential results in 49 out of 50 states. Since then, his website, fivethirtyeight.com (now central to The New York Times's political coverage), has become an essential source of rigorous, objective analysis of voter surveys to predict the Electoral College outcome of presidential campaigns.

After a post-election appearance by Silver on Joe Scarborough's *Morning Joe*,[72] Scarborough published what he called a "(semi) apology," in which he concluded:

> I won't apologize to Mr. Silver for predicting an outcome that I had also been predicting for a

year. But I do need to tell Nate I'm sorry for leaning in too hard and lumping him with pollsters whose methodology is as rigorous as the Simpsons' strip mall physician, Dr. Nick. For those sins (and a multitude of others that I'm sure I don't even know about), I am sorry.

Politics is a messy sport. And just as ball players who drink beer and eat fried chicken in dugouts across America can screw up the smartest sabermatrician's forecast, Nate Silver's formula is sure to let his fervent admirers down from time to time. But judging from what I saw of him this morning, Nate is a grounded guy who admits as much in his book. I was too tough on him and there's a 84.398264% chance I will be less dismissive of his good work in the future.[73][74][75][76]

### U.S. Senate elections

For more details on this topic, see United States Senate elections, 2012.

The FiveThirtyEight model correctly forecasted the outcome of 31 of the 33 U.S. Senate races.

In one unexpected result, the model had estimated that Republican Rick Berg had a 92% chance of winning the Senate seat in North Dakota. However, by a vote margin of less than 1 percentage point, Democrat Heidi Heitkamp won the election.[77] When asked about his forecast in an online chat a week after the election, Silver said: "The polls showed Berg a little bit ahead. But also there weren't very many polls, so the model defaults in those cases toward looking at "state fundamentals", i.e. the fact that you'd bet on the Republican in North Dakota other things being equal. That race should also serve as a reminder that we put the probabilities in our forecasts for a reason. We had Heitkamp with a 8% chance of winning, I think, about the same as we gave Romney. Those 8% chances come up sometimes... they come up 8% of the time, in fact".[47]

In the other unexpected result, the model had estimated that Montana Republican challenger Denny Rehberg had a 66% chance to defeat the Democratic incumbent Jon Tester; but Tester prevailed and kept his seat.[78]

## 26.5   Under ESPN ownership

FiveThirtyEight launched its ESPN-owned stage on March 17, 2014. As of July, it had a staff of 20 writers, editors, data visualization specialists, and others.[538 83] By December 2015, this staff had expanded to 32 listed on the mast-

head, and 7 more listed as contributors.[79] The site produced articles under 5 headings: politics, economics, science and health, (cultural) life, and sports. In addition to feature articles it produced podcasts on a range of subjects.

Monthly traffic to the site grew steadily from about 2.8 million unique visitors in April 2014 to 10.7 million unique visitors in January 2016.[80]

### 26.5.1   2014 U.S. elections

On September 3, 2014, FiveThirtyEight introduced its forecasts for each of the 36 U.S. Senate elections being contested that year.[538 84] At that time, the Republican Party was given a 64 percent chance of holding a majority of the seats in the Senate after the election. However, FiveThirtyEight editor Nate Silver also remarked, "An equally important theme is the high degree of uncertainty around that outcome. A large number of states remain competitive, and Democrats could easily retain the Senate".[538 85] About two weeks later, the forecast showed the Republican chances of holding the majority down to 55 percent.[538 86]

## 26.6   Recognition and awards

- In September 2008, *FiveThirtyEight* became the first blog ever selected as a Notable Narrative by the Nieman Foundation for Journalism at Harvard University. According to the Foundation, "In his posts, former economic analyst and baseball-stats wunderkind Nate Silver explains the presidential race, using the dramatic tension inherent in the run-up to Election Day to drive his narrative. Come November 5, we will have a winner and a loser, but in the meantime, Silver spins his story from the myriad polls that confound us lesser mortals".[81]

- *The New York Times* described *FiveThirtyEight.com* in November 2008 as "one of the breakout online stars of the year".[13]

- *Huffington Post* columnist Jason Linkins named *FiveThirtyEight.com* as No. 1 of "Ten Things that Managed to Not Suck in 2008, Media Edition".[82]

- *FiveThirtyEight.com* is the 2008 Weblog Award Winner for "Best Political Coverage".[83]

- *FiveThirtyEight.com* earned a 2009 "Bloggie" as the "Best Weblog about Politics" in the 9th Annual Weblog Awards.[84]

- In April 2009, Silver was named "Blogger of the Year" in the 6th Annual Opinion Awards of *The Week*, for his work on *FiveThirtyEight.com*.[85]

- In September 2009, *FiveThirtyEight.com*'s predictive model was featured as the cover story in *STATS: The Magazine for Students of Statistics*.[19]

- In November 2009, *FiveThirtyEight.com* was named one of "Our Favorite Blogs of 2009" ("Fifty blogs we just can't get enough of") by PC Magazine.[86]

- In December 2009, *FiveThirtyEight* was recognized by *The New York Times Magazine* in its "Ninth Annual Year in Ideas" for conducting "Forensic Polling Analysis" detective work on the possible falsification of polling data by a major polling firm.[87][lower-alpha 6]

- In November 2010, Editor-in-Chief of *Politico* John F. Harris, writing in *Forbes* magazine, listed Silver as one of seven bloggers among "The Most Powerful People on Earth".[89]

- In June 2011, *Time's* "The Best Blogs of 2011" named *FiveThirtyEight* one of its Essential Blogs.[90]

- May 2012: *FiveThirtyEight* won a Webby Award for "Best Political Blog" from the International Academy of Digital Arts and Sciences in the 16th annual Webby Awards.[91]

- April 2013: FiveThirtyEight won a Webby Award for "Best Political Blog" from the International Academy of Digital Arts and Sciences in the 17th annual Webby Awards.[92]

## 26.7 See also

- Electoral College (United States)

- Electoral-vote.com

- RealClearPolitics

- Statewide opinion polling for the United States presidential election, 2008

## 26.8 Notes

[1] Several national firms use the name "Strategic Vision"; only one has been releasing political polling results to the media.

[2] Berman first worked with *FiveThirtyEight.com* when he made some provocative discoveries of anomalies in the reported results of the 2009 Election in Iran.[25]

[3] Why other writers played only a limited role in FiveThirtyEight/NYT was explained in February 2011 in an article in *Poynter*.[37]

[4] For example, he considers the ratings by Charlie Cook and *Congressional Quarterly*.

[5] Although Silver put a "toss-up" tag on the presidential election in Florida, his interactive electoral map on the website painted the state light blue and stated that there was a 50.3% probability that Obama would win a plurality of the state's votes.

[6] The first of a series of articles challenged Strategic Vision LLC to reveal key information.[88]

## 26.9 References

### General citations

[1] "fivethirtyeight.com Site Overview". Alexa Internet. Retrieved 2016-02-10.

[2] "Nate Silver joins ESPN in multifaceted role". *ESPN.com*.

[3] Andrew Romano,"Making His Pitches: Nate Silver, an all-star in the world of baseball stats, may be the political arena's next big draw," *Newsweek*, June 16, 2008.

[4] "FAQ and Statement of Methodology *FiveThirtyEight.com*". *FiveThirtyEight.com*. June 9, 2008. Retrieved June 19, 2008.

[5] "Poblano's Profile". *Daily Kos*. Retrieved 2015-04-26.

[6] "Mo. Parents Clueless About Kerry". *Daily Kos*.

[7] "Daily Kos: State of the Nation". Archived from the original on February 8, 2008.

[8] "Obama's Path to Victory". *The New York Times*. February 11, 2008.

[9] Blumenthal, Mark (May 8, 2008). "The Poblano Model". *National Journal*. Retrieved 2015-04-26.

[10] Bialik, Carl (June 2, 2008). "Baseball Analyst Draws Fans by Crunching Election Numbers". *The Wall Street Journal*. Retrieved June 19, 2008.

[11] "Rasmussen Reports to Partner with FiveThirtyEight.com".

[12] "Today's Polls: The Bounce hits the Badger State - The Plank". Archived from the original on June 14, 2008.

[13] Clifford, Stephanie (November 9, 2008). "Finding Fame With a Prescient Call for Obama". *The New York Times*. Retrieved April 26, 2015.

[14] "The New York Times Will Incorporate the Blog FiveThirtyEight into the Politics Section of NYTimes.com". MarketWatch.

[15] "Times to Host Blog on Politics and Polls". *The New York Times*. June 4, 2010.

[16] "Nate Silver of FiveThirtyEight Blog Is to Join ESPN Staff". *The New York Times.* July 20, 2013.

[17] Amy Phillips (July 22, 2013). "Nate Silver - Renowned Statistician, Author and Founder of FiveThirtyEight - Joins ESPN in Multi-Faceted Role - ESPN Front Row". *ESPN Front Row.*

[18] "Nate Silver Interview: The New FiveThirtyEight -- NY-Mag". *Daily Intelligencer.*

[19] Felder, Adam (September 2009). "Case study: The FiveThirtyEight.com Predictive Model of the 2008 Presidential Election" (PDF). *STATS* (50). pp. 3–9. ISSN 1053-8607. Retrieved 2015-04-26.

[20] ElectoralVote.com

[21] "Stevens concedes Alaska Senate race".

[22] "Interview with Nate Silver". *Financial Times.*

[23] "Polling Firm's Reprimand Rattles News Media". *The New York Times.* October 3, 2009.

[24] .

[25] "Statistics wizard from Winchester makes a splash in Iran election - The Boston Globe".

[26] Burkeman, Oliver (April 27, 2010). "Baseball nerd who predicted Obama's win foresees Labour meltdown". *The Guardian* (London). Retrieved May 19, 2010..

[27] "Where's the Transparency in Pollster Ratings?". Archived from the original on June 12, 2010.

[28] "Polling". *Daily Kos.*

[29] "National Journal Online - Transparency In Rating". Archived from the original on June 14, 2010.

[30] "Pollster.com".

[31] pollster-ratings on GitHub

[32] Brian Stelter (June 3, 2010). "The Times to Host Political Polling Site FiveThirtyEight". *Media Decoder Blog.* Archived from the original on September 9, 2015.

[33]

[34] "FiveThirtyEight blog gets with the Times". *NY Daily News.* June 8, 2010.

[35] "News Trends Tilt Toward Niche Sites". *The New York Times.* September 12, 2011.

[36] "About FiveThirtyEight". Archived from the original on March 18, 2014.

[37] "FiveThirtyEight's Nate Silver adjusts to New York Times, 6 months after joining the newsroom". *Poynter.*

[38] "The Monkey Cage". *The Monkey Cage.*

[39] "Nate Silver's Tournament Forecast". *The New York Times.* March 18, 2013.

[40] Silver, Nate (August 27, 2011). "Popularity and Pedigree Matter in the B.C.S.".

[41] "Election 2006: Generic Congressional Ballot". *RealClearPolitics.* Retrieved 2015-04-26.

[42] "Larry J. Sabato's Crystal Ball » What to Expect in 2010".

[43] "Forecasting the House of Representatives' Seat Division in the 2010 Midterm Election".

[44] "Some thoughts on election forecasting - Statistical Modeling, Causal Inference, and Social Science". *Statistical Modeling, Causal Inference, and Social Science.*

[45] Silver, Nate (November 3, 2011). "Is Obama Toast? Handicapping the 2012 Election". *The New York Times Magazine.* Retrieved 2015-02-26.

[46] "Why Obama Will Embrace the 99 Percent". *The New York Times.* February 19, 2012.

[47] "Skew Yourselves: Nate Silver Is Here To Answer Your Questions". *Deadspin.* November 14, 2012. Retrieved 2015-04-26.

[48] "Nate Silver Is a One-Man Traffic Machine for the Times". *The New Republic.* Archived from the original on February 16, 2013.

[49] Erik Maza. "Mirror Awards Honor Excellence in Media Reporting". *WWD.*

[50] "Obama's win a big vindication for Nate Silver, king of the quants". *CNET.* CBS Interactive. November 7, 2012.

[51] "Pollster Predictive Performance, 51 out of 51". *The Huffington Post.* November 7, 2012.

[52] Jonathan D. Salant and Laura Curtis. "Nate Silver-Led Statistics Men Crush Pundits in Election". *Businessweek.com.* Archived from the original on November 8, 2012.

[53] "Nobody's perfect: Nate Silver and the imperfect art of prediction (UPDATE)". *Boston.com.*

[54] "538's Uncertainty Estimates Are As Good As They Get".

[55] "Was Nate Silver the Most Accurate 2012 Election Pundit? - CFAR". *CFAR.*

[56] "2012 Presidential prediction rankings". Retrieved 12 November 2012.

[57] "Why Data Wonks Are Wrong About Presidential Elections: Ron Klain". *Bloomberg.* Archived from the original on November 16, 2011.

[58] "Respectfully, Nate Silver Is Still Wrong: The Ticker". *Bloomberg.* Archived from the original on November 18, 2012.

[59] "Underemphasized Points about the Economy and Elections". *The Monkey Cage.*

[60] "Larry J. Sabato's Crystal Ball » Why Barack Obama has a good chance of winning a second term".

[61] Josh Jordan, "Nate Silver's Flawed Model", *National Review,* October 22, 2012.

[62] Byers, Dylan (2015-04-26). "Nate Silver: One-term celebrity?". *Politico.* Retrieved 6 November 2012.

[63] "The Critique of Nate Silver's Pure Reason - National Review Online". *National Review Online.* Archived from the original on October 31, 2013.

[64] "War on Nate Silver: Final After-Action Report: The Flag of Reality Flies Uncontested Over Silvergrad Weblogging".

[65] "Two views of journalism clash in debate over Nate Silver's work". *Poynter.*

[66] "In defense of Nate Silver: Pundits bare their misunderstanding.". Archived from the original on November 10, 2012.

[67] Brett LoGiurato (November 7, 2012). "'Unskewed' Pollster Dean Chambers: 'Nate Silver Was Right' - Business Insider". *Business Insider.*

[68] Zeynep Tufekci (November 2, 2012). "In Defense of Nate Silver, Election Pollsters, and Statistical Predictions". *WIRED.*

[69] "Poll Addict Confesses". *The New York Times.* October 23, 2012.

[70] John Cassidy (October 24, 2012). "Brooks vs. Silver: The Limits of Forecasting Elections". *The New Yorker.*

[71] Samuel Popkin, "Nate Silver, Artist of Uncertainty," *The American Prospect,* October 28, 2012. Retrieved November 4, 2012

[72] "Morning Joe". Archived from the original on January 27, 2013.

[73] "My (semi) apology to Nate Silver". *POLITICO.*

[74] "Joe Scarborough Nate Silver Apology - Nate Silver Continues To Bother Joe Scarborough - Esquire". *Esquire.* Archived from the original on January 11, 2013.

[75] Erik Wemple (November 21, 2012). "Scarborough half-apologizes to Nate Silver". *Washington Post.*

[76] "Joe Scarborough Is Part Of The Problem". *The Dish.* Archived from the original on January 8, 2013.

[77] "Democrat Heitkamp wins Senate race in North Dakota". *Boston.com.* Archived from the original on November 17, 2012.

[78] "Jon Tester Election Results: Montana Democratic Senator Wins Against Denny Rehberg". *The Huffington Post.* November 7, 2012.

[79] "Masthead".

[80] Tweet by @NateSilver538 on February 3, 2016, https://twitter.com/NateSilver538/status/694974558831525888/photo/1

[81] "Electoral Projections Done Right".

[82] "2008: The Year In Media Highlights". *The Huffington Post.* January 24, 2009.

[83] "The 2008 Weblog Awards Winners".

[84] "Ninth Annual Weblog Awards: The 2009 Bloggies".

[85] "THE WEEK Opinion Awards". Archived from the original on January 10, 2010.

[86] "Our Favorite Blogs 2009". *PCMAG.*

[87] NY Times Magazine "Forensic Polling Analysis"

[88] "A Few More Questions for a Sketchy Pollster". *FiveThirtyEight.*

[89] John F. Harris (November 3, 2010). "My Picks: Bloggers". *Forbes.*

[90] "Five Thirty Eight - TIME's 25 Best Blogs of 2011 - TIME". *TIME.com.* June 6, 2011.

[91] "The Webby Awards".

[92] "Blog - Political".

## FiveThirtyEight articles

[1] Silver, Nate (August 7, 2008). "Frequently Asked Questions". *FiveThirtyEight.com.* Retrieved April 26, 2015.

[2] "No, I'm not Chuck Todd". *FiveThirtyEight.*

[3] Quinn, Sean (October 3, 2008). "On the Road: St. Louis County, Missouri". FiveThirtyEight.com.

[4] Quinn, Sean (November 3, 2008). "Site Note". FiveThirtyEight.com.

[5] Silver, Nate (June 3, 2010). "FiveThirtyEight to Partner with New York Times". *FiveThirtyEight.com.* Retrieved June 3, 2010.

[6] Silver, Nate (August 25, 2010). "New Forecast Shows Democrats Losing 6 to 7 Senate Seats". *FiveThirtyEight.* Retrieved 2015-04-26.

[7] "What the Fox Knows". *FiveThirtyEight.*

[8] "Pollster Ratings v3.0". *FiveThirtyEight.*

[9] Senate rankings

[10] "Swing State Analysis". *FiveThirtyEight*.

[11] "Today's Polls and Final Election Projection: Obama 349, McCain 189". *FiveThirtyEight*.

[12] "The End of the Beginning". *FiveThirtyEight*.

[13] "Obama Hits the Road to Sell Stimulus, Steps Up Pressure on Key Senators". *FiveThirtyEight*.

[14] "Appointed Senators Rarely Win Re-Election". *FiveThirtyEight*.

[15] "Daddy, Where Do Senators Come From?". *FiveThirtyEight*.

[16] "Obama's Agenda & The Difference Between Tactics & Strategy". *FiveThirtyEight*.

[17] "What Are the Chances of a Depression?". *FiveThirtyEight*.

[18] "Senate Rankings, January 2009 Edition". *FiveThirtyEight*.

[19] "Are Oklahoma Students Really This Dumb? Or Is Strategic Vision Really This Stupid?". *FiveThirtyEight*.

[20] "Real Oklahoma Students Ace Citizenship Exam; Strategic Vision Survey Was Likely Fabricated". *FiveThirtyEight*.

[21] "Strategic Vision Polls Exhibit Unusual Patterns, Possibly Indicating Fraud". *FiveThirtyEight*.

[22] "An Open Letter to Strategic Vision CEO David Johnson". *FiveThirtyEight*.

[23] "Skipping Elections, Strategic Vision Has Not Polled Since Controversy Arose". *FiveThirtyEight*.

[24] "Polling and Voting in Iran's Friday Election". *FiveThirtyEight*.

[25] "All posts tagged "Iran"". *FiveThirtyEight*. Retrieved 2015-04-26.

[26] "Election Night Overview". *FiveThirtyEight*.

[27] "Independent Voters and Empty Explanations". *FiveThirtyEight*.

[28] "538 Model Posits Brown as 3:1 Favorite". *FiveThirtyEight*.

[29] "UK Seats Projection: Tories 299, Labour 199, LibDems 120". *FiveThirtyEight*.

[30] "A Hung Parliament?   (From the Gallows, Perhaps?)". *FiveThirtyEight*.

[31] "Instant Run-Off Proposed by Brown". *FiveThirtyEight*.

[32] "Getting It "Right" on the UK Numbers". *FiveThirtyEight*.

[33] "Selection bias in UK polling (Part 1):  Cell phones". *FiveThirtyEight*.

[34] "Selection Bias in UK Polling (Part 2): Internet Polling". *FiveThirtyEight*.

[35] "Is the Lib Dem Surge for Real (Part 4:  The meltdown)". *FiveThirtyEight*.

[36] Silver, Nate; Sexton, Renard; Berman, Dan; Dollar, Thomas (May 6, 2010). "Liveblog: UK Election Returns". *FiveThirtyEight*. Retrieved 2015-04-26.

[37] "Final UK Projection: Conservatives 312, Labour 204, Lib-Dems 103". *FiveThirtyEight*.

[38] Silver, Nate (May 11, 2010). "U.K. Forecasting Retrospective". *FiveThirtyEight*. Retrieved 2015-04-26.

[39] "Con-Lib Pact Brings Cameron to PM's Chair". *FiveThirtyEight*.

[40] "Pollster Ratings v4.0: Results". *FiveThirtyEight*.

[41] "On Transparency, Hypocrisy, and Research 2000". *FiveThirtyEight*.

[42] "FiveThirtyEight Establishes Process for Pollsters to Review its Database of Their Polls". *FiveThirtyEight*.

[43] "FiveThirtyEight's Pollster Ratings". *FiveThirtyEight*.

[44] "How FiveThirtyEight Calculates Pollster Ratings". *FiveThirtyEight*.

[45] Nate Silver (August 25, 2010). "Welcome (and Welcome Back) to FiveThirtyEight". *FiveThirtyEight*. Archived from the original on September 7, 2015.

[46] Andrew Gelman (January 3, 2011). "All Politics Is Local? The Debate and the Graphs". *FiveThirtyEight*. Archived from the original on March 21, 2015.

[47] Brian J. McCabe (January 19, 2011). "Grading New York Restaurants: What's in an 'A'?". *FiveThirtyEight*. Archived from the original on May 26, 2015.

[48] Nate Silver (October 10, 2011). "New Hampshire's Contrarian Streak". *FiveThirtyEight*. Archived from the original on September 11, 2015.

[49] Micah Cohen (September 23, 2011). "A Look at PolitiFact Grades of Candidates". *FiveThirtyEight*. Archived from the original on September 10, 2015.

[50] John Sides (September 12, 2011). "Social Status and How the Elected Vote". *FiveThirtyEight*. Archived from the original on September 6, 2015.

[51] Silver, Nate (March 28, 2011). "In Tournament of Upsets, V.C.U. Has Overcome Longest Odds". *FiveThirtyEight*.

[52] Silver, Nate (March 18, 2003). "Parity in N.C.A.A. Means No Commanding Favorite". *FiveThirtyEight*.

[53] Silver, Nate (March 13, 2012). "FiveThirtyEight Picks the N.C.A.A. Bracket". *FiveThirtyEight*.

[54] Silver, Nate (February 22, 2011). "Deal for Anthony May Limit Knicks' Upside". *FiveThirtyEight*.

[55] "Calling Foul on N.B.A.'s Claims of Financial Distress". *FiveThirtyEight*. July 5, 2011.

[56] "Jeremy Lin Is No Fluke". *FiveThirtyEight*. February 11, 2012.

[57] Silver, Nate (May 31, 2011). "As Mets' Image Slumps, So Does Attendance". *FiveThirtyEight*.

[58] Silver, Nate (September 27, 2011). "September Collapse of Red Sox Could Be Worst Ever". *FiveThirtyEight*.

[59] Nate Silver (February 12, 2011). "The Economics of Blogging and The Huffington Post". *FiveThirtyEight*. Archived from the original on December 10, 2015.

[60] Nate Silver (August 8, 2011). "Why S.&P.'s Ratings Are Substandard and Porous". *FiveThirtyEight*. Archived from the original on September 8, 2015.

[61] Nate Silver (September 6, 2011). "In Jobs Data, 'Surprises' Mean Bad News". *FiveThirtyEight*. Archived from the original on September 6, 2015.

[62] Nate Silver (August 26, 2011). "A New York Hurricane Could Be a Multibillion-Dollar Catastrophe". *FiveThirtyEight*. Archived from the original on September 6, 2015.

[63] Nate Silver (August 29, 2011). "How Irene Lived Up to the Hype". *FiveThirtyEight*. Archived from the original on September 6, 2015.

[64] Silver, Nate (October 7, 2011). "Police Clashes Spur Coverage of Wall Street Protests". *FiveThirtyEight*. Retrieved 2015-04-26.

[65] Nate Silver (October 17, 2011). "The Geography of Occupying Wall Street (and Everywhere Else)". *FiveThirtyEight*. Archived from the original on May 9, 2015.

[66] "Senate Rankings: Post-Masspocalypse Edition". *FiveThirtyEight*.

[67] "Methodology". Archived from the original on September 10, 2015.

[68] Nate Silver (November 3, 2010). "Did Polls Underestimate Democrats' Latino Vote?". *FiveThirtyEight*. Archived from the original on September 7, 2015.

[69] Nate Silver (October 16, 2010). "Consensus Points Toward 50-Seat G.O.P. Gain in House - The New York Times". *FiveThirtyEight*. Archived from the original on September 8, 2015.

[70] Nate Silver (October 27, 2010). "It's Not Inevitable That Democrats Lose The House. (It's Merely Quite Likely.) - The New York Times". *FiveThirtyEight*. Archived from the original on September 22, 2015.

[71] Nate Silver (November 1, 2010). "Agreeing to Disagree: Size of Republican Wave Hard to Predict". *FiveThirtyEight*. Archived from the original on December 25, 2015.

[72] Nate Silver (November 1, 2010). "House Forecast: G.O.P. Plus 54-55 Seats; Significantly Larger or Smaller Gains Possible". *FiveThirtyEight*. Archived from the original on December 25, 2015.

[73] Micah Cohen (December 10, 2010). "38 Days Later". *FiveThirtyEight*. Archived from the original on October 11, 2014.

[74] Nate Silver (November 3, 2011). "Choose Obama's Re-Election Adventure". *FiveThirtyEight*. Archived from the original on September 10, 2015.

[75] Nate Silver (February 15, 2012). "The Fundamentals Now Favor Obama". *FiveThirtyEight*. Archived from the original on September 6, 2015.

[76] Nate Silver (December 13, 2011). "A First Iowa Forecast: Race Is Still Wide Open". *FiveThirtyEight*. Archived from the original on September 8, 2015.

[77] Nate Silver (June 7, 2012). "Election Forecast: Obama Begins With Tenuous Advantage". *FiveThirtyEight*. Archived from the original on September 11, 2015.

[78] Nate Silver (June 22, 2012). "Calculating 'House Effects' of Polling Firms". *FiveThirtyEight*. Archived from the original on September 6, 2015.

[79] "FiveThirtyEight blog". *The New York Times*. Retrieved 2015-04-26.

[80] Nate Silver (November 16, 2011). "A 'Radical Centrist' View on Election Forecasting". *FiveThirtyEight*. Archived from the original on April 3, 2015.

[81] Nate Silver (July 5, 2012). "Measuring the Effect of the Economy on Elections". *FiveThirtyEight*. Archived from the original on September 10, 2015.

[82] Micah Cohen (November 19, 2011). "Reads and Reactions". *FiveThirtyEight*. Archived from the original on October 9, 2015.

[83] "Masthead". *FiverThirtyEight*. Retrieved 2015-04-26.

[84] "2014 Senate Forecast". *FiveThirtyEight*. Retrieved 2015-04-26.

[85] "FiveThirtyEight's Senate Model Is Back And It Gives Republicans The Edge". *FiveThirtyEight*.

[86] "Senate Update: Democrats Draw Almost Even. Is It The Money?". *FiveThirtyEight*.

## 26.10 Further reading

- Etim, Bassey (March 22, 2009). "Blogging in a Post-Campaign World". *The New York Times*.

- Bobbie Johnson, Bobbie (November 3, 2008). "America's Hottest Pollster Gives His Final Verdict as US Elections Reach Climax". *The Guardian*.

- Myers, Steve (October 30, 2008) "FiveThirtyEight Combines Polls, Reporting and Baseball". Poynter Institute.

- Rothschild, David (2009). "Forecasting Elections: Comparing Prediction Markets, Polls, and their Biases". *Public Opinion Quarterly*. 73, No. 5. pp. 895–916.

## 26.11  External links

- FiveThirtyEight 2008–2010 (pre-NYT) and August 18, 2013–present (ESPN era)

- FiveThirtyEight at *The New York Times* archive (Aug. 2008-Aug. 2013)

- Nate Silver interview on Bloggingheads.tv (August 21, 2008)

# Chapter 27

# Electoral-vote.com

**Electoral-Vote.com** (formally, **Electoral Vote Predictor**) is a website created by computer scientist Andrew S. Tanenbaum. The site's primary content is poll analysis to project the outcome of U.S. elections. The site also includes commentary on related news stories.

The site was created during the lead-up to the 2004 U.S. Presidential election to predict the winner. The site tries to improve on national polls usually reported in the media, by instead analyzing the most recent polls on the state level, thus simulating the process by which Electoral College votes are determined in the actual election. Updated throughout the campaign, visitors can see who is "ahead" at any time.

Through most of the 2004 campaign Tanenbaum kept his identity a secret, only acknowledging that he personally preferred John Kerry. Tanenbaum, a civil libertarian who is a member of Democrats Abroad, and generally supports Democratic candidates for office, revealed his identity on November 1, 2004, as well as stating his reasons and qualifications for running the website.[1]

## 27.1 History

### 27.1.1 2004 Presidential election

The site began operating on May 24, 2004 with a simple map and a few links to other pages. The information available grew over time, though. During the months leading up to the 2004 U.S. Presidential election, the site was updated daily to reflect new state polls. The site was immensely popular, attracting nearly 700,000 daily visitors as election day neared and was the most popular election site in the country, in the top 1,000 Web sites in the world, and in the top 10 blogs in the world.

The main page consisted of a map of the United States with the individual states colored varying shades of red or blue, based on the polls for that state. For instance, Illinois, a state that was polling strongly for Democrat John Kerry was colored dark blue, whereas Michigan where Kerry's lead

polled by a small margin was colored light blue. Analogously, Texas was dark red during the whole campaign, indicating Bush's strong lead there. All of the polling data were provided in multiple formats, including HTML, Excel, and .csv for downloading. Other features included historical data on previous elections, charts and animations showing the polls over the course of time, cartograms, and links to hundreds of other pages and external Websites with tables, charts, graphs, and other election data and information.

The main algorithm just used the most recent poll(s) in every state. If two polls came out on the same day, they were averaged. This algorithm used all published polls, including those by partisan pollsters such as Strategic Vision (R) and Hart Research (D). A second algorithm used only nonpartisan polls and averaged all polls during the past three days. A third algorithm used historical data to predict how undecided voters would break. Maps for each of the algorithms were given every day, but the first one got most of the publicity since it was on the main page.

The site's final tracking using algorithm 1 posted on Election Day, November 2 gave 262 electoral votes to John Kerry and 261 to George W. Bush, with 15 tossups.[2] The second algorithm (averaging 3 days worth of nonpartisan polls) gave Kerry 245 and Bush 278 with 15 tossups. The third algorithm (predicting the undecideds) predicted 281 for Kerry and 257 for Bush.

The actual vote gave Kerry 252 to Bush's 286. Using nonpartisan polls and averaging a few days worth of polls did best. This algorithm got 47 states plus D.C. right, 1 state (Iowa) wrong, and said New Mexico and Wisconsin were too close to call. The most-recent-poll wins algorithm got 46 right, 4 wrong, and one too close to call.

### 27.1.2 2006 Senate and House elections

On September 6, 2006, the site began tracking the 2006 Congressional elections in the Senate. Shortly thereafter, the House of Representatives was added. The map on the site's front page displayed polling for the 2006 Senate races.[3] For House races, the site featured a "Hot House Races" page with links to Wikipedia articles on the candidates, links to the candidates' official websites, and notes on the races.[4] The relatively small number of House election polls as well as 2004's House vote totals were used to project the makeup of the House on the site's front page.[3] The site correctly predicted the winners in all 33 Senate races.

### 27.1.3    2008 Presidential, Senate, and House elections

In late December 2006, the site began its 2008 coverage, which included the presidential race, all 33 Senate races, and about 40 House races that had been close in 2006 and were expected to be highly contested in 2008. For each of the known presidential, senatorial and House candidates, a photo was given, linked to the candidate's Wikipedia entry, along with a brief description of the candidate and race. The site also had four new maps: one showing the 2004 presidential election, one showing the governors by state, one showing the senate by state and finally one showing the House delegations by state. Polling data was presented daily beginning in December 2007 with data from the primaries.

Polling data was presented daily on the likely outcome of the primaries as well as upcoming trends.[5]

The site's electoral vote prediction for the 2008 election was very close to the actual outcome, correctly projecting the winner of every state except for Indiana, and showing Missouri (won by John McCain by only 0.13% of the vote) as a pure tossup.[6] The Senate projection was also close to the actual outcome, predicting 34 of the 35 decided states correctly, including correctly showing a Democratic pickup in Alaska and incorrectly showing the Republican Senator Norm Coleman holding his seat in Minnesota.[7] The Senate results of the Minnesota election was so close that it was contested until the state supreme court ruled in favor of Al Franken on June 30, 2009.

### 27.1.4    2010 Senate and House elections

In 2010 the site projected 51 seats held by Democrats, 48 by Republicans, and 1 by Lisa Murkowski (a Republican running a write-in campaign). It was incorrect about Colorado and Nevada, which instead went to Democrats. It projected 202 House seats held by Democrats, 216 seats held by Republicans, with 17 too close to call. The actual outcome was 195 Democrats and 240 Republicans.

### 27.1.5    2012 Presidential and Senate elections

In 2012 the site projected the electoral votes for Barack Obama and Mitt Romney, and the Senate. Its final analysis predicted 303 electoral votes for Obama, and 220 for Romney, with 15 votes (North Carolina's) too close to call. The actual outcome was 332 to 206; North Carolina went to Romney, but Florida instead went to Obama. Its final projection for the Senate was 51 seats held by Democrats, 45 by Republicans, 1 by independent Angus King (an ally of the Democrats), and 3 too close to call (Montana, Wyoming, North Dakota); those 3 seats all went to Democrats.

### 27.1.6    2014 Senate elections

In 2014 the site projected 47 Senate seats held by Democrats, 52 by Republicans, and 1 too close to call (Kansas). The actual outcome was 46 Democrats and 54 Republicans, with Kansas and North Carolina instead going to Republicans.

### 27.1.7    2016 Presidential election

Tanenbaum has not committed to performing the same ongoing statistical analysis leading up to the 2016 election,[8] but as of early December 2015 continues to update the site daily with commentary on the presidential candidates of both parties. In September 2015, UCLA-trained historian Christopher Bates starting contributing.

## 27.2    See also

- Fivethirtyeight.com
- Real Clear Politics
- Electoral College (United States)

## 27.3    References

[1]  The Votemaster FAQ

[2]  Electoral Vote Predictor archive from Nov. 2

[3]  Electoral-vote.com

[4]  The Hot House Races at electoral-vote.com

[5]  "It's going to be a photo finish". *The West Georgian*. 2008-01-16.

[6]  http://electoral-vote.com/evp2008/Pres/Maps/Nov04.html

[7] http://www.electoral-vote.com/evp2008/Senate/Maps/Nov04-s.html

[8] Tanenbaum, Andrew. "Announcement". Retrieved 13 August 2015.

## 27.4 External links

- electoral-vote.com

- "Poll Crazy" http://www.guardian.co.uk/salon/story/0,,1331599,00.html 2004-10-20

## 27.5　Text and image sources, contributors, and licenses

### 27.5.1　Text

- **United States presidential election** *Source:* https://en.wikipedia.org/wiki/United_States_presidential_election?oldid=706958479 *Contributors:* RjLesch, The Cunctator, RobLa, DanKeshet, Rmhermen, PierreAbbat, SimonP, Zoe, Soulpatch, Olivier, Mrwojo, Ubiquity, Patrick, Infrogmation, Kidburla, Minesweeper, Radicalsubversiv, Ahoerstemeier, Kingturtle, Jiang, Deisenbe, JamesReyes, John K, Jengod, Smith03, Dan-Tilkin, Guaka, Molinari, Choster, Savantpol, Traal, Tpbradbury, Jeffrey Smith, Eduarodi, Bevo, Topbanana, HarryHenryGebel, AaronSw, Jfruh, Jerzy, Flockmeal, Adam Carr, Slawojarek, Gromlakh, Robbot, Friedo, Postdlf, Ivan~enwiki, Harry Doddema, Mushroom, Mattflaschen, Steve Casburn, Wikilibrarian, Peruvianllama, Bkonrad, Xinoph, Mboverload, Formeruser-83, Jackol, Deus Ex, Neilc, Gadfium, Pgan002, R. fiend, MarkSweep, MisfitToys, OwenBlacker, Dmaftei, Husnock, Sam Hocevar, Neutrality, Joyous!, MementoVivere, Valadius, Jwolfe, Dbaron, Discospinster, Solitude, Rhobite, Guanabot, Bender235, Jnestorius, Brian0918, Phoenix Hacker, Tverbeek, Triona, Spoon!, Tachitsuteto, SNIyer1, La goutte de pluie, Physicistjedi, Pschemp, Rsholmes, Jhjh2004, Terrycojones, Duffman~enwiki, SnowFire, Mlessard, DLJessup, TommyBoy, Samaritan, Wtmitchell, EKMichigan, RainbowOfLight, Cmprince, Zereshk, Kbolino, Kenyon, Nautical Mongoose, Ron Ritzman, Rorschach, Reinoutr, Woohookitty, MK2, Tripodics, Tabletop, Ianweller, Zzyzx11, 🔲🔲🔲🔲🔲, EricE, Palica, Graham87, GoldRingChip, BD2412, Rjwilmsi, Seraphimblade, InFairness, The wub, SNIyer12, Qqqqqq, Ground Zero, Nihiltres, NoSeptember, Supertrouperdc, Atrix20, Awbeal, YurikBot, RussBot, Epolk, Gaius Cornelius, Redspork02, Wimt, NawlinWiki, Bruguiea, Rjensen, Toya, Lexicon, Raven4x4x, T, Madcynic, Vanished user 8488293, Trainra, Wknight94, Zzuuzz, PTSE, Chrishmt0423, Kevin, HereToHelp, Teryx, 🔲🔲🔲 robot, Vanka5, SmackBot, Rrius, Felix Dance, Nickst, Stifle, Renesis, Yamaguchi🔲🔲, Gilliam, Betacommand, Psiphiorg, Chris the speller, Jprg1966, PrimeHunter, Roms85, Deli nk, Darth Panda, Mikker, Gyrobo, GoodDay, EvelinaB, Andy120290, GrahameS, William Quill, JanCeuleers, Danjewell, Wybot, Wizardman, Pats1, Ericl, Mitchumch, Wikizach, SashatoBot, Nishkid64, Potosino, John, The alliance, J 1982, IronGargoyle, Techsmith, Levineps, Iridescent, Joseph Solis in Australia, JoeBot, Igoldste, CapitalR, Eluchil404, Jwood74, Ale jrb, Zarex, Argon233, Vrysxy, AndrewHowse, Reywas92, Gogo Dodo, Alanbly, JiangWei23, Rracecarr, Shirulashem, Dferrantino, Gonzo fan2007, Zalgo, Gimmetrow, CieloEstrellado, Thijs!bot, Epbr123, N5iln, Mojo Hand, Headbomb, Marek69, Basun, Ultegra, Grand51paul, Big Bird, Heroeswithmetaphors, JRRobinson, Northumbrian, Jtmoon, AntiVandalBot, Luna Santin, Opelio, Vantelimus, Farosdaughter, Wisl, Yellowdesk, Res2216firestar, JAnDbot, Captain Planet's Green Mullet, Db099221, Bluerondo, Nevermore27, SteveSims, Bongwarrior, VoABot II, Gang14, Catgut, LW77, W like wiki, MartinBot, Molimo728, Masebrock, Plawler, J.delanoy, Bigzig91090, Numbo3, Turnip281, Vanished user 342562, Loftond3, It Is Me Here, LordAnubisBOT, McSly, JayJasper, Vanished User 4517, Antony-22, D00lim, Potatoswatter, Juliancolton, STBotD, ACBest, WinterSpw, JavierMC, Alain10, Bluecollarchessplayer, Borat fan, That-Vela-Fella, CWii, A.Ou, CSumit, Nburden, Seattle Skier, Jgrdonquixote, Philip Trueman, Conor69, Leafyplant, Broadbot, LeaveSleaves, Ray andrew, Buffs, Mjcoyle, Highground79, BatMiata, Sue Rangell, Deconstructhis, D. Recorder, StAnselm, Sheppa28, Phe-bot, JuWiki2, WRK, Keilana, Sg647112c, Toddst1, Uwmad, Arbor to SJ, Theemes, Pharmregulations, Oxymoron83, Tombomp, Jmj713, LonelyMarble, Geoff Plourde, Nn123645, Pinkadelica, Explicit, Ratemonth, Oneforlogic, ClueBot, The Thing That Should Not Be, Happysomeone, Rjd0060, ZippyGoogle, Der Golem, Agraefe, Blanchardb, Rabidbuzz, Ivnryn, Brettnyy, Atomic Wedgie, NuclearWarfare, Searcher 1990, SockPuppetForTomruen, Fitzburgh, SounderBruce, Dekisugi, Pookman7497, Thingg, Aitias, 7, Belchfire, SF007, Barbaricino~enwiki, Temeku, XLinkBot, Jovianeye, Hillaryforprez, Yraad, Rreagan007, PL290, Nally890, MatthewVanitas, Ga1dal, Addbot, Kelly, ConCompS, Super-Wiki10000, JohnSWren, Blubberboy92, ChairmanNow, Stuwarren, Metsavend, Startstop123, Amrad, KorinoChikara, CanadianLinuxUser, Saberwolf116, Dyadron, Lethalpotato, Debresser, Fireaxe888, Tassedethe, Tide rolls, Zorrobot, Jarble, Ergtwrttqqagqa, Yobot, Granpuff, Alanpip, Tohd8BohaithuGh1, Ptbotgourou, Fraggle81, Gabejgrant, Mmxx, Maxí, Againme, Oneslowlx, Backslash Forwardslash, Piano non troppo, Dsprink, Veristic, Ulric1313, Obamamaniac, Flewis, Luckedout2, Ocexpo, Lucas Leon, Citation bot, Bob Burkhardt, Acts17:6, Rogerrabbitt, Frankenpuppy, ArthurBot, Xqbot, Capricorn42, Khajidha, Tmoy, Rushkid7, Maddie!, Louis XVIII, Raprchju, AlphaRed3, Christian-913-101-, Charles Edwin Shipp, TheVirginiaHistorian, Mahnut, Nezor87, Jusses2, Fat&Happy, BuzzFlood, BluesGal4U, PleaseStand, Tbhotch, RjwilmsiBot, Ripchip Bot, Alison22, R.A. Weber 6 12 03, EmausBot, John of Reading, Cristian.nadler, Evanh2008, ZéroBot, PBS-AWB, Donutcity, HandsomeFella, ClueBot NG, Iamnoone321, Angelmarie87, Vacation9, Widr, Cameron4134, 43hellokitty21, SMD JMP 2011, Kelfman, Prcc27, M0rphzone, Kagundu, Prajcoep, Qwekiop147, BattyBot, Eeelliimmaann, Mediran, Futurist110, Craub, Dexbot, Mogism, Rosepol, NewJerseyNetsfan1982, LlamaDude78, Lugia2453, Jeffrey L Albertson, P4iraTMW, SteenthIWbot, Zziccardi, Epicgenius, William2001, Eyesnore, ArmbrustBot, Matsci2, Monkbot, Chesnaught555, SaltySeas, Ethan817, GeneralizationsAreBad, Cjrawrdan, ProprioMe OW, Sanket Edits Wiki, Rowssusan, Cynstraham and Anonymous: 543

- **Indirect election** *Source:* https://en.wikipedia.org/wiki/Indirect_election?oldid=705719150 *Contributors:* Karada, Jeffq, Wilfried Derksen, Macrakis, Rlquall, Neutrality, Mike Jones, Jnestorius, Man vyi, Mindmatrix, Drachenfyre, Electionworld, Rjwilmsi, DirkvdM, Chobot, Bgwhite, YurikBot, RussBot, Lincolnite, Nanten, PanchoS, Red Jay, SmackBot, Davewild, Bluebot, Bidgee, Bancki, AndySimpson, Mitrius, Beetstra, Dnheff, NaBUru38, CzechOut, Beecheese, InternationalIDEA, Joshua, SteveSims, DerHexer, Jim.henderson, Huzzlet the bot, L'Aquatique, Lulo.it, Hersfold, WarddrBOT, Skikid419, Ceranthor, SPQRobin, SieBot, Swliv, ToePeu.bot, Toddst1, FredrikLähnn, Bee Cliff River Slob, Alexbot, Muro Bot, Addbot, Morannikka, Montgomery '39, MagnusA.Bot, Cambalachero, Numbo3-bot, Zorrobot, Luckas-bot, Lucas Leon, DSisyphBot, Annie Lennox, FrescoBot, MondalorBot, StacyOnEarth, MAXXX-309, EmausBot, Illegitimate Barrister, Mcc1789, ClueBot NG, Littleowljrn, Lanhiaze, Iloilo Wanderer, Monkbot and Anonymous: 46

- **Electoral College (United States)** *Source:* https://en.wikipedia.org/wiki/Electoral_College_(United_States)?oldid=703762063 *Contributors:* Derek Ross, Ansible, Vicki Rosenzweig, Malcolm Farmer, Kowloonese, Phil Bordelon, Roadrunner, Zimriel, Gpietsch, Hephaestos, Soulpatch, Olivier, Bobdobbs1723, Vik-Thor, K.lee, Patrick, Michael Hardy, Gabbe, Hoshie, Menchi, Ixfd64, Seav, Delirium, Mcarling, Davejenk1ns, Minesweeper, Stib, Mpolo, Ahoerstemeier, Baylink, Kingturtle, BigFatBuddha, Susurrus, Jiang, Kaihsu, Jeandré du Toit, Dwo, Jengod, Smith03, Vanished user 5zariu3jisj0j4irj, RickK, Savantpol, Fuzheado, Doradus, Wik, Timc, Radiojon, Tpbradbury, Buckwad, Dinopup, Furrykef, Taxman, Tempshill, Mattworld, Ed g2s, Bevo, Lord Emsworth, Joy, Raul654, AnonMoos, Bcorr, Flockmeal, David.Monniaux, UninvitedCompany, Dimadick, Branddobbe, EdwinHJ, Robbot, Dale Arnett, Josh Cherry, Astronautics~enwiki, Friedo, Moriori, Chrism, Lbs6380, Jredmond, Ikkakujyu, Yelyos, Lowellian, Chris Roy, Drago9034, Postdlf, Stewartadcock, Merovingian, Pingveno, Tualha, Henrygb, Dukeofomnium, Hemanshu, Meelar, Timrollpickering, Pm06420, Andrew Levine, Alex R S, Hadal, UtherSRG, Toiyabe, Tim Bell, Seth Ilys, Diberri, Guy Peters, Rsduhamel, Jord, Davidcannon, David Gerard, Xyzzyva, JamesMLane, Achurch, Inter, Lupin, Ferkelparade, Orpheus, Wwoods, Everyking, Betelgeuse, Curps, Skyshadow, Js coron, Xinoph, Nkocharh, Kainaw, Rchandra, Redux, Solipsist, Uzume, Bobblewik, Deus Ex, JRR Trollkien, Golbez, Stevietheman, Simulcra, M4rk, SoWhy, VoX, Alexf, MikeX, Xmnemonic, Academician, Slowking Man, AHM, Jackms, Antandrus,

DaveJB, Beland, MisfitToys, Kaldari, Rdsmith4, Balcer, Ellsworth, Bumm13, PSzalapski, Chrisn4255, Pmanderson, Atemperman, Gscshoyru, Neutrality, Lacrimosus, Kate, Mike Rosoft, Jwolfe, ClockworkTroll, Ulflarsen, Pmadrid, Juan Ponderas, Dcfleck, Larrybob, Discospinster, Brianhe, Rhobite, Guanabot, Supercoop, Kenj0418, Jonpin, Paulr~enwiki, Deh, Smyth, IlyaHaykinson, Ponder, 1pezguy, Bender235, Gsgeorge, ESkog, Kbh3rd, Fataltourist, Jwalling, Ylee, Croz~enwiki, Mbroooks, Omnibus, Zenohockey, Cg41386, Kross, Tverbeek, Shanes, Tom, Sietse Snel, Leif, Etimbo, SS451, Spoon!, Noren, Grick, Bobo192, Live and let Troll, O18, NetBot, Papercut2a, Richss, Smalljim, Nyenyec, Che fox, Allthewhile, Pgva, Elipongo, Doppelzoo, Chirag, Joshlmay, La goutte de pluie, Zoewscott, VBGFscJUn3, Charonn0, TMS63112, Pschemp, Jonathunder, Katiexkill, Wpopp~enwiki, Disneyfreak96, Eduffy, Msh210, PaulHanson, Neria, Neonumbers, Penwhale, Doopokko, Alessenda~enwiki, Thirtyeyes, Wachtou, SlimVirgin, DLJessup, TommyBoy, Batmanand, Metron4, Scott5114, Snowolf, Wtmitchell, Zantastik, RainbowOfLight, Buoren, Pethr, Geraldshields11, BDD, LukeSurl, Ericl234, Joelfurr, TShilo12, Fdewaele, Matthew238, Nichlemn, Anthony aragorn, GaelicWizard, OwenX, Camw, Guy M, Tripodics, MONGO, Randi75, Kgrr, Nomenclaturist, Terence, KevinOKeeffe, SCEhardt, Zzyzx11, DocRuby, Clarkefreak, Wayward, Prashanthns, Allen3, Behun, Mandarax, Wikimike, Marskell, GoldRingChip, BD2412, Deadcorpse, Levelistchampion, Zzedar, RxS, Jclemens, Jcmo, Sjö, Rjwilmsi, Tim!, Eyu100, Rillian, Joz3d, Nneonneo, Chekaz, Bubba73, Oo64eva, Exeunt, Titoxd, Goclenius, FlaBot, SchuminWeb, RobertG, Ground Zero, CR85747, KarlFrei, Nihiltres, Githlar, RMc, Nivix, Richardbooth, RexNL, Gurch, Leslie Mateus, Wars, NoSeptember, Jrtayloriv, Str1977, DevastatorIIC, Supertrouperdc, Atrix20, Blackberrylaw, Simishag, Karel Anthonissen, Srleffler, Glenn L, King of Hearts, Rosenbluh, Cshay, VolatileChemical, Samwaltz, Joseph11h, The Rambling Man, YurikBot, Wavelength, RobotE, Hairy Dude, RussBot, Red Slash, Robert A West, Zafiroblue05, Pigman, DanMS, Chaser, Casey56, Tonywiki, BillMasen, Gaius Cornelius, Tastywheat, Atwood, NawlinWiki, Kcmurphy88, Lucero del Alba~enwiki, Schlafly, Neutron, Barberio, Cleared as filed, HowardDean, Davemck, Tony1, Mysid, Gadget850, TransUtopian, FF2010, Bdell555, Nightryder84, Knotnic, Closedmouth, Pb30, Red Jay, Scoutersig, Wainstead, Lancer9910, JLaTondre, Scineram, Markustwofour, MagneticFlux, X3210, The 13th 4postle~enwiki, Some guy, GrinBot~enwiki, FrozenPurpleCube, Ant ie, Sardanaphalus, Errickfoxy, SmackBot, WoodenBooks, Kalebdf, Ezratrumpet, Hux, Pfly, Reedy, KnowledgeOfSelf, Mdiamante, DMorpheus, Prototime, Rrius, DWaterson, Pennywisdom2099, Stifle, Anastrophe, Delldot, Pdurland, Orser67, Eloil, Ejeffrey, Gilliam, Senfo, Hmains, Talinus, Andy M. Wang, Laukster, Psiphiorg, Jgog2, Chris the speller, Bluebot, Kurykh, Keegan, Juneappal, SlimJim, Persian Poet Gal, Jgera5, Alexwagner, SchfiftyThree, CSWarren, Baa, Konstable, Szetlan, Darth Panda, AKMask, Gracenotes, Bancki, GoodDay, Muboshgu, Rtbinc, Drycoookiedough, Jennica, RiFraS, Lostinlodos, Folksong, TheKMan, Xiagu, Andy120290, Addshore, Edivorce, Celarnor, Grover cleveland, Mitrius, Overacker, Dejo~enwiki, CanDo, Cybercobra, Royho, Captain Zyrain, Nakon, TGC55, Salt Yeung, A.J.A., BlueGoose, Suimpos, IMaRocketMan, Crd721, BryanG, Michalchik, Scalga, Kukini, Ohconfucius, Will Beback, Esrever, Fifty7, Howdoesthiswo, Microchip08, Eshafoshaf, DLoney, James.S, Daverich313, Green Giant, KenBest, Cielomobile, RandomCritic, JJdude, Pudgenet, Slakr, Shangrilaista, Beetstra, Noah Salzman, Mets501, Funnybunny, Markjdb, Ryulong, Chronicler3, Cerealkiller13, Whosawhatsis, MrDolomite, Andymmu, Isaac Crumm, Levineps, Parsleyij, G1076, Simon12, Iridescent, Joseph Solis in Australia, Shoeofdeath, Dnheff, Cbrown1023, S0me l0ser, Whedonite, CapitalR, Richard75, Lucy-marie, JRtx, Courcelles, Bfoaz, Eluchil404, Hossenfeffer, Tawkerbot2, Coreycubed, Daniel5127, Clyde Miller, Esobocinski, Thomas81, Eastlaw, P-Chan, HDCase, AarrowOM, JForget, Cg-realms, KyleGardiner, Wolfdog, CmdrObot, Ale jrb, TimothyHorrigan, The ed17, KyraVixen, Rwflammang, CWY2190, Orayzio, Shyran, Dgw, Msavidge, Eihjia, Imaginationac, Vrysxy, Cydebot, Korky Day, Bur, ChrisKennedy, Nebular110, Reywas92, MC10, Hawksocc8, Gogo Dodo, Khatru2, TodKarlson, Corpx, CoolCityConsulting, DavidRF, Demomoke, DumbBOT, NaLalina, Sir Grant the Small, Rakf1, EricBetzold, SMP0328, Gonzo fan2007, JohnClarknew, Quaxmonster, Bishop-Berkeley, Taxcheat, BCSWowbagger, Epbr123, Dubc0724, Rockymountains, King Bee, Rev.bayes, Qwyrxian, Rusl, Chitomcgee, 271828182, Sselbor, Vidor, Keraunos, Glennfcowan, Mojo Hand, Tiailds, John254, PJtP, Philippe, Michael A. White, Lutskovp, Radio Guy, Nizamarain, Seacow, Northumbrian, Dzubint, Hmrox, Hires an editor, AntiVandalBot, Luna Santin, Seaphoto, Opelio, Lamontacranston, Mack2, Toohool, SSJPabs, Yellowdesk, AtikuX, Historypre, Pixor, Béka, Gökhan, Res2216firestar, Tomertomer, Twilight, DuncanHill, Komponisto, MER-C, Benjamin22b, Pcubbage, Rearete, Hello32020, Db099221, Thenub314, Nevermore27, Wmcewenjr, Greg Comlish, Makron1n, Beaumont, Kaonslau~enwiki, Joshua, Acroterion, SteveSims, Boris B, Magioladitis, Fitnr, VoABot II, Swpb, Trick311, Velvet elvis81, Jim Nightshade, Wikied~enwiki, Animum, BilCat, Allstarecho, Peterhi, JaGa, PatPeter, Thyroidpsychic, AdamC387, Terrymitchell, TheCheshiresGrin, Bmf 51, Cliff smith, Electiontechnology, Hdt83, MartinBot, Neverlookback75, Nikpapag, Rettetast, Jonathan Hall, Fastman99, R'n'B, Commons-Delinker, Starwarswizard, J.delanoy, Euku, ChrisfromHouston, Tommy11111, SubwayEater, George415, Vrnd05, McSly, Ycdkwm, Audio-books, Veriss1, Gurchzilla, JayJasper, Lilpinoy 82, NewEnglandYankee, Kw0134, SJP, Themoodyblue, BigHairRef, Sunderland06, Julian-colton, Gr8white, Something Original, Mrmuk, Jamesontai, Foofighter20x, Mookabear, TWCarlson, Nat682, RVJ, Andy Marchbanks, Goyston, Idioma-bot, Speciate, VolkovBot, IWhisky, DrDentz, CWii, Infoman99, Mrh30, Jeff G., Indubitably, Katydidit, Station1, Philip Trueman, Skalskal, Blake the bookbinder, Melsaran, LeaveSleaves, Bentley4, UnitedStatesian, Cremepuff222, Frank G Anderson, Wiae, DesmondRavenstone, Buffs, Robbie7256, BlueH2O, Enviroboy, Root Beers, Judgeking, Seresin, Alaniaris, Koldito, Jihinotenshi, T0lk, Why Not A Duck, Truthanado, Mlf107, Qworty, Bitbut, Krakaet, Nagy, Woodeye18, Legoktm, Pokeraddict, Deconstructhis, NerfOne, SieBot, BrainOverfloW, TJRC, Mggrant, Dough4872, Gerakibot, Plinkit, MusicRunnerDebaterGirl, Vanished User 8a9b4725f8376, Pgbochanski, Calabraxthis, Keilana, Flyer22 Reborn, Tiptoety, Radon210, The Evil Spartan, Elcobbola, JSpung, Enos733, Oxymoron83, Judicatus, Baseball Bugs, Lightmouse, Laid-Off, Radzewicz, Conollyb, Lynntoniolondon, Kumioko (renamed), Catrope, Anakin101, Hubertfarnsworth, Sxp151, Motthoangwehuong, SEppley, PerryTachett, Pinkadelica, Randy Kryn, RomanHistorian, Faithlessthewonderboy, Farkeld, Kinkyturnip, Szu, ClueBot, Vrmlguy, LP-mn, Wikievil666, Iman2464, Jeff kuta, Voxpuppet, EoGuy, General Epitaph, Hansbaer, Enthusiast01, FJSchorr2, Farolif, Drmies, The Vegetable Man, Captaincalcium, Dawginroswell, CounterVandalismBot, Cfsenel, Harland1, P. S. Burton, Piledhigheranddeeper, Rprpr, Privatemusings, BlairLTFPM, Excirial, Sebo1, -Midorihana-, Drs3000, Wikipology, Bchaosf, Wordwright, Infallibleflyingzombie, Ember of Light, Ghostking13, Razorflame, Westbranch, Kool200, Jayp1981, La Pianista, Looktothis, Thingg, Bradybee, Silas Maxfield, OddibeKerfeld, Lx 121, BlueDevil, Blow of Light, Profstein2, SoxBot III, Evilinnocence18e, Cglynn, DumZiBoT, Crazy Boris with a red beard, SMP0328., XLinkBot, Jed 20012, Items Year, Tomblikebomb, RRichie, GIVE YOUR MAMA SOME SUGAR!, Atime2think, SilvonenBot, Fzxboy, Uhllhu, Noctibus, WikiDao, Dwilso, Begoodanddontbeevilbutinsteadbegood, Addbot, Tmeryhewjsf35, Roentgenium111, Willking1979, Some jerk on the Internet, DOI bot, Non-dropframe, Wernhervonbraun, KorinoChikara, CanadianLinuxUser, Noozgroop, Chessna13, Epicadam, CarsracBot, Glane23, Bassbonerocks, Lihaas, SalineNasalMist, Amjsjc, Bwrs, Almightyjean, Arbitrarily0, Bartledan, CristoperB, Legobot, Luckas-bot, MileyDavidA, Yobot, 2D, Tohd8BohaithuGh1, Ptbotgourou, Librsh, Mklbtz, Wargo, THEN WHO WAS PHONE?, AnomieBOT, Cochituate, Wes colley~enwiki, Wahoos0595, Piano non troppo, Frontierecs, MindscapesGraphicDesign, Molcont, Flewis, Jaresing, Lucas Leon, Ksferrante, Bob Burkhardt, Neurolysis, Xqbot, YBG, Tomwsulcer, Tyrol5, GrouchoBot, ProtectionTaggingBot, Mark Schierbecker, RibotBOT, ACatRon, Ejrubio, Drdpw, Safiel, Dylan03, Horrid Henry, Otterro, Dougofborg, Thehelpfulbot, Haldraper, Tktru, FrescoBot, CMWrestlemaniaPunkCharlie, TheVirginiaHistorian, PeterEastern, Danhomer, Citation bot 1, Mosemamenti, Skyerise, Jschnur, RedBot, StacyOnEarth, Victor Victoria, Dienacarfire, Lotje, Dinamik-bot, Sgt. R.K. Blue, Reaper Eternal, Sgravn, No One of Consequence, Tbhotch, Minimac, DARTH SIDIOUS 2, Rjwilmsi-

Bot, TheArguer, Ripchip Bot, Thedofc, NerdyScienceDude, Jowa fan, EmausBot, Gfoley4, Dewritech, XinaNicole, NotAnonymous0, K6ka, HiW-Bot, ZéroBot, Lateg, Ὁ οἶστρος, H3llBot, Kilopi, Aichonic, IGeMiNix, L Kensington, Dan56789, MonoAV, Donner60, Clementina, HandsomeFella, Doggy141, Ginsengsniper, Showard506, 28bot, ClueBot NG, Iiii I I I, Logos111, 5thhourclass, Wikiepdiax818, Hurunui99, NextUSprez, PolySciJoe, Curb Chain, Calidum, Jaydoubleuu, Oakb, Kinaro, Jefkitz, BG19bot, Prcc27, Mark Arsten, ErikBly, Compfreak7, Fairlyoddparents1234, Asa Gordon, FatGrover, Polmandc, Doingurmom6my9, Achowat, Jannaapple, Bartonkj, BattyBot, Cyberbot II, Saedon, Kelvinsong, Dylanvt, Makecat-bot, Jeffrey L Albertson, SFK2, Jamesx12345, Rogr101, PinkAmpersand, Epicgenius, Fu7gffeg7456, HerpaDerpaLerpa, BreakfastJr, NottNott, Finnusertop, Postybj, Monkbot, Vieque, Xxbean5xx, BethNaught, Mikeonthenet, Ecm6118, Oranges Juicy, Cewlt, KasparBot, MB298, Cruelmentelpro, JoeSmash and Anonymous: 1280

- **President of the United States** *Source:* https://en.wikipedia.org/wiki/President_of_the_United_States?oldid=707163941 *Contributors:* Damian Yerrick, Magnus Manske, Kpjas, RjLesch, The Epopt, Vulture, Brion VIBBER, Mav, Bryan Derksen, Robert Merkel, The Anome, Berek, Koyaanis Qatsi, RobLa, Taw, Ed Poor, Alex.tan, Eclecticology, Youssefsan, Danny, Shsilver, Sfmontyo, Rmhermen, Toby Bartels, Fubar Obfusco, Nate Silva, DavidLevinson, Shri, Ryguasu, Montrealais, Tzartzam, Hephaestos, Tedernst, Someone else, Hfastedge, Edward, Lorenzarius, Patrick, Infrogmation, D, Erik Zachte, Fred Bauder, Dante Alighieri, Ronincyberpunk, Jtdirl, GUllman, Gabbe, Hoshie, Ixfd64, Dcljr, Eurleif, Paul Benjamin Austin, Delirium, Dori, Minesweeper, Tregoweth, JerryG, Card~enwiki, Ahoerstemeier, Mac, Jimfbleak, Arwel Parry, Snoyes, Angela, Den fjättrade ankan~enwiki, Jebba, ToastyKen, Kingturtle, BigFatBuddha, DropDeadGorgias, Amcaja, LouI, Vzbs34, Susurrus, Kwekubo, Katagelophobia, Jiang, Dod1, Palfrey, Jeandré du Toit, Astudent, GCarty, Wnissen, Ghewgill, Mxn, BRG, Hashar, Jengod, Mulad, Smith03, The Tom, Timwi, Dcoetzee, Reddi, Tedius Zanarukando, Daniel Quinlan, WhisperToMe, Wik, DJ Clayworth, Haukurth, Gepwiki, Vancouverguy, Tpbradbury, Maximus Rex, Saltine, VeryVerily, Ryoho, StinKerr, Bevo, Nricardo, Morven, Lord Emsworth, Mackensen, Kewpid, Fvw, Raul654, AnonMoos, Mtcv, Jerzy, Jusjih, Eugene van der Pijll, Flockmeal, Adam Carr, David.Monniaux, MrWeeble, Pollinator, UninvitedCompany, Critic, Onebyone, Dimadick, Sjorford, Donarreiskoffer, Branddobbe, Dale Arnett, Phil R, Friedo, Jmabel, Goethean, ZimZalaBim, Yelyos, Naddy, Modulatum, Lowellian, Postdlf, Rfc1394, Academic Challenger, Puckly, Desmay, Meelar, Timrollpickering, DHN, Pm06420, Jondel, Acegikmo1, Look upon my works, ye Mighty, and despair!, Hadal, JackofOz, Wereon, Aggelophoros, Lupo, Seth Ilys, Diberri, Guy Peters, Hcheney, Xanzzibar, Oobopshark, Mattflaschen, Dina, Davidcannon, Matt Gies, Alexwcovington, DocWatson42, Christopher Parham, Jacoplane, Rickscholz, Wikilibrarian, Philwelch, Nunh-huh, Cobaltbluetony, Tom harrison, Binadot, Cool Hand Luke, Dissident, Neuro, Peruvianllama, Everyking, Bkonrad, Curps, Gamaliel, Jdavidb, Cantus, Rpyle731, Zaphod Beeblebrox, Pteron, Guanaco, Alensha, Tom-, Iota, Ikari, Solipsist, Dumbo1, Iceberg3k, Gzornenplatz, Steggall, Python eggs, Avala, Pne, AdamJacobMuller, Bobblewik, Deus Ex, Edcolins, Golbez, Sexyfoxboy, Gugganij, OldakQuill, JFKtruth, Stevietheman, Lawrennd, Fishal, Chowbok, Mackeriv, Utcursch, DocSigma, Fys, Joshua Roberts, Lst27, R. fiend, Zeimusu, Proberts2003, Antandrus, Williamb, BozMo, Fredcondo, MarkSweep, Doops, Saline, Jossi, Huntington, Rdsmith4, Kesac, EBB, Krg~enwiki, Ellsworth, Husnock, PFHLai, Simplicius, Burgundavia, Jawed, Satori, Chrisn4255, Pmanderson, Hammersfan, Zfr, Jareha, Howardjp, B.d.mills, An~enwiki, Neutrality, Sam, Joyous!, GreenReaper, M1ss1ontomars2k4, Deleteme42, Zondor, Adashiel, TheObtuseAngleOfDoom, Grunt, Ericg, The stuart, Lacrimosus, Esperant, Jimaginator, Gazpacho, Gamingboy, Mike Rosoft, PRiis, D6, Dbaron, Monkeyman, Pmadrid, RedWordSmith, Lumrs, Erc, PrinceValium, Moverton, Discospinster, Themadmac, William Pietri, Rich Farmbrough, Alsadius, Rhobite, Supercoop, Hydrox, FiP, Wrp103, Vsmith, Ktwsolo, Ahkond, Rorschach567, Xezbeth, Abelson, Erolos, Horkana, SocratesJedi, 1pezguy, LeoDV, Paul August, SpookyMulder, Lachatdelarue, Bender235, ESkog, Carrp, Sc147, Andrejj, Alxt, Kbh3rd, Mateo SA, A purple wikiuser, Kaisershatner, Loren36, Jice, MyNameIsNotBob, Aranel, Ylee, CanisRufus, Mr. Billion, LordHarris, Livajo, Zscout370, Szyslak, Shrike, Kross, Laurascudder, Aude, Shanes, Tom, Art LaPella, RoyBoy, EurekaLott, Djd1219, Coolcaesar, Adambro, Causa sui, Bastique, ParaVach, Bobo192, Vanished user sdfkjertiwoi1212u5mcake, Martey, NetBot, Feitclub, Smalljim, Clawson, John Vandenberg, Fremsley, Old Right, Kevin Myers, JW1805, Arcadian, Howlader, SNIyer1, Joshlmay, Man vyi, Sasquatch, Kbir1, TMS63112, Ardric47, RussBlau, Pperos, Obradovic Goran, Idleguy, MPerel, Sam Korn, Ral315, Pharos, Supersexyspacemonkey, Luckyluke, Matthewcieplak, Jcrocker, Wpopp~enwiki, Shirimasen, Danski14, Musiphil, Defunkt, Chizu, Terrycojones, Alphaboi867, Redxiv, Polarscribe, Jordan117, Jamyskis, Borisblue, Philosophistry, Babajobu, Rlazarowich, Andrewpmk, Craigy144, User6854, AzaToth, Calton, Ekko, WikipediaAdmin, Mattley, Kel-nage, DLJessup, Mac Davis, InShaneee, Gblaz, Cdc, Gerry Edgar, Malo, Katefan0, Stillnotelf, Scott5114, MattWade, Snowolf, Zsero, Sir Joseph, Dreyfus, Angelic Wraith, Dhartung, Dschwen, Captain Seafort, RPH, Fourthords, Andreas C~enwiki, Mike Beidler, Cburnett, Luspari, Evil Monkey, Omphaloscope, Grenavitar, Randy Johnston, TenOfAllTrades, Sciurinæ, Mcmillin24, Pethr, BLueFiSH.as, R6MaY89, Vuo, Kaiser matias, Dominic, Joshbrez, Computerjoe, Ianblair23, Zereshk, Netkinetic, Thore, Dan100, Kbolino, Dismas, CaptainMike, Siafu, KUsam, Stemonitis, The JPS, Rorschach, Jeffrey O. Gustafson, Mário, OwenX, Woohookitty, Doctor Boogaloo, Georgia guy, TigerShark, Anilocra, Derktar, LOL, Tripodics, Scjessey, JustDerek, Pol098, Before My Ken, ^demon, WadeSimMiser, MONGO, Sdgjake, Moormand, Tabletop, Bkwillwm, Dah31, Bbatsell, Damicatz, Bradybd, El Suizo, OCNative, RicJac, Skywriter, Mb1000, Prezboy1, Zzyzx11, EvilOverlordX, TheEvilBlueberryCouncil, Emops, Wayward, Elithea, Doco, BrenDJ, Bad Graphics Ghost, Essjay, LinkTiger, Karam.Anthony.K, Oleg Schultz, Zpb52, Turnstep, Lords Page, Bluefruitbowl, Dysepsion, Youngamerican, Paxsimius, LeoO3, Graham87, KyuuA4, Deltabeignet, Magister Mathematicae, GoldRingChip, Keeves, Johnhpaulin, BD2412, Penguin X, Wachholder0, MaxZolt, Kbdank71, FreplySpang, Cmsg, Plau, Zzedar, RxS, Dennypayne, Electionworld, Unshakeable123, Search4Lancer, Canderson7, Kotukunui, Sjakkalle, Rjwilmsi, Koavf, Rogerd, Dpark, Kinu, Gryffindor, Wikibofh, Vary, Strait, Rillian, Linuxbeak, Seraphimblade, Harro5, MZMcBride, BCV, Funnyhat, Ccson, Oblivious, Cww, ElKevbo, Durin, The wub, Bhadani, MikeJ9919, Fred Bradstadt, GregAsche, Jbamb, Sango123, Ian Moyes, Yamamoto Ichiro, SNIyer12, Sheldrake, Silver1569, Exeunt, Messenger88, Titoxd, FlaBot, Osprey39, Ian Pitchford, DDerby, SchuminWeb, G Clark, Ground Zero, Doc glasgow, Djrobgordon, Cooldoug111, KarlFrei, IceDrake523, Crazycomputers, Bitoffish, Nivix, AJR, Shadow007, Rune.welsh, SportsMaster, RexNL, Gurch, Redwolf24, Wars, NoSeptember, RasputinAXP, Vonspringer, Wolfpackfan72, Pikiwedia~enwiki, Steveo2, EronMain, Alphachimp, Jehb, Tysto, Zotel, Gurubrahma, Snailwalker, Imnotminkus, JonathanFreed, Coolhawks88, Butros, MichaelJBuck, King of Hearts, Scimitar, Chobot, El Slameron, Copperchair, Mhking, JesseGarrett, VolatileChemical, Cactus.man, Hall Monitor, Digitalme, Noble Skuld the Legend Killer, Gwernol, Algebraist, Flcelloguy, The Rambling Man, YurikBot, Wavelength, Borgx, BuddyJesus, Angus Lepper, Grifter84, Lordsutch, Sceptre, NTBot~enwiki, Trainthh, Theredstarswl, Arado, Red Slash, Jtkiefer, Splash, Epolk, CASportsFan, GreatGreg, SluggoOne, SpuriousQ, Todasco, Reddevil0728, GusF, Tonywiki, Nurmsook, Akamad, Stephenb, Jim Campbell, Lord Voldemort, Gaius Cornelius, Rsrikanth05, Wimt, RadioKirk, Flyguy33, Lusanaherandraton, Notchcode, NawlinWiki, Yserarau, Kreia, Dhwani1989, SEWilcoBot, Wiki alf, Cryptoid, Robertvan1, NickBush24, Ou tis, Jaxl, Johann Wolfgang, Rjensen, Darker Dreams, Taco325i, R'son-W, Joelr31, Cybrspunk, Silver149, Jhurlburt, Cleared as filed, JDoorjam, Irishguy, Nick, Retired username, Mshecket, Midnite Critic, Brandon, Cholmes75, Matticus78, Millermz, WiteoutKing, PeepP, BertK, Misza13, DerEikopf, Tony1, DGJM, Gertie, Rodyx, Lockesdonkey, Kyle Barbour, Drumsac, J2kiddj, Arcman, Psy guy, Mddake, Supspirit, Private Butcher, Obi-WanKenobi-2005, Haemo, Brisvegas, Ballodisco, User27091, David Underdown, Wknight94, TransUtopian, Fallout boy, Novasource, FF2010, Newagelink, Sandstein, 21655, Zzuuzz, Shinhan, Mike Dillon, Black Regent, Bayerischermann, Enricoincognito, Barryob, Nikkimaria, Theda, Closedmouth, Spondoolicks, Harrythemaster, Pb30, Th1rt3en, CapitalLetterBeginning, Lynbarn, Jaberwockynmt, Asmallwhitecube, Canley, Sean Whitton, BorgQueen, TheImpossibleMan, Duroy~enwiki, Rlove, JoanneB, TBadger, Vicarious, Alias Flood, Shawnc, WinOne4TheGipper, Peter, Karatenerd, HereToHelp, Whobot, Xil, Jesup, ArielGold, Easter Monkey, Garion96, Staxringold, Ybbor, SunKing, Kungfuadam, CD Random, Le Hibou~enwiki, SDS, Teryx, Philip Stevens, GrinBot~enwiki, SkerHawx, DVD R W, Monsieurtode, Luk, Hiddekel, Kalsermar, Isoxyl, The Wookieepedian, Sardanaphalus, Veinor, Sintonak.X, Remiel, SmackBot, Shadow2700, Wangyunfeng, Tessanoth, H2eddsf3, Unschool, Narson, Monocrat, Feedyourfeet, Saravask, Moeron, Mangoe, Davepape, Jacobrs, Prodego, KnowledgeOfSelf, Chazz88, Melchoir, Bjelleklang, Primetime, Pgk, Matusu, Rrius, Ikip, KocjoBot~enwiki, Davewild, Patrickneil, Setanta747 (locked), DWaterson, Chairman S., Michael Dorosh, Renesis, Dwp49423, Delldot, Eskimbot, KelleyCook, Wizard1022, RobotJcb, BigD527, K8TEK, Bburton, Edgar181, HalfShadow, Relaxing, TypoDotOrg, The Rhymesmith, Notea42, Gilliam, Ohnoitsjamie, Oscarthecat, Skizzik, Political Lefty, Daysleeper47, CmdrClow, Smeggysmeg, Jeffro77, Juve2000, LotteryOhYah, Izehar, Chris the speller, Master Jay, Bluebot, Alexmagnus~enwiki, Keegan, Parajuris, Persian Poet Gal, Josh K, Rmt2m, Swanner, Bonesiii, Tree Biting Conspiracy, Liamdaly620, Lusanders, Ocicat, Norad918, Kemet, Android32̂, Timneu22, BrendelSignature, RayAYang, Comedy240, The Rogue Penguin, Zarf, Breadandcheese, Schi, Baronnet, Roy Al Blue, ArgentiumOutlaw, Everett polanski, Mortel3, AKMask, Gracenotes, Lightspeedchick, GoodDay, John Reaves, Mjl0509, Dethme0w, Can't sleep, clown will eat me, Jakie3, Kristbg, AP1787, VarunGupta, Pher~enwiki, Onorem, Vcrs, Dev1n, Yidisheryid, Malnova, Arod14, Rrburke, Krsont, Andy120290, Dbdb, Bolivian Unicyclist, Coz 11, Elendil's Heir, Blueboar, Grover cleveland, The tooth, AndySimpson, Censorwolf, CharonX, Fonduelazone, Dharmabum420, Jmlk17, Krich, Hypergeometric2F1(a,b,c,x), Flyguy649, Rick man, Smooth O, Hateless, Bowlhover, Nakon, Underbar dk, TedE, Jared, Zen611, Daveserpa, Aelffin, Miked84, Chargh, WaldoJ, Mtmelendez, SnappingTurtle, TrogdorPolitiks, Eran of Arcadia, Anoriega, Brainyiscool, RideThatPony35, Fordzo, LKLIII, Nathans, AshleyHandley, Jklin, Lawsonrob, Fredgoat, DavidSSabb, Kotjze, Ericl, Scalga, Fatla00, Ashi Starshade, Niremetal, Where, Sigma 7, Ligulembot, Attucks, Mwelch, Lph, Kukini, Coat of Arms, Ohconfucius, JLogan, Redlegsfan21, CIS, The undertow, Esrever, Chitoryu12, Nishkid64, Jcembree, DMB, Producercunningham, Jjjjjjjjjj, Fifty7, BrownHairedGirl, Good Intentions, Grizzwald, Zmehlo, John, Dreslough, Jaffer, Abrazame, MrKing84, WhartoX, Mrom, MilborneOne, Armyrifle9, Lukeward, Sir Nicholas de Mimsy-Porpington, MarcusGraly, Miles530, Al1encas1no, Edwy, Coredesat, Robovski, Javit, Bloodpack, Syferus, Ocatecir, Jaywubba1887, IronGargoyle, Archangel127, Marblewonder, Nagle, Alf melmac, The Tramp, Edward.armitage, 041744, Shaoquan, RandomCritic, 16@r, A. Parrot, Jtciszewski, Stupid Corn, Timmeh, Werdan7, Davemcarlson, Beetstra, Fishbowlbob, Freyr35, Hypnosifl, Haslo04, Spejic, Meco, Ductape, Renrenren, AdultSwim, Ravi12346, Onetwo1, Chris.read, Norman bates, Citicat, RMHED, JesusChrist1, Beck162, Varuag doos, PSUMark2006, Ryanjunk, Impm, Chart123, TheMagician, Nsidney, Hectorian, NinjaCharlie, ShakingSpirit, KJS77, TJ Spyke, Isaac Crumm, Levineps, Fan-1967, 293.xx.xxx.xx, NEMT, Michaelbusch, Krick, Joseph Solis in Australia, Shoeofdeath, Gomarlins, Sander Säde, Ludo716, J Di, Scott777, Admiral06, Calebolson, Labz, Shoreranger, Octane, Richard75, Lucy-marie, Hokeman, Civil Engineer III, Courcelles, Lifeverywhere, Mlucasone, Anger22, Eluchil404, Fdp, Tawkerbot2, Shmoogle728, Lincmad, IronChris, Southleft, Eric71186, Thomas81, Jombage, Alexthe5th, SkyWalker, JForget, GeneralIroh, Erazor~enwiki, InvisibleK, Anthony22, Dan0 00, CmdrObot, Mattbr, TimothyHorrigan, Sjmcfarland, Vanished user sojweiorj34i4f, SammyJames, Scohoust, Aherunar, Clindberg, Void23, RedRollerskate, JohnCD, Macg4cubeboy, Munkee madness, Duke of Yarmouth, CWY2190, Schweiwikist, Im.a.lumberjack, KnightLago, Seandog3152, Stenquist, Shyran, Orannis, Dgw, Connect.Media, Carouselambra, Pseudo-Richard, Mctaviix, Ferdiaob, Evilhairyhamster, MarsRover, Moreschi, Neelix, CmdrDan, Chrisahn, Ken Gallager, Ispy1981, MrFish, RagingR2, Hemlock Martinis, Nilfanion, TJDay, Chessmaster3, Vaquero100, Cydebot, Yrodro, Aarondaniel652, Nick Charlton, Reywas92, Computervillan, Zeppelin462, Petercoyl, Gogo Dodo, JFreeman, Flowerpotman, Corpx, DangApricot, Redsox00002, Soetermans, Cuzza, Tawkerbot4, Demomoke, Dragomiloff, Codetiger, Xusmc7, DumbBOT, JCO312, L d allan, GoLeafsGo2626, Shemela, FastLizard4, Allabo, Darkchocobo12, Akcarver, Dinnerbone, Pauljeffersonks, Inkington, Omicronpersei8, DarkAsSin, Longhorn966, Hangovergoblin, LarryQ, RickDC, Emperornortonx, Rougher07, RandomOrca2, MLBbrad, Mercury~enwiki, Signor Pastrini, Bchalfin, LeeG, LactoseTI, Eminemsuperman, ThaWhistle, Colesupperman1, Xela Yrag, IndepIntel, Kablammo, Alfredw, Steve Dufour, 1234567890qwer, Lanky, TK421, Mojo Hand, Coidzor, Oliver202, Id447, Newton2, HirschiHusky05, West Brom 4ever, John254, Tapir Terrific, Neil916, Woody, SomeStranger, Leon7, ThreePointOneFour, Jonny-mt, Jacoblp, Philippe, CharlotteWebb, Therequiembellishere, Michael A. White, Cooljuno411, WhaleyTim, Tree Hugger, Natalie Erin, Scottandrewhutchins, Raditzu, Northumbrian, Escarbot, Eleuther, Danielfolsom, Dantheman531, Libs23, Mentifisto, AntiVandalBot, Gioto, Luna Santin, Heyfunboy, CheckeredFlag200, Rictuar, Opelio, Mab819c, Courtjester555, Prolog, Benny45boy, Autocracy, Edokter, Readro, Catfoo, Naffe, Artjunky, Daniel Villalobos, Fayenatic london, HRHITTER3000, Ktappe, Mark Smith 617, Fmmarianicolon, Superzohar, Danger, Farosdaughter, Blu3d, L0b0t, Zedla, Yellowdesk, Ozgod, Pixelface, Tails Soda, Sima Yi, GTPoompt, Dockurt2k, AubreyEllenShomo, Matthew0820, Bscottbrown, Goran Baotic, Tomertomer, Raukodacil, Serpent's Choice, Erxnmedia, JAnDbot, Winndm31, Leuko, Husond, Jimothytrotter, Wiki0709, MER-C, BlindEagle, Lifthrasir1, Flipfellax1, Sanchom, Hello32020, Db099221, Reticulum, Nevermore27, BenB4, Roleplayer, Hut 8.5, Firefox1975, Dricherby, Fro chill, Biddenden, Billywhack, Knowpedia, Slowhandsd, Kerotan, Joshua, Martan, LittleOldMe, SteveSims, Freshacconci, Joebengo, Huphelmeyer, Penubag, Knowledgesmith, Casmith 789, Magioladitis, Mikemill, Kcilawman, Ztack08, WolfmanSF, Hroðulf, Kelleyo2l, Bongwarrior, VoABot II, MiguelMunoz, Doodoobutter, Vitaminman, AuburnPilot, Chevinki, Wikidudeman, Mlbtaz, Qomak, Conor McManus, Alexander Domanda, JoDB, Doublenickle59, Mbc362, Niathabiti, FMSW, Cryptosquid, Keith H., LafinJack, SwedishConqueror, Armona, Jim Douglas, Nyttend, Jatkins, Brusegadi, Hasbro, KConWiki, Soleado, Catgut, Indon, Kxfz inf, The Mystery Man, Loonymonkey, Terjen, Allstarecho, Kosan~enwiki, Mike Payne, Mr. Bad, Gede, DruPagz44, PoliticalJunkie, Damuna, Just James, Glen, DerHexer, JaGa, BATE Borisov, Huadpe, Mika293, LW77, Fuzzycass, DIEXEL, Markco1, Jonomacdrones, Gjd001, Jdrsmith, Milece, Dr. Morbius, Krinsky, Maverick-X, Hdt83, MartinBot, Socialism forever, Deltawalton, Reconfirm, Jeendan, Akbeancounter, AznElliot518, UnfriendlyFire, Jay Dogg, Braningillespie, Notmyhandle, Rettetast, Sm8900, Actorma, Mschel, CommonsDelinker, AlexiusHoratius, Linkerules, WelshMatt, Smokizzy, Pomte, Yangliu239, Ssolbergj, J.delanoy, GreenRunner0, Cospelero, Nympho1, Colacool, Dingoman, Rex13a, ChrisfromHouston, Ztjank, Ginsengbomb, Eliz81, Jerry, Dave Dial, Skippy-9, Paraparanormal, Zamyatin, Potentially broken, Vanished user 342562, SU Linguist, Zaphodyossarian, Tdadamemd, GreenawayJ, OfficeGirl, Lt. penguin, Coxtastic, Waynehead777, It Is Me Here, Duece22, Katalaveno, Dreko, Natobxl, I do things, Parrotman, Janus Shadowsong, Patrioticanti-american, Starnestommy, S4diStiC, Zedboy, L'Aquatique, OAC, Anetheron589, B64, Monkey.choker, JayJasper, Calder Pegden, Pyrospirit, Noahcs, Comp25, Homesun, Vanished User 4517, Antony-22, Hudrew101, Ajlipp, Aervanath, SJP, Carewser, I love Snake, R-pantheon-7, Ss654, Malerin, KCinDC, Themoodyblue, Carl wilhoyte, Mufka, Shoessss, Linkracer, Sunderland06, Icecreamania, 2help, Mxh2o, Juliancolton, Len124, Dlins24, Salmans801, Burzmali, Foofighter20x, DH85868993, WikiDaily, SBKT, Veghead13, Mookabear, Swinquest, Omnihunter, Jvcdude, Knowledge26, Packerfansam, Dorftrottel, Buendorf, UnitedStatesIndia, Martial75, The Behnam, Xiahou, Yhac, ThePointblank, Donking90~enwiki, Starwars10, Signalhead, Wikieditor06, Spear of fire, Cyphern, Alexdb2005, Egghead06, Lights, X!, G2bambino, Sam Blacketer, Senorpepr, TreasuryTag, CWii, Thedjatclubrock, Aledevries, A.Ou, Infoman99, DarthSci, Lazy fcuk, Jbill007, Imanutting, Jeff G., Regnisied, Grey Blot, Kerrow, Qwerty1212, Linefeed, Kingsley911, Aesopos, Barneca, Olsolino,

Scholarofpastandpresent, Umalee, Irish Pearl, Mike Castle, JayEsJay, RPlunk2853, Charleca, Jerseysurfer99, TheVault, Jwf505, MAtchley911, SeanNovack, Maximillion Pegasus, Spainpink, Moreno Valley User, ProfPhys, Baileypalblue, Malljaja, Amir beckham, Miranda, Obafgkm, Z.E.R.O., Anonymous Dissident, Rigel B, Valencerian, Llamabr, Sean D Martin, Rrhyno, SteveStrummer, Macslacker, Callmewhatyouwill2001, Shindo9Hikaru, Froggy33, Terence7, TheSpeakerOfTruth, Seraphim, Corvus cornix, Adam-machiavelli, Zr970, Leafyplant, Werideatdusk33, Jordan1226, Kirsten07734, Lou.weird, Manchurian candidate, Simon Palmucci, Zsalamander, Cremepuff222, Info999, Harayda, Mjhammerle123, Fattyvajj, Cpatt58, ThrakAttack, Veers117, Romeisburning, Greswik, Doug, Improve~enwiki, Pious7, Complex (de), Feefeefee2, Jwalkrooles, OverMyHead, Happyme22, Comrade Tux, Lilking0028, Kutieangel15118, Bawm79, 9allenride9, Enviroboy, Denvermountains, 82muchman, Bengalbh7325, Sylent, Mrstevencool, Twsimmo, Karlbrezner, Justmeherenow, Miguelkane, The Brown Man, Entirelybs, Vodkationn, Brianga, Secretservgy, Twooars, WelshDoctor, BillyBobChhist, Eli81993, Jophisr, Tvinh, Superphobe75, IndulgentReader, Trisha-1616, Bmds, Nithinaprakash, Red, Johnolsen13, Demmy, The Random Editor, Hackerstatus, Motorcross1100, Crazydude4life, KPB15, CN110893, Coffee, DerekDD92, TJRC, Grant.Alpaugh, Dems on the move, Scarian, Euryalus, Patfan100, Tupac4ever88722, Jauerback, Virtual Cowboy, Smarterchild7, Paddymc68, Tbo 157, Dawn Bard, Caltas, Universe=atom, Gamma180, Sandersonjoe222, Senkei242, Tdfty, Deeznuts555, Triwbe, Eclectic star, Snake4556, Calabraxthis, Kirlin43, Stratman07, Big Dazz, Barliner, Z1216, Vandill 01, Oober349, Keilana, McGrupp10799, Lordokagespencer, HimMan, Quest for Truth, Eenyminy, Radon210, Exert, DanceDanceRevolution, Superscott94, The Evil Spartan, Gqbrown, Jojalozzo, Matthewedwards, BigJimDawsonRules, Mailman9, Darth Kalwejt, Doestube, Ayudante, Jackwsteiner, MamaChicken, Oxymoron83, Moberg23, Monster009, Nuttycoconut, Baseball Bugs, 1.21 jigwatts, Jdaloner, Lochiel, Lightmouse, Hotmama1234, Tombomp, Memorymaster, LuciusValens, Ksuwildcats10, Ambobjill, Int21h, Juhwader, Samkremer, Mk32, Zzjaszz, Fratrep, Gonezales, 13djb13, Musse-kloge, Papenpau000, Kumioko (renamed), Dillard421, Graygreen89, RandomHumanoid, Spindext, Vojvodaen, Maelgwnbot, Presidentman, Gorrrilla5, Lil george walker bush, Hubertfarnsworth, B4L24, William Saturn, Thebigga, EveryDayJoe45, Shekimuli, Superbeecat, Iamwisesun, Lloydpick, Dylan55555, Into The Fray, Pdxx123, Furado, Muhends, Jbloun1, Jw2034, Jamesfranklingresham, Smashville, Faithlessthewonderboy, Bgrimer, ClueBot, Asdfghjkl1991, QueenofBattle, Syco bob1, Bkporter12, Sunfiregx, Matrek, Joeandspank, Mbutts04, Wikievil666, Eric Wester, Adlkjgqafdl, Bob1370, Rjd0060, Jordansean, EoGuy, Dean Wormer, Steve The Steve, Lawrence Cohen, Boo1210, Supertouch, Rise Above the Vile, Arakunem, Mrs.EasterBunny, Gayatri Chauhan, Dalielah, Bobisbob, Michael.Urban, Loks1995, Objective3000, Lantay77, Ventusa, JTBX, Stevesim89, Lightninggremlin, Tmflemi, Kjohnson16, 03ctodd, Matfernan1, Shanewhiting, Evinco, Jlocalled, Thbraith, Cluedo, Phuntsok2000, Grandpallama, Qwerty9999999999, Ahamill, Andy4stacey7, Snocrates, Tonythetiger5, Kev2310, Presidentjiok, GoldenGoose100, Ihatebush1, Ottre, HaloZero00, Savethecheerleaderssavetheworld, Rook2pawn, Lartoven, Readin, Ghostrider, NuclearWarfare, Mjj4, Cenarium, Jwking, 1manfern, StartSh1tUp, JamieS93, Cheatcode2, Cedarkey1, Steven Evens, Twc779, Rtgriffis5, SchreiberBike, Sallicio, John Paul Parks, Aitias, Littleteddy, Versus22, Felix B. C., SDY, Blow of Light, Mythdon, Party, DumZiBoT, Novjunulo, G W BUSH IS A DICTATOR, Pitt, Your mom is hottt, Masher oz, SMP0328., Roots42, Bearsona, HALALpork, SUNAT, Will-B, Rich Baldwin, Anthonym2008, Guy43821, Utkarshshah007, Boulderdash56, Whoischristopher, Presidentdust, Guitarmasters, Rreagan007, Charles Sturm, Facts707, WikHead, Kbx3, Xander66, Luvernfrends, Firebat08, Alexius08, Noctibus, Kinghamza1, Eleven even, FrostyLars, Classy.luke, PeterWD, Hiskett2, AlphOmeGuy, Totlmstr, Rokenrollskater, Anticipation of a New Lover's Arrival, The, Ryan-McCulloch, Kajabla, Addbot, Man with one red shoe, Roentgenium111, I'mnotlame, Casey1817, DesMoinesDude, Tanliste, Jojhutton, Blubberboy92, Drexlerlk, IXavier, Matth942, Laurinavicius, Leszek Jańczuk, Driscoll42, Jordan Timmins, Skittleman42, LinkFA-Bot, Eighteen and a half, Alanscottwalker, Emdrgreg, BennyQuixote, Bhentze, Everyme, MileyDavidA, Yobot, JJARichardson, TaBOT-zerem, AmaraBot, GateKeeper, Jrboi, Vibrantspirit, Squeeze me, Ayrton Prost, AnakngAraw, MHLU, Azcolvin429, Bbb23, Szajci, AnomieBOT, PonileExpress, Jeanpuetz, TJD2, Galoubet, AdjustShift, MovieMan123, Katenbail, Mn6230, Materialscientist, Lucas Leon, Citation bot, ZenCopain, GB fan, B. Fairbairn, Xqbot, Mostlyghostly, Yellowluis, TinucherianBot II, Nash16, Spiretas, Cureden, Antimony Manganide, TracyMcClark, Khajidha, BsaPR1996, Purplebackpack89, Laurence Gilcrest, MarinusPHI, BSCOUT13, The Evil IP address, Tomwsulcer, BritishWatcher, Intelligentlove, RozenGlobetrotter, Typative, Miesianiacal, Mcoupal, Omnipaedista, ConservativeLiberalLiberalConservative, Future2008, Mark Schierbecker, RibotBOT, Mathonius, Erwin Springer, Hero of Time 87, Mirada1923, Yoganate79, Doulos Christos, Phxsuns562, Pinkygirl91, Drdpw, GhalyBot, MerlLinkBot, Howsa12, Dinamyte, Chexandy89, Charles Savard-Daigle, Thehelpfulbot, Cekli829, Tktru, FrescoBot, CMWrestlemaniaPunkCharlie, Gaydenver, HJ Mitchell, Chard513, Citation bot 1, Bjkijkjr83, Fat&Happy, Tkexb173, Lars Washington, Tahir mq, Bilabong205, Brucejoel99, Contributor tom, Crusoe8181, ImmortalYawn, Kildruf, Victor Victoria, Trappist the monk, Khaotika, Vale Dator, FoxBot v3, WCCasey, IRISZOOM, Innotata, Tbhotch, Fry1989, Arathjp, RjwilmsiBot, Lilly granger, Dlambe3, Matt-eee, DRAGON BOOSTER, Nima1024, Never give in, Leemfrank, King-Macca, Primefac, Nations United, GoingBatty, KeithL2156, Gwillhickers, TJ994, Hamish8, Kensta2k9, Italia2006, MageLam, NearThe-Zoo, Illegitimate Barrister, H3llBot, Kira817, Petropetro, Brandmeister, Percepeters, Thewolfchild, Mlang.Finn, ChuispastonBot, Handsome-Fella, Шиманьский Василь, Frizbaloid, ClueBot NG, B633980v, -sche, AeroPsico, Lord Roem, Spartan7W, Suresh 5, North Atlanticist Usonian, NextUSprez, Helpful Pixie Bot, Asdfjkl1235, Tholme, Calidum, Cseanburns, SchroCat, BG19bot, Ceradon, Crocodilesareforwimps, CTF83!, Alt, Drift chambers, Félix Wolf, The Almightey Drill, Medo4, Ernio48, LFevas, Alarbus, Schwarzy1, Brhiba, Wer900, Rileychilds, BattyBot, Pendragon5, Pottinger's cats, Hipposcrashed, Dawn Eastwood, EuroCarGT, IjonTichyIjonTichy, Futurist110, P3Y229, Jisnu, Dexbot, Mogism, Wikignome1213, Timothysandole, PennyDreadful33, Zziccardi, Mungoza28, Rfassbind, Nolanneff555, Vcfahrenbruck, Guycodepoll, Super Nintendo Chalmers, Zdawg1029, WeThePeoples, CapLiber, Billybob2002, IM-yb, YiFeiBot, J-boogie7, FNCwatcher, Archwayh, Estreberto, Monkbot, SA Thomas1994, Mmdvids, Saad Awan 951, UglowT, StanMan87, Anonymous427, Eriwawo, Nightwingandbats!, MrMaximMinkin, Happy Wisdom, Prinsgezinde, KasparBot, Hi, Boy Named Stu, CAPTAIN RAJU, Huritisho, Bduheh, Hunter11701, Spienciak and Anonymous: 2163

- **Vice President of the United States** *Source:* https://en.wikipedia.org/wiki/Vice_President_of_the_United_States?oldid=707009798 *Contributors:* Tobias Hoevekamp, RjLesch, Vicki Rosenzweig, Taw, Jeronimo, Ortolan88, Roadrunner, Zoe, Hephaestos, Ubiquity, Lorenzarius, Michael Hardy, Dante Alighieri, Gabbe, Hoshie, CORNELIUSSEON, Zanimum, IZAK, Delirium, Minesweeper, NicoNet, TUF-KAT, Jebba, Kingturtle, DropDeadGorgias, Vzbs34, Jiang, John K, Hashar, Jengod, Smith03, The Tom, Revolver, Janko, Tedius Zanarukando, Daniel Quinlan, Savantpol, WhisperToMe, DJ Clayworth, Vancouverguy, Tpbradbury, Maximus Rex, Tempshill, Nricardo, Frihet, Jlavezzo, Dpbsmith, Jfruh, Pakaran, Adam Carr, EdwinHJ, Robbot, Sensor, Josh Cherry, Moondyne, Psychonaut, Calmypal, Lowellian, Postdlf, Pobbard, Timrollpickering, Sunray, Hadal, JackofOz, Xanzzibar, Dmn, AmericanCentury21, Davidcannon, Alan Liefting, Centrx, DocWatson42, Marnanel, Morria, NightThree, Meursault2004, Bkonrad, Gamaliel, Pteron, Gilgamesh~enwiki, Bluejay Young, Wronkiew, Bobblewik, Golbez, Stevietheman, Andycjp, Lst27, CryptoDerk, Plutor, AHM, Antandrus, Fredcondo, Huntington, Rdsmith4, Xtreambar, Ellsworth, Husnock, PFHLai, SimonLyall, Jklamo, Neutrality, Jewbacca, Zondor, Acsenray, Lacrimosus, Jwolfe, Freakofnurture, Pmadrid, DanielCD, Mystery-Dog, Discospinster, Themadmac, Alsadius, Guanabot, Orbital, Sahasrahla, Ibagli, Bender235, Jnestorius, Ylee, Kross, Barfooz, Shanes, Tom, TMC1982, Causa sui, Bobo192, SNIyer1, VBGFscJUn3, Keebler, Sam Korn, Krellis, Vanished user azby388723i8jfjh32, Jonathunder, Ranveig, Jumbuck, Shirimasen, Honeycake, Alansohn, Gary, Leonardo Alves, Luke stebbing, SlimVirgin, Mailer diablo, Redfarmer, Scott5114, AverageGuy, Cburnett, Dtcdthingy, RainbowOfLight, Danthemankhan, Ianblair23, Zereshk, Capecodeph, Forteblast, KriZe, Ron Ritzman, Mullet, Bellhalla, TigerShark, ScottDavis, Camw, Muya, PoccilScript, Jftsang, Poiuyt Man, Robert K S, Briangotts, Before My Ken, WadeSimMiser, Ddye, Tabletop, OCNative, RicJac, Vanished895703, Zzyzx11, Emops, MarcoTolo, LinkTiger, Jack Cox, GoldRingChip, James26, Bunchofgrapes, RxS, CheshireKatz, Electionworld, Josh Parris, Rjwilmsi, Nightscream, Koavf, Rogerd, Ctdunstan, Kinu, Vary, Rillian, Blue-Moonlet, Harro5, Elefuntboy, BCV, SNIyer12, FlaBot, CDThieme, SchuminWeb, Ground Zero, KarlFrei, SouthernNights, Mark83, Gurch, Wars, NoSeptember, Str1977, Quuxplusone, TeaDrinker, Pevernagie, Srleffler, Jtmichcock, Chobot, The Shadow Treasurer, Wasted Time R, Bægx, BuddyJesus, RobotE, Alma Pater, Neitherday, Sceptre, Rs09985, Splash, GusF, Stephenb, Flyguy33, Gcapp1959, NawlinWiki, Exir Kamalabadi, Rjensen, MDolson22, Howcheng, Awiseman, Thiseye, Cleared as filed, Anetode, Edwardlalone, Semperf, CrazyLegsKC, Mart-inHagberg~enwiki, Evrik, Antonio Basto, Mistercow, Typer 525, Nick123, Wknight94, 21655, Zzuuzz, Celtic Knight, Silverhorse, SFGiants, Closedmouth, Arthur Rubin, Josh3580, JQF, Dspradau, Mikeygator, Silverhelm, Wasseralm, Spaltavian, Curpsbot-unicodify, Staxringold, Allens, Kb9wte, White Lightning, Teryx, Philip Stevens, JCheng, That Guy, From That Show!, Sacxpert, Sardanaphalus, 6SJ7, SmackBot, Un-school, Dav2008, Griot~enwiki, KnowledgeOfSelf, Melchoir, Lasloo, C.Fred, Rrius, Davewild, Delldot, AnOddName, Septegram, Gilliam, Ohnoitsjamie, Ghosts&empties, The Gnome, Chris the speller, Happywaffle, Bluebot, BullWikiWinkle, Achmelvic, B00P, Mattweng, Schi, Colonies Chris, Dual Freq, Darth Panda, Mexcellent, GoodDay, Royboycrashfan, AP1787, Erayman64, OrphanBot, Onorem, Folksong, TheK-Man, Andy120290, Addshore, Elendil's Heir, Grover cleveland, Mattsea, Cybercobra, Decltype, Noles1984, Ozdaren, NickPenguin, Jsding, Wizardman, Ericl, Scalga, Aftertheend, Raysoller, Ck lostsword, Synthe, UmbertoM, General Ization, Iglew, Ishmaelblues, Neovu79, IronGargoyle, HADRIANVS, A. Parrot, JHunterJ, MarkSutton, Slakr, SQGibbon, Dicklyon, DCNanney, Meco, AdultSwim, Ryulong, Borninbronx10, TPIRFanSteve, Impm, Kevin W., Levineps, BranStark, Iridescent, Clarityfiend, Joseph Solis in Australia, Bjengles3, Pegasus1138, Labz, CapitalR, Richard75, Stereorock, Courcelles, Bfoaz, Tawkerbot2, Dlohcierekim, Bstepp99, Thomas81, Eastlaw, Dan0 00, Clindberg, Seattledude, W guice, Dynzmoar, Mhenneberry, Yaris678, Cydebot, Karichisholm, Aarondaniel652, Reywas92, Henrymrx, Gogo Dodo, Zginder, Khatru2, DangApricot, ST47, Ttenchantr, DavidRF, Chrislk02, JCO312, In Defense of the Artist, Vanished User jdksfajlasd, Rougher07, DavidSteinle, Thijs!bot, Epbr123, Sarner, Barnej, 0dd1, ClosedEyesSeeing, Unzicker, NorwegianBlue, Basement12, D3gtrd, Hcobb, Dgies, Nick Number, Insomniacpuppy, PaulVIF, Dawnseeker2000, Nizamarain, Gevan, Hires an editor, AntiVandalBot, MoogleDan, Majorly, Luna Santin, Seaphoto, CheckeredFlag200, Akkifokkusu, Ozzieboy, Benny45boy, Billscottbob, Cnota, Jayron32, Edokter, Dr who1975, The Sartorialist, North Shore-man, Spencer, Salgueiro~enwiki, Yellowdesk, JAnDbot, Tigga, MER-C, Instinct, Colotfox, JTRH, Jamesedwardsmith, Acroterion, SteveS-ims, Jonpetteroie, Magioladitis, WolfmanSF, Bongwarrior, VoABot II, AndriusG, FMSW, CTF83!, Gang14, Bubba hotep, Zana Dark, Giggy, Animum, Rmburkhead, Ali'i, The Mystery Man, Huadpe, Verdamondo, LW77, S3000, GM11, Kiore, Viperdude908, Roastytoast, Anaxial, Aquafish, Mschel, CommonsDelinker, ASDFGH, Lilac Soul, J.delanoy, Pharaoh of the Wizards, Rhammang, Trusilver, Adavidb, Whaatt, Uncle Dick, Ginsengbomb, NYCRuss, OohBunnies!, NerdyNSK, Tommy11111, BBrucker2, Acalamari, It Is Me Here, Bishzilla, Abhijitsathe, B64, JayJasper, Snake bgd, Alberto2345, Richard D. LeCour, Bobianite, KCinDC, Jjmillerhistorian, Fusek71, Phirazo, Hanacy, Spshu, KylieTastic, STBotD, Foofighter20x, Vanished user 39948282, Ssd175, Namekal, Bob2717, Andy Marchbanks, Sgeureka, Blood Oath Bot, Quiet Silent Bob, Tuttlemsm, Hunt 4 Orange November, Deor, VolkovBot, TreasuryTag, Jeff G., Dyjodee, SHJohnson, WOSlinker, Suprcel, Philip True-man, TXiKiBoT, Oshwah, Zidonuke, SeanNovack, Maximillion Pegasus, Jmio, Vipinhari, Sswonk, Sg2002, Btmachine333667, Jtenenb, JhsBot, Broadbot, LeaveSleaves, Guldenat, Wiae, Mwilso24, Wenli, Improve~enwiki, Skotywa, Finngall, Happyme22, Aron.Foster, Swingline2000, Nla-gatta, Burntsauce, JHBarclay, Nowax, Angelzfromhell, HiDrNick, AlleborgoBot, Sfmammamia, Schonbrunn, Turok 29, Rontrigger, GoShox, SieBot, Veritably, Ipankonin, Oarsome, Ttony21, Pgp688, Jacotto, RJaguar3, Yintan, Derekdavenport, CRock692, Oda Mari, Momo san, Arat645, Joebrenner, EditorInTheRye, Yerpo, Darth Kalwejt, Antonio Lopez, Faradayplank, Jdaloner, Lightmouse, NvemtIffII, Poindexter Pro-pellerhead, Ralphie G, Neoguru12, Presidentman, William Saturn, Motthoangwehuong, Spotty11222, Ken123BOT, Thoughtman, Pinkadelica, HPJoker, Iamwisesun, Denisarona, Wikijsmak, Big BLA, Explicit, ImageRemovalBot, Atif.t2, MBK004, ClueBot, Harryplopper, Ideal gas equation, The Thing That Should Not Be, Simply Agrestic, Rodhullandemu, Jpc1017, Arakunem, Harland1, Excirial, Anonymous101, Jus-dafax, Andy pyro, PixelBot, Estirabot, NuclearWarfare, Antodav2007, Ember of Light, CowboySpartan, Natty sci~enwiki, JasonAQuest, John Paul Parks, Thingg, Pkylie, Aitias, Versus22, SoxBot III, DumZiBoT, HeadCaptain, SMP0328., Joshgreen22, Wertuose, Rankiri, Bradv, Jo-hhtfd, Rreagan007, Springycom, Facts707, Skarebo, WikHead, AntIsNowHere, NellieBly, Moisesencyclopedia, Saxonthedog, SlubGlub, Bazj, Exclarogative, Addbot, Lordoliver, Willking1979, Jojhutton, Atethnekos, Geekmage4292, Ronhjones, TutterMouse, Jncraton, Fieldday-sunday, Cheney123, AJGrossman, Fluffernutter, Tigerguy999, Jordan Timmins, Orangejuicejunkie, LaaknorBot, Glane23, Snag99, LinkFA-Bot, Blay-lockjam10, William (The Bill) Blackstone, Itfc+canes=me, Seeker alpha806, Tharnton345, Tide rolls, Gail, Wildct387, Bhentze, Legobot, Irvid-ing, Luckas-bot, MileyDavidA, TheSuave, Yobot, 2D, O Fenian, Fraggle81, EditorKid, Noobhunterdude, THEN WHO WAS PHONE?, Gong-show, AnimalExtender, KamikazeBot, 101090ABC, IW.HG, TJDishaw6, AnomieBOT, Marauder40, IRP, Doomcookie222, Tucoxn, Piano non troppo, Yangtairan, Shoneen, AdjustShift, Kingpin13, Law, Mn6230, Ulric1313, Greyish7374, Giants27, Materialscientist, Citation bot, Eric Rowland, Maxis ftw, Noraowolf, Moodyjg, Newsboy50, Joey224455, Jonathan321, Gopal81, Dhruvhemmady, Gtwytoalaska47, Capricorn42, EmikoC, Fantaman3000, Mononomic, Purplebackpack89, Acshy, BALLSTOTHEWALLS5, Breakingsilly, Armbrust, Abce2, Riotrocket8676, Miesianiacal, Irviding11, Yoganate79, Alyssa96, Doulos Christos, Drdpw, GhalyBot, Shadowjams, Spinach Monster, Erik9, Tktru, FrescoBot, Fortdj33, Calibrador, Jessxenos, TharsHammar, Holdme8==D, Pdunc, Pxos, Wildboy7, Kwiki, Danhomer, Democraticsystem, WaffleStomp, Chard513, Citation bot 1, GeneLesterisaMan, Pinethicket, I dream of horses, BigDwiki, Jschnur, Bmclaughlin9, Tahir mq, SpaceFlight89, Brucejoel99, Contributor tom, Kimballru, Cnwilliams, Jeffrd10, Weedwhacker128, ThinkEnemies, Jamietw, Fry1989, DARTH SIDIOUS 2, Difu Wu, Atreklin, RjwilmsiBot, WildBot, DASHBot, Steve03Mills, The Hanukkah Moose, EmausBot, Acather96, Gfoley4, Akjar13, Kris tenrebekah, Da500063, Ezperkins, Tachin34, Nations United, GoingBatty, Hitmonchan, Namebigvinsd, AFA7380, The crooked letter - z no better, Dem1995, Hahahah7, Tommy2010, Winner 42, Wikipelli, MageLam, ZéroBot, Susfele, Illegitimate Barrister, Fæ, Kilopi, Seattle, Brand-meister, Donner60, Thewolfchild, Orange Suede Sofa, Meowwwgoesthecat123, EcHoxDarkZ, Petrb, ClueBot NG, Gareth Griffith-Jones, Jack Greenmaven, Editorial111, Spartan7W, Frietjes, Jerzzul, Widr, Crohall, NextUSprez, Helpful Pixie Bot, Eldrad2mustlive, Dreamyeyed, Tholme, Calidum, Wbm1058, 4321sean, HIDECCHI001, MusikAnimal, Mark Arsten, Medo4, LFevas, MrZackAttack, Mom1967, Eduardofeld, Qrhoo, Teammm, Dawn Eastwood, Codeh, Abstractematics, Dexbot, Steinsplitter, TwoTwoHello, Gryphon70, AldezD, Redalert2fan, WayneyP, Lump-man23, FenixFeather, Aaronredsox, RubleuleR, Leoesb1032, Jianhui67, Jackmcbarn, G S Palmer, Zedgefan, Moonboy54, Timmey31, Iwag-ner501, J.bradley.s, Joshualeecampbell304, Jacobdeathhorn, Timhowardawesome, KH-1, X3a7Xr1c8lu6V, Anthan07, Dash9Z, MajesticEli99, Mickey Featherstone, Lizaisaboss, Alina Kozitch, GeneralizationsAreBad, Cnl18, MrMaximMinkin, PresidentJohnsonCunningham, JJMC89, Gabeisapenguin, Fsurroca, CarlM61, Deezeditz, Breasulp24033, Allthefoxes, Jdhudi, Little Big Mighty Mouse, George Bush IV and Anonymous: 1106

- **United States presidential primary** *Source:* https://en.wikipedia.org/wiki/United_States_presidential_primary?oldid=706813409 *Contributors:* William Avery, Minesweeper, Ahoerstemeier, DavidWBrooks, Ciphergoth, Vzbs34, John K, Jengod, Choster, Mrand, AaronSw, Francs2000, KeithH, Chrism, Naddy, Lowellian, Postdlf, Meelar, Timrollpickering, Acegikmo1, Elysdir, Alan Liefting, DocWatson42, Andris, Xinoph, Formeruser-83, Andycjp, Latitude0116, RayBirks, Neutrality, Calwatch, Flex, Discospinster, Rhobite, Smyth, Bobo192, Brim, Giraffedata, Alansohn, SnowFire, Calton, Omphaloscope, Zereshk, Dan100, Matthew238, Superman53142, Dglynch, Zzyzx11, Marudubshinki, GoldRingChip, BD2412, Monk, Rjwilmsi, Nightscream, Cgray4, David the Aspie, Alex20850, Ground Zero, Jbarrett, KarlFrei, DVdm, Gwernol, Awbeal, Wasted Time R, Ravenswing, Akamad, Gaius Cornelius, O^O, Akhristov, Welsh, Trovatore, Rjensen, Falcon9x5, DeadEyeArrow, Pb30, Josh3580, Vogelfrei, Peter, PhS, John Broughton, SmackBot, Unschool, Hux, Rrius, Izehar, Chris the speller, Bluebot, Alan smithee, Deli nk, Sct72, Shunpiker, Krich, WaldoJ, Ericl, Falconsgladiator, Keizaijungakushi, RBPierce, Agent 86, Levineps, Simon12, Abulsme, Pwforaker, Joseph Solis in Australia, JoeBot, Jaksmata, JForget, Zullo74, JohnCD, AndrewHowse, Korky Day, Peripitus, Breedimm, Doug Weller, Kirk Hilliard, Legotech, CharlotteWebb, Radio Guy, Hmrox, Widefox, Kayamon, Spencer, Yellowdesk, Waterthedog, Instinct, PhilKnight, Garion333, Andropod, VoABot II, Rami R, Vksun, Aka042, Eamon1916, DerHexer, MartinBot, Tremello, Xeriphas1994, Whiteman, J.delanoy, Erendwyn, Engunneer, Coppertwig, Spshu, Scott Illini, Fishbert, CardinalDan, Patrekursson, Tlaarschot, Katydidit, Skalskal, Determinist~enwiki, MatthewLiberal, Stope, Yanosaur, Mlf107, Sendmailtojk, Jauerback, Calabraxthis, Flyer22 Reborn, MaynardClark, Lightmouse, KathrynLybarger, Earthere, Knelmes, Kumioko (renamed), MrZeebo, Lafuzion, Anchor Link Bot, Mygerardromance, Motthoangwehuong, Pinkadelica, Hoplon, ClueBot, Simply Agrestic, Iman2464, Niceguyedc, Digby333, Adimovk5, Iamthegod2, Highfly3442, JamieS93, Thingg, Kitaro53085, Bournereality, Thompsontough, Apparition11, DumZiBoT, XLinkBot, Stuart C. Jones, Northwesterner1, Telew, Gwpluim, Noctibus, NonvocalScream, Bookbrad, Addbot, Squash1212, Jojhutton, Brw3sbc, Nohomers48, LAAFan, Roux, Drahcir24, Onedayonevote, Yobot, Truance, Webmgr, Anand011892, Tempodivalse, Synchronism, AnomieBOT, Kingpin13, Citation bot, Maxis ftw, LilHelpa, Capricorn42, William Bower, Tktru, Gullit Torres, Charles Edwin Shipp, Fat&Happy, Xiglofre, Full-date unlinking bot, RjwilmsiBot, Polly Ticker, Hajatvrc, Rollins83, Seattle, Idolgin776, 28bot, ClueBot NG, Benjamin9832, Delusion23, BlueHappy1, Helpful Pixie Bot, APierce87, MusikAnimal, Gotit90, MonkeyKingBar, Polmandc, DuchMarleya, Cup o' Java, Touranushertz, Epicgenius, Eyesnore, Matsci2, Gopreform, KBH96, Areyoufuckingkiddingmeh, YoursT, RobbCilek, Jarmorton, H.dryad, SolarPowerEverything and Anonymous: 295

- **United States presidential nominating convention** *Source:* https://en.wikipedia.org/wiki/United_States_presidential_nominating_convention?oldid=706358835 *Contributors:* Bryan Derksen, Habj, John K, Lukobe, Jengod, Choster, Zoicon5, Ank329, Popageorgio, Dale Arnett, Lowellian, Postdlf, Jxg, Meelar, Beowabbit, DocWatson42, No Guru, Xinoph, Ary29, Calwatch, Trevor MacInnis, D6, Jiy, Discospinster, IKato, Ibagli, Bender235, Shanes, Jpgordon, Pschemp, Plange, Alai, Zereshk, Matthew238, Woohookitty, Tabletop, Zzyzx11, JiMidnite, GoldRingChip, BD2412, Ando228, Rjwilmsi, Koavf, The wub, Ground Zero, Nihiltres, Mrschimpf, Metropolitan90, Wasted Time R, YurikBot, RussBot, Petiatil, Azlib77, Akhristov, Moe Epsilon, Lockesdonkey, C mon, SmackBot, Allixpeeke, Quidam65, Chris the speller, Stripe66506, Darth Panda, Fearfulsymmetry, Zsinj, Stevenmitchell, Warren, Ericl, MusicMaker5376, Producercunningham, Smartyllama, RandomCritic, Stwalkerster, Levineps, Simon12, Iridescent, Joseph Solis in Australia, KerryVeenstra, Yopienso, Bellerophon5685, Tkynerd, Briantw, Thijs!bot, TonyTheTiger, JustAGal, Canadiaqueen, Tom dl, Settler, Mack2, Husond, SteveSims, VoABot II, Clygeric, GM11, R'n'B, Biff2bad, Jevansen, ABF, ToyotaPanasonic, Jeff G., Philip Trueman, Someguy1221, Steven J. Anderson, Figmillenium, Bcharles, CoolKid1993, Flyer22 Reborn, Socal gal at heart, Aragh, GrouchoPython, ClueBot, LAX, IceUnshattered, Asidbrain, Smaatt, Adimovk5, DumZiBoT, Nct26, Addbot, Blubberboy92, Shakescene, Fieldday-sunday, Bassbonerocks, SpBot, Tassedethe, Lightbot, CountryBot, Vegaswikian1, Yobot, Triquetra, Backslash Forwardslash, XL2D, Galoubet, Piano non troppo, LilHelpa, Xqbot, Capricorn42, Purplebackpack89, Carrite, FrescoBot, MNTRT2009, Trust Is All You Need, Calmer Waters, RjwilmsiBot, Otutusaus, John of Reading, GoingBatty, Elee, Peter Karlsen, Rocketrod1960, ClueBot NG, NextUSprez, HMSSolent, SMD JMP 2011, Andyakamiztatwizta, CdePatNoble, Nuitetjour, Lolo Lympian, CsDix, Nøkkenbuer and Anonymous: 134

- **Article Two of the United States Constitution** *Source:* https://en.wikipedia.org/wiki/Article_Two_of_the_United_States_Constitution?oldid=706887006 *Contributors:* RjLesch, Hornlo, Bryan Derksen, Jeronimo, Gabbe, Tompagenet, Wapcaplet, CORNELIUSSEON, Minesweeper, Jebba, Kevin Baas, JamesReyes, Smack, Lord Emsworth, Adam Carr, Jon Roland, Branddobbe, Dale Arnett, Enceladus, Postdlf, Rfc1394, JesseW, Mattflaschen, Snowdog, Quadell, Kaldari, Rdsmith4, Anythingyouwant, Ellsworth, Pmanderson, Neutrality, Pmadrid, Discospinster, Rich Farmbrough, Smyth, Sebmol, Paul August, Bender235, Mateo SA, NetBot, Giraffedata, Mareino, Alansohn, PaulHanson, DavidHoag, Lord Pistachio, DLJessup, SonPraises, TheAznSensation, Versageek, Simetrical, Rorschach, Theloniouszen, Hbdragon88, Tejastheory, Macaddct1984, M412k, GoldRingChip, BD2412, Rjwilmsi, Coemgenus, Syndicate, Rillian, Sdornan, Pruneau, Poshua, KarlFrei, John Z, Andy85719, Shadow007, Russmack, Hairy Dude, RussBot, Thane, Aftermath, ONEder Boy, JPMcGrath, Rktect, Paul Magnussen, JLaTondre, SmackBot, Cdogsimmons, Gilliam, Hmains, Psiphiorg, Quinsareth, Jprg1966, SchfiftyThree, Tobyw, Can't sleep, clown will eat me, Andy120290, Elendil's Heir, Grover cleveland, Jmlk17, PiMaster3, Cybercobra, Savidan, The Kids Aren't Alright, SnappingTurtle, Jfingers88, Lambiam, Esrever, SilverStar, Adamc714, Green Giant, Loadmaster, Fedallah, RHB, PaulGS, Levineps, Shoeofdeath, CapitalR, Courcelles, Eluchil404, Tawkerbot2, Eastlaw, Dycedarg, Bubbynee, Incady, HalJor, Cydebot, Mato, Slagathor, Christian75, Mathew5000, Epbr123, Steve Dufour, Marek69, Mnemeson, Mentifisto, AMittelman, Paul from Michigan, Jj137, Altamel, Ghmyrtle, Res2216firestar, Epeefleche, Jmchambers90, Db099221, JTRH, Karlhahn, VoABot II, Teekbah, Domingo Portales, Textorus, R'n'B, AlexiusHoratius, Koalaroo, J.delanoy, Ed hover~enwiki, MrBell, CraigMonroe, McSly, JayJasper, Fullmetal2887, Tectonics55, SJP, Themoodyblue, KylieTastic, GregJackP, RVJ, Tulpan, TyrellCorp, Fr33kman, Carter, Philip Trueman, TXiKiBoT, Oshwah, Gifted But Twisted, Cremepuff222, Happyme22, SQL, Enviroboy, Anonymos869, Keilana, Flyer22 Reborn, Jojalozzo, Baseball Bugs, RSStockdale, Anchor Link Bot, Mygerardromance, RomanHistorian, Ratemonth, Elassint, ClueBot, The Thing That Should Not Be, DanielDeibler, Trivialist, Arunsingh16, Excirial, NuclearWarfare, Diaa abdelmoneim, BingoDingo, Silas Maxfield, DumZiBoT, SMP0328., XLinkBot, Jovianeye, Bradv, Little Mountain 5, LTIUAFO, Some jerk on the Internet, Tcncv, Jamball77, Glane23, 5 albert square, Xoilovitaly8, Tide rolls, Lightbot, Legobot, Yobot, Wargo, AnomieBOT, DemocraticLuntz, Piano non troppo, Materialscientist, E2eamon, Eumolpo, GB fan, Spacefuzz, Shouran, Surgical Stryke, Jmundo, Srich32977, Hi878, Swift18717, AlasdairEdits, Drdpw, Dogposter, VI, Bobowski, Cubs197, Hschumbley, Thurmant, 14BlaineA, Myownworst, CanadianPenguin, KinkyLipids, EmausBot, John of Reading, RA0808, RenamedUser01302013, Wikipelli, K6ka, AlexaxelA, Barnwell11, John Cline, Fæ, Unreal7, Kevjonesin, L Kensington, Dan56789, Ssgmcwatson, Donner60, Korruski, J. L. Stout, ClueBot NG, Gareth Griffith-Jones, Joefromrandb, Sleddog116, -sche, CopperSquare, Widr, Jeraphine Gryphon, BG19bot, Roberticus, MusikAnimal, Tompars, Mark Arsten, Space fountain, BattyBot, Walkingdistance, Mrt3366, ChrisGualtieri, Objective Reason, Obtund, P3Y229, Spray787, Bulba2036, AdelanteXIV, CSBurksesq, FallingGravity, Ryanabcdefghijklmnop, BethNaught, Wabs3, Thisisgonnabebad, VoidPhantom, Montaire, Thehaystinch and Anonymous: 408

- **Natural-born-citizen clause** *Source:* https://en.wikipedia.org/wiki/Natural-born-citizen_clause?oldid=707161154 *Contributors:* Ed Poor,

Jackfork, Captaincoffee, Uwhoff, Highground79, Insanity Incarnate, However whatever, Austriacus, HGat82ndSt, Dems on the move, Lightmouse, All Hallow's Wraith, Hansbaer, GoLatvia, DumZiBoT, XLinkBot, Laser brain, Coolnation, Addbot, Doniago, Zorrobot, Yobot, Montemonte, Tempodivalse, AnomieBOT, YeshuaDavid, Rdupuy, Racingstripes, Americus55, HRoestBot, Xcvista, Full-date unlinking bot, Rotsapsky, Victor Victoria, DARTH SIDIOUS 2, RjwilmsiBot, Jmannc3, Cymru.lass, ResidentAnthropologist, Diversity8, Petrb, ClueBot NG, BattyBot, AWDaisy, How hot is the sun?, Finnusertop, Ginsuloft, Paradies, Mpj7 and Anonymous: 81

- **Faithless elector** *Source:* https://en.wikipedia.org/wiki/Faithless_elector?oldid=704451100 *Contributors:* Hoshie, John K, WhisperToMe, Jeffq, Orangemike, Xinoph, Kainaw, Gregory Watson, Mike R, DaveJB, JimWae, D6, MarkusSchulze, Rich Farmbrough, Ibagli, Closeapple, Jnestorius, Jpgordon, Causa sui, Bobo192, Leifern, PaulHanson, DLJessup, Lugevas, Fourthords, LukeSurl, Matthew238, Josephf, Lawrence King, GoldRingChip, BD2412, Neoeinstein, Coemgenus, ElKevbo, Fish and karate, Metropolitan90, BillMasen, Gaius Cornelius, FFLaguna, Ryright, Retired username, Sandstein, Sooperhotshiz, SmackBot, Rrius, Xaosflux, Quidam65, Thumperward, Stevage, The Moose, Elendil's Heir, Savidan, Ultraexactzz, Ligulembot, TTE, BillFlis, Levineps, Joseph Solis in Australia, Woodshed, Vitriden, KXL, Crossmr, Vyselink, Instaurare, Brstahl, Ufwuct, Ramseyman, Binarybits, Radio Guy, Oreo Priest, Blue Tie, JonathanCross, Hut 8.5, SteveSims, Magioladitis, Nyttend, Sm8900, R'n'B, USN1977, Ncmvocalist, JayJasper, Seattle Skier, Fagiolonero, Riffraffselbow, Llamasown, Bentley4, Graymornings, Highground79, Bitbut, AlleborgoBot, Lucky Mitch, Presidentman, GrouchoPython, Runner5k, ClueBot, Wikievil666, Enthusiast01, Niceguyedc, Cfsenel, NuclearWarfare, BOTarate, John Paul Parks, MelonBot, MetaBohemian~enwiki, Addbot, Richardpku, LaaknorBot, Epicadam, Yobot, AnomieBOT, A More Perfect Onion, Carolina wren, Ocnn, Xqbot, Themeatpopsicle, RaymondRuptime, JMilty, Brucewh, His male lover, No One of Consequence, Justdave79, Mattwigway, EmausBot, Ajraddatz, AoV2, Solarra, RedSoxFan274, ClueBot NG, Delusion23, Prcc27, Habitmelon, Jeffvarwig, FakirNL, Polmandc, YFdyh-bot, Webclient101, Mogism, Cerabot~enwiki, Foladaniel05, Dixiedemocrat, Gluten is a tent test and Anonymous: 90

- **Federal Election Commission** *Source:* https://en.wikipedia.org/wiki/Federal_Election_Commission?oldid=702533746 *Contributors:* RobLa, DavidWBrooks, Meelar, JamesMLane, Cnhbradley, Foryst, AlistairMcMillan, Allstar86, Deus Ex, GreenReaper, Rich Farmbrough, Stesmo, Man vyi, PaulHanson, Geraldshields11, Seth Goldin, Woohookitty, Scriberius, BD2412, Magidin, Merv, DVdm, Epolk, Gaius Cornelius, Number 57, Sardanaphalus, SmackBot, Dauster, Ohnoitsjamie, Philosopher, Muboshgu, Overacker, John, Gobonobo, Green Giant, Peterbr~enwiki, Joseph Solis in Australia, Theflyer, CapitalR, JRSpriggs, Eastlaw, EABSE, Clindberg, Michael Johnson, Thijs!bot, AntiVandalBot, Czj, Mdotley, Lordmetroid, Yellowdesk, Magioladitis, Bongwarrior, Atb129, Chivista~enwiki, MoxRox, Electiontechnology, VolkovBot, Soliloquial, Bdb484, Gbawden, SieBot, Thehornet, Int21h, Kumioko (renamed), Francvs, ClueBot, Trivialist, Excirial, Noneforall, Dthomsen8, UESPArules, Addbot, DOI bot, Cst17, Yobot, AnomieBOT, Xqbot, Fern 24, DrDanielJackson, Full-date unlinking bot, Grammarxxx, Tibet111, RayneVanDunem, ClueBot NG, Mahir256, Kendall Chadwick, Pbmaise, YFdyh-bot, BuzyBody, WikiUser6813, Monkbot, Rma0406, Gtaboy234, Orduin and Anonymous: 59

- **United States presidential election debates** *Source:*  https://en.wikipedia.org/wiki/United_States_presidential_election_debates?oldid= 703028142 *Contributors:* The Anome, SimonP, Minesweeper, J'raxis, Ciphergoth, Rossami, Vzbs34, Choster, Zoicon5, Wetman, Moncrief, Postdlf, Desmay, Timrollpickering, Acegikmo1, Lupo, Seth Ilys, Laudaka, Angmering, Stevietheman, JimWae, Hammersfan, Neutrality, Cab88, Jwolfe, Lifefeed, Rich Farmbrough, Guanabot, Kdammers, CanisRufus, EurekaLott, Pschemp, Hagerman, Pearle, Rye1967, Deathphoenix, Zereshk, April Arcus, Woohookitty, Kosher Fan, MONGO, ERoss, Zzyzx11, LinkTiger, Deltabeignet, BD2412, Josh Parris, Nightscream, OneWeirdDude, Vary, JHMM13, SchuminWeb, Ground Zero, Mrschimpf, DVdm, Borgx, Stan2525, OldRight, NawlinWiki, Zwobot, Slicing, TheMadBaron, Esprit15d, CWenger, SmackBot, Gilliam, Hmains, Marbehraglaim, Yaf, Savidan, TGoodman, Andrew c, Mitchumch, Robofish, Cpastern, Levineps, Joseph Solis in Australia, Igoldste, CapitalR, Vitriden, Bellerophon5685, Las Casas, Epbr123, SchutteGod, Binarybits, Husond, Wasell, Hroðulf, Jatkins, JLMadrigal, Cgingold, Jcool155, Vigyani, CommonsDelinker, J.delanoy, JayJasper, Wa3pxx, Mike V, Cosmic Latte, Happyme22, The Devil's Advocate, AlleborgoBot, Laoris, SE7, Flyer22 Reborn, Randy Kryn, Revelian, ClueBot, Stevenphil, Brngreenback, P. S. Burton, Adel Hosny, Ericci8996, Thingg, XLinkBot, RyanCross, Jmerchant29, Addbot, Chris19910, Bassbonerocks, Tassedethe, Jarble, Сергей Олегович, Yobot, Marctho, Greentree22, AnomieBOT, Jim1138, RadioBroadcast, Xqbot, Dhruvhemmady, Omnipaedista, Cresix, Tktru, Ormebk, Lionelt, Mheineke, Full-date unlinking bot, Cnwilliams, RjwilmsiBot, ZéroBot, Larast, ClueBot NG, Smtchahal, Rezabot, Helpful Pixie Bot, Cojovo, Strike Eagle, BG19bot, Kendall-K1, Michaelmalak, Werety23, Rutebega, Wmorris79, BattyBot, KhabarNegar, Blix1900, Rfranze, RasBryan, Lugia2453, Mhioh, Marxistfounder, Podiaebba, Watchmeexplode15, Lommes, Whosaidsodotnet and Anonymous: 155

- **Election Day (United States)** *Source:* https://en.wikipedia.org/wiki/Election_Day_(United_States)?oldid=705686629 *Contributors:* SimonP, Docu, Jengod, Mulad, Clipdude, Tpbradbury, Furrykef, Jfruh, Francs2000, Owen, EdwinHJ, Hadal, Walloon, Davidcannon, Centrx, Xinoph, Bobblewik, Cnproudf, PFHLai, Scott Burley, Neutrality, Lacrimosus, D6, KillerChihuahua, Mr. Billion, PPGMD, LostLeviathan, Jonathunder, Mareino, Alansohn, Richard Harvey, Metstotop333, Danhash, Cmprince, Tariqabjotu, TSP, Optichan, Steinbach, Zzyzx11, Graham87, Keeves, Eoghanacht, Dapoloplayer, Nneonneo, The wub, FlaBot, CR85747, Eiad77, Chobot, Flcelloguy, Ravenswing, YurikBot, RussBot, Lincolnite, NawlinWiki, Dforest, Josejose50, Tony1, Lockesdonkey, Marktaff, PS2pcGAMER, DisambigBot, TLSuda, Bdve, Luk, Fritsky~enwiki, SmackBot, PJM, Orser67, Gilliam, Hmains, Allholy1, Hongooi, Krallja, Htra0497, TCY, Deathsythe, Doodle77, G-Bot~enwiki, SilkTork, Rob Zako, Slakr, Publicus, Citicat, Levineps, Joseph Solis in Australia, Tawkerbot2, PuerExMachina, Theleek, JohnCD, CWY2190, Cydebot, Reywas92, JFreeman, AngoraFish, Dchristle, Starionwolf, Wikichange, Qwyrxian, Marek69, Natalie Erin, AntiVandalBot, Luna Santin, Bry456, Joshua, VoABot II, RBBrittain, Jackscarab, Allstarecho, Floria L, Connor Behan, Electiontechnology, MartinBot, Manticore, Inwardexposure, JayJasper, Vicodin addict, Littlepea, Quantling, Flatterworld, Atropos235, Foofighter20x, Davidwr, Schoop, MagicSporkBagel, Logan, Coreyjune12, Matthew Yeager, Oxymoron83, Lightmouse, Ks0stm, JDBravo, Ratemonth, Elassint, ClueBot, LP-mn, The Thing That Should Not Be, Enthusiast01, Mild Bill Hiccup, Piledhigheranddeeper, Trivialist, John J. Bulten, Cenarium, Alexius08, Kbdankbot, Addbot, Fieldday-sunday, CanadianLinuxUser, Cst17, 5 albert square, Tide rolls, Sofresh412, II MusLiM HyBRiD II, Gongshow, AnomieBOT, Floquenbeam, Jim1138, Jayarathina, BruceMiller, Capricorn42, Klarkincooke, Tippythop, Mechanic1c, Lord1023, ProtectionTaggingBot, AtxApril, Kyle Hardgrave, FrescoBot, Kobitate94, Anonomousone, RjwilmsiBot, Orphan Wiki, Gfoley4, Spasquali, JustinTime55, Trickytruck, ZéroBot, SaradominO o, ClueBot NG, Sbradley666, Yurthouses, NextUSprez, M0rphzone, Ceradon, Wastednow, TBrandley, Mouseinthehouse15, Mediran, UsefulWikipedia, Lugia2453, Frosty, 93, Rogr101, KETCHUP6789, William2001, Exoplanetaryscience, Kind Tennis Fan, Rehsjntdz, Tihbsfi, GeoffreyT2000, JJMC89, Leowikileo and Anonymous: 187

- **United States presidential inauguration** *Source:*  https://en.wikipedia.org/wiki/United_States_presidential_inauguration?oldid=700746552 *Contributors:* Rickyrab, Hoshie, Lquilter, Ciphergoth, Jiang, Jeandré du Toit, Jengod, Tpbradbury, AnonMoos, Steffen Löwe Gera, Robbot, JackofOz, JerryFriedman, DocWatson42, Jao, BenFrantzDale, Jcarlock, Bobblewik, Beland, TonyW, Neutrality, Lacrimosus, Bender235,

Kop, O18, AKGhetto, Kbir1, Pschemp, Caeruleancentaur, Mrzaius, Alansohn, Eleland, LtNOWIS, Nulall, TommyBoy, Brookie, PJWirs, Gabriel Kent, PoccilScript, Jacobolus, Knuckles, OCNative, Prezboy1, Zzyzx11, JohnC, Dysepsion, Graham87, Jack Cox, GoldRingChip, Tim!, Rillian, AySz88, Austrian, SNIyer12, FlaBot, SchuminWeb, Nihiltres, Cherubino, Tuneman42, Gurch, NoSeptember, Str1977, Erp, Amchow78, Drcobe, Awbeal, Spleodrach, RussBot, Epolk, Shep9882, Anomalocaris, Joshdboz, MDolson22, Aaron charles, Lockesdonkey, Obi-WanKenobi-2005, Evrik, Antonio Basto, Mike Serfas, Notepadzone, Philip Stevens, Sardanaphalus, SmackBot, Mangoe, Tom Lougheed, Jeppesn, KelleyCook, Imzadi1979, Mauls, Kudzu1, Hraefen, LinguistAtLarge, GregE625, Epastore, GoodDay, Quake20044, Elendil's Heir, Mitrius, NoIdeaNick, Savidan, Gamgee, Mtmelendez, The PIPE, Ericl, Stefano85, Ohconfucius, Autopilot, Arodb, Khazar, Robofish, Wizelf94, Thegreatdr, Ckatz, XP528, MrDolomite, Levineps, Joseph Solis in Australia, SChaos1701, CapitalR, Richard75, Lucy-marie, PGSable, Alfredo Molina, Runningonbrains, DanielRigal, Cydebot, Reywas92, Henrymrx, Chasingsol, Alexfrance250291, Smile Lee, TonyTheTiger, HappyInGeneral, Sarner, Eco84, Marek69, Missvain, JustAGal, Sturm55, Aaron7chicago, Rees11, Phuff, Seaphoto, Emeraldcityserendipity, FHSerkland, DarkAudit, F McGady, FueledbyRamen, Xdeadclancyx, MER-C, Redking7, Propaniac, Magioladitis, Fitnr, LordCobalt, VoABot II, 1995hoo, RBBrittain, JNW, Kinston eagle, KConWiki, Cgingold, Bbigjohnson, JaGa, J.delanoy, Pharaoh of the Wizards, TECH-NOIR, ChrisfromHouston, RoyBatty42, Jjmillerhistorian, Juliancolton, Andy Marchbanks, Wikipeterproject, Lwalt, JGHowes, Eubulides, Happyme22, Jhawkinson, Angelmorph, Legokid, Jwray, TJRC, Dough4872, D420182, Le.Kwyjibo, Matthewedwards, Nopetro, Darth Kalwejt, Oxymoron83, Baseball Bugs, Jdaloner, Macy, Philly jawn, Tannline, Rmh1, Iamwisesun, ClueBot, The Thing That Should Not Be, Mardetanha, BlackbeardK, Manutdglory, Boo1210, Pi zero, Trivialist, Cirt, Erinaceus, Bobopaedia, Alexbot, Jusdafax, Sun Creator, Raulv01, Cousteau69, Redthoreau, Thingg, Versus22, NewYork483, Bellwether BC, DumZiBoT, MonoBot, SMP0328., XLinkBot, Sherreyes, Dan Cavin, Addbot, Freakmighty, Com-ed, Epicadam, Mragsdale, Teles, Zorrobot, Luckas-bot, Yobot, EgbertMcDunk, AnomieBOT, Rubinbot, Flewis, Cyan22, Ewikdjmco, Xqbot, Capricorn42, OmuYasha, Unknown619, Ernest Peiris, Batman4ever, Mrcsisml, Dave Smith, Canalization, Deaflympic, Chickens12, Yoganate79, Shadowjams, Tktru, FrescoBot, Moonshaker, Eagle4000, CircleAdrian, GeneLesterisaMan, Jamescooly, Full-date unlinking bot, Pristino, Kildruf, Kgrad, Wibble1966, Lotje, Weedwhacker128, EmausBot, Gored82, Trickytruck, ZéroBot, RayneVanDunem, ClueBot NG, Angelmarie87, Snotbot, Ezuvian, Dru of Id, Widr, NextUSprez, MS10EL, Rodchen, BG19bot, Michael Barera, Lucullus19, BattyBot, Marino13, Florwoman, SFK2, Jarrettmdrake, Corn cheese, Omri.mor, Epicgenius, Osunga, Govgovgov, Ruserman, Nomads18, Abristola, CHSIV, Kevieman94, Dickbuttmagee, Pawtiko and Anonymous: 255

- **List of Presidents of the United States by previous experience** *Source:* https://en.wikipedia.org/wiki/List_of_Presidents_of_the_United_States_by_previous_experience?oldid=702199309 *Contributors:* Timrollpickering, Jamesdowallen, RPH, Bgwhite, Silverhorse, Gilliam, Hmains, Colonies Chris, Vanis314, Stefan2, MrDolomite, Richard75, Valereee, Erich031985, KConWiki, R'n'B, CommonsDelinker, Tgeairn, Elfelix, ChrisfromHouston, Robertgreer, Calatayudboy, Adam Cuerden, Ratemonth, Mononomic, Armbrust, WCCasey, Brandmeister, SBaker43, Thewolfchild, Pfieffer Latsch, Calabe1992, BG19bot, Krenair, KraigStagg, Marxistfounder, WikiBrainHead, BethNaught, Eriwawo, Doctorwho503, YoursT, Bandaideditor, TroyHay283746373, NCentral05 and Anonymous: 52

- **List of Presidents of the United States by other offices held** *Source:* https://en.wikipedia.org/wiki/List_of_Presidents_of_the_United_States_by_other_offices_held?oldid=693913221 *Contributors:* Rmhermen, Hoshie, Docu, LouI, Jengod, Zoicon5, Dale Arnett, Chrism, Jmabel, Postdlf, Steve Casburn, Bkonrad, Blue387, Neutrality, RobbieFal, Ahkond, Rorschach567, Surachit, Kross, Bobo192, Pschemp, Alansohn, TommyBoy, Cburnett, Jack Cox, GoldRingChip, Ashandarei, NekoDaemon, NoSeptember, Metropolitan90, Neitherday, Black Regent, Curpsbot-unicodify, Sardanaphalus, David Kernow, Hmains, Betacommand, Bluebot, Colonies Chris, Scwlong, Mathmannix, Alcuin, Joseph Solis in Australia, CapitalR, Eluchil404, JustAGal, Libs23, Gopherbone, Ozzieboy, Yellowdesk, Gang14, J.delanoy, ChrisfromHouston, Tdadamemd, Klausdog, Brennan626, OldestManOnMySpace, Tim Thomason, Ratemonth, Plumber, Purplebackpack89, GoingBatty, ClueBot NG, Jack Greenmaven, Widr, Lucullus19, Shaun, Hmainsbot1, GyaroMaguus and Anonymous: 53

- **List of United States presidential elections by Electoral College margin** *Source:* https://en.wikipedia.org/wiki/List_of_United_States_presidential_elections_by_Electoral_College_margin?oldid=706700921 *Contributors:* SimonP, Matt Gies, Spiffy sperry, Bender235, Pschemp, Pearle, DLJessup, Dr Gangrene, Woohookitty, Zzyzx11, GoldRingChip, BD2412, Bubba73, NoSeptember, Bgwhite, Zafiroblue05, Deville, Sardanaphalus, SmackBot, David Kernow, Rrius, Hraefen, Bluebot, Efrainbet, Midnightcomm, Zrulli, Hgilbert, BrownHairedGirl, Tyharvey313, Timmeh, MrDolomite, Levineps, Joseph Solis in Australia, Highway99, Cydebot, Reywas92, RobotG, Magioladitis, W like wiki, ChrisfromHouston, Nedhenry, Hugo999, Clarince63, Sheppa28, Proud Ho, Jmj713, ClueBot, The Thing That Should Not Be, Iohannes Animosus, Roentgenium111, Nolelover, FrescoBot, ElockidAlternate, Vale of Glamorgan, Kaltenmeyer, FoCuSandLeArN, Hmainsbot1, Xwoodsterchinx, CAPTAIN RAJU and Anonymous: 32

- **List of United States presidential elections by popular vote margin** *Source:* https://en.wikipedia.org/wiki/List_of_United_States_presidential_elections_by_popular_vote_margin?oldid=706430791 *Contributors:* Spiffy sperry, Bender235, GoldRingChip, Wasted Time R, Sardanaphalus, WildElf, Orser67, Afasmit, Scwlong, Hoof Hearted, BrownHairedGirl, Potosino, Timmeh, Levineps, Eluchil404, NapoliRoma, Mavwreck, W like wiki, R'n'B, ChrisfromHouston, Bdodo1992, Vanished User 4517, German.Knowitall, Jeff G., Rtr10, Wiae, Klippa, Sheppa28, Ratemonth, Excirial, Thingg, Roentgenium111, Stidmatt, Yobot, HairyPerry, Mkwan79, YBG, Thehelpfulbot, Omniscientest, Tilden76, Serols, Orphan Wiki, Vanished user sfijw8jh4tjkefs, HandsomeFella, GrayFullbuster, ClueBot NG, Spartan7W, Widr, Wbm1058, Kaltenmeyer, BrookKoorb, Cwobeel, Cmckain14, RumorDestroyer38, Snowsuit Wearer, Tara M. Lee, Cerretalogan13, Andreraynal and Anonymous: 43

- **Voter turnout in the United States presidential elections** *Source:* https://en.wikipedia.org/wiki/Voter_turnout_in_the_United_States_presidential_elections?oldid=701841881 *Contributors:* Andrewman327, Prosfilaes, Piotrus, Giraffedata, Lugevas, NCdave, SportsMaster, I Use Dial, SmackBot, Yamaguchi⬜⬜, Potosino, Levineps, Jamesofengland, Jcarle, Candent shlimazel, JayJasper, KylieTastic, Martha Forsyth, Jmj713, Coinmanj, InaMaka, John Paul Parks, Feinoha, Addbot, Yobot, Wikkerp, AnomieBOT, AaronF2, Biograph1985, Jonesey95, Pristino, GoingBatty, ZéroBot, ClueBot NG, Mark Arsten, Garamond Lethe, Joe rickard, Cmckain14, N scarborough, Lennysmouse, Simmons91 and Anonymous: 30

- **Elections in the United States** *Source:* https://en.wikipedia.org/wiki/Elections_in_the_United_States?oldid=706268553 *Contributors:* Lousyd, Ixfd64, Ahoerstemeier, Conti, Furrykef, AnonMoos, KeithH, Chrism, Kagredon, Tobias Bergemann, Davidcannon, Jahaza, Wilfred Derksen, Gamaliel, Jason Quinn, Pascal666, Deus Ex, Stevietheman, Neutrality, Willhsmit, Calwatch, Reinthal, Gedca, Chadlupkes, El C, Laurascudder, EurekaLott, RTucker, Acntx, Scott Ritchie, Deryck Chan, Pperos, Alansohn, DLJessup, Velella, EKMichigan, Evil Monkey, Zereshk, Ceyockey, Dunord~enwiki, Firsfron, Woohookitty, MattGiuca, Ddye, TreveX, Tetraminoe, Zzyzx11, Prinzwilhelm, Obersachse, GoldRingChip, Electionworld, Rjwilmsi, Vegaswikian, Stilgar135, Ground Zero, Mogest, Bdelisle, Gwernol, Borgx, Hairy Dude, Stephenb, Gaius Cornelius, Welsh,

Nutiketaiel, Moe Epsilon, Tony1, Rwalker, Zzuuzz, Sardanaphalus, SmackBot, Prototime, August99, Sam8, Gilliam, Betacommand, Political Lefty, Andy M. Wang, CSWarren, Revchu, -Barry-, Cribananda, Crd721, Didero, The undertow, Green Giant, Ckatz, 16@r, MrDolomite, Levineps, Woodshed, Addict 2006, Neelix, Karenjc, Evil00, Cydebot, Reywas92, Besieged, RightClickSaveAs, JodyB, CieloEstrellado, Figgie123, Blah42, Top.Squark, Dfrg.msc, Wap7223, MER-C, Db099221, Thedudeno7, Bongwarrior, VoABot II, CTF83!, Ronm01, Catgut, Brenji, Kunalpareek, Textorus, Littlepear, Launch3, Electiontechnology, Jnshimko, J.delanoy, Mikael Häggström, Carlosforonda, SmilesALot, Jorfer, Flatterworld, Student7, Juliancolton, Foofighter20x, RVJ, KCMM, StillTrill, Wiae, Locke9k, Sendmailtojk, VVVBot, Flyer22 Reborn, Radon210, Gonezales, Kumioko (renamed), Hubertfarnsworth, ClueBot, Plastikspork, Enthusiast01, Excirial, Kain Nihil, Kaiba, BlueDevil, MairAW, DumZiBoT, Fstickney, Seablade, Maxj96, Addbot, Ronhjones, CarsracBot, SpBot, Pince Nez, Gail, Zorrobot, -iNu-, Yobot, Azcolvin429, AnomieBOT, IRP, Flewis, Ksferrante, Xqbot, Capricorn42, Khajidha, Cekli829, FrescoBot, Charles Edwin Shipp, DrilBot, Calmer Waters, Hamtechperson, Dupont och Dupond, Vrenator, RjwilmsiBot, EmausBot, Thecheesykid, Kkm010, ZéroBot, Wieralee, H3llBot, Sross (Public Policy), L Kensington, Donner60, ClueBot NG, Satellizer, Snotbot, Hazhk, Widr, Crohall, Theopolisme, Wbm1058, Arnavchaudhary, Kaltenmeyer, MusikAnimal, Blackhole008, Pro jack g, TheOriginalTrollMaster, Khazar2, Dexbot, Michael A Bekoff, Wikignome1213, MrSoderpop, Tentinator, Jim Carter, Third party481, Dannyleeodriscoll, Masterblaster31, Wech2443 and Anonymous: 200

- **Most royal candidate theory** *Source:* https://en.wikipedia.org/wiki/Most_royal_candidate_theory?oldid=705346733 *Contributors:* Michael Hardy, Joy, Branddobbe, Nunh-huh, Rich Farmbrough, Pharos, Kazvorpal, Sjakkalle, Cleared as filed, SmackBot, Mangoe, Stifle, JJay, Robofish, Levineps, Cydebot, Bellerophon5685, Michael A. White, Ronweezlee, RainbowCrane, Crubba, Goustien, Geoff Plourde, Rxstar, Trivialist, Good Olfactory, Addbot, Drpickem, Yobot, Gongshow, Mechanic1c, AlphaRed3, ZéroBot, Thargor Orlando, IrregularApocalypse, DoctorKubla, Lchski, Dozei, Boomer Vial and Anonymous: 10

- **PollyVote** *Source:* https://en.wikipedia.org/wiki/PollyVote?oldid=678634728 *Contributors:* Edward, Giftlite, Ground Zero, Zafiroblue05, Shell Kinney, Doncram, SmackBot, Neo-Jay, Noian, Joseph Solis in Australia, Headbomb, Guy Macon, Seleucus, Kimleonard, DadaNeem, Jomasecu, Nancy, Agraefe, NuclearWarfare, Ettrig, Bph2002, BG19bot, Monkbot and Anonymous: 15

- **FiveThirtyEight** *Source:* https://en.wikipedia.org/wiki/FiveThirtyEight?oldid=704729259 *Contributors:* Edward, Voidvector, Bearcat, Schutz, Goethean, HangingCurve, Khaosworks, Dwedit, Oknazevad, Vsmith, D-Notice, Tom, Mareino, Alansohn, Gary, DanielVallstrom, LukeSurl, Bastin, Chardish, Mindmatrix, G.W., Mandarax, Jack Cox, Koavf, Adjusting, MZMcBride, Bfigura, Bgwhite, Arzel, Cardsplayer4life, Arthur Rubin, Dspradau, DoriSmith, SmackBot, Kudzu1, Quidam65, MrNonchalant, Thumperward, Timneu22, Cybercobra, Ratel, Ohconfucius, Fifty7, Gobonobo, Robofish, Timmeh, Spiel496, Rnb, Wslack, CmdrObot, Vision Thing, Cydebot, Reywas92, Studerby, Trident13, Underpants, Mack2, LeedsKing, Skomorokh, Albany NY, Magioladitis, Hroðulf, Dp76764, Lnward87, R'n'B, Richiekim, Dave Dial, Friendofwashoe, RenniePet, Allreet, DadaNeem, Atheuz, Jrytrumpet, Bob103051, Why Not A Duck, Truthanado, TJRC, Hibsch, Rslnerd, LP-mn, Niceguyedc, Not Brit, Blanchardb, Parkwells, Trivialist, Diderot's dreams, Nymf, Sun Creator, NuclearWarfare, Newsroom hierarchies, MelonBot, Aaronsawyer1, The Squicks, Camera123456, CountryBot, Yobot, AnomieBOT, Rjanag, SupermanML, Ring Cinema, Guillermo Ugarte, Ballsinmymouthmonkeybutt, Njbunk, Benevolus257, Cresix, FrescoBot, Winterst, Fat&Happy, Designate, Brandonblattner, Comet Tuttle, RjwilmsiBot, Polly Ticker, Regancy42, Shabidoo, Mukogodo, EmausBot, John of Reading, Iyhberry, GoingBatty, ZéroBot, NathanielTheBold, H3llBot, WoolseyLynn, RayneVanDunem, ClueBot NG, Kcwz, Ypnypn, Helpful Pixie Bot, BG19bot, Dualus, Elisfkc, WikiHannibal, Mike.wasikowski, Epicgenius, Sublim808, Wernstrom and Anonymous: 101

- **Electoral-vote.com** *Source:* https://en.wikipedia.org/wiki/Electoral-vote.com?oldid=694847290 *Contributors:* Minesweeper, Ciphergoth, David Gerard, Oberiko, Fishal, Quarl, Guy Harris, Kocio, Dhartung, Zantastik, Jersyko, Novagabe, Tabletop, TreveX, BD2412, Epitome83, Arzel, Member, NawlinWiki, RL0919, Leontes, NBS525, SmackBot, Eseymour, John, Gobonobo, Vanished user v8n3489h3tkjnsdkq30u3f, Timmeh, Levineps, Joseph Solis in Australia, Gnfnrf, Pyroponce, Mack2, JohnSinteur, Custodiet ipsos custodes, Stealthound, LongView, Tuanomsoc, Plasticup, The Devil's Advocate, ImageRemovalBot, Diderot's dreams, JasonAQuest, Aprock, XLinkBot, Saberwolf116, Interwebs, Yobot, AnomieBOT, Tiller54, Drrll, ClueBot NG, Kaltenmeyer, Futurist110, Schrodingers9Lives and Anonymous: 22

## 27.5.2 Images

- **File:114th_United_States_Senate_(with_independents_outlined_in_blue).svg** *Source:* https://upload.wikimedia.org/wikipedia/commons/b/b4/114th_United_States_Senate_%28with_independents_outlined_in_blue%29.svg *License:* CC BY-SA 4.0 *Contributors:* Own work *Original artist:* Tozian

- **File:1876_Democratic_National_Convention_-_Missouri.jpg** *Source:* https://upload.wikimedia.org/wikipedia/commons/4/41/1876_Democratic_National_Convention_-_Missouri.jpg *License:* CC BY 2.0 *Contributors:* originally posted to **Flickr** as Missouri - The Democratic National Convention *Original artist:* Cornell University Library

- **File:1965_Inauguration_of_President_Lyndon_Johnson.jpg** *Source:* https://upload.wikimedia.org/wikipedia/commons/c/c0/1965_Inauguration_of_President_Lyndon_Johnson.jpg *License:* CC BY 2.0 *Contributors:* 1965-01-20-Inaugural Parade for President Lyndon Johnson-11 *Original artist:* Old Guard Museum

- **File:1976_Republican_National_Convention.jpg** *Source:* https://upload.wikimedia.org/wikipedia/commons/d/d9/1976_Republican_National_Convention.jpg *License:* Public domain *Contributors:* http://www.ford.utexas.edu/images/avproj/pop-ups/B1272-18A.html(Previously uploaded at en.wikipedia; a description page is/was here. 2006-02-14 (upload date) by Ctdunstan) *Original artist:* William Fitz-Patrick

- **File:2004CampaignAttention_(edit).png** *Source:* https://upload.wikimedia.org/wikipedia/commons/8/8c/2004CampaignAttention_%28edit%29.png *License:* Public domain *Contributors:*

- 2004CampaignAttention.png *Original artist:*

- derivative work: ChrisnHouston (<a href='//commons.wikimedia.org/wiki/User_talk:ChrisnHouston' title='User talk:ChrisnHouston'>talk</a>)

- **File:20080825_Michelle_Obama_Close-up_at_2008_Democratic_National_Convention.png** *Source:* https://upload.wikimedia.org/wikipedia/commons/9/93/20080825_Michelle_Obama_Close-up_at_2008_Democratic_National_Convention.png *License:* CC BY 2.0 *Contributors:* http://www.flickr.com/photos/avalowery/2893907715/ *Original artist:* flickr user Ava Lowery

- **File:Flag_of_the_United_States.svg** *Source:* https://upload.wikimedia.org/wikipedia/en/a/a4/Flag_of_the_United_States.svg *License:* PD *Contributors:* ? *Original artist:* ?

- **File:Flag_of_the_Vice_President_of_the_United_States.svg** *Source:* https://upload.wikimedia.org/wikipedia/commons/1/19/Flag_of_the_Vice_President_of_the_United_States.svg *License:* Public domain *Contributors:* Design from the Army Institute of Heraldry and Executive Order 11884 SVG elements from <a href='//commons.wikimedia.org/wiki/File:Flag_of_the_President_of_the_United_States_of_America.svg' class='image'><img alt='Flag of the President of the United States of America.svg' src='https://upload.wikimedia.org/wikipedia/commons/thumb/a/af/Flag_of_the_President_of_the_United_States_of_America.svg/50px-Flag_of_the_President_of_the_United_States_of_America.svg.png' width='50' height='35' srcset='https://upload.wikimedia.org/wikipedia/commons/thumb/a/af/Flag_of_the_President_of_the_United_States_of_America.svg/75px-Flag_of_the_President_of_the_United_States_of_America.svg.png 1.5x, https://upload.wikimedia.org/wikipedia/commons/thumb/a/af/Flag_of_the_President_of_the_United_States_of_America.svg/100px-Flag_of_the_President_of_the_United_States_of_America.svg.png 2x' data-file-width='942' data-file-height='651' /></a> *Original artist:* Ipankonin

- **File:Folder_Hexagonal_Icon.svg** *Source:* https://upload.wikimedia.org/wikipedia/en/4/48/Folder_Hexagonal_Icon.svg *License:* Cc-by-sa-3.0 *Contributors:* ? *Original artist:* ?

- **File:Four_Ruffles_and_Flourishes_(pause)_and_Hail_To_The_Chief_-short_version-.ogg** *Source:* https://upload.wikimedia.org/wikipedia/commons/0/06/Four_Ruffles_and_Flourishes_%28pause%29_and_Hail_To_The_Chief_-short_version-.ogg *License:* Public domain *Contributors:* The United States Air Force Band, originally uploaded to Commons by Remember the dot, converted to Ogg Vorbis format by Mormegil *Original artist:* The United States Air Force Band

- **File:Four_U.S._presidents_in_2013.jpg** *Source:* https://upload.wikimedia.org/wikipedia/commons/b/b3/Four_U.S._presidents_in_2013.jpg *License:* Public domain *Contributors:* White House (P042513PS-0658) *Original artist:* Pete Souza

- **File:Four_ruffles_and_flourishes,_hail_to_the_chief_(long_version).ogg** *Source:* https://upload.wikimedia.org/wikipedia/commons/7/7c/Four_ruffles_and_flourishes%2C_hail_to_the_chief_%28long_version%29.ogg *License:* Public domain *Contributors:* http://www.usarmyband.com/Audio/ceremonial_music_guide.html *Original artist:* U. S. Army Band, James Sanderson

- **File:GOP_Primaries_2012_Calendar.svg** *Source:* https://upload.wikimedia.org/wikipedia/commons/e/eb/GOP_Primaries_2012_Calendar.svg *License:* CC-BY-SA-3.0 *Contributors:* Original map Blank USA, w territories.svg *Original artist:* derivative work: Allstar86

- **File:George-W-Bush.jpeg** *Source:* https://upload.wikimedia.org/wikipedia/commons/d/d4/George-W-Bush.jpeg *License:* Public domain *Contributors:*

  This Image was released by the United States Department of Defense with the ID 030114-O-0000D-001_screen <a class='external text' href='//commons.wikimedia.org/w/index.php?title=Category:Files_created_by_the_United_States_Department_of_Defense_with_known_IDs,<span>,&,</span>,filefrom=030114-O-0000D-001_screen#mw-category-media'>(next)</a>.

  This tag does not indicate the copyright status of the attached work. A normal copyright tag is still required. See Commons:Licensing for more information.

  *Original artist:* White house photo by Eric Draper.

- **File:George-Washington.jpg** *Source:* https://upload.wikimedia.org/wikipedia/commons/2/2e/George-Washington.jpg *License:* Public domain *Contributors:* saucing *Original artist:* Gilbert Stuart

- **File:George_H._W._Bush,_President_of_the_United_States,_1989_official_portrait.jpg** *Source:* https://upload.wikimedia.org/wikipedia/commons/0/0f/George_H._W._Bush%2C_President_of_the_United_States%2C_1989_official_portrait.jpg *License:* Public domain *Contributors:* http://www.dodmedia.osd.mil/DVIC_View/Still_Details.cfm?SDAN=DNSC8905558&JPGPath=/Assets/Still/1989/Navy/DN-SC-89-05558.JPG *Original artist:* N/A, likely POTUS

- **File:George_and_Laura_Bush_during_the_2005_Inaugural_Parade.jpg** *Source:* https://upload.wikimedia.org/wikipedia/commons/3/37/George_and_Laura_Bush_during_the_2005_Inaugural_Parade.jpg *License:* Public domain *Contributors:* White House [1] *Original artist:* White House (Eric Draper)

- **File:Gerald_Ford.jpg** *Source:* https://upload.wikimedia.org/wikipedia/commons/4/4e/Gerald_Ford.jpg *License:* Public domain *Contributors:* http://www.fordlibrarymuseum.gov/images/avproj/pop-ups/A0381.html *Original artist:* David Hume Kennerly

- **File:Gilbert_Stuart_Williamstown_Portrait_of_George_Washington.jpg** *Source:* https://upload.wikimedia.org/wikipedia/commons/b/b6/Gilbert_Stuart_Williamstown_Portrait_of_George_Washington.jpg *License:* Public domain *Contributors:* link *Original artist:* Gilbert Stuart

- **File:Gnome-mime-sound-openclipart.svg** *Source:* https://upload.wikimedia.org/wikipedia/commons/8/87/Gnome-mime-sound-openclipart.svg *License:* Public domain *Contributors:* Own work. Based on File:Gnome-mime-audio-openclipart.svg, which is public domain. *Original artist:* User:Eubulides

- **File:Great_Seal_of_the_United_States_(obverse).svg** *Source:* https://upload.wikimedia.org/wikipedia/commons/5/5c/Great_Seal_of_the_United_States_%28obverse%29.svg *License:* Public domain *Contributors:* Extracted from PDF version of *Our Flag*, available here (direct PDF URL here.) *Original artist:* U.S. Government

- **File:Greater_coat_of_arms_of_the_United_States.svg** *Source:* https://upload.wikimedia.org/wikipedia/commons/5/5b/Greater_coat_of_arms_of_the_United_States.svg *License:* CC BY-SA 3.0 *Contributors:* Own work + File:Seal of the House of Representatives.svg *Original artist:* Ssolbergj

- **File:Green-2008-chicago.jpg** *Source:* https://upload.wikimedia.org/wikipedia/commons/0/03/Green-2008-chicago.jpg *License:* CC BY-SA 3.0 *Contributors:* Own work *Original artist:* MattHucke

- **File:Grover_Cleveland.jpg** *Source:* https://upload.wikimedia.org/wikipedia/commons/9/9c/Grover_Cleveland.jpg *License:* Public domain *Contributors:* This image is available from the United States Library of Congress's Prints and Photographs division under the digital ID ggbain.00828.

  This tag does not indicate the copyright status of the attached work. A normal copyright tag is still required. See Commons:Licensing for more information. *Original artist:* Bain News Service, publisher

- **File:HarryTruman.jpg** *Source:* https://upload.wikimedia.org/wikipedia/commons/e/e6/HarryTruman.jpg *License:* Public domain *Contributors:* Harry S. Truman Library *Original artist:* Greta Kempton

- **File:Harry_S._Truman.jpg** *Source:* https://upload.wikimedia.org/wikipedia/commons/c/cf/Harry_S._Truman.jpg *License:* Public domain *Contributors:* http://www.trumanlibrary.org/photographs/view.php?id=2267 *Original artist:* Frank Gatteri, United States Army Signal Corps

- **File:Herberthoover.jpg** *Source:* https://upload.wikimedia.org/wikipedia/commons/e/e7/Herberthoover.jpg *License:* Public domain *Contributors:* http://www.whitehouse.gov *Original artist:* Elmer Wesley Greene (1907–64), 1956

- **File:Inaugural_invitation_2009.jpg** *Source:* https://upload.wikimedia.org/wikipedia/commons/7/74/Inaugural_invitation_2009.jpg *License:* Public domain *Contributors:* Joint Congressional Committee on Inaugural Ceremonies *Original artist:* Joint Congressional Committee on Inaugural Ceremonies; Precise Contintental, printer; Karl O. Pinc, original uploader of File:Inaugural invitation 2009.png; User:Matthewedwards, uploader of *this* file

- **File:Inaugural_parade_2005.jpg** *Source:* https://upload.wikimedia.org/wikipedia/commons/3/3e/Inaugural_parade_2005.jpg *License:* Public domain *Contributors:* http://www.whitehouse.gov/news/releases/2005/01/images/20050120-1_p44294-010-515h.html *Original artist:* User Minesweeper on en.wikipedia

- **File:Inauguration-01-20-2009.jpg** *Source:* https://upload.wikimedia.org/wikipedia/commons/9/9f/Inauguration-01-20-2009.jpg *License:* CC BY 3.0 *Contributors:* http://www.whitehouse.gov/assets/hero/624x351/inauguration-01-20-2009.jpg *Original artist:* whitehouse.gov

- **File:Increase2.svg** *Source:* https://upload.wikimedia.org/wikipedia/commons/b/b0/Increase2.svg *License:* Public domain *Contributors:* Own work *Original artist:* Sarang

- **File:Invocation_at_1981_Reagan_inauguration.jpg** *Source:* https://upload.wikimedia.org/wikipedia/commons/f/fd/Invocation_at_1981_Reagan_inauguration.jpg *License:* Public domain *Contributors:* http://online.wsj.com/article/SB123215076308292139.html?mod=todays_us_weekend_journal *Original artist:* Photo courtesy Ronald Reagan Library, which states that photos are available for use because they are official government records

- **File:Iowa_City_Caucus.jpg** *Source:* https://upload.wikimedia.org/wikipedia/commons/d/d8/Iowa_City_Caucus.jpg *License:* Public domain *Contributors:* Own work *Original artist:* Citizensharp

- **File:James_A._Garfield.jpg** *Source:* https://upload.wikimedia.org/wikipedia/commons/5/5a/James_A._Garfield.jpg *License:* Public domain *Contributors:* http://www.law.umkc.edu/faculty/projects/Ftrials/guiteau/garfieldj.jpg *Original artist:* Unknown<a href='//www.wikidata. org/wiki/Q4233718' title='wikidata:Q4233718'><img alt='wikidata:Q4233718' src='https://upload.wikimedia.org/wikipedia/commons/thumb/ f/ff/Wikidata-logo.svg/20px-Wikidata-logo.svg.png' width='20' height='11' srcset='https://upload.wikimedia.org/wikipedia/commons/thumb/ f/ff/Wikidata-logo.svg/30px-Wikidata-logo.svg.png 1.5x, https://upload.wikimedia.org/wikipedia/commons/thumb/f/ff/Wikidata-logo.svg/ 40px-Wikidata-logo.svg.png 2x' data-file-width='1050' data-file-height='590' /></a>

- **File:James_Buchanan.jpg** *Source:* https://upload.wikimedia.org/wikipedia/commons/f/fd/James_Buchanan.jpg *License:* Public domain *Contributors:* Library of Congress *Original artist:* From Brady daguerreotype (Mathew Brady) (1822-1896)

- **File:James_K._Polk.jpg** *Source:* https://upload.wikimedia.org/wikipedia/commons/5/56/James_K._Polk.jpg *License:* Public domain *Contributors:* http://inaugural.senate.gov/images/photo-jpolk-1845-loc-07596u-s.jpg *Original artist:* Charles Fenderich

- **File:James_Madison.jpg** *Source:* https://upload.wikimedia.org/wikipedia/commons/1/1d/James_Madison.jpg *License:* Public domain *Contributors:* Ths White House Historical Association. the painting is in the White House collection[1] *Original artist:* John Vanderlyn (1775–1852)

- **File:Jimmy_Carter.jpg** *Source:* https://upload.wikimedia.org/wikipedia/commons/4/4c/Jimmy_Carter.jpg *License:* Public domain *Contributors:* This image is available from the United States Library of Congress's Prints and Photographs division under the digital ID cph.3b52090. This tag does not indicate the copyright status of the attached work. A normal copyright tag is still required. See Commons:Licensing for more information. *Original artist:* Official White House photographer

- **File:Jm5.gif** *Source:* https://upload.wikimedia.org/wikipedia/commons/9/95/James_Monroe_White_House_portrait_1819.gif *License:* Public domain *Contributors:*
*Original artist:* Samuel Morse

- **File:Joe_Biden_and_Dick_Cheney_at_VP_residence.jpg** *Source:* https://upload.wikimedia.org/wikipedia/commons/9/9a/Joe_Biden_and_Dick_Cheney_at_VP_residence.jpg *License:* Public domain *Contributors:* White House *Original artist:* White House photo by David Bohrer

- **File:John_C._Calhoun.jpg** *Source:* https://upload.wikimedia.org/wikipedia/commons/c/ce/John_C._Calhoun.jpg *License:* Public domain *Contributors:*
*Original artist:* John Wesley Jarvis

- **File:John_F._Kennedy,_White_House_color_photo_portrait.jpg** *Source:* https://upload.wikimedia.org/wikipedia/commons/c/c3/John_F. _Kennedy%2C_White_House_color_photo_portrait.jpg *License:* Public domain *Contributors:* This media is available in the holdings of the National Archives and Records Administration, cataloged under the ARC Identifier (National Archives Identifier) **194255**. *Original artist:* Cecil Stoughton, White House

- **File:John_Quincy_Adams.jpg** *Source:* https://upload.wikimedia.org/wikipedia/commons/6/64/John_Quincy_Adams.jpg *License:* Public domain *Contributors:* ? *Original artist:* ?

- **File:John_Tyler.jpg** *Source:* https://upload.wikimedia.org/wikipedia/commons/c/c5/John_Tyler.jpg *License:* Public domain *Contributors:* Library of Congress *Original artist:* unattributed

- **File:Johnadams.jpg** *Source:* https://upload.wikimedia.org/wikipedia/commons/8/88/Johnadams.jpg *License:* Public domain *Contributors:* The Presidents of The Unites States *Original artist:* John Trumbull

- **File:Johnadamsvp.flipped.jpg** *Source:* https://upload.wikimedia.org/wikipedia/commons/9/9e/Johnadamsvp.flipped.jpg *License:* Public domain *Contributors:* http://www.cowboybooks.com.au/pictures/JohnAdams.jpg *Original artist:* Gilbert Stuart

- **File:PartyVotes-PresidentsWhoHadBeenVicePresidents.png**	*Source:*	https://upload.wikimedia.org/wikipedia/commons/2/23/ PartyVotes-PresidentsWhoHadBeenVicePresidents.png *License:* CC0 *Contributors:* File:PartyVotes-Presidents.png *Original artist:* ChrisnHouston

- **File:Pat_Nixon_speaking_at_Republican_National_Convention.jpg** *Source:* https://upload.wikimedia.org/wikipedia/commons/5/50/Pat_ Nixon_speaking_at_Republican_National_Convention.jpg *License:* Public domain *Contributors:* http://images.gmu.edu/luna/servlet/s/t5deap *Original artist:* Oliver Atkins, White House Photo Office

- **File:Permanent_Calendar_gregorian.png** *Source:* https://upload.wikimedia.org/wikipedia/commons/7/74/Permanent_Calendar_gregorian. png *License:* CC BY 3.0 *Contributors:* Own work *Original artist:* Karl Nimtsch

- **File:Photograph_of_the_Four_Presidents_(Reagan,_Carter,_Ford,_Nixon)_toasting_in_the_Blue_Room_prior_to_leaving_ for_Egypt..._-_NARA_-_198522.tif**	*Source:*	https://upload.wikimedia.org/wikipedia/commons/1/18/Photograph_of_the_Four_ Presidents_%28Reagan%2C_Carter%2C_Ford%2C_Nixon%29_toasting_in_the_Blue_Room_prior_to_leaving_for_Egypt... _-_NARA_-_198522.tif *License:* Public domain *Contributors:* U.S. National Archives and Records Administration *Original artist:* Unknown<a href='//www.wikidata.org/wiki/Q4233718' title='wikidata:Q4233718'><img alt='wikidata:Q4233718' src='https://upload.wikimedia.org/wikipedia/commons/thumb/f/ff/Wikidata-logo.svg/20px-Wikidata-logo.svg.png' width='20' height='11' srcset='https://upload.wikimedia.org/wikipedia/commons/thumb/f/ff/Wikidata-logo.svg/30px-Wikidata-logo.svg.png 1.5x, https://upload.wikimedia.org/wikipedia/commons/thumb/f/ff/Wikidata-logo.svg/40px-Wikidata-logo.svg.png 2x' data-file-width='1050' data-file-height='590' /></a> or not provided

- **File:PopWinnerLosesElecVote.png** *Source:* https://upload.wikimedia.org/wikipedia/commons/5/51/PopWinnerLosesElecVote.png *License:* Public domain *Contributors:* Own work *Original artist:* Szu

- **File:Portal-puzzle.svg** *Source:* https://upload.wikimedia.org/wikipedia/en/f/fd/Portal-puzzle.svg *License:* Public domain *Contributors:* ? *Original artist:* ?

- **File:President_George_W._Bush_announcing_the_nomination_of_John_Bolton_as_UN_Ambassador.jpg**	*Source:*	https: //upload.wikimedia.org/wikipedia/commons/3/3c/President_George_W._Bush_announcing_the_nomination_of_John_Bolton_as_UN_ Ambassador.jpg *License:* Public domain *Contributors:* President Appoints John Bolton as Ambassador to the United Nations (direct link) Transferred from en.wikipedia; Transfer was stated to be made by User:jonny-mt. *Original artist:* White House photo by Paul Morse

- **File:President_Rutherford_Hayes_1870_-_1880.jpg**	*Source:*	https://upload.wikimedia.org/wikipedia/commons/9/97/President_ Rutherford_Hayes_1870_-_1880.jpg *License:* Public domain *Contributors:* This image is available from the United States Library of Congress's Prints and Photographs division under the digital ID cwpbh.03606.
This tag does not indicate the copyright status of the attached work. A normal copyright tag is still required. See Commons:Licensing for more information. *Original artist:* Mathew Brady

- **File:President_Woodrow_Wilson_portrait_December_2_1912.jpg**	*Source:*	https://upload.wikimedia.org/wikipedia/commons/2/2d/ President_Woodrow_Wilson_portrait_December_2_1912.jpg *License:* Public domain *Contributors:* This image is available from the United States Library of Congress's Prints and Photographs division under the digital ID cph.3a04218.
This tag does not indicate the copyright status of the attached work. A normal copyright tag is still required. See Commons:Licensing for more information. *Original artist:* Pach Brothers, New York

- **File:Question_book-new.svg** *Source:* https://upload.wikimedia.org/wikipedia/en/9/99/Question_book-new.svg *License:* Cc-by-sa-3.0 *Contributors:*
Created from scratch in Adobe Illustrator. Based on Image:Question book.png created by User:Equazcion *Original artist:*
Tkgd2007

- **File:RNC-interior-Palin-20080903.jpg** *Source:* https://upload.wikimedia.org/wikipedia/commons/7/72/RNC-interior-Palin-20080903.jpg *License:* CC BY 2.0 *Contributors:* http://www.flickr.com/photos/ttoes/2826453919/ *Original artist:* twinkletoez

- **File:Richard_M._Nixon,_ca._1935_-_1982_-_NARA_-_530679.jpg**	*Source:*	https://upload.wikimedia.org/wikipedia/commons/3/ 39/Richard_M._Nixon%2C_ca._1935_-_1982_-_NARA_-_530679.jpg *License:* Public domain *Contributors:* U.S. National Archives and Records Administration *Original artist:* Unknown<a href='//www.wikidata.org/wiki/Q4233718' title='wikidata:Q4233718'><img alt='wikidata:Q4233718' src='https://upload.wikimedia.org/wikipedia/commons/thumb/f/ff/Wikidata-logo.svg/20px-Wikidata-logo.svg.png' width='20' height='11' srcset='https://upload.wikimedia.org/wikipedia/commons/thumb/f/ff/Wikidata-logo.svg/30px-Wikidata-logo.svg.png 1.5x, https://upload.wikimedia.org/wikipedia/commons/thumb/f/ff/Wikidata-logo.svg/40px-Wikidata-logo.svg.png 2x' data-file-width='1050' data-file-height='590' /></a> or not provided

- **File:Roll_call_DNC_2008.jpg** *Source:* https://upload.wikimedia.org/wikipedia/commons/3/39/Roll_call_DNC_2008.jpg *License:* CC BY-SA 3.0 *Contributors:* Transferred from en.wikipedia; transferred to Commons by User:Isthmus using CommonsHelper.
*Original artist:* Qqqqqq (talk). Original uploader was Qqqqqq at en.wikipedia

- **File:Roosevelt-inauguration-1905.jpeg** *Source:* https://upload.wikimedia.org/wikipedia/commons/8/89/Roosevelt-inauguration-1905.jpeg *License:* Public domain *Contributors:* Library of Congress, Prints & Photographs Division, LC-DIG-ppmsca-19619 (digital file from original item), uncompressed archival TIFF version (29 MiB), cropped, minor clone healing in right corners, and converted to JPEG (quality level 88) with the GIMP 2.6.6 *Original artist:* Unknown<a href='//www.wikidata.org/wiki/Q4233718' title='wikidata:Q4233718'><img alt='wikidata:Q4233718' src='https://upload.wikimedia.org/wikipedia/commons/thumb/f/ff/Wikidata-logo.svg/20px-Wikidata-logo.svg.png' width='20' height='11' srcset='https://upload.wikimedia.org/wikipedia/commons/thumb/f/ff/Wikidata-logo.svg/30px-Wikidata-logo.svg.png 1.5x, https://upload.wikimedia.org/wikipedia/commons/thumb/f/ff/Wikidata-logo.svg/40px-Wikidata-logo.svg.png 2x' data-file-width='1050' data-file-height='590' /></a>

- **File:RooseveltTruman1944poster.jpg** *Source:* https://upload.wikimedia.org/wikipedia/commons/a/a5/RooseveltTruman1944poster.jpg *License:* Public domain *Contributors:* Own work *Original artist:* Ianlopez12

- **File:SOU2007.jpg** *Source:* https://upload.wikimedia.org/wikipedia/commons/a/a4/SOU2007.jpg *License:* Public domain *Contributors:* http://www.whitehouse.gov/news/releases/2007/01/images/20070123-2_v012307db-0202w-772v.html *Original artist:* White House photographer David Bohrer

- **File:Seal_Of_The_President_Of_The_United_States_Of_America.svg** *Source:* https://upload.wikimedia.org/wikipedia/commons/3/36/Seal_of_the_President_of_the_United_States.svg *License:* Public domain *Contributors:* Extracted from the title page of PDF document at http://www.whitehouse.gov/nsc/nss.pdf *Original artist:* Unknown<a href='//www.wikidata.org/wiki/Q4233718' title='wikidata:Q4233718'><img alt='wikidata:Q4233718' src='https://upload.wikimedia.org/wikipedia/commons/thumb/f/ff/Wikidata-logo.svg/20px-Wikidata-logo.svg.png' width='20' height='11' srcset='https://upload.wikimedia.org/wikipedia/commons/thumb/f/ff/Wikidata-logo.svg/30px-Wikidata-logo.svg.png 1.5x, https://upload.wikimedia.org/wikipedia/commons/thumb/f/ff/Wikidata-logo.svg/40px-Wikidata-logo.svg.png 2x' data-file-width='1050' data-file-height='590' /></a>

- **File:Seal_of_the_President_of_the_United_States.svg** *Source:* https://upload.wikimedia.org/wikipedia/commons/3/36/Seal_of_the_President_of_the_United_States.svg *License:* Public domain *Contributors:* Extracted from the title page of PDF document at http://www.whitehouse.gov/nsc/nss.pdf *Original artist:* Unknown<a href='//www.wikidata.org/wiki/Q4233718' title='wikidata:Q4233718'><img alt='wikidata:Q4233718' src='https://upload.wikimedia.org/wikipedia/commons/thumb/f/ff/Wikidata-logo.svg/20px-Wikidata-logo.svg.png' width='20' height='11' srcset='https://upload.wikimedia.org/wikipedia/commons/thumb/f/ff/Wikidata-logo.svg/30px-Wikidata-logo.svg.png 1.5x, https://upload.wikimedia.org/wikipedia/commons/thumb/f/ff/Wikidata-logo.svg/40px-Wikidata-logo.svg.png 2x' data-file-width='1050' data-file-height='590' /></a>

- **File:Seal_of_the_US_Presidential_Libraries.svg** *Source:* https://upload.wikimedia.org/wikipedia/commons/8/84/Seal_of_the_US_Presidential_Libraries.svg *License:* Public domain *Contributors:* National Archives and Records Administration *Original artist:* National Archives and Records Administration

- **File:Seal_of_the_United_States_Congress.svg** *Source:* https://upload.wikimedia.org/wikipedia/commons/4/4b/Seal_of_the_United_States_Congress.svg *License:* Public domain *Contributors:* Vectorized from <a href='//commons.wikimedia.org/wiki/File:US_Congress_seal.png' class='image'><img alt='US Congress seal.png' src='https://upload.wikimedia.org/wikipedia/commons/thumb/6/6b/US_Congress_seal.png/50px-US_Congress_seal.png' width='50' height='49' srcset='https://upload.wikimedia.org/wikipedia/commons/thumb/6/6b/US_Congress_seal.png/75px-US_Congress_seal.png 1.5x, https://upload.wikimedia.org/wikipedia/commons/thumb/6/6b/US_Congress_seal.png/100px-US_Congress_seal.png 2x' data-file-width='150' data-file-height='147' /></a> SVG elements from 50px *Original artist:* Ipankonin

- **File:Seal_of_the_United_States_House_of_Representatives.svg** *Source:* https://upload.wikimedia.org/wikipedia/commons/1/1a/Seal_of_the_United_States_House_of_Representatives.svg *License:* Public domain *Contributors:* Vectorized from w:Image:House large seal.png SVG elements from <a href='//commons.wikimedia.org/wiki/File:Great_Seal_of_the_United_States_(obverse).svg' class='image'><img alt='Great Seal of the United States (obverse).svg' src='https://upload.wikimedia.org/wikipedia/commons/thumb/5/5c/Great_Seal_of_the_United_States_%28obverse%29.svg/50px-Great_Seal_of_the_United_States_%28obverse%29.svg.png' width='50' height='50' srcset='https://upload.wikimedia.org/wikipedia/commons/thumb/5/5c/Great_Seal_of_the_United_States_%28obverse%29.svg/75px-Great_Seal_of_the_United_States_%28obverse%29.svg.png 1.5x, https://upload.wikimedia.org/wikipedia/commons/thumb/5/5c/Great_Seal_of_the_United_States_%28obverse%29.svg/100px-Great_Seal_of_the_United_States_%28obverse%29.svg.png 2x' data-file-width='600' data-file-height='600' /></a> *Original artist:* Ipankonin

- **File:Seal_of_the_United_States_Senate.svg** *Source:* https://upload.wikimedia.org/wikipedia/commons/f/f0/Seal_of_the_United_States_Senate.svg *License:* CC BY-SA 2.5-2.0-1.0 *Contributors:* Vectorized from <a href='//commons.wikimedia.org/wiki/File:Senate_cap.PNG' class='image'><img alt='Senate cap.PNG' src='https://upload.wikimedia.org/wikipedia/commons/thumb/4/43/Senate_cap.PNG/50px-Senate_cap.PNG' width='50' height='50' srcset='https://upload.wikimedia.org/wikipedia/commons/thumb/4/43/Senate_cap.PNG/75px-Senate_cap.PNG 1.5x, https://upload.wikimedia.org/wikipedia/commons/thumb/4/43/Senate_cap.PNG/100px-Senate_cap.PNG 2x' data-file-width='232' data-file-height='234' /></a> SVG elements from <a href='//commons.wikimedia.org/wiki/File:Great_Seal_of_the_United_States_(obverse).svg' class='image'><img alt='Great Seal of the United States (obverse).svg' src='https://upload.wikimedia.org/wikipedia/commons/thumb/5/5c/Great_Seal_of_the_United_States_%28obverse%29.svg/50px-Great_Seal_of_the_United_States_%28obverse%29.svg.png' width='50' height='50' srcset='https://upload.wikimedia.org/wikipedia/commons/thumb/5/5c/Great_Seal_of_the_United_States_%28obverse%29.svg/75px-Great_Seal_of_the_United_States_%28obverse%29.svg.png 1.5x, https://upload.wikimedia.org/wikipedia/commons/thumb/5/5c/Great_Seal_of_the_United_States_%28obverse%29.svg/100px-Great_Seal_of_the_United_States_%28obverse%29.svg.png 2x' data-file-width='600' data-file-height='600' /></a> <a href='//commons.wikimedia.org/wiki/File:Blason_Brumath.svg' class='image'><img alt='Blason Brumath.svg' src='https://upload.wikimedia.org/wikipedia/commons/thumb/7/71/Blason_Brumath.svg/50px-Blason_Brumath.svg.png' width='50' height='55' srcset='https://upload.wikimedia.org/wikipedia/commons/thumb/7/71/Blason_Brumath.svg/75px-Blason_Brumath.svg.png 1.5x, https://upload.wikimedia.org/wikipedia/commons/thumb/7/71/Blason_Brumath.svg/100px-Blason_Brumath.svg.png 2x' data-file-width='600' data-file-height='660' /></a> <a href='//commons.wikimedia.org/wiki/File:Coat_of_arms_of_Paraguay_(reverse).svg' class='image'><img alt='Coat of arms of Paraguay (reverse).svg' src='https://upload.wikimedia.org/wikipedia/commons/thumb/9/9c/Coat_of_arms_of_Paraguay_%28reverse%29.svg/50px-Coat_of_arms_of_Paraguay_%28reverse%29.svg.png' width='50' height='50' srcset='https://upload.wikimedia.org/wikipedia/commons/thumb/9/9c/Coat_of_arms_of_Paraguay_%28reverse%29.svg/75px-Coat_of_arms_of_Paraguay_%28reverse%29.svg.png 1.5x, https://upload.wikimedia.org/wikipedia/commons/thumb/9/9c/Coat_of_arms_of_Paraguay_%28reverse%29.svg/100px-Coat_of_arms_of_Paraguay_%28reverse%29.svg.png 2x' data-file-width='600' data-file-height='600' /></a> <a href='//commons.wikimedia.org/wiki/File:Armoiries_r%C3%A9publique_fran%C3%A7aise.svg' class='image'><img alt='Armoiries république française.svg' src='https://upload.wikimedia.org/wikipedia/commons/thumb/b/b7/Armoiries_r%C3%A9publique_fran%C3%A7aise.svg/50px-Armoiries_r%C3%A9publique_fran%C3%A7aise.svg.png' width='50' height='57' srcset='https://upload.wikimedia.org/wikipedia/commons/thumb/b/b7/Armoiries_r%C3%A9publique_fran%C3%A7aise.svg/75px-Armoiries_r%C3%A9publique_fran%C3%A7aise.svg.png 1.5x, https://upload.wikimedia.org/wikipedia/commons/thumb/b/b7/Armoiries_r%C3%A9publique_fran%C3%A7aise.svg/100px-Armoiries_r%C3%A9publique_fran%C3%A7aise.svg.png 2x' data-file-width='175' data-file-height='199' /></a> *Original artist:* Ipankonin

- **File:Seal_of_the_United_States_Supreme_Court.svg** *Source:* https://upload.wikimedia.org/wikipedia/commons/f/f3/Seal_of_the_United_States_Supreme_Court.svg *License:* Public domain *Contributors:* Vectorized from <a href='//commons.wikimedia.org/wiki/File:Seal_of_the_

United_States_Supreme_Court.png' class='image'><img alt='Seal of the United States Supreme Court.png' src='https://upload.wikimedia.org/wikipedia/commons/thumb/3/33/Seal_of_the_United_States_Supreme_Court.png/50px-Seal_of_the_United_States_Supreme_Court.png' width='50' height='50' srcset='https://upload.wikimedia.org/wikipedia/commons/thumb/3/33/Seal_of_the_United_States_Supreme_Court.png/75px-Seal_of_the_United_States_Supreme_Court.png 1.5x, https://upload.wikimedia.org/wikipedia/commons/thumb/3/33/Seal_of_the_United_States_Supreme_Court.png/100px-Seal_of_the_United_States_Supreme_Court.png 2x' data-file-width='341' data-file-height='341' /></a> SVG elements from <a href='//commons.wikimedia.org/wiki/File:Great_Seal_of_the_United_States_(obverse).svg' class='image'><img alt='Great Seal of the United States (obverse).svg' src='https://upload.wikimedia.org/wikipedia/commons/thumb/5/5c/Great_Seal_of_the_United_States_%28obverse%29.svg/50px-Great_Seal_of_the_United_States_%28obverse%29.svg.png' width='50' height='50' srcset='https://upload.wikimedia.org/wikipedia/commons/thumb/5/5c/Great_Seal_of_the_United_States_%28obverse%29.svg/75px-Great_Seal_of_the_United_States_%28obverse%29.svg.png 1.5x, https://upload.wikimedia.org/wikipedia/commons/thumb/5/5c/Great_Seal_of_the_United_States_%28obverse%29.svg/100px-Great_Seal_of_the_United_States_%28obverse%29.svg.png 2x' data-file-width='600' data-file-height='600' /></a> *Original artist:* Ipankonin

- **File:Second_oath_of_office_of_Barack_Obama.jpg** *Source:* https://upload.wikimedia.org/wikipedia/commons/b/b1/Second_oath_of_office_of_Barack_Obama.jpg *License:* Public domain *Contributors:* White House
  *Original artist:* White House (Pete Souza)[1]

- **File:State_population_per_electoral_vote.png** *Source:* https://upload.wikimedia.org/wikipedia/commons/1/14/State_population_per_electoral_vote.png *License:* CC BY-SA 3.0 *Contributors:* Data for the figure used state population & electoral information available on wikipedia. Figure was made using the IDL programming language. *Original artist:* Fzxboy

- **File:Superdome_from_Garage.jpg** *Source:* https://upload.wikimedia.org/wikipedia/commons/d/d8/Superdome_from_Garage.jpg *License:* CC BY-SA 3.0 *Contributors:* Own work *Original artist:* Nwill21

- **File:Swing_states_2012.svg** *Source:* https://upload.wikimedia.org/wikipedia/commons/4/4e/Swing_states_2012.svg *License:* CC-BY-SA-3.0 *Contributors:* This file was derived from Blank US Map.svg: <a href='//commons.wikimedia.org/wiki/File:Blank_US_Map.svg' class='image'><img alt='Blank US Map.svg' src='https://upload.wikimedia.org/wikipedia/commons/thumb/3/32/Blank_US_Map.svg/50px-Blank_US_Map.svg.png' width='50' height='31' srcset='https://upload.wikimedia.org/wikipedia/commons/thumb/3/32/Blank_US_Map.svg/75px-Blank_US_Map.svg.png 1.5x, https://upload.wikimedia.org/wikipedia/commons/thumb/3/32/Blank_US_Map.svg/100px-Blank_US_Map.svg.png 2x' data-file-width='959' data-file-height='593' /></a>
  *Original artist:*

- User:SnowFire

- **File:Symbol_book_class2.svg** *Source:* https://upload.wikimedia.org/wikipedia/commons/8/89/Symbol_book_class2.svg *License:* CC BY-SA 2.5 *Contributors:* Mad by Lokal_Profil by combining: *Original artist:* Lokal_Profil

- **File:Symbol_template_class.svg** *Source:* https://upload.wikimedia.org/wikipedia/en/5/5c/Symbol_template_class.svg *License:* Public domain *Contributors:* ? *Original artist:* ?

- **File:Text_document_with_red_question_mark.svg** *Source:* https://upload.wikimedia.org/wikipedia/commons/a/a4/Text_document_with_red_question_mark.svg *License:* Public domain *Contributors:* Created by bdesham with Inkscape; based upon Text-x-generic.svg from the Tango project. *Original artist:* Benjamin D. Esham (bdesham)

- **File:The_County_Election,_Bingham,_1846.jpg** *Source:* https://upload.wikimedia.org/wikipedia/commons/f/ff/The_County_Election%2C_Bingham%2C_1846.jpg *License:* Public domain *Contributors:* ang.Wikipedia *Original artist:* George Caleb Bingham

- **File:Theodore_Roosevelt.jpg** *Source:* https://upload.wikimedia.org/wikipedia/commons/6/60/Theodore_Roosevelt.jpg *License:* Public domain *Contributors:* ? *Original artist:* ?

- **File:Thomas_Jefferson.jpg** *Source:* https://upload.wikimedia.org/wikipedia/commons/5/50/Thomas_Jefferson.jpg *License:* Public domain *Contributors:* Unknown *Original artist:* Gilbert Stuart

- **File:Tyler_receives_news.jpg** *Source:* https://upload.wikimedia.org/wikipedia/commons/a/a8/Tyler_receives_news.jpg *License:* Public domain *Contributors:* From the Library of Congress see high resolution *Original artist:* Illustrated in Stoddard, William Osborn, 1835-1925. The Lives of the Presidents, v. 5, New York: Frederick A. Stokes & Brother, 1888, between pp. 12-13.

- **File:US-FederalElectionCommission.svg** *Source:* https://upload.wikimedia.org/wikipedia/commons/c/c7/US-FederalElectionCommission.svg *License:* Public domain *Contributors:* Extracted from PDF version of the FEC's 2006 Performance and Accountability Report (direct PDF URL [1]). *Original artist:* U.S. Government

- **File:USHouseBalanceOverTime.png** *Source:* https://upload.wikimedia.org/wikipedia/commons/8/87/USHouseBalanceOverTime.png *License:* Public domain *Contributors:* Own work (Original caption: *"Willhsmit (talk) -Data from public records of the Clerk of the House, chart made by me."*) *Original artist:* Willhsmit at en.wikipedia

- **File:US_Vice_President_Seal.svg** *Source:* https://upload.wikimedia.org/wikipedia/commons/9/90/US_Vice_President_Seal.svg *License:* Public domain *Contributors:* Vectorized from <a href='//commons.wikimedia.org/wiki/File:VPofUSSeal.PNG' class='image'><img alt='VPofUSSeal.PNG' src='https://upload.wikimedia.org/wikipedia/commons/thumb/4/41/VPofUSSeal.PNG/50px-VPofUSSeal.PNG' width='50' height='50' srcset='https://upload.wikimedia.org/wikipedia/commons/thumb/4/41/VPofUSSeal.PNG/75px-VPofUSSeal.PNG 1.5x, https://upload.wikimedia.org/wikipedia/commons/thumb/4/41/VPofUSSeal.PNG/100px-VPofUSSeal.PNG 2x' data-file-width='375' data-file-height='375' /></a> SVG elements from <a href='//commons.wikimedia.org/wiki/File:Seal_of_the_President_of_the_United_States.svg' class='image'><img alt='Seal of the President of the United States.svg' src='https://upload.wikimedia.org/wikipedia/commons/thumb/3/36/Seal_of_the_President_of_the_United_States.svg/50px-Seal_of_the_President_of_the_United_States.svg.png' width='50' height='50' srcset='https://upload.wikimedia.org/wikipedia/commons/thumb/3/36/Seal_of_the_President_of_the_United_States.svg/75px-Seal_of_the_President_of_the_United_States.svg.png 1.5x, https://upload.wikimedia.org/wikipedia/commons/thumb/3/36/Seal_of_the_President_of_the_United_States.svg/100px-Seal_of_the_President_of_the_United_States.svg.png 2x' data-file-width='2424' data-file-height='2425' /></a>
  *Original artist:* Ipankonin

- **File:Ulysses_Grant_1870-1880.jpg** *Source:* https://upload.wikimedia.org/wikipedia/commons/d/d7/Ulysses_Grant_1870-1880.jpg *License:* Public domain *Contributors:* This image is available from the United States Library of Congress's Prints and Photographs division under the digital ID cwpbh.03890.
  This tag does not indicate the copyright status of the attached work. A normal copyright tag is still required. See Commons:Licensing for more information. *Original artist:* Brady-Handy Photograph Collection (Library of Congress)

- **File:Unbalanced_scales.svg** *Source:* https://upload.wikimedia.org/wikipedia/commons/f/fe/Unbalanced_scales.svg *License:* Public domain *Contributors:* ? *Original artist:* ?

- **File:United_States_House_of_Representatives_2015.svg** *Source:* https://upload.wikimedia.org/wikipedia/commons/d/db/United_States_House_of_Representatives_2015.svg *License:* CC BY-SA 4.0 *Contributors:* Own work *Original artist:* Nick.mon

- **File:Vote_icon.svg** *Source:* https://upload.wikimedia.org/wikipedia/commons/4/46/Vote_icon.svg *License:* Public domain *Contributors:* ? *Original artist:* ?

- **File:Voter_Turnout_by_Educational_Attainment,_2008_US_Presidential_Election.png** *Source:* https://upload.wikimedia.org/wikipedia/commons/5/54/Voter_Turnout_by_Educational_Attainment%2C_2008_US_Presidential_Election.png *License:* CC BY 3.0 *Contributors:* Own work *Original artist:* Rcragun

- **File:Voter_Turnout_by_Income,_2008_US_Presidential_Election.png** *Source:* https://upload.wikimedia.org/wikipedia/commons/c/ca/Voter_Turnout_by_Income%2C_2008_US_Presidential_Election.png *License:* CC BY 3.0 *Contributors:* Own work *Original artist:* Rcragun

- **File:Voter_Turnout_by_Race-Ethnicity,_2008_US_Presidential_Election.png** *Source:* https://upload.wikimedia.org/wikipedia/commons/f/fd/Voter_Turnout_by_Race-Ethnicity%2C_2008_US_Presidential_Election.png *License:* CC BY 3.0 *Contributors:* Own work *Original artist:* Rcragun

- **File:Voter_Turnout_by_Sex_and_Age,_2008_US_Presidential_Election.png** *Source:* https://upload.wikimedia.org/wikipedia/commons/b/b9/Voter_Turnout_by_Sex_and_Age%2C_2008_US_Presidential_Election.png *License:* CC BY 3.0 *Contributors:* Own work *Original artist:* Rcragun

- **File:Voter_turnout.png** *Source:* https://upload.wikimedia.org/wikipedia/commons/3/35/Voter_turnout.png *License:* Public domain *Contributors:* http://en.wikipedia.org/wiki/File:Voter_turnout.png *Original artist:* Jmj713

- **File:Warren_G_Harding_portrait_as_senator_June_1920.jpg** *Source:* https://upload.wikimedia.org/wikipedia/commons/8/87/Warren_G_Harding_portrait_as_senator_June_1920.jpg *License:* Public domain *Contributors:* http://hdl.loc.gov/loc.pnp/cph.3a53301 *Original artist:* Copyright by Moffett, Chicago. J241772 U.S. Copyright Office.

- **File:Washington'{}s_Inauguration.jpg** *Source:* https://upload.wikimedia.org/wikipedia/commons/e/e6/Washington%27s_Inauguration.jpg *License:* Public domain *Contributors:* Encyclopedia Britannica *Original artist:* Ramon de Elorriaga

- **File:Wikiquote-logo.svg** *Source:* https://upload.wikimedia.org/wikipedia/commons/f/fa/Wikiquote-logo.svg *License:* Public domain *Contributors:* ? *Original artist:* ?

- **File:Wikisource-logo.svg** *Source:* https://upload.wikimedia.org/wikipedia/commons/4/4c/Wikisource-logo.svg *License:* CC BY-SA 3.0 *Contributors:* Rei-artur *Original artist:* Nicholas Moreau

- **File:William_Henry_Harrison.jpg** *Source:* https://upload.wikimedia.org/wikipedia/commons/e/ea/William_Henry_Harrison.jpg *License:* Public domain *Contributors:* http://lifetussle.files.wordpress.com/2008/03/william-henry-harrison.jpg *Original artist:* Albert Gallatin Hoit, 1809–1856 (source)

- **File:William_Howard_Taft.jpg** *Source:* https://upload.wikimedia.org/wikipedia/commons/8/86/William_Howard_Taft.jpg *License:* Public domain *Contributors:* ? *Original artist:* ?

- **File:Wilson-inaug.jpg** *Source:* https://upload.wikimedia.org/wikipedia/en/e/e6/Wilson-inaug.jpg *License:* PD-US *Contributors:* ? *Original artist:* ?

- **File:Wilson_opening_day_1916.jpg** *Source:* https://upload.wikimedia.org/wikipedia/commons/5/5e/Wilson_opening_day_1916.jpg *License:* Public domain *Contributors:* This image is available from the United States Library of Congress's Prints and Photographs division under the digital ID cph.3a12422.
  This tag does not indicate the copyright status of the attached work. A normal copyright tag is still required. See Commons:Licensing for more information. *Original artist: This work is from the National Photo Company collection at the Library of Congress. According to the library, there are no known copyright restrictions on the use of this work.*

- **File:Zachary_Taylor.jpg** *Source:* https://upload.wikimedia.org/wikipedia/commons/7/7a/Zachary_Taylor.jpg *License:* Public domain *Contributors:* Library of Congress Prints and Photographs Division Washington, D.C. 20540 USA - Reproduction Nr. LC-USZ62-7559 DLC (b&w film copy neg.) *Original artist:* John Sartain

## 27.5.3 Content license

- Creative Commons Attribution-Share Alike 3.0

Made in the USA
Columbia, SC
16 June 2020